THE SECRET LIFE
OF PLANTS

Books by Peter Tompkins

The Secret Life of Plants
(with Christopher Bird)
Secrets of the Great Pyramid
Italy Betrayed
The Murder of Admiral Darlan
The Eunuch and the Virgin
Shaw and Molly Tompkins
A Spy in Rome
To a Young Actress

THE SECRET LIFE OF PLANTS

Peter Tompkins

AND

Christopher Bird

HARPER & ROW, PUBLISHERS

New York, Evanston, San Francisco, London

Portions of this work appeared in the November 1972 issue of *Harper's Magazine*.

THE SECRET LIFE OF PLANTS. Copyright © 1973 by Peter Tompkins and Christopher Bird. All rights reserved. Printed in the United States of America. No part of this book may be used or reproduced in any manner whatsoever without written permission except in the case of brief quotations embodied in critical articles and reviews. For information address Harper & Row, Publishers, Inc., 10 East 53rd Street, New York, N.Y. 10022. Published simultaneously in Canada by Fitzhenry & Whiteside Limited, Toronto.

Designed by Gloria Adelson

Library of Congress Cataloging in Publication Data

Tompkins, Peter.
  The secret life of plants.
  Bibliography: p.
  1. Plants. I. Bird, Christopher, joint
author. II. Title.
QK50.T65 1973   581   72–9160
ISBN 0–06–014326–6

Contents

Acknowledgments

The authors wish to express their gratitude to all who have helped them in the compilation of this book, which required extensive research in Europe, the Soviet Union, and the United States.

They are especially grateful to the staff of the U.S. Library of Congress and in particular to Legare H. B. Obear, Chief of the Loan Division, and to his most helpful assistants. In the Stack and Reader Division, they wish to thank Dudley B. Ball, Roland C. Maheux, William Sartain, Lloyd A. Pauls, and Benjamin Swinson, who saved them much anxiety by caring for their shelved books.

Thanks are also due to Robert V. Allen of the Slavic and Central European Division, and Dolores Moyano Martin, of the Latin American Division, Library of Congress, and to Lida L. Allen of the National Agricultural Library, Beltsville, Maryland.

Very special thanks are due to two Muscovite scientists, biophysicist Dr. Viktor Adamenko, well known for his research on bio-energetics, and Professor Sinikov, Director of Studies of the Timiryazev Academy of Agricultural Sciences, both of whom kindly and promptly replied to requests for data and references unavailable in the United States, as did M. Rostislav Donn, Commercial Counselor of the French Embassy in Moscow.

Lastly the authors are grateful to their respective helpmates, without whom the book would never have reached the printer.

Introduction

Short of Aphrodite, there is nothing lovelier on this planet than a flower, nor more essential than a plant. The true matrix of human life is the greensward covering mother earth. Without green plants we would neither breathe nor eat. On the undersurface of every leaf a million movable lips are engaged in devouring carbon dioxide and expelling oxygen. All together, 25 million square miles of leaf surface are daily engaged in this miracle of photosynthesis, producing oxygen and food for man and beast.

Of the 375 billion tons of food we consume each year the bulk comes from plants, which synthesize it out of air and soil with the help of sunlight. The remainder comes from animal products, which in turn are derived from plants. All the food, drink, intoxicants, drugs and medicines that keep man alive and, if properly used, radiantly healthy are ours through the sweetness of photosynthesis. Sugar produces all our starches, fats, oils, waxes, cellulose. From crib to coffin, man relies on cellulose as the basis for his shelter, clothing, fuel, fibers, basketry, cordage, musical instruments, and the paper on which he scribbles his philosophy. The abundance of plants profitably used by man is indicated by nearly six hundred pages in Uphof's *Dictionary of Economic Plants.* Agriculture—as the economists agree—is the basis for a nation's wealth.

Instinctively aware of the aesthetic vibrations of plants, which are spiritually satisfying, human beings are happiest and most comfortable when living with flora. At birth, marriage, death, blossoms are prerequisites, as they are at mealtime or festivities. We give plants and flowers as tokens of love, of friendship, or homage, and of thanks for hospitality. Our houses are adorned with gardens, our cities with parks, our nations with national preserves. The first thing a woman does to make a room livable is to place a plant in it or a vase of fresh cut flowers. Most men, if pressed, might describe paradise, whether in heaven or on earth, as a garden filled with luxuriant orchids, uncut, frequented by a nymph or two.

Aristotle's dogma that plants have souls but no sensation lasted through the Middle Ages and into the eighteenth century, when Carl von Linné, grandfather of modern botany, declared that plants differ from animals and humans only in their lack of movement, a conceit which was shot down by the great nineteenth-century botanist Charles Darwin, who proved that every tendril has its power of independent movement. As Darwin put it, plants "acquire and display this power only when it is of some advantage to them."

At the beginning of the twentieth century a gifted Viennese biologist with the Gallic name of Raoul Francé put forth the idea, shocking to contemporary natural philosophers, that plants move their bodies as freely, easily, and gracefully as the most skilled animal or human, and that the only reason we don't appreciate the fact is that plants do so at a much slower pace than humans.

The roots of plants, said Francé, burrow inquiringly into the earth, the buds and twigs swing in definite circles, the leaves and blossoms bend and shiver with change, the tendrils circle questingly and reach out with ghostly arms to feel their surroundings. Man, said Francé, merely thinks plants motionless and feelingless because he will not take the time to watch them.

Poets and philosophers such as Johann Wolfgang von Goethe and Rudolf Steiner, who took the trouble to watch plants, discovered that they grow in opposite directions, partly burrowing into the ground as if attracted by gravity, partly shooting up into the air as if pulled by some form of antigravity, or levity.

Wormlike rootlets, which Darwin likened to a brain, burrow constantly downward with thin white threads, crowding themselves firmly into the soil, tasting it as they go. Small hollow chambers in which a ball of starch can rattle indicate to the root tips the direction of the pull of gravity.

When the earth is dry, the roots turn toward moister ground, finding their way into buried pipes, stretching, as in the case of the lowly alfalfa plant, as far as forty feet, developing an energy that can bore through concrete. No one has yet counted the roots of a tree, but a study of a single rye plant indicates a total of over 13 million rootlets with a combined length of 380 miles. On these rootlets of a rye plant are fine root hairs estimated to number some 14 billion with a total length of 6,600 miles, almost the distance from pole to pole.

As the special burrowing cells are worn out by contact with stones, pebbles, and large grains of sand, they are rapidly replaced, but when they reach a source of nourishment they die and are replaced by cells designed to dissolve mineral salts and collect the resulting elements. This basic nourishment is passed from cell to cell up through the plant, which constitutes a single unit of protoplasm, a watery or gelatinous substance considered the basis of physical life.

The root is thus a waterpump, with water acting as a universal solvent, raising elements from root to leaf, evaporating and falling back to earth to act once more as the medium for this chain of life. The leaves of an ordinary sunflower will transpire in a day as much water as a man perspires. On a hot day a single birch can absorb as much as four hundred quarts, exuding cooling moisture through its leaves.

No plant, says Francé, is without movement; all growth is a series of movements; plants are constantly preoccupied with bending, turning and quivering. He describes a summer day with thousands of polyplike arms reaching from a peaceful arbor, trembling, quivering in their eagerness for new support for the heavy stalk that grows behind them. When the tendril, which sweeps a full circle in sixty-seven minutes, finds a perch, within twenty seconds it starts to curve around the object, and within the hour has wound itself so firmly it is hard to tear away. The tendril then curls itself like a corkscrew and in so doing raises the vine to itself.

A climbing plant which needs a prop will creep toward the nearest support. Should this be shifted, the vine, within a few hours, will change its course into the new direction. Can the plant see the pole? Does it sense it in some unfathomed way? If a plant is growing between obstructions and cannot see a potential support it will unerringly grow toward a hidden support, avoiding the area where none exists.

Plants, says Francé, are capable of *intent:* they can stretch toward, or seek out, what they want in ways as mysterious as the most fantastic creations of romance.

Far from existing inertly, the inhabitants of the pasture—or what the ancient Hellenes called *botane*—appear to be able to perceive and to react to what is happening in their environment at a level of sophistication far surpassing that of humans.

The sundew plant will grasp at a fly with infallible accuracy, moving in just the right direction toward where the prey is to be found. Some parasitical plants can recognize the slightest trace of the odor of their victim, and will overcome all obstacles to crawl in its direction.

Plants seem to know which ants will steal their nectar, closing when these ants are about, opening only when there is enough dew on their stems to keep the ants from climbing. The more sophisticated acacia actually enlists the protective services of certain ants which it rewards with nectar in return for the ants' protection against other insects and herbivorous mammals.

Is it chance that plants grow into special shapes to adapt to the idiosyncrasies of insects which will pollinate them, luring these insects with special color and fragrance, rewarding them with their favorite nectar, devising extraordinary canals and floral machinery with which to ensnare a bee so as to release it through a trap door only when the pollination process is completed?

Is it really nothing but a reflex or coincidence that a plant such as the orchid *Trichoceros parviflorus* will grow its petals to imitate the female of a species of fly so exactly that the male attempts to mate with it and in so doing pollinates the orchid? Is it pure chance that night-blossoming flowers grow white the better to attract night moths and night-flying butterflies, emitting a stronger fragrance at dusk, or that the carrion lily develops the smell of rotting meat in areas where only flies abound, whereas flowers which rely on the wind to cross-pollinate the species do not waste energy on making themselves beautiful, fragrant or appealing to insects, but remain relatively unattractive?

To protect themselves plants develop thorns, a bitter taste, or gummy secretions that catch and kill unfriendly insects. The timorous *Mimosa pudica* has a mechanism which reacts whenever a beetle or an ant or a worm crawls up its stem toward its delicate leaves: as the intruder touches a spur the stem raises, the leaves fold up, and the assailant is either rolled off the branch by the unexpected movement or is obliged to draw back in fright.

Some plants, unable to find nitrogen in swampy land, obtain it by devouring living creatures. There are more than five hundred varieties of carnivorous plants, eating any kind of meat from insect to beef, using endlessly cunning methods to capture their prey, from tentacles to sticky hairs to funnel-like traps. The tentacles of carnivorous plants are not only mouths but stomachs raised on poles with which to seize and eat their prey, to digest both meat and blood, and leave nothing but a skeleton.

Insect-devouring sundews pay no attention to pebbles, bits of metal, or other foreign substances placed on their leaves, but are quick to sense the nourishment to be derived from a piece of meat. Darwin found that the sundew can be excited when a piece of thread is laid on it weighing no more than 1/78,000 of a grain. A tendril, which next to the rootlets constitutes the most sensitive portion of a plant, will bend if a piece of silk thread is laid across it weighing but .00025 of a gram.

The ingenuity of plants in devising forms of construction far exceeds that of human engineers. Man-made structures cannot match the supply strength of the long hollow tubes that support fantastic weights against terrific storms. A plant's use of fibers wrapped in spirals is a mechanism of great resistance against tearing not yet developed by human ingenuity. Cells elongate into sausages or flat ribbons locked one to the other to form almost unbreakable cords. As a tree grows upward it scientifically thickens to support the greater weight.

The Australian eucalyptus can raise its head on a slim trunk above the ground 480 feet, or as high as the Great Pyramid of Cheops, and certain walnuts can hold a harvest of 100,000 nuts. The Virginia knotweed can tie a sailor's knot which is put to such a strain when it dries that it snaps, hurling the seeds to germinate as far as possible from mother.

Plants are even sentient to orientation and to the future. Frontiersmen and hunters in the prairies of the Mississippi Valley discovered a sunflower plant, *Silphium laciniatum*, whose leaves accurately indicate the points of the compass. Indian licorice, or *Arbrus precatorius*, is so keenly sensitive to all forms of electrical and magnetic influences it is used as a weather plant. Botanists who first experimented with it in London's Kew Gardens found in it a means for predicting cyclones, hurricanes, tornadoes, earthquakes and volcanic eruptions.

So accurate are alpine flowers about the seasons, they know when spring is coming and bore their way up through lingering snowbanks, developing their own heat with which to melt the snow.

Plants which react so certainly, so variously, and so promptly to the outer world, must, says Francé, have some means of communicating with the outer world, something comparable or superior to our senses. Francé insists that plants are constantly observing and recording events and phenomena of which man—trapped in his anthropocentric view of the world, subjectively revealed to him through his five senses—knows nothing.

Whereas plants have been almost universally looked upon as senseless automata, they have now been found to be able to distinguish between sounds inaudible to the human ear and color wavelengths such as infrared and ultraviolet invisible to the human eye; they are specially sensitive to X-rays and to the high frequency of television.

The whole vegetal world, says Francé, lives responsive to the movement of the earth and its satellite moon, to the movement of the other planets of our solar system, and one day will be shown to be affected by the stars and other cosmic bodies in the universe.

As the external form of a plant is kept a unit and restored whenever part of it is destroyed, Francé assumes there must be some conscious entity supervising the entire form, some intelligence directing the plant, either from within, or from without.

Over half a century ago Francé, who believed plants to be possessed of all the attributes of living creatures including "the most violent reaction against abuse and the most ardent gratitude for favors," could have written a *Secret Life of Plants*, but what he had already put into print was either ignored by the establishment or considered heretically shocking. What shocked them most was his suggestion that the awareness of plants might originate in a supramaterial world of cosmic beings to which, long before the birth of Christ, the Hindu sages referred as "devas," and which, as fairies, elves, gnomes, sylphs and a host of other creatures, were a matter of direct vision and experience to clairvoyants among the Celts and other sensitives. The idea was considered by vegetal scientists to be as charmingly jejune as it was hopelessly romantic.

It has taken the startling discoveries of several scientific minds in the 1960s to bring the plant world sharply back to the attention of mankind. Even so there are skeptics who find it hard to believe that plants may at last be the bridesmaids at a marriage of physics and metaphysics.

Evidence now supports the vision of the poet and the philosopher that plants are living, breathing, communicating creatures, endowed with personality and the attributes of soul. It is only we, in our blindness, who have insisted on considering them automata. Most extraordinary, it now appears that plants may be ready, willing, and able to cooperate with humanity in the Herculean job of turning this planet back into a garden from the squalor and corruption of what England's pioneer ecologist William Cobbett would have called a "wen."

PART I

MODERN RESEARCH

CHAPTER 1

Plants and ESP

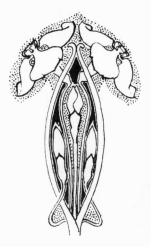

The dust-grimed window of the office building facing New York's Times Square reflected, as through a looking glass, an extraordinary corner of Wonderland. There was no White Rabbit with waistcoat and watch chain, only an elfin-eared fellow called Backster with a galvanometer and a house plant called *Dracaena massangeana*. The galvanometer was there because Cleve Backster was America's foremost lie-detector examiner; the dracaena because Backster's secretary felt the bare office should have a touch of green; Backster was there because of a fatal step taken in the 1960s which radically affected his life, and may equally affect the planet.

Backster's antics with his plants, headlined in the world press, became the subject of skits, cartoons, and lampoons; but the Pandora's box which he opened for science may never again be closed. Backster's discovery that plants appear to be sentient caused strong and varied reaction round the globe, despite the fact that Backster never claimed a discovery, only an uncovering of what has been known and forgotten. Wisely he chose to avoid publicity, and concentrated on establishing the absolute scientific bona fides of what has come to be known as the "Backster Effect."

The adventure started in 1966. Backster had been up all night in his school for polygraph examiners, where he teaches the art of lie detection to policemen and security agents from around the world. On impulse he decided to attach the electrodes of one of his lie detectors to the leaf of his dracaena. The dracaena is a tropical plant similar to a palm tree, with large leaves and a dense cluster of small flowers; it is known as the dragon tree (Latin *draco*) because of the popular myth that its resin yields dragon blood. Backster was curious to see if the leaf would be affected by water poured on its roots, and if so, how, and how soon.

As the plant thirstily sucked water up its stem, the galvanometer, to Backster's surprise, did not indicate less resistance, as might have been expected by the greater electrical conductivity of the moister plant. The pen on the graph paper, instead of trending upward, was trending downward, with a lot of sawtooth motion on the tracing.

A galvanometer is that part of a polygraph lie detector which, when attached to a human being by wires through which a weak current of electricity is run, will cause a needle to move, or a pen to make a tracing on a moving graph of paper, in response to mental images, or the slightest surges of human emotion. Invented at the end of the eighteenth century by a Viennese priest, Father Maximilian Hell, S.J., court astronomer to the Empress Maria Theresa, it was named after Luigi Galvani, the Italian physicist and physiologist who discovered "animal electricity." The galvanometer is now used in conjunction with an electrical circuit called a "Wheatstone bridge," in honor of the English physicist and inventor of the automatic telegraph, Sir Charles Wheatstone.

In simple terms, the bridge balances resistance, so that the human body's electrical potential—or basic charge—can be measured as it fluctuates under the stimulus of thought and emotion. The standard police usage is to feed "carefully structured" questions to a suspect and watch for those which cause the needle to jump. Veteran examiners, such as Backster, claim they can identify deception from the patterns produced on the graph.

Backster's dragon tree, to his amazement, was giving him a reaction very similar to that of a human being experiencing an emotional stimulus of short duration. Could the plant be displaying emotion?

What happened to Backster in the next ten minutes was to revolutionize his life.

The most effective way to trigger in a human being a reaction strong enough to make the galvanometer jump is to threaten his or her well-being. Backster decided to do just that to the plant: he dunked a leaf of the dracaena in the cup of hot coffee perennially in his hand. There was no reaction to speak of on the meter. Backster studied the problem several minutes, then conceived a worse threat: he would burn the actual leaf to which the electrodes were attached. The instant he got the picture of flame in his mind, and before he could move for a match, there was a dramatic change in the tracing pattern on the graph in the form of a prolonged upward sweep of the recording pen. Backster had not moved, either toward the plant or toward the recording machine. Could the plant have been reading his mind?

When Backster left the room and returned with some matches, he found another sudden surge had registered on the chart, evidently caused by his determination to carry out the threat. Reluctantly he set about burning the leaf. This time there was a lower peak of reaction on the graph. Later, as he went through the motions of pretending he would burn the leaf, there was no reaction whatsoever. The plant appeared to be able to differentiate between real and pretended intent.

Backster felt like running into the street and shouting to the world, "Plants can think!" Instead he plunged into the most meticulous investigation of the phenomena in order to establish just how the plant was reacting to his thoughts, and through what medium.

His first move was to make sure he had not overlooked any logical explanation for the occurrence. Was there something extraordinary about the plant? About him? About the particular polygraph instrument?

When he and his collaborators, using other plants and other instruments in other locations all over the country, were able to make similar observations, the matter warranted further study. More than twenty-five different varieties of plants and fruits were tested, including lettuce, onions, oranges, and bananas. The observations, each similar to the others, required a new view of life, with some explosive connotations for science. Heretofore the debate between scientists and parapsychologists on the existence of ESP, or extrasensory perception, has been fierce, largely because of the difficulty of establishing unequivocally when such a phenomenon is actually occurring. The best that has been achieved so far in the field, by Dr. J. B. Rhine, who initiated his experiments in ESP at Duke University, has been to establish that with human beings the phenomenon seems to occur with greater odds than are attributable to chance.

Backster first considered his plants' capacity for picking up his intention to be some form of ESP; then he quarreled with the term. ESP is held to mean perception above and beyond varieties of the established five sensory perceptions of touch, sight, sound, smell, and taste. As plants give no evidence of eyes, ears, nose, or mouth, and as botanists since Darwin's time have never credited them with a nervous system, Backster concluded that the perceiving sense must be more basic.

This led him to hypothesize that the five senses in humans might be limiting factors overlying a more "primary perception," possibly common to all nature. "Maybe plants see better *without* eyes," Backster surmised: "better than humans do with them." With the five basic senses, humans have the choice, at will, of perceiving, perceiving poorly, not perceiving at all. "If you don't like the looks of something," said Backster, "you can look the other way, or not look. If everyone were to be in everyone else's mind all the time it would be chaos."

To discover what his plants could sense or feel, Backster enlarged his office, and set about creating a proper scientific laboratory, worthy of the space age.

During the next few months, chart after chart was obtained from all sorts of plants. The phenomenon appeared to persist even if the plant leaf was detached from the plant, or if it was trimmed to the size of the electrodes; amazingly, even if a leaf was shredded and redistributed between the electrode surfaces there was still a reaction on the chart. The plants reacted not only to threats from human beings, but to unformulated threats, such as the sudden appearance of a dog in the room or of a person who did not wish them well.

Backster was able to demonstrate to a group at Yale that the movements of a spider in the same room with a plant wired to his equipment could cause dramatic changes in the recorded pattern generated by the plant just *before* the spider started to scamper away from a human attempting to restrict its movement. "It seems," said Backster, "as if each of the spider's decisions to escape was being picked up by the plant, causing a reaction in the leaf."

Under normal circumstances, plants may be attuned to each other, said Backster, though when encountering animal life they tend to pay less attention to what another plant may be up to. "The last thing a plant expects is another plant to give it trouble. So long as there is animal life around, they seem to be attuned to animal life. Animals and people are mobile, and could need careful monitoring."

If a plant is threatened with overwhelming danger or damage, Backster observed that it reacts self-defensively in a way similar to an opossum—or, indeed, to a human being—by "passing out," or going into a deep faint. The phenomenon was dramatically demonstrated one day when a physiologist from Canada came to Backster's lab to witness the reaction of his plants. The first plant gave no response whatsoever. Nor did the second; nor the third. Backster checked his polygraph instruments, and tried a fourth and a fifth plant; still no success. Finally, on the sixth, there was enough reaction to demonstrate the phenomenon.

Curious to discover what could have influenced the other plants, Backster asked: "Does any part of your work involve harming plants?"

"Yes," the physiologist replied. "I terminate the plants I work with. I put them in an oven and roast them to obtain their dry weight for my analysis."

Forty-five minutes after the physiologist was safely on the way to the airport, each of Backster's plants once more responded fluidly on the graph.

This experience helped to bring Backster to the realization that plants could intentionally be put into a faint, or mesmerized, by humans, that something similar could be involved in the ritual of the slaughterer before an animal is killed in the kosher manner. Communicating with the victim, the killer may tranquilize it into a quiet death, also preventing its flesh from having a residue of "chemical fear," disagreeable to the palate and perhaps noxious to the consumer. This brought up the possibility that plants and succulent fruits might *wish* to be eaten, but only in a sort of loving ritual, with a real communication between the eater and the eaten—somehow akin to the Christian rite of Communion —instead of the usual heartless carnage.

"It may be," says Backster, "that a vegetable appreciates becoming part of another form of life rather than rotting on the ground, just as a human at death may experience relief to find himself in a higher realm of being."

On one occasion, to show that plants and single cells were picking up signals through some unexplained medium of communication, Backster provided a demonstration for the author of an article appearing in the Baltimore *Sun*, subsequently condensed in the *Reader's Digest*. Backster hooked a galvanometer to his philodendron, then addressed the writer as if it were *he* who was on the meter, and interrogated him about his year of birth.

Backster named each of seven years between 1925 and 1931 to which the reporter was instructed to answer with a uniform "No." Backster then selected from the chart the correct date, which had been indicated by the plant with an extra high flourish.

The same experiment was duplicated by a professional psychiatrist, the medical director of the research ward at Rockland State Hospital in Orangeburg, New York, Dr. Aristide H. Esser. He and his collaborator, Douglas Dean, a chemist at Newark College of Engineering, experimented with a male subject who brought along a philodendron he had nursed from a seedling and had cared for tenderly.

The two scientists attached a polygraph to the plant and then asked the owner a series of questions, to some of which he had been instructed to give false answers. The plant had no difficulty indicating through the galvanometer the questions which were falsely answered; Dr. Esser, who at first had laughed at Backster's claim, admitted, "I've had to eat my own words."

To see if a plant could display memory, a scheme was devised whereby Backster was to try to identify the secret killer of one of two plants. Six of Backster's polygraph students volunteered for the experiment, some of them veteran policemen. Blindfolded, the students drew from a hat folded slips of paper, on one of which were instructions to root up, stamp on, and thoroughly destroy one of two plants in a room. The criminal was to commit the crime in secret; neither Backster nor any of the other students was to know his identity; only the second plant would be a witness.

By attaching the surviving plant to a polygraph and parading the students one by one before it, Backster was able to establish the culprit. Sure enough, the plant gave no reaction to five of the students, but caused the meter to go wild whenever the actual culprit approached. Backster was careful to point out that the plant could have picked up and reflected the guilt feelings of the culprit; but as the villain had acted in the interests of science, and was not particularly guilty, it left the possibility that a plant could remember and recognize the source of severe harm to its fellow.

In another series of observations, Backster noted that a special communion or bond of affinity appeared to be created between a plant and its keeper, unaffected by distance. With the use of synchronized stopwatches, Backster was able to note that his plants continued to react to his thought and attention from the next room, from down the hall, even from several buildings away. Back from a fifteen-mile trip to New Jersey, Backster was able to establish that his plants had perked up and shown definite and positive signs of response—whether it was relief or welcome he could not tell—at the very moment he had decided to return to New York.

When Backster was away on a lecture tour and talked about his initial

1966 observation, showing a slide of the original dracaena, the plant, back in his office, would show a reaction on the chart at the very time he projected the slide.

Once attuned to a particular person, plants appeared to be able to maintain a link with that person, no matter where he went, even among thousands of people. On New Year's Eve in New York City, Backster went out into the bedlam of Times Square armed with a notebook and stopwatch. Mingling with the crowd, he noted his various actions, such as walking, running, going underground by way of subway stairs, nearly getting run over, and having a mild fracas with a news vendor. Back at the lab, he found that each of three plants, monitored independently, showed similar reactions to his slight emotional adventures.

To see if he could get a reaction from plants at a much greater distance, Backster experimented with a female friend to establish whether her plants remained attuned to her on a seven-hundred-mile plane ride across the United States. From synchronized clocks they found a definite reaction from the plants to the friend's emotional stress each time the plane touched down for its landing.

To test a plant's reaction at still greater distances, even millions of miles, to see if space is a limit to the "primary perception" of his plants, Backster would like the Mars probers to place a plant with a galvanometer on or near that planet so as to check by telemeter the plant's reaction to emotional changes in its caretaker at ground control on earth.

Since "telemetered" radio or TV signals traveling via electromagnetic waves at the speed of light take between six and six and one-half minutes to reach Mars and as many to return to Earth, the question was whether an emotional signal from an earthbound human would reach Mars faster than an electromagnetic wave or, as Backster suspects, the very instant it was sent. Were the round-trip time for a telemetered message to be cut in half it would indicate that mental or emotional messages operate outside time as we conceive it, and beyond the electromagnetic spectrum.

"We keep hearing about non-time-consuming communication from Eastern philosophic sources," says Backster. "They tell us that the universe is in balance; if it happens to go out of balance someplace, you can't wait a hundred light-years for the imbalance to be detected and corrected. This non-time-consuming communication, this oneness among all living things, could be the answer."

Backster has no idea what kind of energy wave may carry man's thoughts or internal feelings to a plant. He has tried to screen a plant by placing it in a Faraday cage as well as in a lead container. Neither shield appeared in any way to block or jam the communication channel linking the plant to the human being. The carrier-wave equivalent, whatever it might be, Backster concluded, must somehow operate beyond the electromagnetic spectrum. It also appeared to operate from the macrocosm down to the microcosm.

One day when Backster happened to cut his finger and dabbed it with iodine, the plant that was being monitored on the polygraph immediately reacted, apparently to the death of some cells in Backster's finger. Though it might have been reacting to his emotional state at the sight of his own blood, or to the stinging of the iodine, Backster soon found a recognizable pattern in the graph whenever a plant was witnessing the death of some living tissue.

Could the plant, Backster wondered, be sensitive on a cellular level all the way down to the death of individual cells in its environment?

On another occasion the typical graph appeared as Backster was preparing to eat a cup of yogurt. This puzzled him till he realized there was a chemical preservative in the jam he was mixing into the yogurt that was terminating some of the live yogurt bacilli. Another inexplicable pattern on the chart was finally explained when it was realized the plants were reacting to hot water being poured down the drain, which was killing bacteria in the sink.

Backster's medical consultant, the New Jersey cytologist Dr. Howard Miller, concluded that some sort of "cellular consciousness" must be common to all life.

To explore this hypothesis Backster found a way of attaching electrodes to infusions of all sorts of single cells, such as amoeba, paramecium, yeast, mold cultures, scrapings from the human mouth, blood, and even sperm. All were subject to being monitored on the polygraph with charts just as interesting as those produced by the plants.

Sperm cells turned out to be surprisingly canny in that they seemed to be capable of identifying and reacting to the presence of their own donor, ignoring the presence of other males. Such observations seem to imply that some sort of total memory may go down to the single cell, and by inference that the brain may be just a switching mechanism, not necessarily a memory storage organ.

"Sentience," says Backster, "does not seem to stop at the cellular level. It may go down to the molecular, the atomic and even the subatomic. All sorts of things which have been conventionally considered to be inanimate may have to be re-evaluated."

Convinced of being on the track of a phenomenon of major importance to science, Backster was anxious to publish his findings in a scientific journal so that other scientists could check his results. Scientific methodology requires that a recorded reaction be repeatable by other scientists at other locations, with an adequate number of repetitions. This made the problem more difficult than anticipated.

To begin with, Backster found that plants can quickly become so attuned to human beings that it is not always possible to obtain exactly the same reactions with different experimenters. Incidents such as the "fainting" which occurred with the Canadian physiologist sometimes made it look as if there were no such thing as the Backster Effect. Personal involvement with an experiment, and even prior knowledge of the exact time an event was scheduled, was often enough to "tip off" a plant into noncooperation. This led Backster to the conclusion that animals subjected to excruciating vivisection may pick up the intent of their torturers and thus produce for them the very effects required in order to end the ordeal as rapidly as possible. Backster found that even if he and his colleagues discussed a project in their waiting room, the plants, three rooms away, could be affected by the imagery apparently generated by their conversation.

To make his point, Backster realized, he would have to devise an experiment in which all human involvement was removed. The entire process would have to be automated. Altogether it took Backster two and a half years and several thousand dollars, some of it provided by the Parapsychology Foundation, Inc., then headed by the late Eileen Garrett, to devise the right experiment and perfect the fully automated equipment necessary to carry it out. Different scientists of varying disciplines suggested an elaborate system of experimental controls.

The test Backster finally chose was to kill live cells by an automatic mechanism at a random time when no humans were in or near the office, and see if the plants reacted.

As sacrificial scapegoats Backster hit upon brine shrimp of the variety sold as food for tropical fish. It was important to the test that the victims demonstrate great vitality because it had been noted that tissue that is unhealthy or has begun to die no longer acts as a remote stimulus, is no longer capable of transmitting some type of warning. To see that brine shrimp are in good form is easy: in a normal condition, the males spend their whole time chasing and mounting females.

The device for "terminating" these playboy creatures consisted of a small dish which would automatically tip them into a pot of boiling water. A mechanical programmer actuated the device on a randomly selected occasion so that it was impossible for Backster or his assistants to know when the event would occur. As a control precaution against the actual mechanism of dumping registering on the charts, dishes were programmed at other times to dump plain water containing no brine shrimp.

Three plants would be attached to three separate galvanometers in three separate rooms. A fourth galvanometer was to be attached to a fixed-value resistor to indicate possible random variations caused by fluctuations in the power supply, or by electromagnetic disturbances occurring near or within the experiment's environment. Light and temperature would be kept uniform on all plants, which, as an extra precaution, would be brought from an outside source, passed through staging areas, and hardly handled before the experiment.

Plants selected for the experiment were of the *Philodendron cordatum* species because of its nice large leaves, firm enough to withstand comfortably the pressure of electrodes. Different plants of the same species would be used on successive test runs.

The scientific hypothesis which Backster wished to pursue was, properly phrased in the vernacular of science, that *"there exists an as yet undefined primary perception in plant life, that animal life termination can serve as a remotely located stimulus to demonstrate this perception capability, and that this perception facility in plants can be shown to function independently of human involvement."*

The experimental results showed that the plants did react strongly and synchronously to the death of the shrimp in boiling water. The automated monitoring system, checked by visiting scientists, showed that plants reacted consistently to the death of the shrimp in a ratio that was five to one against the possibility of chance.

The whole procedure of the experiment and its results were written up in a scientific paper published in the winter of 1968 in Volume X of *The International Journal of Parapsychology* under the title "Evidence of Primary Perception in Plant Life." It was now up to other scientists to see if they could repeat Backster's experiment and obtain the same results.

More than seven thousand scientists asked for reprints of the report on Backster's original research. Students and scientists at some two dozen American universities indicated they intended to attempt to duplicate Backster's experiments as soon as they could obtain the necessary equipment.* Foundations expressed interest in funding further experiments. The news media, which at first ignored Backster's paper, went into a flurry of excitement over the story once *National Wildlife* had the courage to take the plunge in February of 1969 with a feature article. This attracted such worldwide attention that secretaries and housewives began talking to their plants, and *Dracaena massangeana* became a household word.

Readers seemed to be most intrigued by the thought that an oak tree could actually quake at the approach of an axman, or that a carrot could shiver at the sight of rabbits, while the editors of *National Wildlife* were concerned that some of the applications of Backster's phenomenon to medical diagnosis, criminal investigation, and such fields as espionage were so fantastic that they dared not as yet repeat them in print.

Medical World News of March 21, 1969, commented that at last

*Backster has been loath to give out the names and places of these establishments so as not to have them importuned by outsiders until they have accomplished their tests and can make pondered announcements of their results at times of their own choosing.

ESP research might be "on the verge of achieving the scientific respectability that investigators of psychic phenomena have sought in vain since 1882 when the British Society for Psychical Research was founded in Cambridge."

William M. Bondurant, an executive of the Mary Reynolds Babcock Foundation in Winston-Salem, North Carolina, produced a grant of $10,000 for Backster to pursue his research, commenting: "His work indicates there may be a primary form of instantaneous communication among all living things that transcends the physical laws we know now —and that seems to warrant looking into."

Backster was thus able to invest in more expensive equipment, including electrocardiographs and electroencephalographs. These instruments, normally used for measuring electrical emissions from heart and brain, had the advantage of not putting current through the plants, merely recording the difference in potential they discharged. The cardiograph enabled Backster to obtain readings more sensitive than the polygraph; the encephalograph gave him readings ten times more sensitive than the cardiograph.

A fortuitous occurrence led Backster into another whole realm of research. One evening, as he was about to feed a raw egg to his Doberman pinscher, Backster noticed that as he cracked the egg one of his plants attached to a polygraph reacted strenuously. The next evening he watched again as the same thing happened. Curious to see what the egg might be feeling, Backster attached it to a galvanometer, and was once more up to his ears in research.

For nine hours Backster got an active chart recording from the egg, corresponding to the rhythm of the heartbeats of the chicken embryo, the frequency being between 160 and 170 beats per minute, appropriate to an embryo three or four days along in incubation. Only the egg was store-bought, acquired at the local delicatessen, and was unfertilized. Later, breaking the egg and dissecting it, Backster was astonished to find that it contained no physical circulatory structure of any sort to account for the pulsation. He appeared to have tapped into some sort of force field not conventionally understood within the present body of scientific knowledge.

The only hint as to what sort of world he had wandered into came to Backster from the amazing experiments in the energy fields around plants, trees, humans, and even cells, carried out at the Yale Medical School in the 1930s and 1940s by the late Professor Harold Saxton Burr, which are only just beginning to be recognized and understood.

With these considerations Backster temporarily abandoned his experiments with plants to explore the implications of his egg discoveries, which appeared to have profound implications for the origin-of-life research—and are the makings of another whole book.

CHAPTER 2

Plants Can
Read Your Mind

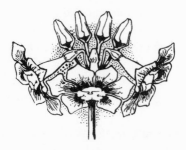

While Backster was developing his experiments in the eastern United States, a heavy-set research chemist working with International Business Machines in Los Gatos, California, was challenged to give a course in "creativity" for IBM engineers and scientists. It was only after Marcel Vogel had taken on the job that he realized the enormity of it. "How does one define creativity?" he found himself asking. "What is a creative person?" To answer these questions, Vogel, who had studied for years to become a Franciscan priest, began writing an outline for twelve two-hour seminars which he hoped would represent an ultimate challenge to his students.

Vogel's own probings into the realm of creativity had started when he was a boy, curious to know what caused the light in fireflies and glowworms. Finding little on luminescence in the libraries, Vogel informed his mother that he would write a book on the subject. Ten years later *Luminescence in Liquids and Solids and Their Practical Application* was published by Vogel in collaboration with Chicago University's Dr. Peter Pringsheim. Two years after that, Vogel incorporated his own company, called Vogel Luminescence, in San Francisco, which became a leader in the field. Over a period of fifteen years Vogel's firm developed a variety of new products: the red color seen on television screens; fluorescent crayons; tags for insecticides; a "black light" inspection kit to determine, from their urine, the secret trackways of rodents in cellars, sewers, and slums; and the psychedelic colors popular in "new age" posters.

By the mid-1950s Vogel became bored with his day-to-day tasks of administering a company and sold it to go to work for IBM. There he was able to devote his full time to research, delving into magnetics, optic-electrical devices, and liquid crystal systems, developing and patenting inventions of crucial significance to the storage of information in computers, and winning awards which adorn the walls of his San Jose home.

The turning point in the creativity course which Vogel was asked to give at IBM came when one of his students gave him an *Argosy* magazine with an article on Backster's work entitled "Do Plants Have Emotions?" Vogel's first reaction was to throw the article into the wastebasket, convinced that Backster was just another charlatan unworthy of serious consideration. Yet something about the idea gnawed at his mind. A few days later, Vogel retrieved the article, and completely reversed his opinion.

The article, read aloud to his seminar students, aroused both derision and curiosity. Out of this ruckus came the unanimous decision to experiment with plants. That same evening, one student called Vogel to announce that the latest issue of *Popular Electronics* referred to Backster's work, and included a wiring diagram for an instrument called a "psychanalyser," which would pick up and amplify reactions from plants and could be built for less than twenty-five dollars.

Vogel divided his class into three groups and challenged them to repeat some of Backster's accomplishments. By the end of the seminar, not one of the three teams had achieved any success. Vogel, on the other hand, was able to report that he had duplicated certain of Backster's results, and proceeded to demonstrate how plants anticipate the act of having their leaves torn, react with even greater alarm to the threat of being burnt or uprooted—more so even than if they are actually torn, burnt, or otherwise brutalized. Vogel wondered why he alone seemed to be successful. As a boy, he had been interested in anything which might explain the workings of the human mind. After dipping into books on magic, spiritualism, and hypnotic technique, he had given stage demonstrations as a teen-age hypnotist.

What particularly fascinated Vogel were Mesmer's theory of a universal fluid whose equilibrium or disturbance explained health or disease, Coué's ideas of autosuggestion as they related to painless childbirth and self-betterment, and the postulates of various writers on "psychic energy," a term popularized by Carl Jung, who, though he differentiated it from physical energy, believed it to be incommensurable.

Vogel reasoned that, if there was a "psychic energy," it must, like other forms of energy, be storable. But in what? Staring at the many chemicals on the shelves of his IBM laboratory, Vogel wondered which of them could be used to store this energy.

In his dilemma, he asked a spiritually gifted friend, Vivian Wiley, who went through the chemicals laid out for her and said that, in her judgment, none offered any promise of a solution for Vogel's problem. Vogel suggested she ignore his preconceived ideas about chemicals and use anything which might intuitively occur to her. Back in her garden, Vivian Wiley picked two leaves from a saxifrage, one of which she placed on her bedside table, the other in the living room. "Each day when I get up," she told Vogel, "I will look at the leaf by my bed and *will* that it continue to live; but I will pay no attention to the other. We will see what happens."

A month later, she asked Vogel to come to her house and bring a camera to photograph the leaves. Vogel could hardly believe what he saw. The leaf to which his friend had paid no attention was flaccid, turning brown and beginning to decay. The leaf on which she had focused daily attention was radiantly vital and green, just as if it had been freshly plucked from the garden. Some power appeared to be defying natural law, keeping the leaf in a healthy state. Curious to see if he could get the same results as his friend, Vogel picked three leaves from an elm outside his IBM laboratory; at home he laid them on a plate of glass near his bed.

Each day, before breakfast, Vogel stared concentratedly at the two outer leaves on the glass for about one minute, exhorting them lovingly to continue to live; the center leaf he assiduously ignored. In a week, the center leaf had turned brown and shriveled. The outer leaves were still green and healthy-looking. Most interesting to Vogel, the severed stems of the live leaves appeared to have healed the wounds caused by being ripped from the tree. Vivian Wiley continued her experiments and later showed Vogel the saxifrage leaf which she had kept green and alive for two long months while the control leaf was completely dehydrated and brown.

Vogel was convinced that he was witnessing the power of "psychic energy" in action. If the power of the mind could keep a leaf green way past its time, Vogel wondered what its effect might be on liquid crystals, an intensive study of which he was pursuing for IBM.

Trained in microscopy, Vogel had taken hundreds of color slides of liquid crystal behavior magnified up to three hundred times; when screened, they rival the works of a gifted abstract artist. While making the slides, Vogel realized that, by "relaxing his mind," he could sense activity not visually revealed in the microscopic field.

"I began to pick up things at the microscope which eluded others, not with ocular vision but with my mind's eye. After becoming aware of them," says Vogel, "I was led by some form of higher sensory awareness to adjust the lighting conditions to allow these phenomena to be optically recordable to the human eye or to a camera."

The conclusion at which Vogel arrived is that crystals are brought into a solid, or physical, state of existence by *pre-forms*, or ghost images of pure energy which *anticipate* the solids. Since plants could pick up intentions from a human, that of burning them, for example, there was no doubt in Vogel's mind that intent produced some kind of energy field.

By the fall of 1971, finding that his microscopic work was taking up most of his time, Vogel abandoned his research on plants. But when an article on this research quoting Dr. Gina Cerminara, psychologist and author of a popular book on the seer Edgar Cayce, appeared in the San Jose *Mercury*, and was wired by the Associated Press throughout the world, Vogel was besieged on the telephone for information, and was thus stimulated to continue.

Vogel realized that before he could observe with precision the effects on plants of human thoughts and emotion he would have to improve his technique of affixing electrodes to the plant leaves in such a way as to eliminate random electromagnetic frequencies, such as the hum of near-by vacuum cleaners, major sources of spurious data—or engineer's "noise"—which could cause the pen recorder to drift on the chart, and which obliged Backster to conduct most of his experiments between midnight and dawn.

Vogel also found that some of the philodendrons he worked with responded faster, others more slowly, some very distinctly, others less distinctly, and that not only plants but their individual leaves had their own unique personality and individuality. Leaves with a large electrical resistance were especially difficult to work with; fleshy leaves with a high water content were the best. Plants appeared to go through phases of activity and inactivity, full of response at certain times of the day or days of the month, "sluggish" or "morose" at other times.

To make sure that none of these recording effects was the result of faulty electroding, Vogel developed a mucilaginous substance composed of a solution of agar, with a thickener of karri gum, and salt. This paste he brushed onto the leaves before gently applying carefully polished one-by-one-and-a-half-inch stainless-steel electrodes. When the agar jelly hardened around the edges of the electronic pickups, it sealed their faces into a moist interior, virtually eliminating all the variability in signal output caused by pressure on leaves when clamped between ordinary electrodes. This system produced for Vogel a base line on the chart that was perfectly straight, without oscillations.

Having eliminated random influences, Vogel began a new round of experiments in the spring of 1971 to see if he could establish the exact moment when a philodendron entered into recordable communication with a human being. With a philodendron attached to a galvanometer which produced a straight base line, Vogel stood before the plant, completely relaxed, breathing deeply and almost touching it with outspread fingers. At the same time, he began to shower the plant with the same kind of affectionate emotion he would flow to a friend. Each time he did this, a series of ascending oscillations was described on the chart by the pen holder. At the same time Vogel could tangibly feel, on the palms of his hands, an outpouring from the plant of some sort of energy.

After three to five minutes, further release of emotion on Vogel's part evoked no further action from the plant, which seemed to have "discharged all its energy" in response to his ministrations. To Vogel, the interreaction between himself and the philodendron appeared to be on the same order as that evoked when lovers or close friends meet, the intensity of mutual response evoking a surge of energy until it is finally expended and must be recharged. Like lovers, both Vogel and the plant appeared to remain suffused with joy and contentment.

In a botanical nursery, Vogel found that he could easily pick out a particularly sensitive plant by running his hands over a group until he felt a slight cooling sensation followed by what he describes as a series of electrical pulses, indicating a powerful field. Increasing the distance between himself and the plant, Vogel found, like Backster, that he could get a similar reaction from it, first from outside the house, then from down the block, and even from his laboratory in Los Gatos, eight miles away.

In another experiment, Vogel wired two plants to the same recording machine and snipped a leaf from the first plant. The second plant responded to the hurt being inflicted on its neighbor, but *only when Vogel was paying attention to it!* If Vogel cut off a leaf while ignoring the second plant, the response was lacking. It was as if Vogel and the plant were lovers on a park bench, oblivious of passers-by until the attention of one lover became distracted from the other.

From his own experience, Vogel knew that masters of the art of Yoga, and teachers of other forms of deep meditation such as Zen, are unaware of disturbing influences around them when in meditative states. An electroencephalograph picks up from them quite a different set of brain waves than when the same persons are alert to the everyday world around them. It became clearer to Vogel that a certain focused state of consciousness on his part seemed to become an integral and balancing part of the circuitry required to monitor his plants. A plant could be awakened from somnolence to sensitivity by his giving up his normally conscious state and focusing a seemingly extra-conscious part of his mind on the exact notion that the plant be happy and feel loved, that it be blessed with healthy growth. In this way, man and plant seemed to interact, and, as a unit, pick up sensations from events, or third parties, which became recordable through the plant. The process of sensitizing both himself and the plant, Vogel found, could take only a few minutes or up to a half hour.

Asked to describe the process in detail, Vogel said that first he quiets the sensory responses of his body organs, then he becomes aware of an energetic relationship between the plant and himself. When a state of balance between the bioelectrical potential of both the plant and himself is achieved, the plant is no longer sensitive to noise, temperature, the normal electrical fields surrounding it, or other plants. It responds only to Vogel, who has effectively tuned himself to it—or perhaps simply hypnotizes it.

Vogel now felt confident enough to accept an invitation to make a public demonstration with a plant. On a local TV program in San Francisco, the plant, coupled to a pen recorder, gave a live illustration of varying states of Vogel's mind, running from irritation at an interviewer's questions to quiet tracings established when Vogel was in harmonious intercommunication with the plant. For the producer of ABC's television program *You Asked for It,* Vogel also demonstrated the plant's response to his or another person's thoughts, including a sudden release of strong emotion on command, followed by the act of his quieting the plant to normal reactions to its environment.

Invited to lecture to audiences who had heard of his experimentation, Vogel said unequivocally: "It is fact: man can and does communicate with plant life. Plants are living objects, sensitive, rooted in space. They may be blind, deaf, and dumb in the human sense, but there is no doubt in my mind that they are extremely sensitive instruments for measuring man's emotions. They radiate energy forces that are beneficial to man. One can feel these forces! They feed into one's own force field, which in turn feeds back energy to the plant." The American Indians, says Vogel, were keenly aware of these faculties. When in need, they would go into the woods. With their arms extended, they would place their backs to a pine tree in order to replenish themselves with its power.

When Vogel began to demonstrate plants' sensitivity to "states of attention" different from the supposed awareness which most humans like to call consciousness, he discovered that the reaction of skeptics or hostile observers could produce strange effects on him. By paying attention to negative attitudes emanating from an audience, Vogel found he could isolate the individuals emitting them and counter their effect with a deep breath, learned in Yoga instruction. He would then switch his mind to another mental image just as if he were turning a dial to a different setting.

"The feeling of hostility, of negativity, in an audience," says Vogel, "is one of the main barriers to effective communication. To counteract this force is one of the most difficult tasks in public demonstration of these plant experiments. If one cannot do this, the plant and therefore the equipment will 'go dead' and there is no response until a positive tie can be reestablished.

"It seems," he says, "that I act as a filtering system which limits the response of a plant to the outside environment. I can turn it off or on, so that people and plant become mutually responsive. By charging the plant with some energy within me, I can cause the plant to build up a sensitivity for this kind of work. It is extremely important that one understand that the plant's response is, in my opinion, not that of an intelligence in plant form, but that the plant becomes an extension of oneself. One can then interact with the bioelectric field of the plant, or through it, with the thought processes and emotions in a third person."

Vogel concluded that a Life Force, or Cosmic Energy, surrounding all living things is sharable among plants, animals, and humans. Through such sharing, a person and a plant become one. "This oneness is what makes possible a mutual sensitivity allowing plant and man not only to intercommunicate, but to record these communications via the plant on a recording chart."

Because his observations indicated there was an interchange, even a commingling or fusion of energies when plant and man commune, Vogel wondered whether an exceptionally sensitive individual could get *into* a plant, as was reported of the sixteenth-century German mystic Jakob Boehme, who, as a young man, became illumined and described being able to see in another dimension.

Boehme said he could look at a growing plant and suddenly, by willing to do so, mingle with that plant, be part of the plant, feel its life "struggling toward the light." He said he was able to share the simple ambitions of the plant and "rejoice with a joyously growing leaf."

One day Vogel was visited in San Jose by Debbie Sapp, a quiet, self-effacing girl who impressed Vogel with her initial ability to enter into instant rapport with his philodendron, as established by his instrumentation.

When the plant was entirely calm, he asked her, point blank: "Can you get into that plant?" Debbie nodded assent, and her face took on an attitude of quiet repose, of detachment, as if she were far away in another universe. Immediately the recording pen began to trace a pattern of undulations revealing to Vogel that the plant was receiving an unusual amount of energy.

Debbie later described what happened in writing:

> Mr. Vogel asked me to relax and project myself into the philodendron. Several things took place as I began to carry out his request.
>
> First, I wondered exactly how I could get inside a plant. I made a conscious decision to let my imagination take over and found myself entering the main stem through a doorway at its base. Once inside, I saw the moving cells and water traveling upward through the stem, and let myself move with this upward flow.
>
> Approaching the spreading leaves in my imagination, I could feel myself being drawn from an imaginary world into a realm over which I had no control. There were no mental pictures, but rather a feeling that I was becoming part of, and filling out, a broad expansive surface. This seemed to me to be describable only as pure consciousness.
>
> I felt acceptance and positive protection by the plant. There was no sense of time, just a feeling of unity in existence and in space. I smiled spontaneously and let myself be one with the plant.
>
> Then Mr. Vogel asked me to relax. When he said this, I realized I was very tired but peaceful. All of my energy had been with the plant.

Vogel, who was observing the recording on the chart, noticed an abrupt stop when the girl "came out" of the plant. On later occasions, when the girl "re-entered" the plant, she was able to describe the inner makeup of its cells and their structure in detail. She specifically noted that one of the leaves had been badly burned by an electrode. When Vogel detached the electrode, he found a hole almost all the way through the leaf.

Vogel has since tried the same experiment with dozens of other people, having them go into a single leaf and look at the individual cells within it. All gave consistent descriptions of various parts of the cellular body down to the detailed organization of the DNA molecules. From the experiment, Vogel came to the conclusion: "We can move into individual cells in our own bodies and, depending on our state of mind, affect them in various ways. One day, this may explain the cause of disease."

The ability to go into a plant and analyze what part of it is hurt was demonstrated on TV film on Good Friday, 1973, when Vogel and Dr. Tom Montelbono, who had been working with him for over a year, were filmed during plant experimentation by a TV production team from CBS. It was highly embarrassing to both researchers that the plant seemed not to respond. Vogel asked Montelbono to see if there was something wrong with the electroding. Instead of tampering with the electrodes, Montelbono, to the astonishment of the CBS technicians, sat where he was and after a moment's concentration announced that damaged cells in the upper right-hand corner of the electroded part of the leaf were shorting the electrical circuit. In the presence of the TV men the electrodes were removed and the leaf was found to be damaged exactly where Montelbono had said.

Because Vogel knows that, among all humans, children are the most "open-minded," he has begun to teach children how to interact with plants. First, he asks them to feel a leaf, describe its temperature, consistency, and texture in detail. Next, he lets them bend leaves and become aware of their resilience before going on to pet the leaves gently by stroking their upper and under sides. If his pupils take pleasure in describing to him the sensations they feel, Vogel asks them to take their hands away from the leaves and try to feel a force or energy emanating from them. Many of the children instantly described a rippling or tingling sensation.

Vogel noticed that those children who felt the strongest sensations were wholly engrossed in what they were doing. Once they felt the tingling, he would say: "Now completely relax and feel the give-and-take of the energy. When you feel it pulsing, gently move your hand up and down over the leaf." Following his directions, the young experimenters could easily see that, when they brought their hands down, the leaves fell away. By continued repetition of this motion, the leaves would begin to oscillate. With the use of both hands, the experimenters could actually get a plant to sway. As they gained confidence, Vogel urged them to move further and further away from the plant.

"This is basic training," says Vogel, "to develop an expanded awareness of a force which is not visible. The awareness established, they see they can operate with this force."

Adults, according to Vogel, are much less successful than children, which leads him to surmise that many scientists are not going to be able to repeat his or Backster's experiments in laboratories. "If they approach the experimentation in a mechanistic way," says Vogel, "and don't enter into mutual communication with their plants and treat them as friends, they will fail. It is essential to have an open mind that eliminates all preconceptions before beginning experiments." Indeed, Vogel was told by one doctor working at the California Psychical Society that he had had not a single result, though he had worked for months. The same is true for one of Denver's most renowned psychoanalysts.

"Hundreds of laboratory workers around the world," says Vogel, "are going to be just as frustrated and disappointed as these men until they appreciate that the empathy between plant and human is the *key*, and learn how to establish it. No amount of checking in laboratories is going to prove a thing until the experiments are done by properly trained observers. Spiritual development is indispensable. But this runs counter to the philosophy of many scientists, who do not realize that creative experimentation means that the *experimenters must become part of their experiments.*"

This highlights the difference in approach between Vogel and Backster, indicating, perhaps, that Vogel is establishing a type of hypnotic control over his plants, whereas Backster says that his plants, left strictly alone, will quite normally react to their environment.

Vogel says that even when a person *can* affect a plant, the result is not always a happy one. He asked one of his friends, a clinical psychologist, who had come to see for himself if there was any truth to the plant research, to project a strong emotion to a philodendron fifteen feet away. The plant surged into an instantaneous and intense reaction and then, suddenly, "went dead." When Vogel asked the psychologist what had gone through his mind, the man answered that he had mentally compared Vogel's plant with his own philodendron at home, and thought how inferior Vogel's was to his. The "feelings" of Vogel's plant were evidently so badly hurt that it refused to respond for the rest of the day; in fact, it sulked for almost two weeks. Vogel could not doubt that plants have a definite aversion to certain humans, or, more exactly, to what those humans are thinking.

This being true, Vogel considered it possible, one day, to read a person's thoughts through a plant. Something of the sort had already taken place. Vogel had asked a nuclear physicist to mentally "work" on a technical problem. As the man was cogitating, Vogel's plant registered a series of tracings on the recorder for 118 seconds. When the tracing fell back to base line, Vogel informed his scientist friend that he had stopped his train of thought. The friend corroborated.

Vogel wondered if he had actually captured a process on a chart via a plant. After a few minutes, he asked the physicist to think of his wife. When the physicist did so, the plant again recorded a tracing, this time for 105 seconds. It seemed to Vogel that, right before him in his living room, a plant was picking up and passing on a man's mental impressions of his wife. If one could interpret such tracings, could one not know what the man was thinking?

After a break for a cup of coffee, Vogel almost casually asked his friend to think once more of his wife in the same way he had thought of her before. The plant registered another 105-second-long tracing very similar to the first. To Vogel this was the first time a plant seemed to have recorded a similar thought spectrogram and duplicated it.

"By pursuing such experiments," says Vogel, "we may have a means of technically identifying energies coming from the human mind, translating them, and feeding them back into an as yet undeveloped device. A whole evening of thinking may be made explicit."

Entertaining a group of skeptical psychologists, medical doctors, and computer programmers at his house, Vogel let them look over his equipment for hidden devices and gimmicks which they insisted must exist, then asked them to sit in a circle and talk so as to see what reactions the plant might pick up. For an hour the group conversed on several topics with hardly a response from the plant. Just as they had all concluded that the whole thing was a fake, one of them said: "How about sex?" To their mutual surprise, the plant came to life, the pen recorder oscillating wildly on the chart. This led to speculation that talking of sex could stir up in the atmosphere some sort of sexual energy such as the "orgone" discovered and described by Dr. Wilhelm Reich, and that the ancient fertility rites in which humans had sexual intercourse in freshly seeded fields might indeed have stimulated plants to grow.

The plant also responded to spooky stories told in a darkened room lit only by a red-shaded candle. At certain points in a story, such as: "The door of the mysterious cabin in the forest began slowly to open," or, "Suddenly there appeared around the corner a strange man with a knife in his hand," or "Charles bent down and raised the lid of the coffin," the plant seemed to pay closer attention. To Vogel, this was evidence that a plant can measure "figments of the imagination," being converted to energy by the group as a whole.

Dr. Hal Puthoff, a physicist at the Stanford Research Institute in Palo Alto, invited Vogel and five other scientists to witness the effects he was getting by hooking up a chicken egg to the electro-psychometer, or "E-meter," developed by L. Ron Hubbard, the founder of Scientology. The E-meter's function is almost identical to that of the psychoanalyzer which Vogel had first used with his seminar students. Puthoff attempted to demonstrate that the egg wired to the E-meter would respond when another egg was broken. He broke three separate eggs, but nothing happened. After asking Puthoff if he could try, Vogel put his hand over an egg and related to it exactly as he had learned to relate to his plants. In one minute, the needle on the E-meter's galvanometer dial began to move and finally "pinned." Vogel backed ten feet away and got gyrations from the needle by opening and closing his hands. Though Puthoff and several others present tried to do the same, all failed.

The needle's movement, once thought to be affected by resistance on the skin of humans attached to electrodes, is known as Galvanic Skin Response, or GSR. Since plants have no skin, in the human sense, the term for the effect on plants has been changed to Psycho-Galvanic Response, or PGR.

"The PGR," says Vogel, "exists not only in plants, but in all living forms. The directive action of the mind focuses this energy and, on command, releases the force in a series of pulses which can pass through glass, metals, and other materials. No one yet knows exactly what they are."

In Russia, a psychic called Nina Kulagina can turn the needle of a compass without touching it but she has to do it with her hands near the compass; more impressive feats have been demonstrated at Stanford University, especially by the remarkably sensitive Ingo Swann, who attributes his success to techniques he learned in Scientology. With nothing but his will power, Swann has been able to affect a mechanism in the university's most thoroughly shielded "quark" chamber, buried deep underground in a vault of liquid helium, impenetrable to any known wave length of the electromagnetic spectrum, astonishing the academic physicists who watched him perform what they considered to be an impossible feat.

Vogel stresses that experiments with plants can be extremely dangerous to those who do not have the ability properly to alter their states of consciousness. "Focused thought," says Vogel, "can exert a tremendous effect on the body of a person in a higher mental state, if he lets his emotions interfere."

No one, says Vogel, who is not in sound bodily health should become involved with plants or any other kind of psychic research. Though he has not been able to prove it, Vogel feels that a special diet of vegetables, fruits, and nuts, rich in minerals and proteins, allows the body to build the kind of energy necessary for such work. "One draws energy at high levels," he said, "and this requires good nutrition."

Asked how the higher energies, such as thought, might operate on the physical bodies of living organisms, Vogel says he has now begun to speculate on the strange properties of water. As a crystallographer, he is interested in the fact that, unlike most salts, which have one crystalline form, core samples of glacier ice have more than thirty different forms. "Uninitiated persons, when first looking at them," says Vogel, "could conclude that they were observing as many different substances. And they would be right in their own way because water is a real mystery."

Vogel makes the prediction, which he stresses is as yet far from established fact, that since living things all have a high water content, the vitality of a person must be in some way related to the rate of respiration. As water moves around the body and through its pores, charges are built. Vogel's first clue about his postulate on water came from the fact that some "psychics" have lost several pounds of body weight during sessions in which they expended vital, or psychic, energy. "If we could weigh a person doing psychic research on a sensitive scale," suggests Vogel, "we would find that there is a loss of weight in each case. It is a water loss, as it is in persons who go on crash diets."

Whatever the future brings, Vogel believes that his research with plants can help man to the recognition of long-ignored truths. By developing simple training kits, which he is presently designing, he thinks he can teach children to release their emotions and watch the effects in a measurable way.

"They can thus learn the art of *loving,*" says Vogel, "and know truly that when they think a thought they release a tremendous power or force in space. By knowing that they *are* their thoughts, they will know how to use thinking to achieve spiritual, emotional, and intellectual growth.

"This is no machine to measure brain waves or any gimmick to help people to become seers or mystics," Vogel insists, "but one to help children to become *simple, honest human beings.*"

Asked to sum up the importance of his research with plants, Vogel replied: "So much of the ills and suffering in life comes from our inability to release stresses and forces within us. When a person rejects us, we rebel inside and we *hold on to this rejection.* This builds a stress which, as Dr. Wilhelm Reich showed so long ago, becomes locked in as muscular tension, and if not unlocked, depletes the body's energy field and alters its chemistry. My research with plants indicates one pathway to deliverance."

For Marcel Vogel, plants have opened new horizons. The vegetal kingdom seems capable of picking up messages of intent, benign or malicious, that are inherently more truthful than when translated into words—a talent which all human beings may share but which they have momentarily occluded.

Two young Californian students of humanistic psychology and Hindu philosophy, Randall Fontes and Robert Swanson, have now pursued Vogel's quarry into unbeaten ground. Using sophisticated equipment lent them by the IBM researcher, they have made a series of discoveries so surprising that despite their youth they have been granted funds and equipment by established universities to further probe the mysteries of plant communication.

Fontes' and Swanson's first discovery came virtually by accident when one noticed that the other's yawning was being picked up by a plant in the form of energy surges. Instead of ignoring the phenomenon as improbable, the two students followed up the clue remembering that in ancient Hindu texts an exaggerated yawn was considered a means by which a tired person could be recharged with vivifying *shakhti*, a postulated energy filling the universe.

With the help of Dr. Norman Goldstein, a professor of biology at State University in Hayward, California, Fontes went on to discover an electrical potential traveling from cell to cell in the ivy philodendron which gives a strong indication of the presence of a hitherto unsuspected simple nervous system. As a result, Fontes has been invited to direct a project at the Science Unlimited Research Foundation in San Antonio, Texas, on the effects of human consciousness on living organisms. Meanwhile, Swanson is cooperating in the setting up of a parapsychologically oriented counseling center at the John F. Kennedy University in Martinez, California, where one of Swanson's goals is to determine just which people affect plants telepathically and which do not.

CHAPTER 3

Plants That Open Doors

Next to probe the mysteries of plant communication was an "electronics specialist" from West Paterson, New Jersey, who happened to hear Backster interviewed on a radio program hosted by Long John Nebel. An assiduous investigator of ESP and of the phenomenon of remote hypnotism, Pierre Paul Sauvin was equally at home in the "state of the art" and "feasibility considerations" of the engineer, mostly because of his training and employment for several large corporations, including Aerospace and International Telephone and Telegraph.

When Long John—a professional skeptic—roped Backster into a corner to get him to describe some practical uses for his discovery of primary perception in plants, Backster first suggested the exotic notion that in jungle warfare soldiers in dangerous territory could wire up the local plants to act as "stress alarm indicators" and avoid being ambushed. "But if you really want to make a psychologist sit up and take notice," Backster told Long John, "you could instrument a plant to activate a small electric train, getting it to move back and forth on no other command than that of human emotion."

This notion, though singularly impractical, could be spelled out in Sauvin's electronics jargon as an "anxiety response device," and so fired him that he turned his bachelor quarters in a house overlooking the Passaic River into a Merlin's cave of electronic equipment.

Sauvin claims that many of his insights and ideas for inventions come to him in psychic flashes, as if he were merely acting as a medium. He says he sometimes gets the factual data necessary for an invention without fully understanding the principle, or how it relates to the whole, and must get further details by questions addressed to "levels beyond."

Using high-voltage generators which produce the sort of lightning arcs usually associated with Dr. Frankenstein, Sauvin can put 27,000 volts through his body and remotely activate a large doughnut bulb filled with helium to serve as an electronic ouija board, its dark rings flowing in one direction or the other in answer to his questions. He also developed a system guaranteed to hypnotize *anyone*, even the most recalcitrant, by placing the subject on an unstable platform in a pitch-black room and swaying before him a rainbow pattern of light that causes him to lose his balance.

With such exotic expertise it was not long before Sauvin had a toy electric train running round a track and reversing its direction through nothing but his thought and emotion relayed to a plant. He was able not only successfully to demonstrate the phenomenon before an audience of sixty in Madison, New Jersey, but to make the train start and stop at will under the klieg lights of a television studio.

As the engine moved around the track it would activate a switch leading to Sauvin's body in such a way as to give him a sharp electric shock. Just ahead on the track, another switch was wired to a galvanometer attached to an ordinary philodendron. As the philodendron picked up Sauvin's emotional reaction at being shocked, the galvanometer needle would jump and throw the switch, reversing the train. The next step was for Sauvin simply to remember the sensation of being shocked and project it in order for the plant to activate the switch.

Though Sauvin had long been interested in parapsychology and was fascinated with the psychological implications of a plant responding to human thought and emotion, his main preoccupation was the development of a foolproof plant device that could be activated by any human being. For Sauvin's purposes it did not matter whether the plant was in any way rational or feeling, so long as it could reliably pick up his emotional signal and trigger the switch. Whether plants were "conscious" or not, Sauvin was convinced they had an energy field similar to the energy field generated by a human being, and that somehow an interaction of these fields could be put to use. The problem was to develop equipment sensitive enough to take advantage of the phenomenon in an absolutely reliable way.

Perusing the endless stream of trade journals that passed across his desk as a technical writer for ITT, Sauvin was struck by a series of articles in *Popular Electronics,* on unusual electronic circuits and exotic weaponry, by a mysterious writer named L. George Lawrence. The author, intrigued by the Russian development of animal guidance systems for training cats to pilot nonjammable air-to-air missiles right onto target, speculated in his articles on training plants to respond to the presence of selected objects and images, evidently for a similar purpose. Rumored to be a high government official involved in security research writing under a pseudonym, Lawrence is in fact a European-born engineer, formerly a professor of audio-visual arts at San Bernardino College in California, presently the director of his own independent research institute.

Unfortunately, the components for sophisticated circuits such as those devised by Lawrence—though worth mere pennies, in terms of materials—would cost thousands of dollars of engineering man-hours to produce, and were in any case not available on the market. But from one of Sauvin's jobs as a specifications engineer on a large government contract he had salvaged what might be just the right pieces—some phase-looplocked discriminators pressed into microelectronic silicon wafers that had been junked by the lab as unfit for the temperature requirements of space.

With these "chips" Sauvin was able to build a Wheatstone bridge for measuring electrical potential with alternating instead of direct current, and an automatic gain control circuit by means of which he hoped to be able to distinguish very fine changes in the energy fields of plants. The sensitivity achieved was one hundred times greater than could be obtained with Backster's galvanometer and eliminated enormous amounts of electronic "noise."

What Sauvin was now measuring was no longer voltage amplitude but phase shift, or the fine lag between two running voltages. The result gave Sauvin an instrument roughly comparable to an ordinary light-dimmer switch, in which a plant leaf acted as the switch. Variations of apparent resistance in the leaf would cause a light to get brighter or dimmer depending on the response of the plant to outside effects.

As soon as his device was functioning, Sauvin set about monitoring plants around the clock. To catch the tiniest nuances of phase shift Sauvin hooked his plants to an oscilloscope, a big electronic green eye with a figure eight of light whose loops changed shape as the current from a plant varied, making patterns much like the fluttering of the wings of a butterfly. Simultaneously, a varying tone was produced by current run through an amplified tone oscillator which enabled Sauvin to hear minute changes in vibrations, and know how his plants were reacting. A bank of tape recorders kept a permanent record of this oscillating tone, along with a monotonous beep every second from a WWV international time-signal broadcast. With a stopwatch Sauvin could run a check on the effect he was having on his plants from a distance, whether down the street, at ITT, or off on a holiday.

Some of Sauvin's Merlin equipment now came into its own, especially a complex system of automatic phone-answering and recording devices. For some years Sauvin had been carrying on a moonlighting operation, writing for various specialized magazines, under various pseudonyms, while retaining his regular job. To keep his cover and not arouse the displeasure of his masters at ITT and yet be able to consult with his editors and answer their queries any time during the day, Sauvin had devised an ingenious system. By means of a small radio transmitter strapped to his leg and a battery of automated and preprogrammed tape machines at home he could communicate via his home phone, receiving messages and giving answers, all from his desk at ITT. For various editors to identify themselves to Sauvin's automatic equipment he developed such simple tricks as having an editor run his finger along a pocket comb close to the phone mouthpiece, generating an easily identifiable sound wave which would trigger from the automatic equipment the appropriate reply. As a cover for his own low-toned conversations from his desk, Sauvin developed the habit of humming to himself most of the time he was at work, soon becoming known as the "hummer" of ITT.

This Rube Goldberg equipment served Sauvin admirably for remote-controlled communication with his plants. He could call his own number and speak to his plants directly; he could monitor the tones of their response via the amplified audio-oscillator, and from wherever he might be he could control the light, color, temperature, or recording equipment in his quarters.

When electroding his plants Sauvin gradually realized that like Vogel he could obtain the best results from plants with which he established a special mental rapport. This he would accomplish by putting himself into a light trance, wishing the plant well, tenderly touching or washing its leaves, till he could feel his own energy emanations entering and interplaying with those of the plant.

Like Backster, Sauvin found that his plants reacted most strongly to the death of living cells in their environment, and most consistently to the death of human cells. He also found in the course of his various experiments that the simplest signal he could transmit to his plants, extrasensorily, to which they would respond with a sharp enough reaction, was to give himself a light electric shock, the very simplest method being to swivel his desk chair and then ground the accumulated static charge by touching his finger to his metal desk. His plants several miles away would react with an instant surge. Just as with the train experiment, Sauvin eventually found that he merely needed to remember or re-feel a shock for his plants to pick up the signal, even from as far away as his holiday cottage eighty miles north of his West Paterson lab.

As Sauvin's main problem remained that of getting his plants to be sharply attuned to his person rather than to their immediate environment, when he was away for several days, he had to devise some means of attracting his plants' attention even more effectively than addressing them over the long-distance phone. As his plants reacted most strongly to any damage done to himself or to any part of his own energy field, he experimented with *remotely* killing a few cells of his body in the presence of the plants. The system worked admirably. The problem was to obtain cells that would remain alive for protracted periods. Blood worked well enough, hair was difficult to kill, but sperm worked best of all, because, as Sauvin explained, it was easier to obtain than bleeding, and much less painful.

These experiments led Sauvin to wonder if plants might not react just as well to emotions of pleasure and joy as to pain and shock. Not only was he tired of shocking himself, he was afraid that repeated shocks to his plants, even indirect ones, might be unpleasantly loading his karma. Sauvin soon found that his plants did react to joy and pleasure, but with wave patterns that were not sharp enough to trigger a switch reliably. Undaunted, Sauvin decided on a more daring experiment. During a holiday with a girl friend at his lakeside cottage he established that his plants, eighty miles away, would react with very high peaks on the tone oscillator to the acute pleasure of sexual climax, going right off the top at the moment of orgasm. All of which was very interesting and could be turned into a commercially marketable device for jealous wives to monitor their philandering husbands, by means of a potted begonia. But it was not yet conducive to a simple, foolproof system of getting a plant to trigger a switch consistently.

There was no question in Sauvin's mind that he could affect a plant at a distance; but he could not rely on the system for any really sensitive fail-safe purpose because his plant might at any time react to some stimulus in its own environment, such as the sudden appearance of a cat or of a bird outside the window snapping up an insect. Sauvin therefore wired three plants, each set in a different room, and thus in a different environment, to a single circuit which could only be activated if all three plants reacted synchronously. By keeping the plants in separate environments Sauvin hoped the required stimulus would be synchronous only when it came from him, wherever he might be. This was still not positively foolproof, because at times one plant or the other might not fully react to the stimulus, but it was a step forward in that it prevented any random stimulus from affecting all three plants at once.

Sauvin was now anxious to release his data confirming Backster's findings and to make public his own contribution to a science which he felt had a potential for the world no less great than Marconi's use of radio waves. But in a country where government and industrial executives are less interested in the quaint notion of communing with nature than in developing sophisticated weapons of offense and the gadgetry of mind surveillance, Sauvin had a hard time finding either a sponsor or an audience.

Unable to interest the mass media, or such conservative journals as *Science* or *Scientific American,* Sauvin decided to angle his material to the engineering and mechanical journals to which he was already a regular contributor. To incite the interest of the editor of a car magazine he concocted a story about a device that would enable him to start his car by remote control by means of thought waves to a plant. With the help of a small radio transmitter this proved to be a simple enough operation, the only technical difficulty being the designing of a gadget that would give just the right pressure to the ignition key, repeat the pressure if the engine failed to catch, and release pressure the moment it did.

The device was designed to appeal to a citizen with the prospect of being able to wake up on a frosty morning and get his car and heater started while still comfortably enjoying his breakfast. But for Sauvin there was one defect: a plant was not really needed; the device could be operated directly by radio. To include his beloved plants in a worthwhile gadget attractive to automobile and home owners, Sauvin cooked up a system whereby a man returning on a snowy night could approach his garage and signal his pet philodendron to open the doors. Here the plant's function of responding only to its master would make it admirably burglar-proof.

To arouse the interest of serious scientists who might wish to provide Sauvin with the necessary funds for a proper lab, Sauvin hit upon the idea of showing that an airplane could be flown by thought control with the aid of his plants attached to his sensitive devices. For years Sauvin, already a licensed pilot, had enjoyed the hobby of flying model planes, some with a wing spread as large as six feet, controlling them entirely from the ground by radio signals, getting them to bank, loop, speed up, slow down, and even land. By a slight adaptation to his transmitter equipment Sauvin is able to start, stop, or affect the speed of a model plane in flight by transmitting a thought to a plant.

In the sensitivity of plants Sauvin also saw a means of detecting a potential hijacker at an airport before such a criminal could board a plane and endanger passengers. He therefore suggested "Operation Sky-jack," a system whereby plants could be used in conjunction with galva-nometers and other sensitive devices to pick up the turbulent emotions of a hijacker being screened by security, the problem at an airport being to safeguard not only the lives of passengers but their rights as citizens not to be subjected to unwarranted search.

Already the U.S. Army has taken an interest in the project. At Fort Belvoir, Virginia, funds have been provided for research on plants. The Army is interested in devising ways of measuring the emotional re-sponses of people via plants, without having to sensitize the plants to a special person beforehand.

The Navy is also showing interest. Eldon Byrd, an operations analyst with the Advanced Planning and Analysis Staff of the Naval Ordnance Laboratory in Silver Spring, Maryland, has been duplicating Backster's experiments with some success. A member of the American Society for Cybernetics and senior member of the Institute for Electrical and Elec-tronic Engineers, Byrd attached the electrodes of a polygraph to the leaves of a plant, and has been observing definite fluctuations of the polygraph needle as the plant responds to various stimuli. Like Backster, Byrd found that by merely thinking of harming a plant's leaf it was possible to make the polygraph needle jump. Byrd's experiments in-volved monitoring a plant's reaction to stimuli from water, infrared and ultraviolet light, fire, physical stress, and dismemberment.

Byrd believes the galvanometrical effect produced by a plant is not caused by electrical resistance in the leaf, but by a change of biopotential in the cells from outside to the inside membrane, as defined by the Swedish Dr. L. Karlson, who has shown that a cluster of cells can change polarity, though the energy which causes cells to become polarized is not known. Byrd believes that a voltage change in the cells is what is being measured, and that it is the mechanism of consciousness which causes the change in potential.

Byrd's research supports Backster's observations that plants exhibit a quality of awareness and an empathy to other organisms that are stimulated in their presence. Like Backster, Byrd also found a major problem in his experiments to be the plants' tendency to "faint" under excess stress, suddenly ceasing to respond even to the most basic stimuli, such as light and heat. Like Backster and Sauvin, Byrd was able to demonstrate on television a plant's reaction to various stimuli, including his *intent* to burn it. On camera Byrd got a plant to respond to his shaking a spider in a pill box. The plant responded with about a second's delay, the response continuing as long as a minute. He also got a strong reaction when cutting the leaf from another plant.

Byrd, who has a master's degree in medical engineering from George Washington University and is a member of Mensa, a worldwide organization whose primary requirement is an extremely high intelligence quotient, has no ready solution to explain the apparent response of plants to human thoughts, and is open to widely disparate explanations, including alterations of the earth's magnetic field, supernatural and spiritual phenomena, and the mysterious mechanics of bioplasma. In a paper presented in 1972 to the American Society of Cybernetics, Byrd reviewed numerous Russian experiments with thought transmission via "bioplasma," which certain Soviet scientists claim to be a previously undiscovered form of energy.

In May, 1973, Byrd began to set up an experiment to instrument the tiny leaves of *Mimosa pudica*, which are so sensitive that they collapse when touched. Byrd believes that, by using a thin wire barely touching a mimosa leaf, he can pick up through a special amplifier minute changes in voltage or resistance. Also available to Byrd is one of the world's finest chart recorders, made in West Germany by Siemens, which shoots out more than three feet of recording paper per second with the patterns recorded by a jet of ink only a few microns wide. With these devices Byrd hopes to be able to pick up plant reactions which have hitherto gone unnoticed.

Byrd is also planning to work with a primitive marine alga, *Acetabularia cremulata*, which, though two inches long, is made up of only a single cell. If this monocellular plant exhibits the "Backster Effect," Byrd will then surgically remove its nucleus. If it then fails to respond, Byrd hopes this will offer proof that the genetic material in the nuclei of plant cells is chiefly responsible for plant response.

A revolutionary new lie-detector device known as a Psychological Stress Evaluator has also been made available to Byrd, along with lab space and facilities, by Allan Bell, inventor of the device, who is president of Dektor Counter Intelligence Systems, a firm he recently formed with two other ex-intelligence officers. The device, tested by monitoring twenty-five segments of the television program *To Tell the Truth*, is said to have picked the persons who were telling the truth with 94.7 percent accuracy. The theory behind the device is that the human voice normally operates in both audible frequencies and inaudible frequency modulations, except when a person is under stress. According to the inventors of the device, when the inaudible FM vibrations disappear from the voice under stress, the ear does not note the difference, but the machine can trace the fluctuations on a chart. Byrd is now working on a means of adapting the device for employment in conjunction with plants.

In Japan a soft-spoken doctor of philosophy and successful electronics engineer from Kamakura, a charmingly gardened retreat not far from Yokohama harbor, has developed a similar lie detector into a device with the most fabulous results yet achieved in the plant kingdom. A regular consultant on lie detection for the Japanese police, Dr. Ken Hashimoto read about Backster's laboratory experiments and decided to wire one of the family cactuses to an ordinary polygraph by means of acupuncture needles.

His intent was more revolutionary than Backster's, Sauvin's or Byrd's. He hoped to enter into actual conversation with a plant; to do so he counted on an improvement he had made in the Japanese procedure for lie detection. To simplify and make less expensive the process of police interrogation, Dr. Hashimoto developed a system, similar to Dektor's, whereby nothing more than a cassette tape is needed to record the reactions of a suspect. Electronically transposing the modulations of the suspect's voice, Hashimoto was able to produce on a paper a running graph reliable enough to pass muster in a Japanese law court.

It now dawned on Hashimoto that by reversing the system he might be able to transform the tracings from a graph into modulated sounds, giving voice to a plant. His first experiments with a cactus similar to the giant saguaro of California and the Arizona desert, but much smaller, were a failure. Loath to conclude that either Backster's reports or his own equipment was defective, Hashimoto decided that it might be he who was having trouble communicating with the plant, despite the fact that he is one of Japan's leading researchers into psychic phenomena.

His wife, on the other hand, who loves plants and is renowned for her "green thumb," soon got sensational results. As Mrs. Hashimoto assured the plant that she loved it, there was an instant response from the cactus. Transformed and amplified by Dr. Hashimoto's electronic equipment, the sound produced by the plant was like the high-pitched hum of very-high-voltage wires heard from a distance, except that it was more like a song, the rhythm and tone being varied and pleasant, at times even warm and almost jolly.

John Francis Dougherty, a young American from Marina Del Rey, California, who witnessed one of these conversations, says it sounded as if Mrs. Hashimoto, speaking in modulated Japanese, was being answered by the plant in modulated "cactese." Dougherty further reports that the Hashimotos became so intimate with their plant that they were soon able to teach it to count and add up to twenty. In answer to a query as to how much two and two make, the plant would respond with sounds which, when transcribed back into inked tracings, produced four distinct and conjoined peaks.

Dr. Hashimoto, who got his doctorate from Tokyo University, and is chief of the Hashimoto Electronics Research Center, as well as managing director and chief of research for the Fuji Electronic Industries—which produce the huge animated electrical signs that illumine Tokyo

—has since demonstrated the adding capacities of his cactus to audiences all over Japan.

Asked to explain the phenomenon of his talking and adding cactus, Dr. Hashimoto, who is also, surprisingly, one of Japan's best-selling authors—his *Introduction to ESP* is in its sixtieth printing and his *Mystery of the Fourth Dimensional World* is in its eightieth—answered that there are many phenomena that cannot be explained by the theories of present-day physics. He believes there is a world beyond the present three-dimensional world defined by physics, that this three-dimensional world is merely a shadow of a fourth-dimensional, nonmaterial world. He further believes that this fourth-dimensional world controls the three-dimensional material world through what he calls "mind concentration" or what others call psychokinesis, or mind-over-matter.

The possibilities of such mind control being used for either good or evil on this planet is the problem now facing these researchers. Since Sauvin's ordination as a minister at the Psychic Science Temple of Metaphysics, he has become a strong pacifist, abhorrent of the use of thought-controlled weapons against animals and plants as well as humans. Though he has taken out business certificates on such devices—which put him on record as the inventor—he is loath to disclose his most sensitive invention, code-named Device 13, for fear that it could quickly be developed by the Department of Defense into a foolproof thought-controlled guided missile. The temple's spiritual leader, the Reverend R. William Daut, is a trumpet medium, one who communicates with those who have departed by going into trance and having a trumpet levitate in a semidarkened room; through it the voices of the departed speak. Made of three pieces of aluminum in the shape of a cheerleader's megaphone, the trumpet has no electronic or other gimmicks. The voices simply seem to materialize out of thin air, at times recognizable as individuals known to the listeners and at others as guiding spirits; often included are such extraneous sound effects as the distant barking of dogs.

Sauvin says the purpose of the exercise is to convey enlightenment, to give profound and beautiful inspirational messages on wisdom, love, and the continuity of life. True religion, says Dr. Daut, is universal intelligence. "There is no death. There are no dead. Reformation is never denied us, here or hereafter."

The trumpet system, says Sauvin, is no more unusual than that of the Oracle at Delphi or of the talking statues of the initiate priests of ancient Egypt; the doctrines, familiar since the erection of temples, include: the fatherhood of God, the brotherhood of man, immortality of the soul, communication between departed human spirits and living mortals, personal responsibility with compensation and retribution, a path of eternal progress open to every soul by the path of eternal good, nature's laws, both spiritual and physical, and now communion with plants.

If communication of nonverbal messages turns out, as the evidence hints, to transcend limitations of time and space, and to take place via some spectrum of energies which is unrelated to what humans call "electromagnetic," the idea of a dialogue with unseen intelligences active in planes beyond that of man's self-limitations, such as was practiced by mystics of the caliber of Jakob Boehme, may no longer seem far-fetched. If we find the means to receive such messages we may reopen the doors to the cosmos.

CHAPTER 4

Visitors from Space

One day late in October of 1971, a blue Volkswagen "bug" carrying some unusual scientific equipment drove into Oak Grove Park near Temecula, a tiny southern California village near the Pechenga Indian Reservation, not far from the famous Mount Palomar Observatory. Out of the driver's seat stepped a forty-seven-year-old Silesian-born electronics engineer—L. George Lawrence. With a field assistant he had come to this remote desertlike spot to record signals from wild-growing oak trees, cacti, and yuccas. Lawrence chose the park because, in his words, it is "an electromagnetic 'deep-fringe' area, with no man-made interferences, and thus ideal for getting clean, uncontaminated plant reactions."

An important difference between Lawrence's apparatus for capturing plant signals and that of Backster, Vogel and Sauvin is that it incorporates, in a temperature-controlled bath, living vegetal tissue shielded behind a Faraday tube that screens out even the slightest electromagnetic interference. Lawrence found that living vegetal tissue is able to perceive signals far more delicately than electronic sensors. It is his belief that *biological* radiations transmitted by living things are best received by a *biological* medium.

Lawrence's equipment also differs significantly from that of the other experimenters in that it dispenses with the need to use electrodes on plants if they are far enough away from their neighbors to rule out signal interference, as is usually the case in desert areas. Instead, Lawrence simply trains a lensless tube with a wide aperture—the optical axes of which parallel the design axis of the Faraday tube—at a target plant. At greater distances he substitutes a telescope for the lensless tube, and makes the plant more visible by hanging a white cloth on it.

Lawrence's living tissue can pick up a directional signal from distances up to *one mile away.* To stimulate his plant subjects into distinct reactions he "dumps a premeasured quantity of electricity into them," activating the stimulus by remote control with a timer which allows him to walk or drive back to the sensing station. His exploratory experiments are made during colder seasons when most vegetation is dormant, so as to be doubly sure that spurious signals from other plants are not garbling his measurements.

Perturbations in the living tissue of his recorder are detected, not visually through a penrecorder, but aurally by means of a continuous, low even whistle, similar to that produced by a sine-wave generator, which changes into a series of distinct pulses whenever it is disturbed by signals from a plant.

On the day of their arrival at Oak Grove Park in 1971 Lawrence and his assistant took a break for a late-afternoon snack, seating themselves about ten yards from their instrument, which was left pointing randomly at the sky.

As Lawrence bit into a Hebrew National knockwurst, the steady whistling sound from his equipment was interrupted by a series of distinct pulsations. Lawrence, who had not yet digested the knockwurst, but had well digested the Backster effect, thought the signals might have been caused by his killing some of the cells in the sausage. Second thoughts reminded him that kosher sausage is biologically dead. As Lawrence checked his instrumentation, the audio signal, to his amazement, continued to produce a distinct chain of pulses for over half an hour before the even whistle returned, indicating that nothing more was being received. The signals had to be coming from somewhere, and since his device had been continuously pointed upward toward the heavens, Lawrence was faced with the fantastic thought that *something or someone was transmitting from outer space.*

The implications of the phenomenon were such that on their way home Lawrence and his partner could not avoid discussing them though, for the moment, they decided not to make public their finding in the event that not true signals but "bugs" in their equipment could have produced what they had heard. The possibility of life beyond earth was both disturbing and exciting to them. Hints about life elsewhere have so far been vague, including the discovery of "organized elements" or organisms in meteorites, and infrared spectra on Mars, which imply organic molecules. There are also rare nonrandom radio interstellar signals whose reception was claimed by Tesla and Marconi, but they were so ridiculed that they were finally reduced to silence; and there are intergalactic radio emissions from pulsars.

Loath to jump to a premature conclusion that he had picked up an intelligent signal from trillions of miles away through a plant tissue, Lawrence spent several months improving his equipment into what he termed a "biodynamic field station designed for interstellar signal reception."

By April of 1972, his equipment was sufficiently refined for him to attempt to point it once more in the same direction which had brought the reaction at the time of the sausage biting. As a laser expert and author of the first technical book on that subject to appear in Europe, Lawrence had carefully noted the direction in which his apparatus had been pointing and had determined that it was aligned on Ursa Major, a seven-star constellation in the region of the north celestial pole, popularly called the Big Dipper. To insure that the equipment would be located as far away from life forms as possible, Lawrence drove out to the Pisgah Crater, a volcanic butte at twenty-three-hundred-feet elevation in the middle of the arid Mojave Desert. The crater is surrounded by some thirty square miles of flat lava beds with not so much as a blade of grass. Aligning his telescope—coupled with the Faraday tube, a camera, an electromagnetic interference monitor, and the tissue chamber—to celestial coordinates 10 hours 40 minutes plus 56 degrees, which gave him the general direction for Ursa Major, Lawrence switched on his audio signal. After a ninety-minute interval, his equipment again picked up a recognizable, though briefer, pattern of signals. According to Lawrence, the periods between rapid series of pulses ranged from approximately three to ten minutes over a stretch of several hours as he monitored a single spot in the heavens.

Having thus successfully repeated his 1971 observations, Lawrence began to wonder whether he had not accidentally stumbled on a scientific discovery of major proportions. He had no idea from where the signals might be coming or what or who was sending them, but it seemed to him highly possible that galactic drift played some role in their origin. "The signals might be spilling over from the galactic equator, which has a dense star population," said Lawrence. "We could be getting something from that area rather than from the Big Dipper."

After the Mojave Desert confirmation of his first observations, Lawrence continued tests from his residence-laboratory, pointing his machine at the same coordinates, leaving it on round the clock. Lawrence says that he had to wait weeks and sometimes months for the signals to come through but, when they did, the reception of something was unmistakable. One signal produced a brr-r-r-r-r beep-beep-beep type of audio pulse which Lawrence maintains no earthly entity has achieved.

Pressed to speculate on the nature of the strange signals, Lawrence stated: "I don't believe they are directed at earthlings. I think we are dealing with transmissions between peer groups, and because we don't know anything about *biological communications* we are simply excluded from these 'conversations.' I also believe that the energy transmitted must be fantastically high since our instrumentation is not at all sophisticated and it would take a tremendous amount of power to create any response in it from such astronomical distances. The signals, therefore, may be of an emergency nature. Something may be happening up there and someone may be desperately calling for help."

Deciding that his findings may be of crucial significance and could herald a new and as yet unimagined system of communication, Lawrence has sent a copy of his October, 1971, tape, together with a seven-page report, to the Smithsonian Institution in Washington, D.C., where it is preserved as a potentially historical scientific document. The report concludes:

> An apparent train of interstellar communication signals of unknown origin and destination has been observed. Since interception was made by biological sensors, a biological-type signal transmission must be assumed. Test experiments were conducted in an electromagnetic deep-fringe area, the equipment itself being impervious to electromagnetic radiation. Follow-up tests revealed no equipment defects. Because interstellar listening experiments are not conducted on a routine basis, the suggestion is advanced that verification tests should be conducted elsewhere, possibly on a global scale. The phenomenon is too important to be ignored.

Lawrence says the instrumentation tape, as a mere audio presentation, is unpleasant to listen to, but reviewers of the tape have conceded that "a fascinating degree of enchantment" tends to emerge after the tape has been played back three or more times, typically over a period of weeks.

The tape contains a short, incremental series of deep harmonious oscillations resembling nonsense chatter or background modulations. An intelligent character of the overall pulse train is implied by discrete spacing patterns, apparent repetitions of sequences, and highly attenuated electromagnetic noise.

Lawrence looks forward to the day when he can arrange for computer analysis of the taped signals, which might be able to provide additional clues to their nature. They are far too rapid to allow manual extraction of the data. Even so, he is not too optimistic that such analysis can produce concrete results. "If the signals are of a personal nature, no means known to modern computer technology will be able to decipher them," he says. "We simply do not have today bionic-type computers which could collect seemingly random data and come up with a concise and rational readout."

Lawrence's most important conclusion, that biological-type sensors are needed in order to intercept biological signals, applies particularly to communications from outer space. As he puts it: "Standard electronics are next to worthless here, since 'bio-signals' apparently reside outside of the known electromagnetic spectrum."

Lawrence points out that in the 1950s scientists who had previously insisted that our small planet was unique in the universe began to admit, on the basis of careful celestial observations and other inferences, that we may not be alone in the cosmic immensity, and to concede the possible existence of extraterrestrials, whose development might be far superior to our own.

In the early nineteenth century Karl Friedrich Gauss—the German mathematician and physicist for whom an electromagnetic unit of magnetic flux density is named—proposed that man might make known his presence on earth to cosmic beings by cutting huge swaths hundreds of miles long in the Siberian taiga to form a right angle. This was followed by the suggestion of the Austrian astronomer J. J. von Littrow that geometric canals be dug in the Sahara, filled with kerosene, and set aflame at night; and the recommendation of the French scientist Charles Gros that a vast mirror be built to reflect sunlight directly at Mars.

These farfetched ideas were updated when, in the summer of 1927, radio observations were made which in the framework of then existing knowledge seemed to imply that earth might be under the scrutiny of communications satellites of extraterrestrial origin. Jorgen Hals, a Norwegian radio engineer, while listening to a short-wave radio station transmitting from Eindhoven in the Netherlands, heard weird echoes for which he could not account. Nor could a number of Dutch and British professors and technicians who carried out a series of experiments to confirm Hals's findings.

The puzzling anomaly was all but forgotten until the early 1950s, when various specialists began to put forward a theory of extraterrestrial interference to explain it. The theorists intrepidly assumed the intermittent existence of an interstellar communications probe designed, first, to monitor solar systems for intelligent life, then retransmit radio-frequency emanations from such life, including earthlings, back to a distant "home-world." Though these far-out interpretations were discounted, even mocked, by the mainstream of scientific opinion, their critics became far less vocal when another series of observations was made, this time involving a television signal which appeared to have been received after a mysterious delay of over three years.

In September, 1953, C. W. Bradley of London picked up the call letters of the American station KLEE-TV in Houston, Texas, on his living-room television tube. Over the next several months the same letters were observed on TV screens in the offices of Atlantic Electronics Ltd. in the English city of Lancaster. What was eerie about these receptions was not that the TV signal had been sent from so far away, since this happens often enough to cause no surprise, but that the signal had been sent about three years prior to the time of its reception, the call letters KLEE having been changed to KPRC in 1950. Explanations that the signals could have been stored in a "plasma cloud" hovering above the earth which released the data in a broadcast for all to see gave no reasons as to how this could have been done or why, and suggestions that the whole thing was merely a meaningless—though extremely expensive—hoax seem far-fetched.

Spurred by the mysteries of these phenomena, American researchers began seriously to consider interstellar communications via radio. But radio was soon ruled out after it was realized that its wavelengths could be absorbed by interstellar gas clouds and nebulae, blocked by various shielding layers around hoped-for faraway target planets, or affected by cosmic radio noise. Only one possible wavelength remained to reach such targets, the much shorter and more penetrating one emitted by neutral galactic hydrogen.

But terrestrials still hoped to receive radio waves from space. In 1960 Dr. Frank Drake initiated Project Ozma—named for the princess who became ruler of the fictional kingdom of Oz—which used a huge circular radio telescope eighty-five feet in diameter at the National Radio Astronomy Observatory near Greenbank, West Virginia. Drake and his colleagues hoped to detect possible intelligent extraterrestrial transmissions from the regions of two nearby stars, Tau Ceti and Epsilon Eridani. Only recently was it discovered that orbiting Epsilon Eridani is a massive planet six times the weight of Jupiter, largest of the nine planets now known to revolve around the sun.

Although Ozma failed to obtain results, scientists are still hotly pursuing the subject of communication with extraterrestrial intelligences, the phrase being now shortened into the acronym CETI.

In the summer of 1971, a group of American scientists at the National Aeronautics and Space Administration's Ames Research Center completed studies for a new Project Cyclops, which proposed a network of ten thousand radio dish telescopes, forming a collective surface of several square kilometers, to be mounted on rails and spread across one hundred square miles of the New Mexican desert. Requiring a cybernetic "nervous system" of brand-new supercomputers, Cyclops was estimated by Charles Seeger of New Mexico State University to cost five billion dollars. In light of the stringent cutbacks in the U.S. space-research funding, it is unlikely that Cyclops will become a reality. This leaves the field to a huge radio telescope more than half a kilometer in diameter currently under construction at the Astrophysical Observatory in the Soviet Crimea.

All of these projects, Lawrence complains, assume that signals must come by radio since that is the most efficient means of communication known to the scientists of this planet. If they converted to his idea of receiving biological signals, Lawrence feels they would have a much better chance. The notion is echoed by Joseph F. Goodavage, author of *Astrology: The Space Age Science,* who, in an article for *Saga* magazine (January, 1973), stated: "Rigid enforcement of established Scientific Method, as a kind of quasi-religion—with its burdensome ritual and tradition—may be the most serious obstacle in the path of direct communication between *Homo sapiens* and other civilizations that may be thriving throughout interstellar, intergalactic space."

Employed as an instrumentation engineer for a Los Angeles space-science corporation, Lawrence decided to design some more sophisticated transducers—or converters of one type of input energy into another type of output energy. Knowing that a mechanical device which could use heat, environmental pressure, electrostatic fields, and gravitational changes simultaneously was not up to the task, he theorized that a plant might be able to turn the trick because it had the necessary components built in by nature.

When he began to study the problem in 1963, Lawrence found he could get no help from plant specialists and biologists because none of them knew enough physics, and especially electronics, to visualize what he was driving at. In his search for a biological system for radiating and receiving signals, Lawrence began by going over the experiments made in the 1920s by the Russian histologist Alexander Gurwitsch and his wife, who proclaimed that all living cells produce an invisible radiation. Gurwitsch had noticed that the cells in the tips of onion roots seemed to be dividing at a definite rhythm. Believing this due to an extra unexplained source of physical energy, Gurwitsch wondered whether it might not come from nearby cells.

To test out his theory he mounted one root tip in a horizontally oriented thin glass tube to act as a ray gun. This he pointed at a similar onion root tip, also protected in a tube, but with a small area on one side exposed naked to serve as a target. After three hours of exposure, Gurwitsch examined sections from the target root under his microscope. When he compared the number of cell divisions, he found 25 percent more in the exposed, irradiated area. The receiver root had seemingly picked up a vital energy from its sender neighbor.

To try to block the emission, Gurwitsch repeated the experiment with a thin shield of quartz between the roots, but obtained essentially the same results. However, when the quartz was coated with gelatin, or a simple sheet of glass was substituted, no enhanced cell division could be observed. Since glass and gelatin were known to block various ultraviolet frequencies on the electromagnetic spectrum, Gurwitsch concluded that the rays emitted by the cells of an onion root tip must be as short as or shorter than ultraviolet. Because they apparently increased cell division, or "mitosis," he called them "mitogenetic rays."

Gurwitsch's findings had created a furor in the scientific world as laboratories hastened to check them. Since the wavelengths claimed for the new rays were more powerful than the ultraviolet frequencies which reach the earth from the sun, many biologists could not believe that living processes were capable of generating them. In Paris two researchers reported similar results; in Moscow one of Gurwitsch's own countrymen showed that he could increase the budding of yeast more than 25 percent by exposing it to "mitogenetic" rays from onion roots.

A pair of scientists at the Siemens and Halske Electric Company near Berlin came to the verdict that the radiation was a fact; and in Frankfort, a researcher actually succeeded in measuring it, not through its effect on vegetal life, but with electrical instruments. On the other hand, equally reliable Anglo-Saxon investigators could detect no effects. In the United States, when the prestigious Academy of Sciences issued a report that Gurwitsch's discovery was not replicable, and therefore strongly suggested it might be the product of his imagination, Gurwitsch was sped into limbo.

Though Lawrence lacked an ultraviolet spectrometer to detect "mitogenetic" radiation, he was fascinated by Gurwitsch's system of *directing* the energy. His observations also nudged Lawrence almost involuntarily to the position that there was a psychological, or "mental," factor involved in Gurwitsch's maverick work. Continuing to probe further with a sensitive high-impedance device of his own design, Lawrence sought to discover whether individual cells in a quarter-inch slice of onion, attached to a Wheatstone bridge and an electrometer, would react to various stimuli. He found that they seemed to respond to irritations such as a puff of smoke, or even to his mental image of their destruction, in about one hundred milliseconds, or one tenth of a second.

What seemed most odd to Lawrence was that the reaction of the onion tissue seemed to change depending on whether he, or someone else, was directing thought at it. People with "psychic gifts" seemed to elicit much stronger responses than the practical-minded Lawrence. As he commented: "If one can cause, or get something to cause, harm to a cell—assuming that the cell has a cellular consciousness—the reaction pattern in it will change from experimenter to experimenter."

About this time Lawrence came across Backster's work and decided to build a sophisticated psycho-galvanic analyzer or plant response detector. With his new equipment, Lawrence got a series of "wild" tracings from his plants; but, because of what he retrospectively calls his "ignorance and classical Prussian orthodoxy," he ascribed these effects to faults in his instrumentation. Nevertheless, his suspicion that plant tissues could pick up human thought and emotion slowly became more concrete in the light of Backster's achievements. Lawrence was reminded that years previously Sir James Jeans, the British astronomer, had written that "the stream of human knowledge is impartially heading toward a non-mechanical reality: the Universe begins to look more like a great *thought* than a great machine. Mind no longer appears as an accidental intruder into the realm of matter. We are beginning to suspect that we ought rather to hail it as the creator and governor of this realm."

In October of 1969, Lawrence began to publish a series of popular articles based on his reading and research, the first of which appeared as "Electronics and the Living Plant" in *Electronics World.* Lawrence told his readers that, for the first time in the millennia since the first green leaves poked their heads out of Paleozoic swamps, plants were at last beginning to be studied for their "electrodynamic properties."

Four main questions, said Lawrence, were starting to attract serious attention: Could plants be integrated with electronic readouts to form major data sensors and transducers? Could they be trained to respond to the presence of selected objects and images? Were their alleged supersensory perceptions verifiable? Of the 350,000 plant species known to science, which were the most promising from the electronic point of view?

Providing detailed instructions for investigating the behavior of living plant cells with microelectrodes, Lawrence also reported that in the "Moon Garden" developed by Republic Aviation at Farmingdale, New York, scientists had been able in the 1960s to induce what appeared to be "nervous breakdown" and "complete frustration" in plants being tested as possible space foods and that, even earlier, in his laboratory at East Grinstead, Sussex, England, L. Ron Hubbard, founder of Scientology, had noted that plants dislike certain types of artificial light, such as the cold light emitted by sodium street lamps, which can cause them to come out in a cold sweat clearly visible on their foliage.

Lawrence warned his readers that work with plants was not just a matter of electronic expertise and that working with the Backster Effect involved much more than the mere ability to construct top-quality electronic equipment. "There are certain qualities here," he wrote, "which do not enter into normal experimental situations. According to those experimenting in this area, it is necessary to have a 'green thumb' and, most important, a genuine love for plants."

Half a year later Lawrence followed up his revelations with an even more controversial article in the same magazine, entitled "Electronics and Parapsychology." Lawrence's article began by asking: "Does man possess latent sensitivities that have been stifled by modern communications systems?" He then pointed out that although the fledgling science of parapsychology, long suspect because of an occult background, was having to fight for acceptance, the application of electronic instruments was permitting dramatic new experiments and bringing forth stunning discoveries which might rival the orthodox communications arts and sciences currently in use.

Stressing that the need for machine systems capable of testing ESP in an unbiased, impartial manner had been recognized fifty years ago, when an Italian scientist, Federico Cazzamalli, developed an ultra-high-frequency apparatus for testing human telepathy, Lawrence reported that the Italian's experiments had never been repeated because the Fascist dictator Benito Mussolini had declared the work secret.

A fascinating offspring of Cazzamalli's ideas and machine, continued Lawrence, is an apparatus called the "Integratron," researched by George W. van Tassel, a self-taught inventor living in Yucca Valley, California, not far from the Giant Rock airport. Developed over twenty years, and still under construction, van Tassel's contrivance is housed in a non-metallic domelike structure thirty-eight feet high and fifty-eight feet in diameter, which looks like an astronomical observatory. It is an electrostatic, magnetic generator with armatures over four times larger than any others in existence. The *Proceedings* of van Tassel's College of Universal Wisdom state that the fields generated by his machine encompass its entire structure and this is why the dome contains no nails, bolts, or metal but is held together like a Chinese puzzle and is six times stronger than the commercial building code requires. When completed it promises, says van Tassel, not only to help solve the problem of extraterrestrial communication, but to afford such possibilities as rejuvenation of body cells, an antigravity force, and the ultimate of psychic experiences: time travel.

What puzzles orthodox scientists and makes skeptics of many of them is a lack of any working theory to cover this kind of phenomenon. One scientist, Dr. W. G. Roll, in his presidential address to the 7th Annual Convention of the Parapsychological Association held in Oxford, England, in 1964, postulated "psi-fields," which might be analogous to electromagnetic or gravitational fields, possibly possessed by all objects, living and nonliving, which could react with known physical fields and with one another. Another theory, put forward by Dr. G. D. Wasserman at the Ciba Foundation Symposium in 1956, leans on quantum mechanics. Wasserman suggests that "psi-fields," which enable persons to have paranormal experiences, are due to the reception of inconceivably small "quanta of energy," far more minute than those which can be absorbed by matter fields of classical physics.

The Backster Effect and other related considerations, says Lawrence, "lead to the idea that psi is but a part of a so-called 'paranormal matrix' —a unique communications grid which binds all life together. Its phenomena apparently work on a multi-input basis which operates beyond currently known physical laws." Within this framework, says Lawrence, plants, after sensitization or conditioning by their owners, can reach a state of communication in which they are able to react to their owners' emotions or states of mind even when they are far away.

In the June, 1971, issue of *Popular Electronics*, Lawrence provided any researcher wishing to investigate communication with plants with detailed diagrams and a parts list for a "response detector" allowing for extremely sensitive tests.

Warning that constant repetition was an important factor in such testing, Lawrence stated that if a plant specimen is stimulated continuously, badly injured, or infrequently watered, it would tire quickly, or even lapse into shock and die. Researchers were therefore cautioned to be gentle with their plants and allow them to recuperate after experimentation. The area in which plants live must be quiet, added Lawrence, "so that the stimuli can be effectively applied with a minimum of power-line noise or disturbances from radio-frequency transmission to cause faulty indications."

Lawrence's ideas about plants were corroborated and elaborated by the experience of a Czech publisher and student of physiological psychology, Jan Merta, now living in Canada, whose psychic gifts allow him to plunge an iron bar into a blacksmith's forge, heat it to incandescence, then calmly brush sparks off its white-hot end with his bare hand as easily as he would rub dust from a shelf.

Freshly settled in Canada, Merta supported himself for two months by working as a troubleshooter for a large Montreal grower and importer of tropical plants. When clients in office and residential buildings complained that their plants were getting sick, Merta was sent to ascertain the trouble. Because he also took care of thousands of plants in the firm's extensive greenhouses, Merta noticed that the effects of loneliness produced when a plant is taken away from hundreds of its friends often caused it such a shock that it would pine, even die; however, when returned to the greenhouse, it immediately perked up and regained its normal green health.

As the result of hundreds of "house calls," Merta noticed that plants throve better when constantly communicated with by office workers and home owners than if left to themselves. Examples of the majestic *Ficus benjamini*, nearly thirty feet tall, transported from Florida, though in excellent condition upon arrival, when placed around a fountain in a shopping center's indoor circular solarium started to wilt within two days in spite of careful watering and feeding. Yet those in heavily traveled passageways leading to the solarium retained their radiant vigor. To Merta this was a sure sign that the *Ficus* enjoyed being admired by the passers-by.

In 1970, when Lawrence read that in the Ukraine radio frequencies and ultrasonic vibrations had been used to stimulate cereal grain seeds to produce higher yields as far back as the early 1930s and that the United States Department of Agriculture had successfully experimented in the same way, he gave up his college position and set about independently developing advanced equipment with which he hopes that seed grains can be provoked, on a commercial scale, to grow better and faster. "If a plant seedling can be stimulated on a parapsychological basis, as the famous plant breeder Luther Burbank knew, then I don't see why," says Lawrence, "we can't transmit specific signals to whole fields of crops to stimulate their growth without all these damned soil-killing fertilizers."

In the February, 1971, issue of *Popular Electronics* Lawrence presented his own experimental arrangement to test his theories about stimulating plant growth in an extremely high-voltage electrostatic field. It is the invention and use of cheap chemical fertilizers, he asserted, which has suppressed the ideas of countless engineers about how to nourish plants electrically. With nitrate pollution from these fertilizers threatening the world's ecological panorama and its water supply, he urges that these ideas be revived.

Acting on his own advice, Lawrence is working up patent applications on special sound-type plant stimulation techniques, which he is combining with Backster Effect methods in order to stimulate his plants in a wireless fashion. This effort has turned Lawrence the engineer into Lawrence the philosopher. "There was a time, when I was a child, when the whole world seemed alive and knowing," he wrote in *Organic Gardening and Farming*. "Trees were friends and as George Eliot put it: 'Flowers see us and know what we're thinking about.' Then came a time when plants just grew, silently and without emotion. But today, I'm entering a second childhood, as least as far as plants are concerned."

Lawrence, torn between his interest in stimulating plant growth electrically and his projects to achieve interstellar communication, feels that the effort to contact extraterrestrial life is more important in the long run because "if routine results can be achieved in CETI, many questions attached to riddles in the plant kingdom will be answered as a consequence.

On June 5, 1973, the research division of Anchor College of Truth in San Bernardino announced that it was inaugurating the world's first biological-type interstellar communications observatory under the direction of L. George Lawrence, now also a vice-president of Anchor. For the new research program Lawrence has designed what he calls a Stellartron, which combines in one three-ton instrument the features of a radio telescope and the biological signal-receiving system of the biodynamic field station.

Anchor president, Ed Johnson, told the press that since radio astronomy had failed to detect intelligent signals from space, the college was backing Lawrence's idea that radio transmission was out of date and that biological communication should be given a trial.

Pointing out that in our own galaxy alone there are some 200 billion stars, Lawrence says that if one assumed each of them to have at least five companion planets, a total of one trillion might consequently be available for study. Even if only one planet in a thousand has intelligent life this would amount to one billion in our galaxy alone. Multiplied by the ten billion galaxies believed to comprise the observable universe, then there may be 10,000,000,000,000,000,000 planets capable of sending some kind of signal to Earth.

Anchor's founder, Reverend Alvin M. Harrell, thinks that contact with another race in the universe will trigger a tremendous explosion of knowledge. As Harrell says: "Given the destructive brutality of humankind, we may expect any newly discovered civilization to be infinitely more loving and compassionate than we are."

"Perhaps plants are the true extraterrestrials," Lawrence observes, "for they converted an early mineral world into a habitat suitable for man by processes that border on near-perfect magic! What remains to be done now is to remove all traces of occultism and make plant response, including communications phenomena, a verifiable component of orthodox physics. Our instrumentation concepts reflect this effort."

If Lawrence is on the right track, the ardently desired prospect of producing hardware to move man into the vastness of interstellar space on Columbian voyages of discovery will be rendered as obsolete as Columbus's flagship, *Santa Maria*. Lawrence's research, suggesting as it does that intelligences are communicating instantly across distances requiring millions of light-years to reach, indicates that what is needed is not spaceships but the proper "telephone numbers" to contact them. Though the work is still in an exploratory stage, his biodynamic field station may be a step toward plugging into the universal switchboard, with plants as the pretty, cheerful and efficient co-operators.

CHAPTER 5

Latest Soviet Discoveries

In Russia, millions of newspaper readers were introduced to the ideas that plants communicate their feelings to man in October, 1970, when *Pravda* published an article entitled "What Leaves Tell Us."

"Plants talk . . . yes, they scream," declared the official organ of the Communist party. "It only *seems* that they accept their misfortunes submissively and silently bear pain." *Pravda's* reporter, V. Chertkov, tells how he witnessed these extraordinary goings-on in Moscow when he visited the Laboratory for Artificial Climate at the renowned Timiryazev Academy of Agricultural Sciences.

Before my eyes a barley sprout literally cried out when its roots were plunged into hot water. True, the plant's "voice" was registered only by a special and extremely sensitive electronic instrument which revealed a "bottomless vale of tears" on a broad paper band. As though it had gone crazy, the recording pen wriggled out on the white track the death agony of the barley sprout, although, to look at the little plant itself, one would never have guessed what it was going through. While its leaves, green as ever, stood upright, the plant's "organism" was already dying. Some kind of "brain" cells within it were telling us what was happening.

Pravda's reporter also interviewed Professor Ivan Isidorovich Gunar, head of the academy's Department of Plant Physiology, who, together with his staff, had performed hundreds of experiments, all of which confirm the presence of electrical impulses in plants similar to the well-known nerve impulses in man. The *Pravda* article noted that Gunar talked about plants as he would about people, distinguishing their individual habits, characteristics, and proclivities. "He even appears to converse with them," Chertkov wrote, "and it seems to me that his plants pay attention to this good, graying man. Only persons invested with certain power are like this. I have even been told of a test pilot who talked to his misbehaving airplane, and I myself have met an old captain who talked with his ship."

When Gunar's chief assistant, Leonid A. Panishkin, a former engineer, was asked by the *Pravda* reporter why he gave up the technology in which he was trained in order to work in Gunar's laboratory, he replied: "Well, there I used to be involved with metallurgy; here there is life." He was echoed by another young laboratory worker, Tatiana Tsimbalist, who affirmed that since she had come to work with Gunar she had "learned to look at nature with different eyes."

Panishkin said he was particularly interested in searching out those conditions which might best suit the specific needs of plants and how "our green friends"—as the *Pravda* reporter termed them—react to light and darkness. By using a special lamp which shone with the same intensity as the sun's rays reaching earth he had found that plants tired in an overextended day and needed rest at night. He hoped that it might one day be possible for plants to turn lights on or off in a greenhouse at will: "a live electric relay."

The studies of the Gunar team may open up new vistas in plant breeding, since in their laboratory it has been found that individual plants more resistant to heat, cold, and other climatological factors can be "selected" within minutes by testing them with their instruments, although these qualities have heretofore taken geneticists years to establish.

In the summer of 1971, an American delegation from the Association for Research and Enlightenment (ARE), founded by the seer and healer Edgar Cayce at Virginia Beach, Virginia, visited Russia. The Americans —four medical doctors, two psychologists, one physicist, and two educators—were shown a film by Panishkin entitled *Are Plants Sentient?* The film demonstrated effects produced on plants by environmental factors such as sunlight, wind, clouds, the dark of night, the tactual stimulus from flies and bees, injuries produced by chemicals and burning, and even the very proximity of a vine to a structure to which it might cling. The film showed further that the immersion of a plant in chloroform vapor eliminates the characteristic biopotential pulse normally apparent when a leaf is given a sharp blow; it also indicated that the Russians are now studying the characteristics of these pulses to establish the relative degree of a plant's health.

One of the American doctors, William McGarey, head of the ARE medical research center in Phoenix, Arizona, stated in his report that the intriguing part of the movie was the method used to record the data. Time-lapse photography made the plants seem to dance as they grew. Flowers opened and closed with the coming of darkness as if they were creatures living in a different time zone. All injury-induced changes were recorded by a sensitive polygraph attached to the plants.

In April, 1972, *Weltwoche,* a Swiss newspaper published in Zurich, came out with an account of both Backster's and Gunar's work which it said had taken place simultaneously and independently. That same week the Swiss article was translated into Russian in a weekly review of the foreign press, *Za Rubezhom (Abroad)* published in Moscow by the USSR's Union of Journalists, under the caption: "The Wonderful World of Plants." These scientists, said the Russian version, are "proposing that plants receive signals and transmit them through special channels to a given center, where they process the information and prepare answering reactions. This nervous center could be located in root tissues which expand and contract like heart muscle in man. The experiments showed that plants have a definite life rhythm and die when they don't get regular periods of rest and quiet."

The *Weltwoche* article also caught the attention of the editors of the Moscow newspaper *Izvestiya*, who assigned their reporter M. Matveyev to do a story for the paper's weekly magazine supplement. Though the newsman referred to Backster's suggestion that plants might have memory, language, and even rudiments of altruism, he strangely omitted Backster's most startling discovery, that his philodendron had perceived his *intent* to harm it.

Deciding (the *Izvestiya* reporter told his readers) that a "sensation was being propagated in Western newspapers," Matveyev traveled to Leningrad, where he interviewed Vladimir Grigorievich Karamanov, director of the Laboratory of Biocybernetics of the Institute of Agrophysics, in order to get an authoritative opinion.

The Institute of Agrophysics was founded over forty years ago at the behest of the renowned solid-state physicist, Academician Abram Feodorovich Ioffe, who became particularly interested in the practical application of physics to the design of new products, first in industry, then in agriculture. After the institute opened its doors, Karamanov, then a young biologist, was inspired by Ioffe to familiarize himself with the world of semiconductors and cybernetics and, in due course, began building microthermistors, weight tensiometers, and other instruments to register the temperature of plants, the flow rate of fluid in their stems and leaves, the intensity of their transpiration, their growth rates, and characteristics of their radiation. He was soon picking up detailed information on when and how much a plant wants to drink, whether it craves more nourishment or is too hot or cold. In the first issue of *Reports of the USSR Academy of Sciences* for 1959, Karamanov published "The Application of Automation and Cybernetics to Plant Husbandry."

According to the *Izvestiya* reporter, Karamanov showed that an ordinary bean plant had acquired the equivalent of "hands" to signal an instrumental brain how much light it needed. When the brain sent the "hands" signals, "they had only to press a switch, and the plant was thus afforded the capability of independently establishing the optimal length of its 'day' and 'night.'" Later, the same bean plant, having acquired the equivalent of "legs," was able instrumentally to signal whenever it wanted water. "Showing itself to be a fully rational being," the account continued, "it did not guzzle the water indiscriminately but limited itself to a two-minute drink each hour, thus regulating its water need with the help of an artificial mechanism.

"This was a genuine scientific and technical sensation," concluded the *Izvestiya* reporter, "a clear demonstration of twentieth-century man's technical abilities."

Asked whether he thought Backster had discovered something new, Karamanov somewhat condescendingly replied: "Nothing of the sort! That plants are able to perceive the surrounding world is a truth as old as the world itself. Without perception, adaptation does not and cannot exist. If plants had no sense organs and didn't have a means of transmitting and processing information with their own language and memory, they would inevitably perish."

Karamanov, who throughout the interview made not a single comment on plants' ability to perceive human thought and emotion— Backster's really sensational discovery—and seemed oblivious of Backster's success in getting his philodendron to recognize a "plant assassin," rhetorically asked the *Izvestiya* reporter: "Can plants discern shapes? Can they, for instance, differentiate a man causing them hurt from another who waters them?" Replying to his own question, while at the same time putting Backster into what he considered to be a proper perspective for Soviet readers, Karamanov said: "Today I cannot answer such a question. And not because I doubt that Backster's experiments were immaculately set up and repeatedly performed, though perhaps a door slammed, or a draft wafted into the room, or something else. The fact is that neither he, nor we, nor anyone else in the world is yet ready to decipher *all* plant responses, hear and understand what they 'say' to one another, or what they 'shout' at us."

Karamanov also predicted that in the long run it would be possible cybernetically to direct all the physiological processes of plants not, as he put it, "for the sake of sensation, but for the advantage of plants themselves." When plants are able to auto-regulate their environment and establish optimal conditions for their own growth with the help of electronic instruments, said Karamanov, this should be a long step toward larger harvests of cereal grains, vegetables, and fruits. Making clear that the achievements were not just around the corner, Karamanov added, "We are not still learning to talk with plants and understand their peculiar language. We are working out criteria which will help us to control the life of plants. Along this difficult but fascinating road, a multitude of surprises still await us."

The *Izvestiya* article was followed that summer by a story in the monthly magazine *Nauka i Religiya* (*Science and Religion*), which has the dual aim of putting forward the latest findings in world science while at the same time playing down—in a section headed "The Theory and Practice of Atheism"—the church-defended notion of a spiritual world hierarchically beyond that of man.

The article's author, engineer A. Merkulov, going further than the *Izvestiya* weekend supplement, recounted how the plant of the "American criminologist" Backster had not only responded to the scalding death of brine shrimp but also to the killer of its vegetal neighbor. Such response to people's moods, added Merkulov, had also been detected at the state university in Alma Ata, capital of the Soviet Kazakh Republic, the apple orchard of the Soviet Union. There scientists have found that plants repeatedly react to their owners' illnesses and to their emotional states.

Noting that plants had long ago been shown to have "short-term memory," Merkulov said that this fact too had been confirmed by the Kazakh scientists. Beans, potatoes, wheat, and crowfoot (*Ranunculus*) after proper "instruction" seemed to have the capability of remembering the frequency of flashes from a xenon-hydrogen lamp. The plants repeated the pulsations with what Merkulov called "exceptional accuracy," and since crowfoot was able to repeat a given frequency after a pause as long as eighteen hours it was possible to speak of "long-term" memory in plants.

The scientists next went on, according to Merkulov, to condition a philodendron to recognize when a piece of mineralized rock was put beside it. Using the system developed by Pavlov with dogs, whereby he discovered the "conditioned reflex," the Kazakh scientists simultaneously "punished" a philodendron with an electrical shock each time a mineralized ore was placed next to it. They reported that, after conditioning, the same plant, anticipating the hurtful shock, would get "emotionally upset" whenever the block of ore was put beside it. Furthermore, said the Kazakh scientists, the plant could distinguish between mineralized ore and a similar piece of barren rock containing no minerals, a feat which might indicate that plants will one day be used in geological prospecting.

Merkulov concluded his reportage with the idea that the *control* of all processes in plant growth was the ultimate goal of all the new experimentation. In an institute of physics in the Siberian city of Krasnoyarsk, he wrote, "Physicists are even now regulating the growth of a monocellular seaweed, *Chlorella.* Experiments are continuing and becoming increasingly complex, and there is no doubt that in the not-distant future scientists will be able to control the growth, not only of the simplest, but of higher plants."

Merkulov beguiled his readers with the idea that this control might well be possible over great distances. "By studying how to 'understand' plants," he prophesied, "man may create automatic contrivances which themselves will watch over fields in such a way that, at any given moment, they can satisfy the every need of crops. The day is not far away when scientists will also work out a theory on the adaptation and resistance of plants to unpleasant conditions in their environment which will encompass how they react to irritants, and to stimulators and herbicides as well."

Toward the end of 1972 Soviet readers were given more food for thought in an article "Flower Recall" published in the popular color-illustrated *Znaniya Sila* (*Knowledge Is Power*), one of the many magazines issued by the Knowledge Society, the leading organization for popular science in the USSR. This time its author was not a news-hungry journalist or an inspired engineer but a professor and doctor of psychological sciences, V. N. Pushkin. Far from suggesting that the

American criminologist Backster had really not discovered anything new, Pushkin began with a complete description of Backster's shrimp experiment. He then let his readers in on the fact that one of his young colleagues, V. M. Fetisov, had made him aware of Backster's accomplishments in the first place, and had been so determined to work with the Backster Effect that he had persuaded Pushkin to take part in the experiments. Fetisov brought an ordinary potted geranium from his home and attached it to an encephalograph.

As Fetisov was making his first attempts to get a response from his pet plant, Georgi Angushev, a Bulgarian student working up a dissertation in psychology at the Lenin Pedagogical Institute in Moscow, heard about the Fetisov-Pushkin experiments and came to their laboratory to see what was going on. Pushkin described Angushev as a talented researcher with many qualities, the most important of which to their "psycho-botanical experiments," as he termed them, was the fact that the Bulgarian was an excellent hypnotist.

Fetisov and Pushkin surmised that a hypnotized person should be able to send emotions to a plant more directly and spontaneously than a person in a normal state. Hypnotizing a young girl by the name of Tanya, who was described by Pushkin as of "lively temperament and spontaneous emotionality," they first implanted in her the notion that she was one of the most beautiful women in the world, then the notion that she was freezing in harsh raw weather. At each change in the girl's mood the plant, which was attached to an encephalograph, responded with an appropriate pattern on the graph. "We were able," says Pushkin, "to get an electrical reaction as many times as we worked, even to the most arbitrary commands."

To obviate criticism that the plant's response was only the result of chance events taking place in the room, the Muscovite psychologists switched on their encephalograph and let it run for long periods between their experiments. But the instrument never registered any reaction of the kind evoked in the plant by the emotions suggested to a hypnotized subject.

Pushkin and Fetisov decided to see whether the plant could detect a lie, as Backster had claimed. It was suggested to Tanya that she think of a number from 1 to 10. At the same time she was told she would never reveal the number, even if pressed to do so. When the researchers counted slowly from 1 to 10, pausing after each digit to inquire whether it was the one she had thought of, each time Tanya responded with a decisive "No!" Though the psychologists could not see any difference in her answers, the plant gave a specific and clear reaction to her internal state when the number 5 was counted. It was the number which Tanya had selected and promised not to reveal.

In his conclusion Pushkin stated that he felt strongly that by pursuing the course initiated by Backster it might be possible to make advances into the thorny problem of the human brain's functioning, which Pavlov over half a century ago had called the "crown of earthly nature." Seizing the opportunity for a political remark, Pushkin reminded those who might look askance at his and Fetisov's new research that at the opening of Moscow Institute of Psychology in 1914 Pavlov had declared that the task of unlocking the mysteries of the brain and its activity was "so unexpressibly enormous and complex that it depends on the totality of thought's resources, namely, complete freedom, and bold deviation from set patterns of research."

Using Pavlov as a shield against what he obviously thought would be attacks from his professional colleagues, Pushkin stressed that the renowned physiologist's statement was as up to date in 1972 as when he had made it. Lest his message not ring clear, he added: "Experience in the development of natural sciences, especially physics, has shown that one should not fear new discoveries, however paradoxical they might seem at first glance."

In his conclusion, the Moscow professor speculated that vegetal cells in the flower react to processes taking place in the nervous system of human subjects or in what is vaguely referred to as their "emotional states." Seeking a meaning for the flower's reaction, Pushkin wrote: "Perhaps between two informational systems, the plant cells and the nervous system, a specific link exists. The language of the plant cell may be related to that of the nerve cell. These wholly different living cells seemed to be able to 'understand' one another."

Pushkin further theorized that in the cells of a flower there take place processes somehow related to mentation and asserted that man's psyche —a word which he says is as yet entirely undefined even by the "ologists" of his own discipline—and the perception, thought, and memory connected to it are all just a specialization of processes existing at the level of vegetal cells.

Pushkin asserts that this conclusion is most important since it will open new thinking about the origin of the nervous system. Noting that in the development of science many different answers have been proposed for what constitutes the actual informational material in human thought, Pushkin skipped lightly over various theories, ranging from the one that holds nerve cells to be elements of a living cybernetic computer to the one which claims that not the cells but the molecules of matter within them may be the basic informational units.

"What is actually irritating the flower?" asked Pushkin, then answered that it might turn out to be some kind of biophysical structure, the ejection of which beyond the confines of the human organism takes place the moment a marked emotional state is reached and carries information about the person from whom it is ejected. Whatever the truth may turn out to be, continued Pushkin, one thing is sure: "Research into the plant and man interrelationships can shed light on some of the most urgent problems in contemporary psychology."

The magic and mystery of the world of plants lying behind these scientific doings have also recently become the subject of a new book entitled *Grass* by a popular slavophile writer, Vladimir Soloukhin, which appeared in four issues of the three-million-circulation magazine *Nauka i Zhizn (Science and Life)* at the end of 1972. Born a country boy in a village outside the ancient city of Vladimir in northern Russia, Soloukhin became fascinated with the *Pravda* account of Gunar's work and wondered why it had not evoked more excitement among his fellow Russians.

"Perhaps the elements of memory in plants are superficially treated," he writes, "but at least there they are in black and white! Yet no one calls his friends or neighbors, no one shouts in a drunken voice over the telephone: Have you heard the news? Plants can feel! They can feel pain! They cry out! Plants remember everything!"

When Soloukhin began to telephone his own friends in excitement he learned from one of them that a prominent member of the Soviet Academy of Sciences, working in Akademgorodok, the new town inhabited almost exclusively by research scientists on the outskirts of Siberia's largest industrial center, Novosibirsk, had stated:

> Don't be amazed! We too are carrying out many experiments of this kind and they all point to one thing: plants have memory. They are able to gather impressions and retain them over long periods. We had a man molest, even torture, a geranium for several days in a row. He pinched it, tore it, pricked its leaves with a needle, dripped acid on its living tissues, burned it with a lighted match, and cut its roots. Another man took tender care of the same geranium, watered it, worked its soil, sprayed it with fresh water, supported its heavy branches, and treated its burns and wounds. When we electroded our instruments to the plant, what do you think? No sooner did the torturer come near the plant than the recorder of the instrument began to go wild. The plant didn't just get "nervous"; it was afraid, it was horrified. If it could have, it would have either thrown itself out the window or attacked its torturer. Hardly had this inquisitor left and the good man taken his place near the plant than the geranium was appeased, its impulses died down, the recorder traced out smooth— one might almost say tender—lines on the graph.

In addition to a plant's ability to recognize friend and foe, Soviet researchers also noted that one plant supplied with water can somehow share it with a deprived neighbor. In one institute of research a cornstalk planted in a glass container was denied water for several weeks. Yet it did not die; it remained as healthy as other cornstalks planted in normal conditions nearby. In some way, say Soviet botanists, water was transferred from healthy plants to the "prisoner" in the jar. Yet they have no idea how this was accomplished.

As fantastic as this may seem, a kind of plant-to-plant transfer has been taking place in England in experiments begun in 1972 by Dr. A. R. Bailey. Two plants in an artificially lit greenhouse in which temperature, humidity, and light were carefully controlled were suffering from lack of water. Bailey and his collaborator measured the voltages generated between two parts of both plants. When one plant was watered from the outside through plastic tubes, the other plant reacted. As Bailey told the British Society of Dowsers: "There was no electrical connection between them, no physical connection whatsoever, but somehow one plant picked up what was going on with the other."

Soloukhin, in his book *Grass*, the title of which conveys, as with Carl Sandburg, Walt Whitman, or Pete Seeger, the most extended meaning of the word "grass," or indeed everything growing, took to task the lack of sensitivity to the vegetal world around them on the part of the Soviet populace. Targets of his criticism included agricultural bureaucrats, individual collective farmers, lumber executives, and even salesgirls in Moscow flower shops.

"Human observation," writes Soloukhin ironically in the opening chapter of *Grass*, "is so precise that we begin to notice the very air we breathe only when it is insufficient for our needs. More exactly, I should say 'value' rather than 'notice.' We do not really value air, or even think about it, so long as we can breathe normally, without difficulty." He adds that, though man prides himself on his vast array of knowledge, he is like a radio technician who knows how to repair a receiver without understanding the theoretical essence of radio waves, or like our cavemen ancestors who put fire to use while unaware of the process of rapid oxidation. Even today, says Soloukhin, we squander heat and light yet have not the slightest clue to, or interest in, their original essence.

Man is equally callous, says Soloukhin, about the fact that the land around him is green. "We trample grasses into dirt, we strip the land with bulldozers and caterpillar treads, we cover it with concrete and hot asphalt. Disposing of wastes from our infernal industrial machines we dump upon it crude oil, rubbish, acids, alkalis, and other poisons. But is there that much grass? I, for one, can imagine man in a boundless, grassless wilderness, the product of a cosmic, or perhaps humanly noncosmic, catastrophe."

Seeking to re-evoke wonder for nature in the hearts of an overurbanized Soviet youth, Soloukhin tells the story of a prisoner who, incarcerated in a dank cell, finds among the pages of an old book, given him by a kindly jailer, a tiny seed smaller than a pinhead. Overcome with emotion at the first visible sign of real life he has seen for years, the prisoner imagines that the microscopic seed is all that remains from the former luxuriant and festive plant kingdom in the great world outside the prison. Planting the seed in a bit of earth in the sole corner of the cell afforded a ray of sunlight, and watering it with his tears, the prisoner waits for a wonder to unfold.

Soloukhin accepts this wonder as a true miracle ignored by man only because it is repeated thousands of billions of times daily. Even if all the world's chemical and physical laboratories with their complex reagents, precise analyses, and electronic microscopes were placed at the prisoner's disposal, he continues, even if the prisoner studied the seed's every cell, atom, and atomic nucleus, he still would not be able to read the mysterious program lying within the seed, to lift the impenetrable veil which could cause it to transform itself into a juicy carrot, a branch of sweet-scented dill, or a radiant-colored aster.

Soloukhin was fascinated with the statement by I. Zabelin, doctor of geographical sciences and Moscow University professor, who in his article "Dangerous Delusions" in one of the USSR's leading opinion forums, *Literaturnaya Gazeta*, wrote: "We are only beginning to comprehend the language of nature, its soul, its reason. The 'inner world' of plants is hidden from our gaze behind seventy-seven seals." Though these lines were in no way emphasized in the printed column, says Soloukhin, "they appeared to me as bold-face type."

During a trip to Paris, Soloukhin was happy to observe florist shops scattered in all, and even the poorest, districts of the French capital. Finding a decent bouquet of flowers in the Soviet capital, he says, can become the object of a day-long search.

Soloukhin has recently attacked the obtuse views of Soviet agricultural officials. Writing in the October, 1972, issue of *Literaturnaya Gazeta*, he deplores the abandon with which generations-old natural Russian meadowlands have been allowed to deteriorate while fields needed for cereal crops are being plowed and planted to grasses for animal fodder. "We could cover Europe with hay and green grass from our meadows and build a haystack extending from the Mediterranean to Scandinavia," writes Soloukhin. "Well, why don't we?" His rhetorical question only provoked an angry rebuttal from the USSR's Deputy Minister of Agriculture, who insisted on upholding the status quo.

In a battle similar to that taking place in the United States and other countries, Soloukhin is unremittingly denouncing unecologically minded industrialists in his country, who are turning the rivers and lakes into cesspools, and despoiling its forests, all in the name of increased production. Seeking to reverse a half century of Communist dicta, this "passionate lover of nature, its defender and bard"—to quote one of Soloukhin's publishers—exhorts his countrymen to cooperate with, rather than subdue, nature.

That the Soviets are bent on introducing the idea of substituting for the burning of coal, oil, and natural gas—three forms of preserved solar energy originally captured by plants—new, more direct, and pollution-free ways to tap the sun was revealed by an article in the first 1973 issue of *Khimiya i Zhizn (Chemistry and Life)*. The article pointed to the research of the American Nobel Prize winner Melvin Calvin in photosynthesis, wherein he discovered that plant chlorophyll under the influence of the sun's rays can give up electrons to a semiconductor such as zinc oxide. Melvin and his co-workers created a "green photoelement," which produced a current of approximately 0.1 microamperes per square centimeter. After several minutes, said the Soviet magazine, the plant chlorophyll becomes desensitized or "exhausted," but its life could be extended by the addition of hydroquinone to the salt solution which acts as an electrolyte. The chlorophyll seems to act as a kind of electron pump passing electrons from the hydroquinone to the semiconductor.

Calvin has calculated that a chlorophyll photoelement with an area of ten square meters could yield a kilowatt of power. He has theorized that in the next quarter century such photoelements could be manufactured on an industrial scale and would be a hundred times cheaper than silicone solar batteries now being experimented with.

Even if the direct conversion of sunlight into energy via plant chlorophyll is not realized by the year 2000, says *Chemistry and Life*, it wouldn't put too much of a burden on man to wait a few decades longer when he considers the millions of years it took to convert plants into coal.

As Soviet readers were being offered the notion that plants could one day directly produce energy for man's needs from the sun, Professor Gunar, together with an increasing number of young Soviet scientists, was continuing to probe the awareness of plants to determine, for instance, how their reactions may serve as an index of frost, cold, and heat resistance in varieties of barley and cucumbers and of disease potentials in potatoes.

A clue to where Professor Gunar got the original inspiration to launch his series of detailed and ongoing studies on plants, which were to have such repercussions throughout the Soviet republics, is to be found in an article published in 1958 by A. M. Sinyukhin. This colleague of Gunar's refers to an outstanding Indian physiologist and biophysicist whose work was buried during his lifetime by Western science and hardly ever cited since his death. As early as 1920 Kliment Arkadievich Timiryazev, in whose honor the Moscow Agricultural Academy is named, heralded this work as introducing a new epoch in the development of world science. This unheralded genius, wrote Timiryazev, developed an apparatus, startling in its simplicity and sensitivity, to counter the entrenched idea of the German botanists that communication in plant tissue was simply hydrostatic. In so doing, he was able to measure in hundredths of a second the time needed for a signal to travel along the stems of various plants.

Sinyukhin made clear that the USSR's plant men were so impressed by the achievements of this Indian scientist that they were going to mount a research campaign based directly upon his long-ignored conclusions. In December, 1958, a pontifical meeting was held in the main conference hall of the USSR Academy of Sciences in celebration of the hundredth anniversary of the Indian sage's birth. Three leading academicians summed up for the huge crowd assembled the fantastic breakthroughs which the Indian had made not only in plant physiology but in physics and in the vital and up to then unheard-of links between these distinct disciplines.

"Many years, during the course of which whirlwind developments have taken place in biophysics," said A. V. Lebedinskii, one of the leading Russian pioneers in radiobiology and space medicine, "separate us from the time this Indian's work appeared. But, reading his works today, one still senses in them an unexpected and fruitful source of a whole chain of ideas in contemporary science."

In this great work, said another speaker, "The green world of plants, seeming to us so immobile and insensitive, came miraculously to life and appeared no less, and often even more, sensitive than animals and man."

Six years later the Soviet Union honored this neglected scientist by publishing in two handsomely illustrated volumes his selected works, together with copious commentaries including one entire book which had first made its appearance over half a century before, in 1902: *Response in the Living and Non-Living*. In these works Sir Jagadis Chandra Bose managed to accomplish the essential requirement of the twentieth century: an amalgamation of the wisdom of the ancient East with the precise scientific techniques and language of the modern West.

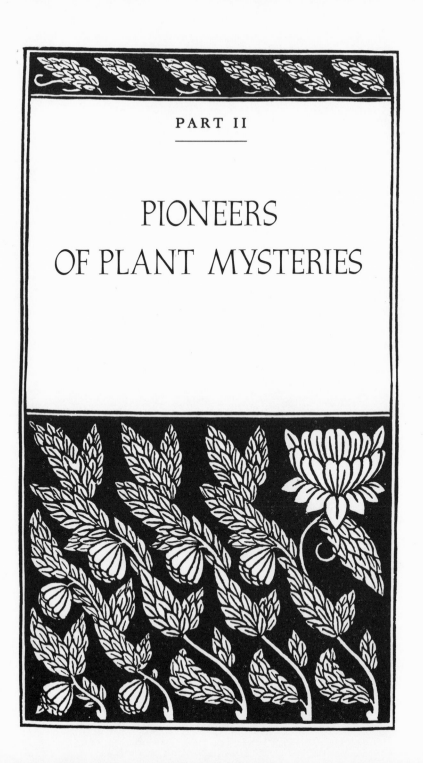

PART II

PIONEERS
OF PLANT MYSTERIES

CHAPTER 6

Plant Life Magnified
100 Million Times

On the eastern coast of the subcontinent of India, in the old state of Bengal, there stands on four acres of ground off the Acharya Prafulla-chandra Road, north of Calcutta University, a complex of buildings made of fine grayish and purple sandstone in the classical design of pre-Mohammedan India. The main edifice, known as the Indian Temple of Science, bears an inscription: "This temple is dedicated to the feet of God for bringing honor to India and happiness to the world."

Just inside the entrance are glass cases containing a series of intriguing instruments devised more than fifty years ago to measure the growth and behavior of plants, down to their minutest detail, by magnification of these processes up to 100 million times. The instruments stand in their cases, in mute testimony to the genius of a great Bengali scientist whose work united in one man the fields of physics, physiology, and psychology, and who found out more about plants than anyone before and perhaps after him, but who remains almost unmentioned in classical histories of subjects in which he specialized.

The buildings and their gardens are the Institute of Research built by Sir Jagadis Chandra Bose, of whose work in the field of plant physiology the *Encyclopaedia Britannica* could only say, nearly half a century after his death, that it was so much in advance of his time it could not be precisely evaluated.

When Bose was still a child, his father had already painfully discerned in 1852 the main impact of the British education system on Indian children: the imposition of a slavish and monotonous imitation of all things Western and the requirement to learn by rote. The senior Bose, therefore, sent his son to a simple village *pathasala* rather than a colonial primary school.

At the age of four the boy was carried to his classroom on the shoulders of a reformed gang robber, or *dacoit,* who could find employment after a long jail term with no one but Bose's father. From this *dacoit* the boy absorbed stories of savage battles and adventurous escapades, but was also exposed to the natural goodness of a man who had been befriended after being rejected by society as a criminal. "No nurse," Bose wrote in his later life, "could have been kinder than this leader of lawless men. Though he scoffed at the juridical strictures of society, he had the deepest veneration for natural moral law."

Bose's early contacts with the peasantry also were crucial to his own appreciation of the world. Much later he told an academic gathering: "It was from those who till the ground and make the land blossom with green verdure, from the sons of fisher-folk who told stories of the strange creatures that frequented the depths of mighty rivers and of stagnant pools, that I first derived a lesson of that which constituted true manhood. From them, too, I drew my love of nature."

When Bose graduated from St. Xavier's College, his brilliant teacher Father Lafont was so impressed by the young man's aptitude in physics and mathematics that he wanted him to go to England and read for the Civil Service examinations. Bose's father, who had personally experienced the deadening nature of that profession, advised his son to become, not an administrator, but a scholar, with the prospect of ruling nobody but himself.

At Christ College Bose was taught physics, chemistry, and botanical sciences by such luminaries as Lord Rayleigh, discoverer of argon in the air, and Francis Darwin, son of the evolutionary theorist. Having passed his tripos examinations, Bose went on to take a bachelor's degree in science the following year at London University. But when Bose was appointed professor of physics at Calcutta's Presidency College, reputedly the best in India, the appointment was protested by the college's principal and by the director of Bengal's public instruction, who maintained the all too usual view that no Indian was competent to teach science.

To get back at Bose for being recommended over their heads by a letter from the Postmaster General to the Viceroy, they offered him a special appointment at a salary only half that of the English professors, and gave him no facilities to carry on research. In protest Bose refused to touch his monthly salary check for three years, which obliged him to live in bitter deprivation, the more so as his father had fallen heavily into debt.

That Bose was brilliant as a teacher was attested by the fact that no roll call had to be instituted in his classroom, which was always packed to the walls. Bowing to his obvious talents, the authorities who had snubbed him finally gave him a position at full pay.

Although Bose had no resources other than his own salary, a twenty-square-foot room to serve as a laboratory, and an illiterate tinsmith whom he trained as his mechanic, he began work in 1894 to see if he could improve the instruments recently devised by Heinrich Rudolph Hertz to transmit "Hertzian" or radio waves through the air. Hertz, who died that same year at the premature age of thirty-seven, had startled the world of physics by fulfilling in his laboratory the prediction of the Scottish physicist James Clerk Maxwell, nearly twenty years before, that the waves of any "electrical disturbance in the ether"—the variety and scope of which was far from known—would, like those of visible light, be reflective, refractible, and polarizable.

While Marconi in Bologna was still trying to transmit electric signals through space without wires, a race he was to win officially against similar efforts by Lodge in England, Muirhead in the United States, and Popov in Russia, Bose had already succeeded. In 1895, the year before Marconi's patent was issued, at a meeting in the Calcutta town hall, presided over by Sir Alexander Mackenzie, the lieutenant-governor of Bengal, Bose transmitted electric waves from the lecture hall through three intervening walls—and Mackenzie's portly body—to a room seventy-five feet away, where they tripped a relay which threw a heavy iron ball, fired off a pistol, and blew up a small mine.

Bose's accomplishments now began to attract the attention of the British Royal Society (equivalent of the academy of sciences in other countries), which, at Lord Rayleigh's behest, invited Bose to publish a paper in its proceedings on the "Determination of the Wave Length of Electric Radiation," and offered him a subsidy from its parliamentary grant for the advancement of science. This was followed by Bose's being awarded a doctorate of science by London University.

The *Electrician*, leading journal in its field, came forward to suggest that, on the basis of Bose's work, it might now become practical to place electromagnetic transmitters in lighthouses and receivers on ships to offer mariners a "third eye" capable of penetrating fog.

In England Bose gave a lecture on his apparatus for investigating electromagnetic waves before a meeting of the British Association for the Advancement of Science in Liverpool, which so impressed Lord Kelvin that he limped up to the ladies' gallery to congratulate Bose's beautiful wife in the most glowing terms on her husband's brilliant work. This triumph was followed in January, 1897, by an invitation to address the Royal Institution at one of its Friday Evening Discourses, which, since the institute's establishment, had become the principal venue for announcements of fresh and momentous investigations and discoveries.

Of Bose's address the *Times* wrote: "The originality of the achievement is enhanced by the fact that Dr. Bose had to do the work in addition to his incessant duties and with apparatus and appliances which in this country would be deemed altogether inadequate." The *Spectator*, echoing this accolade, announced: "There is something of rare interest in the spectacle of a Bengali of the purest descent lecturing in London to an audience of appreciative European savants upon one of the most recondite branches of modern physical science."

Back in India, Bose was buoyed to find that a communication signed by Lord Lister, president of the Royal Society, and by other scientific luminaries, had been sent to the Secretary of State for India, recommending that a center for research and advanced teaching in physics "worthy of that great Empire" be established under Bose's direction at Presidency College.

Despite this recommendation, and an immediate grant by the Imperial Government of £40,000 to set up the center forthwith, mean-minded, jealous functionaries in the Bengal Education Department succeeded in so tying up the project that it never came to fruition. Only the gesture of his fellow Bengali, the poet Rabindranath Tagore, later to win the Nobel Prize for literature, alleviated Bose's disappointment: Tagore came specially to greet him and not finding him at home left a huge magnolia blossom in token of his tribute.

Doggedly pursuing his research whenever the press of his teaching duties in the backbiting climate of the college offered him a spare moment, Bose published in 1898 four papers on the behavior of electric waves, in the *Proceedings of the Royal Society* and in Great Britain's foremost popular scientific journal, *Nature*.

In 1899 Bose noticed the strange fact that his metallic coherer for receiving radio waves became less sensitive if continuously used but returned to normal after a period of rest. This led him to the conclusion that metals, however inconceivably, might exhibit a recovery from fatigue similar to that which took place in tired animals and people. Further work began to convince Bose that the boundary line between so-called "nonliving" metals and "living" organisms was tenuous indeed. Spontaneously moving from the domain of physics into that of physiology, Bose began a comparative study of the curves of molecular reaction in inorganic substance and those in living animal tissue.

To his awe and surprise, the curves produced by slightly warmed magnetic oxide of iron showed striking resemblance to those of muscles. In both, response and recovery diminished with exertion, and the consequent fatigue could be removed by gentle massage or by exposure to a bath of warm water. Other metal components reacted in animal-like ways. A metal surface etched with acid when polished to remove all trace of the etching exhibited reactions in its acid-treated sections which could not be elicited in those nontreated. Bose ascribed to the affected sections some kind of lingering memory of the treatment. In potassium he found that the power of recovery was almost totally lost if it was treated with various foreign substances; this seemed to parallel the reactions of muscular tissue to poisons.

In a presentation to the International Congress of Physics, held in 1900 at the Paris Exhibition, entitled "De la Généralité des Phénomènes Moléculaires Produits par l'Electricité sur la Matière Inorganique et sur la Matière Vivante," Bose stressed the "fundamental unity among the apparent diversity of nature," concluding that "it is difficult to draw a line and say that here the physical phenomenon ends and here the physiological begins." The congress was *"bouleversé"* by Bose's earth-shaking suggestion that the gulf between the animate and inanimate might not be as broad and unspannable as generally believed; its secretary declared himself "stunned."

The enthusiasm of his fellow physicists was, however, not matched by the coterie of physiologists who were invited the following September to a meeting of the physics section of the British Association for the Advancement of Science at Bradford. Because Bose's research overlapped onto territory which they considered their private preserve, the physiologists listened with hostile silence while Bose read a paper contending that Hertzian waves could be used as a stimulating agent on tissues, and that metal response was analogous to that of tissues. To meet the physiologists on their ground, Bose meticulously adapted his experiments to an accepted "electromotive variation" to which they were accustomed, and again got similar curves of muscles and metals responding to the effects of fatigue or of stimulating, depressing, and poisoning drugs.

Shortly thereafter it dawned on Bose that if the striking continuity between such extremes as metals and animal life were real he should also be able to get similar effects in ordinary vegetable plants, which, because they were held to have no nervous systems, were universally reckoned as unresponsive. Picking several horse-chestnut leaves from a tree in the garden next to his lab, Bose found that they responded to various "blows" in much the same way as had his metals and muscles. Excited by the results, he betook himself to his greengrocer and purchased a bag of carrots and turnips, which, of all vegetables, appeared the most stolidly nonsentient, and found them to be highly sensitive. When he chloroformed plants, Bose discovered that they were as successfully anesthetized as animals, and that when the narcotic vapor was blown away by fresh air like animals they revived. Using chloroform to tranquilize a huge pine tree, Bose was able to uproot it and transplant it without the usually fatal shock of such operations.

When Sir Michael Foster, secretary of the Royal Society, came to Bose's laboratory one morning to see for himself what was happening and Bose showed the Cambridge veteran some of his recordings, the older man said jocularly: "Come now, Bose, what is the novelty of this curve? We have known it for at least half a century!"

"But what do you think it is?" Bose persisted quietly.

"Why, a curve of muscle response, of course!" said Foster testily.

Looking at the professor from the depths of his haunting brown eyes, Bose said firmly: "Pardon me, but it is the response of metallic tin!"

Foster was aghast. "What?" he shouted, jumping from his chair, "Tin? Did you say tin?"

When Bose showed him all his results, Foster was as thrilled as he was astounded. On the spot, he invited Bose to give an account of his discoveries at another Friday Evening Discourse at the Royal Institution and offered to communicate his paper personally to the Royal Society in order to secure his priority. At the evening meeting of May 10, 1901, Bose marshaled all the results obtained over four years and demonstrated each one of them with a comprehensive series of experiments before ending with a peroration:

> I have shown you this evening autographic records of the history of stress and strain in the living and non-living. How similar are the writings! So similar indeed that you cannot tell one apart from the other. Among such phenomena, how can we draw a line of demarcation and say, here

the physical ends, and there the physiological begins? Such absolute barriers do not exist.

It was when I came upon the mute witness of these self-made records, and perceived in them one phase of a pervading unity that bears within it all things—the mote that quivers in ripples of light, the teeming life upon our earth, and the radiant suns that shine above us—it was then that I understood for the first time a little of that message proclaimed by my ancestors on the banks of the Ganges thirty centuries ago: "They who see but one, in all the changing manifoldness of this universe, unto them belongs Eternal Truth—unto none else, unto none else!"

Bose's lecture was warmly received and to his surprise his views went unchallenged, despite the metaphysical note at its end. Sir William Crookes even urged that the last quotation not be omitted when the address was published. Sir Robert Austen, one of the world's authorities on metals, praised Bose for his faultless arguments, saying, "I have all my life studied the properties of metals and am happy to think that they have life." He confessed confidentially that he had formed a similar opinion but had been rebuffed when he had once hesitantly hinted at it before the Royal Institution.

A month later, when Bose repeated his lecture and demonstrations before the Royal Society, he received an unexpected blow from "the grand old man of physiological science in England," Sir John Burdon-Sanderson, whose principal work had been a study of muscle behavior and the movements of the Venus's flytrap to which Darwin had first called his attention. As Burdon-Sanderson was *the* authority on electrophysiology, all turned to him to open the discussion which followed Bose's speech.

Burdon-Sanderson began by complimenting Bose on his acknowledged work in physics but followed with the remark that it was "a great pity" that he had wandered from his own field of study to areas which belonged properly to the physiologist. Since Bose's paper was still under consideration for publication he suggested that its title be changed from "Electrical Response in . . ." to "Certain Physical Reactions in . . . ," thus leaving to the physiologists the term "response" with which physicists should not be concerned. As for the electrical responses of ordinary plants, which Bose had described at the end of his address, Burdon-

Sanderson denied categorically that such were possible, since "he himself had tried for many years past to obtain them and had never succeeded."

In his reply Bose said candidly he understood that the *facts* experimentally demonstrated were not questioned by his critic. If, therefore, he was not being impugned on the basis of this evidence, but was being asked to make modifications which altered the whole purpose and meaning of his presentation, on the basis of *authority* alone, he would have to decline. It seemed to Bose inexplicable, he said, that any doctrine could be advocated before the Royal Society which suggested that knowledge could not advance beyond known bounds. Unless he was shown on scientific grounds where his experiments were faulty or defective, he would insist his paper be published as he had written it. At the end of his rebuttal, when no one rose to break the icy silence which hung over the hall, the meeting was adjourned.

Because of doubt thrown on his work by so eminent an expert as Burdon-Sanderson, and to put down a younger man who had so outspokenly challenged his senior, the society voted not to follow up Bose's "preliminary notice" with the full publication of his paper in its *Proceedings,* and instead buried it in its archives, a fate which had befallen other notable papers in the past. To Bose, who all his life had listened to Britishers lecture against the evils of the Indian caste system, the vote seemed to evidence the existence of a not dissimilar system within British science itself. At the institution's laboratories, Bose was consoled by Lord Rayleigh, who told him that he too had been subjected to ceaseless attacks from chemists because, as a physicist, he had had the temerity to predict that a hitherto unsuspected new element would be found in air, a prediction shortly to be verified by his discovery, with the help of Sir William Ramsay, of argon.

The controversy with the physiologists elicited the interest of Bose's former teacher Professor Sidney Howard Vines, the well-known botanist and vegetable physiologist at Oxford, who called on Bose and asked if he could witness Bose's experiments. Vines brought with him T. K. Howes, who had succeeded T. H. Huxley at the British Museum's Department of Botany at South Kensington. When the men saw Bose's plant respond to stimulus, Howes exclaimed: "Huxley would have given years of his life to see this experiment." As secretary of the Linnean Society, he told Bose that, since his paper had been refused for publication by the Royal Society, not only would the Linnean accept it but also he would invite Bose to repeat all his experiments before the physiologists, particularly his opponents.*

As a result of this new presentation to the Linnean Society, on February 21, 1902, Bose was able to write to his friend Tagore: "Victory! I stood there alone, ready for hosts of opponents, but in fifteen minutes the hall was resounding with applause. After the paper, Professor Howes told me that as he saw each experiment, he tried to get out of it by thinking of a loophole of explanation, but my next experiment closed that hole." The president of the Linnean Society wrote Bose a few days later: "It seems to me that your experiments make it clear beyond doubt that all parts of plants—not merely those which are known to be motile —are irritable, and manifest their irritability by an electrical response to stimulation. This is an important step in advance, and will, I hope, be the starting point for further researches to elucidate what is the nature of the molecular condition which constitutes irritability, and the nature of the molecular change induced by a stimulus. This would doubtless lead to some important generalities as to the properties of matter, not only living matter, but non-living matter as well."

Since ordinary plants and their different organs exhibited electrical response indicative of excitation under mechanical and other stimuli, it puzzled Bose that they gave no sign of this excitement by *visible movement.* Unlike the mimosa leaf, which, if irritated, abruptly collapses, owing to a contraction of its cushion-shaped base, or pulvinus, other plants seem, at least to the eye, placidly unconcerned when scraped, burned, or otherwise interfered with. Back home in Calcutta, it suddenly hit Bose that the contraction in the mimosa was magnified by its long leaf stalk. To similarly magnify a suspected contraction in other plants,

*The Linnean Society, named after Carl von Linné or Linnaeus (1707–1778), the great Swedish botanist whose *Genera Plantorum* is considered the starting point of modern systematic botany, was organized at the end of the eighteenth century when Sir J. E. Smith, its first president, acquired Linnaeus' botanical library from his widow.

he designed a special optical lever with which he was able to demonstrate visually that *all the characteristics of the responses exhibited by animal tissues were also found in those of plants.*

Bose communicated the results of these new and extended investigations in December, 1903, in a series of seven papers to the Royal Society, which immediately planned their publication the following year in its "Philosophical Transactions," a series reserved for only the most significant and momentous scientific findings. However, as the papers were being readied for the printer, underhanded intrigues and prejudicial insinuations, which had almost suppressed his Linnean Society offering, began anew and, with Bose unable to refute them from far-off India, won the day.

Convinced by Bose's opponents that his theories should not be officially printed, and without waiting for his detailed records, the society changed its august mind and once again filed Bose's papers in its archives. To Bose this vacillation by the society only justified his decision, taken two years before, no longer to rely wholly upon the acceptance of others before presenting his astonishing discoveries to the world. "Although," as he put it, "I thought I was much too lazy to write books, I was forced into it." To guarantee that the substance of the lectures he had given in London, Paris, and Berlin should receive the widest possible circulation, Bose completed a book-length account of all his experimentation up to the middle of 1902, which was published the same year under the title *Response in the Living and Non-Living.*

Herbert Spencer, the great British synthetic philosopher, very much alive to the important scientific advances of his time, despite his entry at eighty-three into the last year of his life, personally acknowledged Bose's volume with the regret that it was too late for him to incorporate its data into his own massive *Principles of Biology.* Two years later, Professor Waller, one of Bose's most adamant opponents, quietly inserted into his new book, without even mentioning Bose's name, the Bengali's assertion that "any vegetable protoplasm gives electrical response."

Bose then began to concentrate on determining how *mechanical* movements in plants might be similar to those in animals and humans.

Since he knew that in plants there was respiration without gills or lungs, digestion without a stomach, and movements without muscles, it seemed plausible to Bose that there could be the same kind of excitation as in higher animals but without a complicated nervous system.

Bose concluded that the only way to find out about the "unseen changes which take place in plants" and tell if they were "excited or depressed" would be to measure visually their responses to what he called "definite testing blows" or shocks. "In order to succeed in this," he wrote, "we have to discover some compulsive force which will make the plant give an answering signal. Secondly, we have to supply the means for an automatic conversion of these signals into an intelligent script. And, last of all, we have ourselves to learn the nature of these hieroglyphics." In this single statement Bose mapped out for himself a course for the next two decades.

He first began by improving his optical lever into an optical pulse recorder. Consisting of a pair of drums over which revolved a continuous paper band driven by clockwork, this device picked up movements in the plant which were translated through a movable lever attached to a set of mirrors which reflected a beam of light onto the paper. The excursion of the shifting spot of light, followed by means of a sliding inkwell with an ink sponge protruding from it, made visible for the first time movements in plant organs which had thus far remained hidden to the scientific world.

With the aid of this instrument, Bose was able to show how the skins of lizards, tortoises, and frogs as well as those of grapes, tomatoes, and other fruits and vegetables behaved similarly. He found that the vegetal digestive organs in insectivorous plants, from the tentacle of a sundew to the hair-lined flap of a pitcher plant, were analogous to animal stomachs. He discovered close parallels between the response to light in leaves and in the retinas of animal eyes. With his magnifier he proved that plants become as fatigued by continuous stimulation as animal muscles, whether they were hypersensitive mimosas or undemonstrative radishes.

Working with the *Desmodium gyrans*, a species whose continuously oscillating leaves recall the motion of semaphore flags and led to its common appellation, telegraph plant, Bose found that the poison which could stop its automatic ceaseless pulsation would also stop an animal heart and that the antidote for this poison could bring both organisms back to life.

Bose demonstrated the characteristics of a nerve system in mimosa, a plant whose leaflets are symmetrically arranged on each leaf with several leaves stemming from more or less the same point, the whole leaf system borne on small branchlets or petioles issuing from the main stem.

When Bose electrically shocked the stem or touched it with a hot wire, the base of the nearest petiole collapsed within seconds, to be followed, after another interval, by the folding of the leaves at its end. Connecting a galvanometer to the petiole, Bose recorded an electrical disturbance between these two points of reaction. If he touched the tip of a leaf with a hot object, first the leaflets closed and then the base segment drooped.

Bose interpreted these actions as due to electrical excitation, which, in turn, produced mechanical responses; this was also what happened in the animal nerve-muscle unit, where the nerve carried the electric impulse and the muscle contracted in response. Bose later proved that identical results could be produced in both plant and animal systems by cold, anesthesia, or the passage of a weak current.

Bose showed that in mimosa there exists the same kind of "reflex arc" which causes us to withdraw our fingers instantly from a hot stove before pain can be felt. When Bose touched the tip of one leaf on a three-leaf petiole he saw that the leaflets of the disturbed leaf gradually closed, starting from the tip; then the petiole collapsed; lastly, the other two leaves closed from the base upward.

In *Desmodium gyrans,* or the telegraph plant, Bose found that if the cut end of a detached leaflet was dipped in water in a bent glass tube it recovered from the shock of its amputation and began to pulsate anew. Was this not like an excised animal heart which can be kept beating in Ringer's solution? Just as the heart stops beating when blood pressure is lowered and starts again when pressure is raised, Bose found the same was true for the pulsation of the *Desmodium* when the sap pressure was increased or decreased.

Bose experimented with heat and cold to ascertain the optimal conditions under which plant movement was best elicited. One day he found that when all motion stopped in his plant, it suddenly shuddered in a way reminiscent of the death spasm in animals. To determine exactly the critical temperature at which death occurred, he invented a morograph, or death recorder. While many plants met their end at sixty degrees Centigrade, individual plants exhibited variations depending on their previous histories and ages. If their power of resistance was artificially depressed by fatigue, or poison, the death spasm would take place with temperatures as low as twenty-three degrees Centigrade. At death, the plant threw off a huge electrical force. Five hundred green peas could develop five hundred volts, said Bose, enough to fulminate a cook but for the fact that peas are seldom connected in series.

Though it had been thought that plants liked unlimited quantities of carbon dioxide, Bose found that too much of this gas could suffocate them, but that they could then be revived, just like animals, with oxygen. Like human beings, plants became intoxicated when given shots of whiskey or gin, swayed like any barroom drunkard, passed out, and eventually revived, with definite signs of a hangover. These findings together with hundreds of other data were published in two massive volumes in 1906 and 1907.

Plant Response as a Means of Physiological Investigation ran to 781 pages and detailed 315 separate experiments. These went against an entrenched notion, which Bose thus explained: "From the plausible analogy of the firing off of a gun by pulling a trigger, or the action of a combustion engine, it has been customary to suppose that all response to stimulus must be of the nature of an explosive chemical change, accompanied by an inevitable rundown of energy." Bose's experiments, on the contrary, showed him that in plants their movement, the ascent of their sap, and their growth were due to energy absorbed from their surroundings, which they could hold latent or store for future use.

These revolutionary ideas, and especially the finding that plants had nerves, were received with veiled hostility among botanists. The *Botanical Gazette* commended Bose for a path-breaking achievement, but held that his book was "not without errors into which the author has fallen by reason of some unfamiliarity with his materials."

Even as the botanists grumbled, Bose sent to the printer a second, equally massive, volume, *Comparative Electro-Physiology*, setting forth 321 additional experiments; its findings also clashed with current teaching and doctrine. Instead of emphasizing the accepted wide range of specific differences between the reactions of various plant and animal tissues, Bose consistently pointed to a real continuity between them. The nerve, universally held to be typically nonmotile, he showed capable of indisputable movement, which could more delicately be ascertained by mechanical than by electrical means. Whereas plants were considered to lack all power of conducting true excitation, Bose showed they were in fact possessed of this power.

Even more heretically, Bose held that the isolated vegetal nerve is indistinguishable from animal nerve: "So complete, indeed, has that similarity between the responses of plant and animal, of which this is an instance, been found," wrote Bose, "that the discovery of a given responsive characteristic in one case has proved a sure guide to its observation in the other, and that the explanation of a phenomenon, under the simpler conditions of the plant, has been found fully sufficient for its elucidation under the more complex circumstances of the animal."

Going even further, Bose maintained that when electromotive intensity was above or below a certain range the law of polar effects of currents, established by Pflüger, was overturned; in addition, a nervous impulse, supposed to lie beyond any conceivable power of visual scrutiny, attended by a change of form, was entirely capable of direct observation.

The authoritative scientific magazine *Nature*, left gasping by both volumes, wrote of the first: "In fact, the whole book abounds in interesting matter skillfully woven together and would be recommended as of great value if it did not continually arouse our incredulity." Of the second, *Nature* was equally ambivalent in its attitude. "The student of plant physiology," said the reviewer, "who has some acquaintance with the main classical ideas of his subject, will feel at first extreme bewilderment as he peruses this book. It proceeds so smoothly and logically, and yet it does not start from any place in the existing 'corpus' of knowledge, and never attaches itself with any firm adherence. This effect of detachment is heightened by the complete absence of precise reference to the work of other investigators." There were, of course, no other investigators; and the reviewer, limited by the compartmentalized science of his day, had no way of knowing he was dealing with a genius half a century ahead of his time.

In a short statement Bose summed up his philosophy: "This vast abode of nature is built in many wings, each with its own portal. The physicist, the chemist and the biologist come in by different doors, each one his own department of knowledge, and each comes to think that this is his special domain unconnected with that of any other. Hence has arisen our present division of phenomena into the worlds of inorganic, vegetal and sentient. This philosophical attitude of mind may be denied. We must remember that all inquiries have as their goal the attainment of knowledge in its entirety."

One of the blocks to the acceptance by plant physiologists of Bose's revolutionary findings was their inability to construct the delicate instruments he had devised. Yet the mounting opposition to his basic thesis that responses in plants are similar to those due to the nervous system of animals convinced Bose that he should develop an even more refined set of instruments for automatic stimulation and recording of response. He therefore designed a resonant recorder, capable of measuring time up to 1/1000 of a second, to make rapid movement in plants apparent, and an oscillating recorder to reveal the slowest movement in plants.

With the assistance of his new recorder Bose got results on the nervous impulse so convincing that this time they were published in the Royal Society's *Philosophical Transactions.* In the same year Bose published his third massive volume of experimentation, *Researches in Irritability of Plants;* 376 pages; 180 experiments.

In 1914, Bose left for Europe on a fourth scientific mission, this time carrying not only his various instruments but specimens of *Mimosa pudica* and *Desmodium gyrans* to illustrate his lectures. In England he demonstrated before audiences at Oxford and Cambridge how a plant touched on one side would shiver and react on the other. He addressed evening meetings of both the Royal Institution and the Royal Society of Medicine, where Sir Lauder Brunton, who had made experiments on insectivorous plants for Charles Darwin in 1875, remarked that all the subsequent physiological experimentation he had seen since then was "crude in comparison with yours in which you show what a marvellous resemblance there is between the reactions of plants and animals."

The vegetarian and antivivisectionist George Bernard Shaw, having witnessed in Bose's laboratory, through one of Bose's magnifiers, a cabbage leaf going through violent paroxysms as it was scalded to death, dedicated his own collected works to Bose, inscribing them: "From the least to the greatest living biologist." A repentant animal physiologist who had cast the single vote preventing publication of plant research by the Royal Society came up to Bose to confess his misdeed and said, "I could not believe that such things were possible and thought your oriental imagination had led you astray. Now, I fully confess that you have been right all along." Bose, letting bygones be bygones, never divulged his name.

Bose's research was for the first time vividly recorded for the public in the British publication *Nation:*

> In a room near Maida Vale there is an unfortunate carrot strapped to the table of an unlicensed vivisector. Wires pass through two glass tubes full of a white substance; they are like two legs, whose feet are buried in the flesh of the carrot. When the vegetable is pinched with a pair of forceps, it winces. It is so strapped that its electric shudder of pain pulls the long arm of a very delicate level which actuates a tiny mirror. This casts a beam of light on the frieze at the other end of the room, and thus enormously exaggerates the tremor of the carrot. A pinch near the right-hand tube sends the beam seven or eight feet to the right, and a stab near the other wire sends it far to the left. Thus can science reveal the feelings of even so stolid a vegetable as the carrot.

The acclaim which came in the British Isles was repeated in Vienna, where it was the consensus of eminent German and Austrian scientists that "Calcutta was far ahead of us in these new lines of investigation."

Back in India, where the governor of Bengal had arranged for a huge meeting, headed by the sheriff of Calcutta to greet him, Bose spoke of the pursuit, under extreme difficulty, of his investigation of the extraordinary slowness of growth in plants. To conceive of this it is only necessary to state that if the annual growth of a tree is liberally estimated to be five feet, it would take one thousand years to cover a mile.

In 1917, at a huge meeting of students held to honor the knighthood bestowed upon Bose, the chairman remarked that he should be looked upon not as a mere discoverer of scientific truths, but as a Yuga Pravartak, or one who has brought about a new epoch of synthesis in scientific development. This compliment was to Bose small music compared to the opening of his own Institute for Research on the thirtieth of November, on the occasion of his fifty-ninth birthday.

During his speech at the ceremony, Bose, who had declined to patent the device which could have made him, instead of Marconi, the inventor of wireless telegraphy, and had consistently resisted the blandishments of industrial representatives to turn his ideas into profits, stated that it was his particular desire that any discoveries made at his new institute would become public property and that no patents would ever be taken out on them. "Not in matter, but in thought, not in possessions, but in ideas, are to be found the seeds of immortality," Bose told the assembled crowd. "Not through material acquisitions, but in generous diffusion of ideas can the true empire of humanity be established. Thus, the spirit of our national culture demands that we should forever be free from the desire of utilizing knowledge for personal gain."

A year after the foundation of the institute, Bose convened a meeting, sponsored by the governor of Bengal, to announce that, after eight years of struggle, he had finally been able to devise a brand-new instrument, the crescograph. Through the use of two levers, this extraordinary invention not only produced a ten-thousand-fold magnification of movement, far beyond the powers of the strongest microscope, but could automatically record the rate of growth of plants and their changes in a period as short as a minute.

With this instrument Bose showed the remarkable fact that in countless plants, growth proceeds in rhythmic pulses, each pulse exhibiting a rapid uplift and then a slower partial recoil of about a fourth the distance gained. The pulses in Calcutta averaged about three per minute. By watching the progress of the movement on the chart of his new invention, Bose found that growth in some plants could be retarded and even halted by merely touching them, and that in others rough handling stimulated growth, especially if they were sluggish and morose.

To determine a method which would allow him *instantly* to show the acceleration or retardation of a plant's growth in response to a stimulant, Bose now devised what he called a "balanced crescograph," which would allow the plant to be lowered *at the same rate* at which it was growing upward, thus reducing the marking of its growth on the chart to a horizontal line and allowing any changes in *the rate* to express themselves as curves. The method was so extremely sensitive that Bose was able to detect variation of the rate of growth as hyper-minimal as 1/1500 millionths of an inch per second.

In America, *Scientific American*, referring to the significance of Bose's findings for agriculture, wrote: "What is the tale of Aladdin and his wonderful lamp compared to the possibilities of Dr. Bose's Crescograph? In less than a quarter of an hour the action of fertilizers, food, electric currents and various stimulants can be fully determined."

Bose also elucidated the mysteries of tropistic movements in plants, or their tendency to move in response to an external stimulus. At the time of his research, botanists could no more explain these tropisms than could Molière's medical student who passed his exam by answering the question "Why does opium make one sleep?" with the tautology "Because it has a dormitive virtue."

The roots of plants are called "geotropic," because they burrow into the soil. Because their shoots flee the earth they are said to be imbued with "negative geotropism." To heighten this nonsense, branches are said to start out laterally from the shoot by "diageotropism." Leaves turn to light because they are "heliotropic" or "phototropic." If, disobeying this rule, they turn away from light, then they are "negatively phototropic." Roots questing water are described as "hydrotropic," and those bending against the flow of a stream "rheotropic." The tendril's touch is known as its "thigmotropism."

As the botanist Sir Patrick Geddes wrote: "Intellectual activities have their verbalisms, their confusions and misdirections and these may also accumulate into what are practically diseases. Every science, of course, needs its technical terminology but all have suffered from the verbosity of nomenclatures and, notoriously, botany most of all. Thus—apart from the systematic names for each and every species and order which are of course indispensable—there are some fifteen or twenty thousand technical terms in the botanical dictionaries of which many have survived into modern textbooks to the perplexity of the student." In an essay, commenting on the strange power of big words like "heliotropism," Bose said that they usually acted like some malevolent magic to kill curiosity.

Though it was beginning to be finally accepted that plants did possess conducting tissue analogous to animal nerve, it was now urged by plant specialists that the sensibility of plants was, if it did in fact exist, of a very low order. Bose demonstrated that this was not the case.

He showed the tropism exhibited by tendrils to be the result of two fundamental reactions: a direct stimulus inducing contraction and an indirect stimulus causing expansion. In the curvature of the plant organ, the convex side was electrically positive, the concave side negative. Since the human organ most readily available and most sensitive to the perception of electric current is the tip of the tongue, Bose decided to match its detective ability against that of the sensitive leaflet of the *Biophytum* plant. Hooking up a tongue and a leaflet, he passed a current through both organs, gradually increasing the amperage. When the current reached an intensity of 1.5 micro-amperes, or 1 1/2 millionths of the standard electrical unit of current, the leaflet shimmered in response but the overrated tongue had nothing to relate about the current until the intensity had been increased threefold.

With the same instrumentation, Bose showed that plants of all kinds are sensitive. He found "a stoutish tree will give its response in a slow and lordly fashion whereas a thin one attains the acme of its excitement in an incredibly short time."

During Bose's trip to London and Europe in 1919 and 1920, the distinguished scientist Professor John Arthur Thomson wrote in the *New Statesman:* "It is in accordance with the genius of India that the investigator should press further towards unity than we have yet hinted at, should seek to correlate responses and memory expression in the living with their analogs in organic matter, and should see in anticipation the lines of Physics and Physiology and of Psychology converging and meeting. These are questionings of a prince of experimenters whom we are proud to welcome in our midst today."

The usually reserved *Times* wrote: "While we in England were still steeped in the rude empiricism of barbaric life, the subtle Easterner had swept the universe into a synthesis and had seen the *one* in all its changing manifestations." But even those bold statements and the announcement that Bose was to be made a fellow of the Royal Society, in May, 1920, could not stem the all-too-familiar intimations of the doubters and pedants. Bose's old adversary Professor Waller, upsetting the general atmosphere of cordiality and recognition, wrote to the *Times* to question the reliability of Bose's magnetic crescograph and to ask for a demonstration of it in a physiological laboratory before experts. When the demonstration, which took place at London University on April 23, 1920, was a complete success, Lord Rayleigh joined with several colleagues in a letter to the *Times* stating: "We are satisfied that the growth of plant tissues is correctly recorded by this instrument and at magnification of one million to more than ten million times."

Bose wrote to the *Times* on May 5:

Criticism which transgresses the limit of fairness must inevitably hinder the progress of knowledge. My special investigations have by their nature presented extraordinary difficulties. I regret to say that during a period of twenty years, these difficulties have been greatly aggravated by misrepresentation and worse. The obstacles deliberately placed in my path I can now ignore and forget. If the result of my work, by upsetting any particular theory, has aroused the hostility here and there of an individual, I can take comfort in the warm welcome which has been extended to me by the great body of scientific men in this country.

During still another trip to Europe in 1923, the year that saw the publication of Bose's detailed 227-page work *The Physiology of the Ascent of Sap,* the French philosopher Henri Bergson said, after hearing Bose lecture at the Sorbonne: "The dumb plants had by Bose's marvelous inventions been rendered the most eloquent witnesses of their hitherto unexpressed life story. Nature has at last been forced to yield her most jealously guarded secrets." More Gallicly humorous, *Le Matin* stated: "After this discovery we begin to have misgivings, when we strike a woman with a blossom, which of them suffers more, the woman or the flower?"

In 1924 and 1926 there appeared two more volumes of experiments totaling more than five hundred pages: *The Physiology of Photosynthesis* and *The Nervous Mechanism of Plants.* In 1926 Bose was nominated a member of the League of Nations Committee on Intercultural Cooperation, along with a physicist, Albert Einstein, a mathematician, H. A. Lorentz, and a Greek literary scholar, Gilbert Murray. The assignment had the advantage of taking Bose to Europe annually. Still the Indian Government had to be jolted into awareness of the importance of Bose's work. In 1926 Sir Charles Sherrington, president of the Royal Society, Lord Rayleigh, Sir Oliver Lodge, and Julian Huxley all signed a memorial to the Viceroy of India pleading for the expansion of the institute.

Back in Europe in 1927, the year which saw the appearance of his *Plant Autographs and Their Revelations,* Bose was presented by Romain Rolland with a signed copy of his new novel, *Jean Christophe,* inscribed "To the Revealer of a New World." Later, comparing Bose to Siegfried, who had learned the language of birds, Rolland said: "In the European scientist the steeling of the mind to the interpretation of nature has often been accompanied by a withering of the feeling for beauty. Darwin bitterly lamented the fact that his research in biology had completely atrophied his appreciation of poetry. With Bose it is otherwise."

In 1928, the same year that Bose brought out his last book, the 429-page *Motor Mechanisms of Plants,* one of the greatest plant physiologists of modern times, Professor Hans Molisch of Vienna, decided, after hearing Bose lecture in the Austrian capital, to go to India and work with the Bengali. Before leaving the subcontinent he wrote to *Nature:* "I saw the plant writing down its rate of assimilation of gaseous food. I also observed the speed of the impulse of the excitement in plants being recorded by the resonant recorder. All these are more wonderful than fairytales."

All his life Bose had stressed to a scientific community steeped in a mechanistic and materialistic outlook, and increasingly divided and subdivided into specialized cubbyholes, the idea that all of nature pulsed with life and that each of the interrelated entities in the natural kingdom might reveal untold secrets could man but learn how to communicate with them. In the lecture hall of his institute, under a bronze, silver, and gold relief of the Hindu sun god rising in his chariot for his daily cosmic fight against the powers of darkness—which Bose had first seen depicted in an ancient cave fresco at Ajanta—Bose, now in retirement, summed up his scientific philosophy.

In my investigations on the action of forces on matter, I was amazed to find boundary lines vanishing and to discover points of contact emerging between the Living and the non-Living. My first work in the region of invisible lights made me realize how in the midst of luminous ocean we stood almost blind. Just as in following light from visible to invisible our range of investigation transcends our physical sight, so also the problem of the great mystery of Life and Death is brought a little nearer solution, when, in the realm of the Living, we pass from the Voiced to the Unvoiced.

Is there any possible relation between our own life and that of the plant world? The question is not one of speculation but of actual demonstration by some method that is unimpeachable. This means that we should abandon all our preconceptions, most of which are afterward found to be absolutely groundless and contrary to facts. The final appeal must be made to the plant itself and no evidence should be accepted unless it bears the plant's own signature.

CHAPTER 7

The Metamorphosis
of Plants

Why botany, a potentially fascinating subject dealing with plants, living and extinct, their uses, classification, anatomy, physiology, geographical distribution, should have been from the beginning reduced to a dull taxonomy, an endless Latin dirge, in which progress is measured more by the number of corpses cataloged than by the number of blossoms cherished, is perhaps the greatest mystery in the study of plant life.

While young botanists still struggle today through the jungles of Central Africa and along the Amazon in search of polysyllabic victims to add to the 350,000 already on the books, what makes plants live, or why, does not appear to be the purview of the science, nor has it been since the fourth century B.C. when Theophrastus, the Lesbian disciple of Aristotle, first cataloged a couple of hundred species in his nine books *On the History of Plants* and six *On the Causes of Plants*. The Christian era merely raised the rolls to four hundred medicinal plants with the publication of *De Materia Medica* by a Greek physician to the Roman army, Dioscorides, shortly after the Crucifixion, an event which put the quietus on the subject for another thousand years. Throughout the Dark Ages, the books of Theophrastus and Dioscorides remained the standard texts in botany. Even though the Renaissance brought aesthetics into the field, with lovely woodcuts in large herbals such as those of Hieronymus Bock, it could not rip botany from the rigorous grip of the taxonomist.

By 1583 a Florentine, Andreas Caesalpinus, had classified 1,520 plants into fifteen classes, distinguished by seed and fruit. He was followed by the Frenchman Joseph Pitton de Tournefort, who described some 8,000 species of plants in twenty-two classes, chiefly according to the form of corolla—the colored petals of the flower. This brought sex into the picture. Although Herodotus had reported almost half a millennium before Christ that the Babylonians distinguished two sorts of palms, and would sprinkle the pollen from one onto the flower of the other in order to secure the production of fruit, it was not till the end of the seventeenth century that it was realized that plants were sexual creatures with a flourishing sex life of their own.

The first botanist to demonstrate that flowering plants have sex and that pollen is necessary for fertilization and seed formation was a German, Rudolf Jakob Camerarius, a professor of medicine and director of the botanical gardens at Tübingen, who published his *De Sexu Plantorum Epistula* in 1694. The idea that there could be a sexual difference in plants caused general astonishment, and Camerarius' theory was fiercely combated by the current establishment. It was considered "the wildest and most singular invention that ever evolved from a poet's mind." A heated controversy lasted almost a generation before it was finally established that plants had sexual organs and could therefore be elevated to a higher sphere of creation.

Even so, that plants have female organs in the form of vulva, vagina, uterus, and ovaries, serving precisely the same functions as they do in woman, as well as distinct male organs in the form of penis, glans, and testes, designed to sprinkle the air with billions of spermatozoa, were facts quickly covered by the eighteenth-century establishment with an almost impenetrable veil of Latin nomenclature, which stigmatized the labiate vulva, and mis-styled the vagina; the former being called "stigma," the latter "style." Penis and glans were equally disfigured into "filament" and "anther."

Whereas plants had been going through countless millennia of improvement to their sexual organs, often in the face of staggering climatic changes, and had invented the most ingenious methods for fecundating each other and for spreading their fertile seed, students of botany, who might have delighted in the sexuality of plants, were frustrated by such terms as "stamens" for the male and "pistils" for the female organs. Schoolchildren might have been fascinated to learn that each corn kernel on a cob in summer is a separate ovule, that each strand on the pubic corn silk tufted around the cob is an individual vagina ready to suck up the pollen sperm brought to it on the wind, that it may wriggle the entire length of the stylized vagina to impregnate each kernel on the cob, that every single seed produced on a plant is the result of a separate independent impregnation. Instead of struggling with archaic nomenclature, teenagers might be interested to learn that each pollen grain impregnates but one womb, which contains but one seed, that a capsule of tobacco contains, on an average, 2,500 seeds, which require 2,500 impregnations, all of which must be effected within a period of 24 hours in a space less than one-sixteenth of an inch in diameter. Instead of using the wonders of nature to stimulate the budding minds of their pupils, Victorian teachers misused the birds and the bees to denature their own sexuality.

How many universities even now draw the parallel between the hermaphroditic nature of plants, which bear both penis and vagina in the same body, with the "ancient wisdom" which relates that man is descended from an androgynous predecessor? The ingenuity of some plants in avoiding self-fertilization is uncanny. Some kinds of palm trees even bear staminate flowers one year and pistillate the next. Whereas in grasses and cereals cross-fertilization is insured by the action of the wind, most other plants are cross-fertilized by birds and insects. Like animals and women, flowers exude a powerful and seductive odor when ready for mating. This causes a multitude of bees, birds, and butterflies to join in a Saturnalian rite of fecundation. Flowers that remain unfertilized emit a strong fragrance for as many as eight days or until the flower withers and falls; yet once impregnated, the flower ceases to exude its fragrance, usually in less than half an hour. As in humans, sexual frustration can gradually turn fragrance into fetor. Similarly, when a plant is ready for impregnation, there is an evolution of heat in the female organ. This was first noted by the celebrated French botanist Adolphe Théodore Brongniart in examining a flower of the *Colocasia odorata,* a tropical plant grown in greenhouses for the beauty of its foliage. This plant, at the time of flowering, presents an increase of temperature that Brongniart compared to an attack of fever, repeating the phenomenon for six days, daily from three to six in the afternoon. At the proper time for impregnation Brongniart found that a small thermometer fastened to the female organ marked a temperature eleven degrees Centigrade higher than any other part of the plant.

The pollen of most plants has a highly inflammable character; when thrown on a red-hot surface it will ignite as quickly as gunpowder. Artificial lightning was formerly produced on the theatrical stage by throwing the pollen grains of the *Lycopodium* or club mosses onto a hot shovel. In many plants the pollen diffuses an odor bearing the most striking resemblance to the seminal emission of animals and man. Pollen, which performs the same function in almost precisely the same manner as does the semen of animals and men, enters the folds of the plant vulva and traverses the whole length of the vagina, until it enters the ovary and comes in contact with the ovule. Pollen tubes elongate themselves by a most remarkable process. As with animals and humans, the sexuality of certain plants is guided by taste. The spermatozoa of certain mosses carried in the morning dew in search of females, is guided by its taste for malic acid toward the delicate cups at the bottom of which lie moss eggs to be fertilized. The spermatozoa of ferns, on the other hand, liking sugar, find their females in pools of sweetened water.

The Metamorphosis of Plants   107

Camerarius' discovery of sex in plants set the stage for the generator of systematic botany, Carl von Linné, who dubbed the corolla petals "curtains of the nuptial bed." A Swede, who latinized his name to Linnaeus from a favorite linden tree while studying for the priesthood, he divided the plant world into species principally on the basis of variations in the male sexual organ or pollen-bearing stamens of each plant. With his penchant for looking, Linnaeus recognized some six thousand different species of plants. His system, referred to as the "sexual system," was considered "a great stimulus to students of botany." But his monumental method of latinized classification turned out to be as sterile as that of any voyeur who only looks at bodies. Still in use today under the unwieldy title of "binomial nomenclature," the system grants to each plant a Latin name for species and genus, to which is added the name of the person responsible for first naming it; thus the garden pea you eat with chops is the *Pisum sativum Linnaeum.*

This mania for registration was but a hangover of scholasticism. As Raoul Francé, true lover of plants, described Linné's efforts, "Wherever he went the laughing brook died, the glory of the flowers withered, the grace and joy of the meadows was transformed into withered corpses whose crushed and discolored bodies were described in a thousand minute Latin terms. The blooming fields and the storied woods disappeared during a botanical hour into a dusty herbarium, into a dreary catalogue of Greek and Latin labels. It became the hour for the practice of tiresome dialectic, filled with discussions about the number of stamens, the shape of leaves, all of which we learnt only to forget. When the work was over we stood disenchanted and estranged from nature."

To break away from this taxonomania, to put life and love and sex back into the plant world, took real poetic genius. In September of 1786, eight years after the death of Linnaeus, a tall, handsome man of thirty-seven, extremely attractive to women, who had been spending his holidays at Karlsbad taking the waters and strolling with the ladies in the woods on long botanical expeditions, suddenly rebelled against the whole system. "Secretly and stealthily" he abandoned mistress and friends to go south toward the Alps. Incognito, with only his servant aware that they were heading for *das Land wo die Citronen bluehen,* the traveler, in real life privy councilor and director of mines for the Duchy of Saxe-Weimar, was delighted at the beauty and variety of the southern vegetation beyond the Brenner Pass. This secret trip to Italy, the culmination of years of longing, was to constitute a climax in the life of Germany's greatest poet, Johann Wolfgang von Goethe.

On his way to Venice he stopped to visit the botanical gardens of the University of Padua. Strolling among the luxuriant verdure, most of which grew only in hothouses in his native Germany, Goethe was overcome with a sudden poetic vision; it was to give him insight into the very nature of plants. It was also to give him a place in the history of science as the precursor of Darwin's theory of organic development, an achievement as little appreciated by his compeers as it was extolled by a later generation. The great biologist Ernst Haeckel considered Goethe to stand with Jean Lamarck "at the head of all the great philosophers of nature who first established a theory of organic development, and who are the illustrious fellow workers of Darwin." For years Goethe had been distressed by the limitations involved in a merely analytical and intellectual approach to the plant world, typified by the cataloging mind of the eighteenth century, and of a theory of physics, then triumphant, which submitted the world to blind laws of mechanics, to a *"jeu de rouages et de ressorts sans vie."*

While still at the university in Leipzig, Goethe had rebelled against an arbitrary division of knowledge into faculties which cut up science into rival disciplines. In Goethe's nostrils university science had the stench of a corpse whose limbs have rotted apart. Disgusted at the petty contradictions of university savants, the young poet, whose early verses glowed with a passionate delight in nature, sought knowledge elsewhere, avidly studying galvanism and mesmerism and pursuing the electrical experiments of Winkler. Already as a child he had been fascinated by the phenomena of electricity and magnetism, struck by the extraordinary phenomenon of polarity. Cured in his late teens of a dangerous throat infection by a Rosicrucian doctor, Johann Friedrich Metz, Goethe was suddenly overwhelmed by the urge to apprehend the tremendous secret displayed all around him in constant creation and annihilation; he was thus led to books on mysticism and alchemy in pursuit of the secret forces of nature. There he discovered Paracelsus, Jakob Boehme, Giordano Bruno, Spinoza, and Gottfried Arnold.

To Goethe's delight he found magic and alchemy "quite other than obscure superstitious practices with the object of creating illusion or malefice." It was then, according to Christian Lepinte, author of *Goethe et l'occultisme,* that Goethe began "to aspire with all his strength to shatter the framework of a mechanized universe, to find the living science capable of revealing to him the ultimate secret of nature." From Philippus Aureolus Theophrastus Bombastus von Hohenheim, or Paracelsus, Goethe learned that the occult, because it deals with living reality and not dead catalogs, might come closer to the truth than science, and that the sage unveiling the secrets of nature was not necessarily profaning a forbidden sanctuary but might be walking in the footsteps of divinity, a person privileged to look deeply into the mystery of souls and of cosmic forces.

Above all, Goethe learned that the treasures of nature are not discovered by one who is not in sympathy with nature. He realized that the normal techniques of botany could not get near to the living being of a plant as an organism in a cycle of growth. Some other form of looking was needed which could unite itself with the life of the plant. To obtain a clearer picture of a plant, Goethe would tranquilize himself at night before going to sleep by visualizing the entire cycle of a plant's development through its various stages from seed to seed. In the splendid ducal gardens at Weimar, in the Gartenhaus quarters given to him by the Duke, Goethe developed an acute interest in living plants, an interest which was sharpened by his friendship with the sole local apothecary, Wilhelm Heinrich Sebastian Buchholz, who kept a garden of medicinal herbs and plants of special interest and with whom Goethe built up a private botanical garden.

In the grander botanical gardens of Padua, where Paracelsus had preceded him, Goethe was most impressed by a high, broad wall of fiery red bells, *Bignonia radicans,* that glowed enchantingly. He was also attracted by a palm because he was able to discern in its fanlike quality a complete development from the simple lance-shaped leaves near the ground, through successive separations, up to a spatulate sheaf where a branchlet of blossoms emerged, strangely unrelated to the preceding growth. From the observation of this complex series of transitional forms Goethe obtained the inspiration for what was to become his doctrine of the *metamorphosis of plants.* In a flash he realized what had been accumulating in his mind through long years of association with plants: the fan palm showed clear, living proof that *all* the lateral outgrowths of the plant were simply variations of a single structure: the leaf.* Goethe saw that propagation and prolification of one organ into another was simply a process of metamorphosis. He saw that each organ though outwardly changed from a similarity to a dissimilarity had a virtual inner identity.

At Goethe's request the Padua gardener cut from the fan palm an entire sequence of modifications which Goethe carried away with him in several pasteboard containers, where they lasted several years. As for the palm tree, it still stands in the Padua botanical gardens despite numerous intervening wars and revolutions.

With his new way of looking at plants Goethe came to the conclusion that nature, by bringing forth one part through another, could achieve the most diversified forms through modification of a single organ. "The variation of plant forms, whose unique course I had long been following, now awakened in me more and more the idea that the plant forms round about us are not predetermined, but are happily mobile and flexible, enabling them to adapt to the many conditions throughout the world, which influence them, and to be formed and re-formed with them."

Goethe also recognized that the process of development and refinement of form in plants worked through a threefold cycle of expansion and contraction. The expansion of foliage was followed by a contraction into calyx and bracts; there followed a splendid expansion into the petals of the corolla and a contraction into the meeting point of stamen and stigma; finally there came a swelling into fruit followed by a contraction into seed. This six-step cycle completed, the essential plant was ready to start all over again.

Ernst Lehrs' thoughtful evaluation of Goethe in *Man or Matter* says

---

*Sir George Trevelyan in a chapter on Goethe's plant metamorphosis in his forthcoming book on architecture, points out that by "leaf" Goethe did not mean the stem leaf, which is itself a manifestation of the basic organ. Some other word, says Trevelyan, is needed, such as "phyllome," to imply the archetypal ideal organ which underlies every organ of the plant and is able to transfer one part into another.

that another natural principle is implicit in this cycle for which Goethe did not coin a specific term, "although he shows through other utterances that he was well aware of it, and of its universal significance for all life." Lehrs calls this principle that of renunciation.

In the life of the plant this principle shows itself most conspicuously where the green leaf is heightened into the flower. While progressing from leaf to flower the plant undergoes a decisive ebb in its vitality. Compared with the leaf, the flower is a dying organ. This dying, however, is of a kind we may aptly call a "dying into being." Life in its mere vegetative form is here seen withdrawing in order that a higher manifestation of the spirit may take place. The same principle can be seen at work in the insect kingdom when the caterpillar's tremendous vitality passes over into the short-lived beauty of the butterfly. In the human being it is responsible for that metamorphosis or organic process which occurs on the path from the metabolic to the nervous system, and which we came to recognize as the precondition for the appearance of consciousness within the organism.

Lehrs marvels at the powerful forces which must be at work in the plant organism at the point of transition from its green to its colored parts. They enforce, says Lehrs, a complete halt upon the juices that rise up right into the calyx, so that these bring nothing of their life-bearing activity into the formation of the flower, but undergo a complete transmutation, not gradually, but with a sudden leap.

After achieving its masterpiece in the flower, the plant once more goes through a process of withdrawal, this time into the tiny organs of fertilization. After fertilization, the fruit begins to swell: once more the plant produces an organ with a more or less conspicuous spatial extension. This is followed by a final and extreme contraction in the forming of the seed inside the fruit. In the seed the plant gives up all outer appearance to such a degree that nothing seems to remain but a small, insignificant speck of organized matter. Yet this tiny, inconspicuous thing bears in it the power of bringing forth a whole new plant.

Lehrs points out that in its three successive rhythms of expansion and contraction the plant reveals the basic rule of its existence.

During each expansion, the active principle of the plant presses forth into visible *appearance;* during each contraction it withdraws from outer embodiment into what we may describe as a more formless pure state of *being.* We thus find the spiritual principle of the plant engaged in a kind of breathing rhythm, now appearing, now disappearing, now assuming power over matter; now withdrawing from it again.

Goethe saw in the changeableness of all the external characteristics of plants nothing but appearance; he drew the conclusion that the nature of the plant was not to be found in these characteristics, but had to be sought at a deeper level. The thought became more and more alive in him that it might be possible to develop all plants from a single one. This small conceit was destined to transform the science of botany, indeed the whole concept of the world: with it came the idea of *evolution*. Metamorphosis was to become the key to the whole alphabet of nature. But, whereas Darwin was to assume that external influences, like mechanical causes, work upon the nature of an organism and modify it accordingly, to Goethe the single alterations were various expressions of the archetypal organism *(Urorganismus)*, which possesses within itself the capacity to take on manifold forms, and which at a particular time takes on that form which is best suited to the conditions of the external environing world. Goethe's *Urorganismus* is a sort of Platonic idea in the eye of the created mind.

Aristotle's philosophy teaches that, besides original matter, another principle is necessary to complete the triune nature of every particle, and this is form: an invisible, but still, in an ontological sense of the word, a substantial being, really distinct from matter proper. Thus, as the theosophist Helena Blavatsky interprets Aristotle, in an animal or a plant, besides the bones, the flesh, the nerves, the brains, and the blood, in the former, and besides the pulpy matter, tissues, fibers, and juice in the latter, there must be a substantial form, which Aristotle named, in the horse, the horse's *soul;* which Proclus identified as the *demon* of every mineral, plant, or animal; and which was later categorized by medieval philosophers as the *elementary spirits* of the four kingdoms.

Trevelyan explains the kernel of Goethe's philosophy as lying in a metaphysical concept of nature.

> The godhead is at work in the living, not in the dead; it is present in everything in the process of development and transformation, not in what has already taken shape and rigidified. Thus, reason in its strivings towards the divine is concerned with putting to use what has already developed and grown torpid.

Seeing that every part of the plant is a metamorphosis of the archetypal "leaf" organ, Goethe came to the conception of an *archetypal* plant, or *Ur-pflanze*, a supersensible force capable of developing into myriad different forms. This, says Trevelyan, is no single plant, but a force that holds the potentiality of every plant form within it.

> All plants are thus seen as specific manifestations of the archetypal plant which controls the entire plant kingdom and gives the value to nature's artistry in creating forms. It is in ceaseless play within the world of plant form, capable of moving backwards and forwards, up and down, in and out, through the scale of forms.

Summing up his discovery, Goethe asked, "If all plants were not modeled on one pattern, how could I recognize that they are plants?" Filled with delight, Goethe declared he could now invent plant forms, even if they had never been realized on earth before.

From Naples Goethe wrote to his friend and fellow poet in Weimar, Johann Gottfried von Herder: "I must tell you confidentially that I am very close to the secret of the creation of plants, and that it is the simplest thing one could imagine. The archetypal plant will be the strangest creature in the world, which nature herself ought to envy me. With this model and the key to it, one can invent plants endlessly which must be consistent—that is, if they did not exist, yet they could exist, and not some artistic or poetic shadows and appearances but possessing inner truth and inevitability. The same law can be applied to everything living." Goethe now pursued the idea "with joy and ecstasy, lovingly immersing myself in it in Naples and Sicily," applying the idea to every plant he saw, writing reports to Herder on what took place "with as much enthusiasm as was manifested over the finding of the lost silver piece in the gospel parable."

For two years Goethe observed, collected, studied phenomena in detail, made many sketches and accurate drawings. "I pursued my botanical studies, into which I was guided, driven, forced—and then held captive by my interest." Back in Germany after two years in Italy, Goethe found that the new vision of life he had acquired was incomprehensible to his fellow countrymen.

From Italy, rich in forms, I was plunged back into formless Germany, exchanging a sunny sky for a gloomy one. My friends, instead of comforting me and drawing me back to them, drove me to despair. My delight in things remote and almost unknown to them, my sorrow and grief over what I had lost, seemed to offend them. I received no sympathy, no one understood my language. I could not adjust myself to this distressing situation, so great was the loss to which my exterior senses must become reconciled. But gradually my spirit returned and sought to preserve itself intact.

Goethe set his thoughts on paper in a first essay, "On the Metamorphosis of Plants," in which he traced "the manifold specific phenomena in the magnificent garden of the universe back to one simple general principle," and stressed nature's method of "producing in accord with definite laws, a living structure that is a model of everything artistic." The essay, which was to generate the science of morphology in plants, was written in an unusual style, different from contemporary scientific writings in that it did not pursue each idea to its full conclusion but, in a cryptic manner, left room for interpretation. "Well satisfied with my brochure," says Goethe, "I was flattered to believe myself auspiciously launched on a career in science. But the same thing happened to me that I had experienced in purely literary work; once more, at the very outset, I was repulsed."

Goethe's regular publisher refused the manuscript, telling him he was a literary man, not a scientist. Goethe found it hard to understand why the publisher would not print the brochure when, "merely by risking six sheets of paper at the very most he might have retained for himself a prolific, reliable, easily satisfied author, who was just getting a fresh start." When the brochure was printed elsewhere Goethe was further surprised to find it completely ignored by botanist and public alike.

The public [said Goethe] demand that every man remain in his own field. Nowhere would anyone grant that science and poetry can be united. People forgot that science had developed from poetry and they failed to take into consideration that a swing of the pendulum might beneficently reunite the two, at a higher level and to mutual advantage.

Goethe then made the mistake of giving away copies of the brochure to friends outside his immediate circle. These friends, said he, were by no means tactful in their comments.

> No one dared to accommodate himself to my method of expressing myself. It is most tormenting not to be understood when one feels sure himself, after a great stress and strain, that one understands both one's self and one's subject. It drove one to insanity to hear repeated again and again a mistake from which one has himself just escaped by a hair's breadth, and nothing is more painful than to have the things that should unite us with informed and intelligent men give rise instead to unbridgeable separation.

To his newly acquired friend and fellow poet Johann Christoph Friedrich von Schiller, Goethe gave a spirited explanation of his theory of the metamorphosis of plants, with graphic pen sketches of a symbolic plant. "He listened and looked with great interest, with unerring comprehension, but when I had ended he shook his head, saying: 'That is not an experience, that is an idea.' " Goethe was taken aback and a little irritated. Controlling himself he said: "How splendid that I have ideas without knowing it, and can see them before my eyes." From the argument Goethe was left with the philosophic concept that ideas must be clearly independent of space and time, whereas experience is restricted to space and time. "The simultaneous and successive are therefore intimately bound together in an idea, whereas they are always separated in experience."

It was eighteen years after the Congress of Vienna before references to the metamorphosis of plants began to appear in botanical texts and other writings, and thirty years before it was fully accepted by botanists. When the essay became known in Switzerland and France people were astonished to find that a poet "normally occupied with moral phenomena associated with feeling and power and imagination, could have achieved such an important discovery."

Late in life Goethe added another basic idea to the science of botany. With his perception carefully attuned to nature he realized—a generation before Darwin was to approach the same subject—that vegetation had a tendency to grow in two distinct ways: vertically and spirally. With his poet's intuition Goethe labeled the vertical tendency, with its sustaining principle, male; the spiral tendency, which conceals itself during the development of the plant but predominates during blossoming and fruiting, he labeled female. "When we see," said Goethe, "that the vertical system is definitely male and the spiral definitely female, we will be able to conceive of all vegetation as androgynous from the root up. In the course of the transformation of growth the two systems are separated, and take opposite courses to be reunited on a higher level."

Goethe held a lofty and comprehensive view of the significance of the male and female principles as spiritual opposites in the cosmos. Lehrs elaborated on it: "In order that spiritual continuity may be maintained within the coming and going multitude of nature's creations, the physical stream must suffer discontinuity at certain intervals. In the case of the plant this discontinuity is achieved by the breaking asunder of the male and female growth-principles. When they have reunited, the type begins to abandon either the entire old plant or at least part of it, according to whether the species is an annual or a perennial one, in order to concentrate on the tiny seed, setting, as it were, its living seal on it."

To Goethe the fact that the action of the root of a plant is directed earthward toward moisture and darkness, whereas the stem or trunk strives skyward in the opposite direction toward the light and the air, was a truly magical phenomenon. To explain it Goethe postulated a force opposite, or polar, to Newton's gravity, to which he gave the name "levity." "Newton," says Lehrs, "explained to you—or at least was once supposed to explain, why an apple fell; but he never thought of explaining the exact correlative but infinitely more difficult question, how the apple got up there." The concept led Goethe to a picture of the earth as being surrounded and penetrated by a field of force in every respect the opposite of the earth's gravitational field.

"As the gravity field decreases in strength," says Lehrs, "with increasing distance from the center of the field, that is, in the outward direction, so does the levity-field decrease in strength with increasing distance from its periphery, or in the inward direction. . . . This is why things 'fall' under the influence of gravity and 'rise' under the influence of levity." Lehrs adds that if there were no field working outward toward the cosmic periphery, the entire material content of the earthly realm would be reduced by gravitation to a spaceless point, just as under the sole influence of the peripheral field of levity it would dissipate into the universe. "Just as in volcanic activity heavy matter is suddenly and swiftly driven heavenwards under the influence of levity, so in a storm does light matter stream earthwards under the influence of gravity."

Goethe, taking his inspiration from the Rosicrucian Aurea Catena of 1781, presumed to be authored by Herwerd von Forchenbrun, saw the whole universe as being moved by opposite polar forces which manifest as light and dark, or plus and minus in electricity, or oxidation and reduction in chemistry.

In his old age Goethe conceived the earth to be an organism animated by the same rhythm of inspiration and evaporation as a plant or an animal. He compared the earth and her hydrosphere, in which he included the humid atmosphere and its clouds, to a great living being perpetually inhaling and exhaling. He said:

> If she inhales, she draws the hydrosphere to her, so that, coming near her surface, it is condensed to clouds and rain. This state I call water-affirmative [*Wasser-Bejahung*]. Should it continue for an indefinite period, the earth would be drowned. This the earth does not allow, but exhales again, and sends the watery vapours upwards, where they are dissipated through the whole space of the higher atmosphere. These become so rarefied that not only does the sun penetrate them with its brilliance, but the eternal darkness of infinite space is seen through them as a fresh blue. This state of the atmosphere I call water-negative [*Wasser-Verneinung*]. For, just as under the contrary influence, not only does water come profusely from above, but also the moisture of the earth cannot be dried and dissipated—so, on the contrary, in this state not only does no moisture come from above, but the damp of the earth itself flies upwards; so that, if this should continue for an indefinite period, the earth, even if the sun did not shine, would be in danger of drying up.

The actual phenomenon of light Goethe considered to be inscrutable, but disagreed with Newton's concept that light waves were light itself and that light was composed of various colors. Goethe considered light waves to be the physical manifestation of eternal light. He saw light and dark to be polar opposites, with a series of colors formed by their interaction: darkness was not complete passive absence of light: it was something active, something that opposed itself to light and interplayed with it. He imagined light and dark as being related like the north and south poles of a magnet. If darkness were absolute void, said Goethe, there would be no perception looking into the dark. The importance Goethe attached to his theory of color is clear from his statement late in life that "I do not attach importance to my work as a poet, but I do claim to be alone in my time in apprehending the true nature of color."

When Goethe died on March 22, 1832, twenty-seven years before Darwin was to proclaim his principle of organic evolution, he was considered Germany's greatest poet, with a universal mind capable of compassing every domain of human activity and knowledge. But as a scientist he was considered a layman.

Though a genus of plants, the Goethea, was named for him, as was a mineral, goethite, it was as a courtesy to a great man more than to a scientist. In due course Goethe was credited with having coined the word "morphology" and of having formulated the concept of botanical morphology which persists to this day. He was credited with the discovery of the volcanic origin of mountains, with establishing the first system of weather stations, with being interested in connecting the Gulf of Mexico with the Pacific Ocean, and with wanting to build steamships and flying machines; but the scope of Goethe's formulation of the metamorphosis of plants had to await the advent of Darwin to be fully appreciated, and even then it was largely misunderstood.

As Rudolf Steiner was to write, almost a hundred years later,

> It was from observations similar to those of Goethe that Darwin proceeded when he asserted his doubt as to the constancy of the external forms of genera and species. But the conclusions which the two thinkers reached were entirely unlike. Whereas Darwin considered that the whole nature of the organism was, in fact, comprised in these characteristics, and came to the conclusion, therefore, that there is nothing constant in the life of the plant, Goethe went deeper and drew the inference that, since those characteristics are not constant, what is constant must be sought in something else which lies beneath changeable externalities.

CHAPTER 8

Plants Will Grow
to Please You

Goethe's poetic notion that a spiritual essence lies behind the material form of plants was put on a firmer basis by a medical doctor and a professor of physics at the University of Leipzig. Credited with over forty papers on such subjects as the measurement of electrical currents and the perceptions of colors, Gustav Theodor Fechner came to his profound understanding of plants in a totally unexpected way. In 1839 he began to stare at the sun in the hope of discovering the nature of afterimages, those strange pictures which seem to persist on the retina of the eye even after the cessation of normal visual stimulus.

A few days later, Fechner was horrified to realize that he was going blind. Exhausted from overwork, and unable in his new affliction to face his friends and colleagues, he retired to a darkened room with a mask over his face, to live in solitude praying for recovery.

One spring morning three years later, sensing that his sight had been restored, he emerged into the light of day. Joyously walking along the Mulde River he instantly recognized that flowers and trees along its banks were what he called be-souled. "As I stood by the water and watched a flower, it was as though I saw its soul lift itself from the bloom and, drifting through the mist, become clearer until the spiritual form hung clearly above it. Perhaps it wanted to stand on the roof of its budding house in order better to enjoy the sun. Believing itself invisible, it was quite surprised when a little child appeared."

While still in semi-seclusion Fechner began setting down a series of similar remarkable impressions. The result was *Nanna, or the Soul-Life of Plants,* published in Leipzig in 1848, which though scathingly rejected by his fellow academicians, became so popular that it was still being printed in Germany three-quarters of a century later.

In his introduction, Fechner explained that he happened on the title by accident. At first he thought of calling his new book *Flora,* after the Roman goddess of flowers, or *Hamadryas,* after the wood nymphs which the Hellenes recognized as living only as long as the trees of which they were the spirit. But he rejected the first as too botanical, the second as too classically stiff and antiquarian. One day, while reading Teutonic mythology, Fechner learned that Baldur, god of light, had, like Actaeon peeping at Diana, secretly gazed upon the naked form of the flower princess Nanna as she bathed in a stream. When her natural loveliness was enhanced by the energy over which Baldur ruled, his heart, said the legend, was pierced, and the marriage of Light and Flowers became a foregone conclusion.

Fechner's awakening to the soul life of plants turned him from professing physics to professing philosophy, of which branch of knowledge he was given a chair at Leipzig the same year that *Nanna* appeared. However, even before his realization that plants had undreamed-of sensitivity, Fechner had concerned himself with cosmic problems in his *Little Book of Life After Death,* posthumously published in Dresden in

1936, and in *Comparative Anatomy of the Angels*, a work which he considered so risqué that he wrote it under the pseudonym of Dr. Mises.

In the *Little Book* Fechner put forward the idea that human life was lived in three stages: one of continuous sleep from conception to birth; one of half wakefulness, which humans called terrestrial life; and one of fuller alertness, which began only after death. In *Comparative Anatomy* he traced the path of evolution from monocellular organisms through man on to angelic higher beings spherical in form and capable of seeing universal gravitation as ordinary humans perceive light, of communicating not acoustically but through luminous symbols.

Fechner introduced *Nanna* with the concept that believing whether plants have a soul or not changes one's whole insight into nature. If man admitted to an omnipresent, all-knowing, and almighty god who bestowed animation on all things, then nothing in the world could be excluded from this munificence, neither plant nor stone nor crystal nor wave. Why would universal spirit, he asked, sit less firmly in nature than in human beings, and not be as much in command of nature's power as it is of human bodies?

Anticipating Bose's work, Fechner further reasoned that if plants have life and soul, they must have some sort of nervous system, hidden perhaps in their strange spiral fibers. Going beyond the limitation of today's mechanistic physiology, Fechner referred to "spiritual nerves" in the universe, one expression of which was the interconnection of celestial bodies, not with "long ropes," but with a unified web of light, gravity, and forces as yet unknown. The soul, said Fechner, receives sensations, in a manner analogous to that of a spider which is alerted to outside influences by its web. It seemed reasonable to Fechner to accept the idea that plants have nerves, their purported absence being due to man's ignorance rather than to any innate vegetal deficiency.

According to Fechner, the psyche of plants is no more linked to their nervous system than is the soul of man to a human body. Both are diffused throughout, yet separated from all the organs which they direct. "None of my limbs anticipates anything for itself," wrote Fechner, "only I, the spirit of my whole, sense everything that happens to me."

Fechner created a new branch of learning called *psychophysics*, which abolished the artificial separation between mind and body and held the two entities to be only different sides of one reality, the mind appearing subjectively, the body objectively, as a circle is either concave or convex depending on whether the observer stands inside it or outside. The confusion resulted, said Fechner, because it was difficult to hold both points of view simultaneously. To Fechner all things express in different ways the same *anima mundi*, or cosmic soul, which came into existence with the universe, is its conscience, and will die when and if the universe dies. Basic to his animate philosophy was the axiom that all life is *one* and simply takes up different shapes in order to divert itself. The highest good and supreme end of all action is the maximum pleasure not of the individual but of all, said Fechner, and on this he based all his rules for morals.

Since spirit to Fechner was a deistic universal, it was useless to refer to souls as wholly individual, whether vegetal or human. Nonetheless souls provided the only criteria for forming a conception of other souls and making themselves known to them by outward physical signs. To the undoubted irritation of today's prevalent school of behaviorist, "carrot-and-stick" psychology, Fechner also maintained that in its soul alone was the true freedom of any creature.

Because a plant is rooted, it necessarily has less freedom of movement than an animal, Fechner declared, though by moving its branches, leaves, and tendrils as it sees fit it behaves much like an animal which opens its claws upon capture or runs away when frightened.

More than a century before experiments in the Soviet Union apparently convinced the Russians that plants can regulate their own needs with the help of man-designed instrumentation, Fechner asked, "Why should we believe that a plant is not any less aware of hunger and thirst than an animal? The animal searches for food with its whole body, the plant with portions of it, guided not with nose, eyes or ears but with other senses." It seemed to Fechner that "plant people," calmly living their lives in the spots of their rooting, might well wonder why human bipeds keep rushing about. "In addition to souls which run and shriek and devour, might there not be souls which bloom in stillness, exhale fragrance and satisfy their thirst with dew and their impulses by their burgeoning?" Could not flowers, Fechner asked, communicate with each other by the very perfumes they exude, becoming aware of each other's presence by a means more delightful than the verbiage and breath of humans, which is seldom delicate or fragrant except, by coincidence, in lovers?

"From *inside* comes the voice," wrote Fechner, "and from inside comes the scent. Just as one can tell human beings in the dark from the tone of their voices, so in the dark, every flower can be recognized by its scent. Each carries the soul of its progenitor." Flowers having no fragrance he likened to animals which live alone in the wilds, and those with perfume to gregarious beasts. In the end, posited this German sage, was it not one of the ultimate purposes of human bodies to serve vegetal life, surrounding it by emitting carbon dioxide for the plants to breathe, and manuring them with human bodies after death? Did not flowers and trees finally consume man and, by combining his remains together with raw earth, water, air, and sunlight, transform and transmute human bodies into the most glorious forms and colors?

Fechner's "animism," for which he was so wrathfully castigated by his contemporaries, led him to issue, two years after *Nanna*, a book on atomic theory, in which, long before the birth of particle physics, he argued that atoms were centers of pure energy and the lowest elements in a spiritual hierarchy. The following year he brought out *Zendavesta*, its title inspired by the sacred writings of the ancient Zoroastrians, who claimed that their great religious leader Zarathustra had taught his people how to breed the food plants that still today form our chief source of nourishment. The original *Zendavesta* might be considered the first textbook on agriculture. Fechner's work was characterized by the younger American philosopher William James as a "wonderful book by a wonderful genius." Its fascinating and complex philosophy contained such concepts as that of "mental energy," which appealed strongly to Sigmund Freud and without which the edifice of psychoanalysis might never have been built.

Though Fechner heroically attempted to put forward what his contemporaries, and many present-day philosophers, would call "an idealistic view of reality," he ceaselessly tried to reconcile it with the methodology of modern science, in which he was trained.

Perhaps this was why the Leipzig physician and physicist, character-ized as one of the most versatile thinkers of the nineteenth century, was so excellent an observer of the details of the vegetable world surrounding him. In *Nanna* he described the sex organs of plants—which in humans St. Paul considered so uncomely—as marvels of beauty, lyricizing on the manner in which plants lure insects to wriggle into their genitalia to drink the hidden nectar and thus shake fertilizing pollen from the anthers of some distant blossom onto the stigma of their petals. Fechner marveled at how plants could devise the most sophisticated systems to spread their species, how the puffball waits to be trodden upon in order to produce a cloud of minute spores which are carried a great distance by the wind, how the maple casts off propeller seeds that spin away with a passing breeze, how fruit trees seduce birds, beasts, and man into distributing their seeds afar, neatly packaged in nourishing manure, how viviparous water lilies and ferns reproduce tiny but perfect plants on the surface of their leaves.

Fechner also expatiated on plant roots, the sensitive tips of which enable plants to maintain a sense of direction, and on the climbing tendrils of plants which, searching for purchase, repeat perfect circles in the air.

Though Fechner's work was not taken seriously in his own time, one Englishman, whose life ran parallel to Fechner's, had the daring to recognize that some mysterious force in plants had the characteristics of sentience or intelligence. After publishing his earthshaking *Origin of Species* in 1859, Charles Robert Darwin devoted the greater part of his remaining twenty-three years not only to an elaboration on his theory of evolution but to a meticulous study of the behavior of plants.

In his 575-page *The Power of Movement in Plants,* published just before his death, Darwin developed in a more scientific way than Fechner the idea that the habit of moving at certain times of day was the common inheritance of both plants and animals. The most striking part of this similarity, he wrote, was "the localization of their sensitive-ness, and the transmission of an influence from the excited part to another which consequently moves."

Though this seemed to imply that Fechner might have been correct in stating that plants, like animals, had nervous systems, Darwin stopped short of making this assertion because he could find no such system. Nevertheless, he could not get out of his mind that plants must have sentient ability. In the very last sentence of his massive volume, referring to the properties of a plant's radicle—that part of its embryo which develops into the primary root—he stated boldly: "It is hardly an exaggeration to say that the tip of the radicle acts like the brain of one of the lower animals: the brain being seated within the anterior end of the body, receiving impressions from the sense organs, and directing the several movements."

In an earlier book, *The Fertilization of Orchids,* published in 1862, one of the most masterful and complete studies on a single species of plant life ever to appear, Darwin set forth in highly technical language the way insects caused the fertilization of those unusual flowers, which he had learned of by sitting on the grass for hours and patiently watching the process.

In more than a dozen years of experiments conducted on fifty-seven species of plants Darwin found that products of cross-pollination resulted in more numerous, larger, heavier, more vigorous and more fertile offspring, even in species that are normally self-pollinating, and he put his finger on the secret of the production of such copious amounts of pollen. Though the odds were millions to one against it, if the pollen of an immobile plant could mix with a faraway relative, its offspring were likely to attain what came to be known as "hybrid vigor." Of this Darwin wrote that "the advantages of cross-fertilization do not follow from some mysterious virtue in the mere union of two distinct individuals, but from such individuals having been subjected during previous generations to different conditions, or to their having varied in a manner commonly called spontaneous, so that in either case their sexual elements have been in some degree differentiated."

For all his academic preciseness, the thrust of Darwin's theory of evolution and of the survival of the fittest indicated that something more than chance was in play. That this something might accommodate to the wish of man was the next extraordinary development.

In 1892, ten years after Darwin's death and five years after Fechner's, a fifty-two-page nurseryman's catalog, *New Creations in Fruits and Flow-*

ers, published in Santa Rosa, California, created a sensation in the United States. Unlike similar booklets, which had thus far included not more than half a dozen novelties among the hundreds advertised, this catalog contained not a single plant known to man.

Among its horticultural marvels were a hardwood giant Paradox walnut, which, growing as fast as a spongy pulpwood, could form a hedge tall enough to screen a house within a few years; a giant daisy, named for Mount Shasta, with mammoth snow-white petals; an apple, sweet on one side and sour on the other; and a cross between a strawberry and a raspberry which, though it did not fruit, seemed as strange to followers of the theory of natural selection as would the mating of a chicken with an owl.

When the catalog finally made its way six thousand miles to the Netherlands, it caught the eye of an Amsterdam professor, Hugo De Vries, in the process of rediscovering the modern science of genetics—originated in the mid-nineteenth century by the Austrian monk Gregor Johann Mendel, but buried during his lifetime in the shelves of his monastery library. De Vries, later to be celebrated for carrying forward Darwin's life work with his own theory of mutation, was flabbergasted by the catalog and the apparent ability of one man to bring into the world botanical specimens undreamed of by nature. To satisfy his curiosity, De Vries set off across the world to visit the catalog's publisher, who turned out to be a New England transplant to California, Luther Burbank, whose feats with plants led to the new transitive verb *to burbank,** and his reputation as the "Wizard of Horticulture" was to infuriate botanists unable to understand the magic of his methods.

When De Vries came to Santa Rosa and saw growing in the "wizard's" front yard a fourteen-year-old Paradox walnut larger than the Persian variety four times its age and a monkey-puzzle tree which could stun passers-by by dropping twenty-pound nuts on their heads, he was dumbstruck that in the little cottage where Burbank worked there was

* *Webster's New International Dictionary,* 2d ed., lists: "Burbank, *v.t.* To modify and improve (plants or animals) esp. by selective breeding. Also to cross or graft (a plant). Hence, figuratively, to improve (anything, as a process or institution) by a selecting of good features and rejecting of bad, or by adding good features.

neither library nor laboratory and that Burbank's work notes were kept on tearings from brown-paper bags or the backs of letters and envelopes.

Throughout the evening the bewildered De Vries, who had expected files of carefully recorded data which might reveal Burbank's secrets, questioned the plant breeder, only to be told that his art was basically "a matter of concentration and the rapid elimination of non-essentials." As for his laboratory, Burbank told De Vries: "I keep it in my head."

The Dutch scientist was no more perplexed than were hundreds of his American confrères who, lacking any rational explanation for Burbank's methodology, often branded the wizard a charlatan. Burbank's own evaluation of the botanical fraternity did little to appease their collective ire. In 1901 Burbank told the San Francisco Floral Congress:

> The chief work of the botanists of yesterday was the study and classification of dried, shriveled plant mummies whose souls had fled. They thought their classified species were more fixed and unchangeable than anything in heaven or earth that we can now imagine. We have learned that they are as plastic in our hands as clay in the hands of the potter or color on the artists' canvas and can readily be molded into more beautiful forms and colors than any painter or sculptor can ever hope to bring forth.

Unlike the narrower minds which such simple and truthful statements drove to frenzy, De Vries, accepting Burbank as a natural-born genius, wrote of his work that "its value for the doctrine of evolution compels our highest admiration."

As his biographers almost inadvertently make clear, Burbank was and remains an enigma. Born in 1849 in the rural Massachusetts village of Lunenburg, the lasting impressions from his schooling came from his reading of Henry David Thoreau and of the other great naturalists Alexander von Humboldt and Louis Agassiz. But even these were overshadowed when he devoured, shortly after its publication in 1868, Charles Darwin's massive two-volume *The Variation of Animals and Plants Under Domestication.* Burbank was deeply impressed by its theme that organisms, when removed from their natural conditions, vary.

While still in Massachusetts, Burbank one day happened upon a seed ball in his patch of potatoes—a vegetable which almost never sets seed and is therefore propagated from the buds, or "eyes," of its tuber. Because he knew that potato seeds, if they could be found, would not grow tubers true to type, and instead would produce a curious batch of mongrels, he excitedly thought that one of them might develop into a potato miracle. One of the twenty-three seeds in the ball gave rise to an offspring that managed to double the average yield. Smooth, plump, an excellent baker, the new potato, unlike its red-skinned progenitor, was creamy-white.

Burbank received $150 from a Marblehead seedman for his discovery and the compliment that it was the best potato the seedman had ever eaten. Christened the "Burbank," it was later widely planted by growers in the San Joaquin River delta town of Stockton, California, who gratefully presented to Burbank its solid gold miniature replica. Today it dominates the U.S. potato market. Three days after the original sale—following the terse advice he later gave to a New England farmer who asked him what he should raise on some newly acquired acreage, "Enough money to go to California"—Burbank was on a cross-continental train.

Shortly after Burbank's arrival in Santa Rosa, Darwin's *The Effects of Cross and Self Fertilisation in the Vegetable Kingdom* came out, and Burbank was particularly struck by a challenging introductory statement: "As plants are adapted by such diversified and effective means for cross-fertilization, it might have been inferred from this fact alone that they derived some great advantage from the process." To Burbank, this sentence seemed both a blueprint and a command. If Darwin had drawn plans, he would carry them out.

Burbank's first chance for fame came in the spring of 1882 when a variety of plums known as prunes were coming into their own in hundreds of California orchards as a new money-making fruit, easily dried and thus easily shipped and slow to spoil. In March a canny banker in the neighboring town of Petaluma, fearful lest he miss the bonanza, asked Burbank if he could deliver twenty thousand young prune trees for a two-hundred-acre planting by December. Everyone else, said the worried banker, had told him this was impossible. Burbank knew that if the man had given him two years nothing would have been simpler than to sprout plum trees from seed, bud them with prunes in the late summer, and after cutting off the original plum tops, watch them develop into prune seedlings the year following. How, he asked himself, could he turn the same trick in eight months?

It then struck Burbank that almonds, a member of the genus *Prunus*, would sprout much faster than the hard stones of plums. After buying a sackful of the oval-shaped nuts, Burbank forced them to sprout in warm water, copying a method he had used with corn in Massachusetts, which allowed him to beat other farmers to the market by more than a week. Even so, the little seedlings were not ready for budding until June, and time was running short. With a cash advance from the banker, Burbank hired all available nursery help in the region. They worked around the clock; when the job was finished, Burbank prayed that his tiny seedlings would grow into trees as tall as the average woman in the four months remaining before the contract called for delivery. His luck held; before Christmas he was able to deliver 19,500 trees to the overjoyed banker. Other nurserymen were left gasping at the feat, which not only produced a $6,000 windfall for Burbank but taught him that mass production was one of the keys to prodding out of nature secrets she was normally unwilling to give up.

Thus began Burbank's pomological revolution, which led to the development of new prunes and plums—including one, the Climax, which tasted like a pineapple, and another which tasted like a pear—that today still account for over half of California's giant crop; the ever-popular Burbank July Elberta peach, a luscious Burbank Flaming Gold nectarine, a bush-type chestnut, which bore a crop six months after its seed was put in the ground, a white blackberry the color of an icicle, and two quinces that were so good that most nurseries still stock no other.

In developing new fruit, Burbank was so adept and fast that he could race through thousands of cross-pollinations while orthodox plant specialists in laboratories were pedantically poring over sheaves of notes involving only a few dozen. It was no wonder that the schoolmen increasingly accused him of trickery, mainly of buying his "new creations" abroad. For Burbank, convinced that plants, like people, would behave differently when away from home, would order, from as far away as Japan and New Zealand, experimental varieties to cross with home-grown standbys. Burbank introduced over a thousand new plants, which, if evenly spaced over his working career, would have amounted to a never-before-seen specimen every three weeks. Despite the backbiting cavils from envious and narrow-minded scientists, this miracle making was heralded by professional experts big enough to recognize genius when they saw it, even if it passed their understanding.

Liberty Hyde Bailey, the universally recognized dean of American botany, who had earlier told a world horticultural congress that "man could not do much to produce variations in plants," came from Cornell University to see what Burbank was doing to create such a furor. He left Santa Rosa stupefied and wrote the same year in an issue of *World's Work* magazine:

> Luther Burbank is a breeder of plants by profession, and in this business he stands almost alone in this country. So many and so striking have been the new plants that he has given to the world that he has been called the "Wizard of Horticulture." This sobriquet has prejudiced a good many people against his work. Luther Burbank is not a wizard. He is an honest, straight-forward, careful, inquisitive and persistent man. He believes that causes produce results. He has no other magic than that of patient inquiry, abiding enthusiasm, an unprejudiced mind, and a remarkably acute judgement of the merits and capabilities of plants.

This was a delight to Burbank, who smarted from the ugly rumors circulated about his work in the halls of academe. He told a packed lecture hall at Stanford University that "Orthodoxy is ankylosis—nobody at home: ring up the undertaker for further information!" Professor H. J. Webber, a geneticist in charge of plant breeding at the U.S. Department of Agriculture, maintained that Burbank had single-handedly saved the world nearly a quarter of a century in plant-breeding time. David Fairchild, who spent years exploring the world for new plants which might prove commercially useful in the United States, though baffled by Burbank's methods, summed up his impressions of his visit to Santa Rosa in a letter to a friend: "There are those who say Burbank is not scientific. It is true only in the sense that he has tried to do so much, and has been so fascinated by the desire to create that he has not always noted and labeled the footsteps which he has taken."

Just watching Burbank at work took the breath away from countless observers. On his experimental farm in nearby Sebastopol, where forty thousand Japanese plums or a quarter of a million flowering bulbs could be seen growing at the same time, Burbank would walk down a row of thousands of plants—whether tiny seedlings just breaking ground or chest-high flowers nearing maturity—and without breaking his stride pick out those likely to succeed. One wide-eyed county farm adviser described this in his own words: "He'd go along a row of gladioli, yanking out the ones he didn't want as fast as he could pull them up. He seemed to have an instinct that told him if a tiny plant would grow up to bear the kind of fruit or flowers he wanted. I couldn't see any difference between them, even if I stooped and looked closely, but Burbank did no more than glance at them."

Burbank's catalogs described his results in such a way that readers could imagine he had thousands of workers and several genies helping him: "Six new gladioli, the best of a million seedlings." "The growing of 10,000 hybrid clematis plants for several years to get a final six good ones." "Discarding 18,000 calla lilies in order to get one plant." "My Royal Walnut can outgrow ordinary walnuts eight to one and promises to revolutionize the furniture business and also perhaps the cord-wood industry."

When, on the 18th day of April, 1906, the same earthquake which all but devastated San Francisco reduced Santa Rosa to a mass of flaming splinters and rubble, the overwhelmed citizens were further stunned that not a pane of glass in Burbank's huge greenhouse not far from the center of town was even cracked.

Burbank was less amazed than his fellow townsmen, though careful not to broach the subject directly in public, surmising that his communing with the forces of nature and the cosmos and his success with plants might well have protected his greenhouse.

His indirect allusions to the personalization of his plants are illustrated by an article he wrote in 1906 for *Century Magazine:*

> The most stubborn living thing in this world, the most difficult to swerve [he asserted] is a plant once fixed in certain habits. Remember that this plant has preserved its individuality all through the ages; perhaps it is one which can be traced backward through eons of time in the very

rocks themselves. Do you suppose, after all these ages of repetition, the plant does not become possessed of a will, if you so choose to call it, of unparalleled tenacity?

To Manly P. Hall, founder and president of the Philosophical Research Society of Los Angeles and a student of comparative religion, mythology, and esoterica, Burbank revealed that when he wanted his plants to develop in some particular and peculiar way not common to their kind he would get down on his knees and talk to them. Burbank also mentioned that plants have over twenty sensory perceptions but, because they are different from ours, we cannot recognize them. "He was not sure," wrote Hall, "that the shrubs and flowers understood his words, but he was convinced that by some telepathy, they could comprehend his meaning."

Hall later confirmed what Burbank told the famous yogi, Paramahansa Yogananda, about his development of the spineless cactus, a years-long procedure during which Burbank at first had to pull thousands of cactus thorns from his hands with pliers, though in the end the cacti grew without thorns. "While I was conducting my experiments with cacti," said Burbank, "I often talked to the plants to create a vibration of love. 'You have nothing to fear,' I would tell them. 'You don't need your defensive thorns. I will protect you.'" Burbank's power of love, reported Hall, "greater than any other, was a subtle kind of nourishment that made everything grow better and bear fruit more abundantly. Burbank explained to me that in all his experimentation he took plants into his confidence, asked them to help, and assured them that he held their small lives in deepest regard and affection."

Helen Keller, deaf and blind, after a visit to Burbank, wrote in *Outlook for the Blind:* "He has the rarest of gifts, the receptive spirit of a child. When plants talk to him, he listens. Only a wise child can understand the language of flowers and trees." Her observation was particularly apt since all his life Burbank loved children. In his essay "Training of the Human Plant," later published as a book, he anticipated the more humane attitudes of a later day and shocked authoritarian parents by saying, "It is more important for a child to have a good nervous system than to try to 'force' it along the line of book knowledge at the expense of its spontaneity, its play. A child should learn through a medium of pleasure, not of pain. Most of the things that are really useful in later life come to the children through play and through association with nature."

Burbank, like other geniuses, realized that his successes came from having conserved the exuberance of a small boy and his wonder for everything around him. He told one of his biographers: "I'm almost seventy-seven, and I can still go over a gate or run a foot race or kick the chandelier. That's because my body is no older than my mind—and my mind is adolescent. It has never grown up and I hope it never will."

It was this quality which so puzzled the dour scientists who looked askance at his power of creation and bedeviled audiences who expected him to be explicit as to how he produced so many horticultural wonders. Most of them were as disappointed as the members of the American Pomological Society, gathered to hear Burbank tell "all" during a lecture entitled "How to Produce New Fruits and Flowers," who sat agape as they heard him say:

> In pursuing the study of any of the universal and everlasting laws of nature, whether relating to the life, growth, structure and movements of a giant planet, the tiniest plant or of the psychological movements of the human brain, some conditions are necessary before we can become one of nature's interpreters or the creator of any valuable work for the world. Preconceived notions, dogmas and all personal prejudice and bias must be laid aside. Listen patiently, quietly and reverently to the lessons, one by one, which Mother Nature has to teach, shedding light on that which was before a mystery, so that all who will, may see and know. She conveys her truths only to those who are passive and receptive. Accepting these truths as suggested, wherever they may lead, then we have the whole universe in harmony with us. At last man has found a solid foundation for science, having discovered that he is part of a universe which is eternally unstable in form, eternally immutable in substance.

Had he known of Fechner, Burbank would have agreed with him "that it is a dark and cold world we sit in if we will not open the inward eyes of the spirit to the inward flame of nature."

CHAPTER 9

Wizard of Tuskegee

That plants were able to reveal their hidden secrets upon request was accepted as normal and natural by a remarkable genius born just before the Civil War, the agricultural chemist George Washington Carver, who overcame the handicap of his slave descent to be heralded in his own lifetime as the "Black Leonardo."

During a stunningly creative career, with methods as incomprehensible to his fellow scientists as were those of his professional forebears the alchemists, Carver turned the lowly peanut, considered useful only as hog food, and the unknown sweet potato into hundreds of separate products, ranging from cosmetics and axle grease to printer's ink and coffee.

From the time he was able to get about by himself in the countryside young Carver began to display an uncanny knowledge of all growing things. Local farmers in Diamond Grove, a tiny community in the foothills of the Ozarks in southwestern Missouri, remembered the weak-looking boy roving for hours through their holdings, examining plants and bringing back certain varieties with which he could miraculously heal sick animals. On his own, the child planted a private garden in a remote and unused bit of bottomland. With the remnants of coldframes and other stray material he built a secret greenhouse in the woods. Asked what he was forever doing all by himself so far from the farmyard, Carver replied firmly if enigmatically, "I go to my garden hospital and take care of hundreds of sick plants."

Farmers' wives from all over the countryside began bringing him their ailing house plants, begging him to make them bloom. Gently caring for them in his own way, Carver often sang to them in the same squeaky voice which characterized him in manhood, put them in tin cans with special soil of his own concoction, tenderly covered them at night, and took them out to "play in the sun" during the day. When he returned the plants to their owners, and repeatedly was asked how he could work his miracles, Carver only said softly: "All flowers talk to me and so do hundreds of little living things in the woods. I learn what I know by watching and loving everything."

Enrolling in Simpson College in Indianola, Iowa, Carver supported himself through his skill as a laundryman by doing shirts for students, then transferred to the Iowa State College of Agriculture. There among his most lasting impressions was the statement of his best-loved teacher, Henry Cantwell Wallace, editor of the popular *Wallace's Farmer*, that "nations endure only as long as their topsoil." Carrying a heavy load of course work and employed by churches as an entirely self-taught organ-ist, Carver found time to take Wallace's six-year-old grandson on long walks into the woods to talk with plants and fairies, little suspecting that the hand he was holding would be that of a Secretary of Agriculture, and later, two years before Carver's own death, Vice President of the United States.

By 1896, Carver had his master's degree and was invited to join the faculty. However, when the founder and president of the Normal and Industrial Institute, Booker T. Washington, who had heard of Carver's brilliance, asked him to come to Tuskegee, Alabama, and run the institute's agricultural department, Carver decided, like Sir Jagadis Chandra Bose, that he could not let the prospect of a comfortable and well-paying post on the Iowa State faculty dissuade him from serving his own people. So he accepted.

Carver had not been back in the South more than a few weeks when he discerned that the main problem facing the flat land spreading out in hundreds of square miles around him was its slow poisoning through monotonous planting year in year out of a single crop, cotton, which for generations had been sucking fertility out of the soil. To counteract the despoliation by thousands of sharecroppers, he decided to set up an experimental station. There he had a private laboratory, christened "God's Little Workshop," in which he would sit for hours communing with plants and into which he never allowed a single book to penetrate.

For his students at Tuskegee he made his lectures as simple and yet as thoroughgoing as possible. When the chancellor of the University of Georgia, W. B. Hill, came to Tuskegee to see for himself if it was true that a Negro professor was as brilliant as rumor had reported, he declared that Carver's presentation on the problem of Southern agriculture was "the best lecture that it has ever been my privilege to attend." Carver's students were greatly impressed that each morning he would rise at four o'clock to walk in the woods before the start of the working day and bring back countless plants with which to illustrate his lectures. Explaining this habit to friends, Carver said, "Nature is the greatest teacher and I learn from her best when others are asleep. In the still dark hours before sunrise God tells me of the plans I am to fulfill."

For more than a decade Carver worked daily on experimental plots of soil trying to discover exactly how to change Alabama's enthrallment by "ol' debbil cotton." On one nineteen-acre plot he put no commercial fertilizer, benefiting it instead with nothing but old dead leaves from the forest, rich muck from the swamps, and barnyard manure. The plot furnished such bountiful harvests of rotated crops that Carver came to the conclusion that "in Alabama the very fertilizers which existed in almost unlimited supply were allowed to go to waste in favor of commercially sold products."

As a horticulturalist, Carver had noticed that the peanut was incredibly self-sufficient and could grow well in poor soil. As a chemist, he discovered that it equaled sirloin steaks in protein and potatoes in carbohydrates. Late one evening while pondering the problem in his workshop Carver stared at a peanut plant and asked, "Why did the Lord make you?" In a flash, he received the briefest of answers: "You have three things to go by: compatibility, temperature, and pressure."

With this slim advice Carver locked himself in his laboratory. There, throughout a sleepless week, he began breaking down the peanut into its chemical components and exposing them by trial and error to different conditions of temperature and pressure. To his satisfaction he found that one-third of the little nut was made up of seven different varieties of oil. Working round the clock, he analyzed and synthesized, took apart and recombined, broke down and built up the chemically differentiable parts of the peanut until at last he had two dozen bottles, each containing a brand-new product.

Leaving his laboratory, he convoked a meeting of farmers and agricultural specialists and showed them what he had been able to do in seven days and seven nights. He begged his audience to plow under the soil-destroying cotton and plant peanuts in its stead, assuring them that it would produce a cash crop far more valuable than its sole existing use as food for pigs might indicate.

The audience was doubtful, the more so when Carver, asked to explain his methods, replied that he never groped for them but that they came to him in flashes of inspiration while walking in the woods. To allay their doubts he began to issue bulletins, one of which stated incredibly that rich, nutritious, and highly palatable butter could be made from the peanut, and that whereas it took one hundred pounds of dairy milk to make ten pounds of butter, a hundred pounds of peanuts could produce thirty-five pounds of peanut butter. Other bulletins showed how a cornucopia of products could also be extracted from the sweet potato, a tropical vine of which most Americans had never heard, that throve in the South's cotton-debased soil. When World War I broke out, and the shortage of dyestuffs presented itself as a serious national problem, Carver rambled at daybreak through the mist and dew, inquiring of his plant friends which of them could alleviate the deficit. From the leaves, roots, stems, and fruits of twenty-eight volunteers he coaxed 536 separate dyes, which could be used to color wool, cotton, linen, silk, and even leather, producing 49 of them from the scuppernong grape alone.

At last his labors attracted national attention. When it was bruited that at Tuskegee Institute they were saving two hundred pounds of wheat per day by mixing two parts of ordinary flour with a new flour derived from sweet potatoes, a flock of dieticians and food writers interested in cooperating with the wartime drive to economize on wheat came to investigate. They were served delicious breads made from the mixed flours, along with a sumptuous lunch of five courses each made from peanuts or sweet potatoes, or, like Carver's "mock chicken," from the two combined. The only other vegetables on the table were sheep sorrel, pepper grass, wild chicory, and dandelions, served as a salad to illustrate Carver's assertion that plants growing in nature were far better than those from which the natural vitality had been removed in cultivation. The food experts, who realized that Carver's contributions might go a long way to helping the war effort, rushed to telephone their papers, and Carver, who had become known to scientists the year before when he was elected a fellow of Great Britain's famous Royal Society, now appeared in the headlines.

Invited to Washington, Carver dazzled government officials with dozens of products, including a starch valuable to the textile industry which later became a component in the glue of billions of U.S. postage stamps.

Next it came to Carver that peanut oil could help the atrophied muscles of polio victims. Results were so astonishing that he had to set aside one day each month to treat patients who came to his laboratory on stretchers, crutches, or canes. This feat remained as unheralded in medicine as the application of castor-oil packs, recommended about the same time by the "sleeping prophet," Edgar Cayce, with which doctors of an intrepidly investigative frame of mind are only today beginning to achieve startling, and wholly inexplicable cures.

By 1930, the peanut's one-time worthlessness had been converted, through Carver's clairvoyance, into a quarter of a billion dollars for Southern farmers, and had created a huge industry. Peanut oil alone was valued at $60 million a year and peanut butter was establishing itself as one of the favorite foods of even the poorest American child. Not satisfied with his achievements, Carver went on to make paper from a local Southern pine tree which ultimately helped to spur lumberers to cover millions of Southern acres with productive forests where only scrub woods had existed.

In the midst of the depression, Carver was again invited to Washington to testify before the powerful Ways and Means Committee of the U.S. Senate, which was considering the Smoot-Hawley tariff bill designed to protect struggling American manufacturers. Dressed in his usual, seemingly eternally durable, two-dollar black suit, with an ever-present flower in its buttonhole and a home-made necktie, Carver, upon his arrival at Union Station, was rebuffed by a waiting porter who, when Carver asked him to help him with his bags and direct him to Congress, replied: "Sorry, Pop, I ain't got time for you now. I'm expecting an important colored scientist coming from Alabama." Patiently Carver hefted his own bags to a taxi which took him to Capitol Hill.

Though the committee had accorded him no more than ten minutes to testify, when he began his presentations and took from his bag face powders, petroleum substitutes, shampoos, creosote, vinegar, woodstains, and other samples of the countless creations concocted in his laboratories, the Vice President of the United States, testy "Cactus Jack" Garner from Texas, overruled protocol and told Carver he could have as much time as he liked because his demonstration was the best that he had ever seen presented to a Senate committee.

In half a lifetime of research Carver, though he created fortunes for thousands, rarely took out a patent on any of his ideas. When practical-minded industrialists and politicians reminded him of the money he might have made had he only afforded himself this protection, he replied simply: "God did not charge me or you for making peanuts. Why should I profit from their products?" Like Bose, Carver believed that the fruit of his mind, however valuable, should be granted free of charge to mankind.

Thomas A. Edison told his associates that "Carver is worth a fortune" and backed up his statement by offering to employ the black chemist at an astronomically high salary. Carver turned down the offer. Henry Ford, who thought Carver "the greatest scientist living," tried to get him to come to his River Rouge establishment, with an equal lack of success.

Because of the strangely unaccountable source from which his magic with plant products sprang, his methods continued to be as wholly inscrutable as Burbank's to scientists and to the general public. Visitors finding Carver puttering at his workbench amid a confusing clutter of molds, soils, plants, and insects were baffled by the utter and, to many of them, meaningless simplicity of his replies to their persistent pleas for him to reveal his secrets.

To one puzzled interlocutor he said: "The secrets are in the plants. To elicit them you have to love them enough."

"But why do so few people have your power?" the man persisted. "Who besides you can do these things?"

"Everyone can," said Carver, "if only they believe it." Tapping a large Bible on a table, he added, "The secrets are all here. In God's promises. These promises are real, as real as, and more infinitely solid and substantial than, this table which the materialist so thoroughly believes in."

In a celebrated public lecture, Carver related how he had been able to call forth from the low mountains of Alabama hundreds of natural colors from clays and other earths, including a rare pigment of deep blue which amazed Egyptologists, who saw rediscovered in it the blue color found in the tomb of Tutankhamen, as bright and fresh after so many centuries as it was when it had been first applied.

When Carver was eighty or thereabouts—his exact date of birth never having been established since no records were kept for slave children—he addressed a meeting of chemists in New York as World War II was erupting in Europe.

"The ideal chemist of the future," said Carver, "will not be satisfied with humdrum day-to-day analysis, but is one who dares to think and work with an independence not permissible heretofore, unfolding before our eyes a veritable mystic maze of new and useful products from material almost or quite beneath our feet and now considered of little or no value."

Not long before Carver's death a visitor to his laboratory saw him reach out his long sensitive fingers to a little flower on his workbench. "When I touch that flower," he said rapturously, "I am touching infinity. It existed long before there were human beings on this earth and will continue to exist for millions of years to come. Through the flower, I talk to the Infinite, which is only a silent force. This is not a physical contact. It is not in the earthquake, wind or fire. It is in the invisible world. It is that still small voice that calls up the fairies."

He suddenly stopped and after a moment of reflection smiled at his visitor. "Many people know this instinctively," he said, "and none better than Tennyson when he wrote:

> "Flower in the crannied wall,
> I pluck you out of the crannies,
> I hold you here, root and all, in my hand,
> Little flower—but *if* I could understand
> What you are, root and all, and all in all,
> I should know what God and man is."

PART III

TUNED TO THE
MUSIC OF THE SPHERES

CHAPTER 10

The Harmonic Life of Plants

The strangest experiment Charles Darwin ever performed on a plant was to sit before his *Mimosa pudica*, or touch-me-not, and play to it his bassoon in close enough proximity to see if he could stimulate its pinnae, or feathery leaflets, into movement. The experiment failed but was exotic enough to stimulate the renowned German plant physiologist Wilhelm Pfeffer, author of the classic *Handbuch der Pflanzenphysiologie*, into attempting, also unsuccessfully, to provoke stamens of *Cynararea*, a small genus of erect herbs, into response by means of sound.

In 1950 when Professor Julian Huxley, the biologist grandson of Thomas Henry Huxley and brother of novelist Aldous, was visiting Dr.

T. C. Singh, head of the department of botany at Annamalai University south of the Tamil-speaking city of Madras, he found his host studying through a microscope the live streaming of protoplasm in the cells of *Hydrilla verticillata,* an aquatic plant of Asian origin with long transparent leaves. Aware of both Darwin's and Pfeffer's experiments, Huxley was struck by the idea that the magnification might be sufficient for his host to see if the streaming process could be affected by sound.

Because the streaming of protoplasm in vegetation begins to speed up after sunrise, Singh placed an electrically operated tuning fork six feet from a *Hydrilla,* and microscopically observed that the fork's note, broadcast for half an hour just before 6 A.M., caused the protoplasm to stream at a speed normally attained only much later in the day.

Singh next asked his young assistant, Stella Ponniah, an accomplished dancer and violinist, if she would play notes on her instrument while standing near a *Hydrilla.* When the girl stroked her strings at a certain pitch, the protoplasm's streaming was again accelerated.

Because the *raga,* a traditional form of South Indian devotional song, has a tonal system which can produce a deep religious feeling and specific emotions in a listener, Singh decided to try its tones on the *Hydrilla.*

Lord Krishna, the eighth and principal avatar and incarnation of the Hindu deity Vishnu, was reputed to have promoted with music enthralling growth and bewitching verdure in Vrindavan, a city on the banks of the Jamuna River in north-central India long famous for its saint-musicians. Much later a courtier of the famous Moghul emperor Akbar is reported to have been able to perform such miracles with his songs as to bring on rain, light oil lamps, vernalize plants and induce them to blossom simply by intoning *ragas* at them. This appealing idea is confirmed in Tamil literature, which refers to the eyes, or buds, of sugar cane growing vigorously in response to the mellifluous buzzing of speckled beetles and to the profuse oozing of sugary nectar from the golden flowers of *Cassia fistula* when serenaded with heart-melting melodies.

Knowing this ancient lore, Singh asked his assistant to play the South Indian tune *"Maya-malava-gaula raga"* to mimosas. After a fortnight, to Singh's intense excitement, he discovered that the number of stomata per unit area in the experimental plants was 66 percent higher, the epidermal walls were thicker, the palisade cells were longer and broader than in control plants, sometimes by as much as 50 percent.

Encouraged to further experimentation, Singh requested Gouri Kumari, a lecturer at Annamalai's Music College, to play a *raga* known as the *"Kara-hara-priya"* to some balsam plants. Kumari, a virtuoso, played for twenty-five minutes each day, on a fretted lutelike instrument usually fitted with seven strings, the *veena* traditionally associated with Saraswati, goddess of wisdom. During the fifth week, the experimental balsams began to shoot ahead of their unserenaded neighbors and, at the end of December, had produced an average of 72 percent more leaves than the control plants, and had grown 20 percent higher.

Singh then experimented on a vast number of species, such as common asters, petunias, cosmos, and white spider lilies, along with such economic plants as onions, sesame, radishes, sweet potatoes, and tapioca.

Each of these species Singh entertained for several weeks just before sunrise with more than half a dozen separate *ragas*, one per experiment, played on the flute, violin, harmonium, and *veena;* the music lasted a half hour daily, scaled at a high pitch, with frequencies between one hundred and six hundred cycles per second. From all this experimentation Singh was able to state, in the magazine of the Bihar Agricultural College at Sabour, that he had "proven beyond any shadow of doubt that harmonic sound waves affect the growth, flowering, fruiting, and seed-yields of plants."

As a result of his success, Singh began wondering whether sound, properly prescribed, could spur field crops to greater yields. From 1960 to 1963 he piped the *"Charukesi raga"* on a gramophone via a loudspeaker to six varieties of early, medium, and late paddy rice growing in the fields of seven villages located in the state of Madras and in Pondicherry on the Bay of Bengal, and got harvests ranging consistently from 25 to 60 percent higher than the regional average. He also was able musically to provoke peanuts and chewing tobacco into producing nearly 50 percent more than normal. Singh further reported that merely by dancing the *"Bharata-Natyam,"* India's most ancient dance style, without musical accompaniment and executed by girls without trinkets on their ankles, the growth of Michaelmas daisies, marigolds, and petunias was very much accelerated, causing them to flower as much as a fortnight earlier than controls, presumably because of the rhythm of the footwork transmitted through the earth.

Replying to a question which he thought would "naturally bristle up" in the minds of his readers, as to exactly what caused the effect on plants, Singh explained that in his laboratories he could visually demonstrate that the fundamental metabolic processes of plants in relation to transpiration and carbon assimilation under the excitation of musical sound or rhythmic beat were very much accelerated and increased over 200 percent compared to controls. "The stimulated plants," wrote Singh, "are energized to synthesize greater quantities of food during a given period of time, which naturally leads to greater yields." Singh also reported that his method of musical stimulation has even increased the chromosome count of certain species of water plants and the nicotine content of tobacco leaves.

Though the Indians of the subcontinent, both ancient and modern, appear to have been the first to produce a significant effect on plants with music or sound, they are by no means the only ones. In the Milwaukee, Wisconsin, suburb of Wauwatosa, a florist, Arthur Locker, began piping music into his greenhouses in the late 1950s. The difference he observed in flower production before and after the broadcasts was sufficiently marked to convince Locker that music powerfully contributed to horticulture. "My plants grew straighter, germinated quicker, bloomed more abundantly," he said. "The colors of the flowers were more striking to the eye, and the blooms lasted longer than usual."

At about the same time a Canadian engineer and gentleman farmer, Eugene Canby, of Wainfleet, Ontario, broadcast the violin sonatas of Johann Sebastian Bach to a test plot of wheat and produced a crop not only 66 percent greater than average but with larger and heavier seeds. Since the wheat growing in those areas of the plot where the soil was inferior did just as well as those growing in the richest earth, it seemed to Canby that Bach's musical genius was as good as or better than nutrients.

In 1960 in the agricultural community of Normal, Illinois, a botanist and agricultural researcher, George E. Smith, learned of Singh's experiments while chatting with the farm editor of his local newspaper. The following spring, Smith, somewhat skeptically, planted corn and soybeans in flats and divided them between two identical greenhouses, both kept precisely at the same level of temperature and humidity. In one of the greenhouses he installed a small record player, its speaker directed toward the experimental plants, and played George Gershwin's "Rhapsody in Blue" twenty-four hours a day. According to Smith's report to his employer, Mangelsdorf and Bros., Inc., wholesale field seed suppliers in St. Louis, Missouri, the Gershwin-inspired seedlings sprouted earlier than those given the silent treatment, and their stems were thicker, tougher, and greener.

Smith, still skeptical, was not satisfied with his subjective observations. Removing ten corn and ten soybean plants from each of the greenhouses, he carefully cut them at ground level and immediately weighed them on apothecary scales. To his surprise the ten corn plants which had been enjoying Gershwin's music weighed 40 grams and those deprived of it only 28 grams; the corresponding soybean plants' weights were 31 and 25 grams respectively.

The following year Smith continuously broadcast music to a small plot of Embro 44XE hybrid corn from the day of its planting to harvest time. The plot produced 137 bushels to the acre as against only 117 bushels for an untreated plot of similar corn growing under the same conditions. Smith noted that the musically entertained corn also grew more rapidly and uniformly and silked earlier. The larger yield per acre was due not to an increase per plant but to a greater survival of plants in the plot. To make sure that his tests were not due to chance, Smith laid out four corn plots in 1962 planted not only with the same Embro 44XE but also with another highly prolific hybrid, Embro Departure. The first plot was treated to the previous year's music, the second left silent, and the third and fourth offered only ear-splitting continuous notes, one with a high pitch of 1,800 cycles a second, the other with a low pitch of 450. At harvest time the Departure plants stimulated with music produced 186 bushels per acre as against only 171 for the silent plot. But those exposed to the high note outdid themselves to achieve nearly 198 bushels; those subjected to the low note topped 200. Gains for the Embro 44XE were less pronounced, though Smith had no idea why.

Pressed by his neighbors from several counties around to explain his results, Smith speculated that sound energy might increase molecular activity in the corn, and added that thermometers placed in the plots indicated that soil temperature was inexplicably two degrees higher directly in front of the loudspeaker. Smith was perplexed that the edges of the leaves of those corn plants growing in the slightly heated earth appeared a little burned, but thought this might be due to excessive exposure to musical vibrations. There were many unresolved mysteries, said Smith, one of whose Kansas friends had told him that high-frequency waves had been used successfully to control insects in stored wheat and that the same wheat planted later germinated faster than untreated grain.

The frequencies on the so-called sonic spectrum, unlike those on the so-called electromagnetic spectrum, relate to vibrations in matter, the medium in which they travel, and result from the rate of its compression and expansion. Thus a sound wave can pass through air, water, and other fluids, an iron bar, a table top, a human being, or a plant. Because human ears can pick up only those frequencies from 16 to about 20,000 cycles per second, they are known as "audio," or "sonic," frequencies. Below them are inaudible subsonic frequencies, some of which result from pressure applied slowly, such as that produced with a hydraulic jack, which become so slow they are measured not in cycles per second but in seconds per cycle. Above them are ultrasonic frequencies also inaudible to the human ear but affecting man's being in a variety of ways which are not fully known. Extremely high frequencies on this spectrum, ranging from hundreds to thousands of millions of cycles per second, can be perceived as heat on the skin and are therefore termed "thermal," though because they too cannot be audially detected could just as well be considered ultrasonic.

After his experimentation was given publicity all over North America, Smith received a letter from Peter Belton of the research branch of Canada's Department of Agriculture, who informed him that he had broadcast ultrasonic waves to control the European corn-borer moth, whose larvae extensively damage growing corn. "At first we tested the hearing ability of this moth," wrote Belton. "It was obvious that moths could hear sounds at about 50,000 cycles. These high-pitched sounds are much like those made by bats, the moth's natural enemy. We planted two plots of corn, each ten feet by twenty, and divided them with sheets of plastic eight feet tall, capable of stopping this sound frequency. Then we broadcast the bat-like sound across two of the half-plots from dusk till dawn throughout the period the moths lay their eggs." Belton informed Smith that nearly 50 percent of his ripe corn ears were damaged by larvae in the silent plots but only 5 percent suffered injury in the plots where the moths had supposedly suspected bats might be lurking. A careful count also revealed 60 percent fewer larvae in the sound plots, and the corn was three inches taller.

In the mid-1960s the varied efforts of Singh and Smith aroused the curiosity of two researchers at Canada's University of Ottawa, Mary Measures and Pearl Weinberger. Like L. George Lawrence, they were conversant with discoveries by Russians, Canadians, and Americans that ultrasonic frequencies markedly affect the germination and growth of barley, sunflower, spruce, Jack pine, Siberian pea tree, and other seeds and seedlings. The experiments indicated, albeit inexplicably, that enzyme activity and respiration rates in plants and their seeds increased when they were stimulated by ultrasonic frequencies. However, the very frequencies which stimulated some plant species inhibited others. Measures and Weinberger wondered whether specific *audible* frequencies in the sonic range would be as effective as music in enhancing the growth of wheat.

In a series of experiments lasting more than four years, the two biologists exposed the grains and seedlings of spring Marquis and winter Rideau wheat to high-frequency vibrations. They found that, depending on how long the wheat seeds had been vernalized, the plants responded best to a frequency of 5,000 cycles a second.

Baffled by their results, the two researchers could not explain why audible sound had resulted in accelerated growth so striking that it seemed to promise to double wheat harvests. The effect could not have been produced by breaking chemical bonds in the seeds, they wrote in the *Canadian Journal of Botany,* since, to do this, one billion times as much energy as was added by the sound frequencies would be required. Instead, they suggested that sound waves might produce a resonant effect in the plant cells, enabling the energy to accumulate and affect the plant's metabolism. In the July, 1968, issue of *Prevention* magazine J. I. Rodale reported that Weinberger "is coming to believe that basic farm equipment of the future will include an oscillator for production of sound waves and a speaker."

Asked to confirm whether her experiments might result in application of sound to wheat seed planted in extended acreage, Dr. Weinberger stated in 1973 that large-scale tests were going forward in Canada, the United States, and Europe to determine the practicability of their idea.

Weinberger's observations are echoed by four scientists at the University of North Carolina at Greensboro, who have discovered that experimental "pink" noise, which, at 20 to 20,000 cycles per second and 100 decibels, sounds to the ear about the same as the noise received 100 feet away from a 727 jet plane about to take off, caused turnips to sprout much faster than those left silently in the ground. Professor Gaylord T. Hageseth, a physicist and leader of the research team, says that his findings have stirred up interest at the U.S. Department of Agriculture, which is studying the team's proposals to awaken seeds planted in hot regions such as California's San Joaquin Valley, where temperatures ranging above 100 degrees Fahrenheit induce dormancy in lettuce seeds. If awakened by sound irradiation, lettuce might produce two crops per season instead of one, say Hageseth and his colleagues, who also suggest that sound waves could be used to make weeds germinate before a field is planted. The weeds could then be plowed under to allow a crop to grow in a weed-free field.

Since broadcasting airport-level noise all over the countryside is hardly appealing, the North Carolina team has been working, like Measures and Weinberger, to find particular wavelengths or combinations to produce the desired effects at lower decibel levels. By the beginning of 1973 they had discovered that the germination rate in turnips seemed to speed up when the turnips were exposed to a frequency of 4,000 cycles per second.

An interesting and eventually very controversial series of experiments on the effects of music on plants began in 1968 when Dorothy Retallack, a professional organist and mezzo soprano, who gave concerts at Denver's Beacon Supper Club from 1947 to 1952, felt herself at loose ends when her eight children went off to college. Not to be the sole member of the family without a degree, Mrs. Retallack surprised her hardworking physician husband with the announcement of her own enrollment for a degree in music at Temple Buell College. Required to come up with a laboratory experiment in biology, Mrs. Retallack vaguely recalled reading an article about George Smith's playing disc jockey to his cornfields.

Following Smith's lead, Mrs. Retallack teamed with a fellow student, whose family provided an empty room at home and furnished two groups of plants, which included philodendron, corn, radishes, geraniums, and African violets. The neophyte experimenters suspended Gro-Lux lights over one group and played the taped musical notes B and D struck on the piano every second, alternating five minutes of those wearisomely repetitive sounds with five minutes of silence. The tape played continuously twelve hours a day. During the first week, the African violets, drooping at the start of the experiment, revived and began to flower. For ten days all the plants in the sound group seemed to thrive; but at the end of two weeks the geranium leaves began to yellow. By the end of the third week all the plants, some of which had been actually leaning away from the source of the sound as if blown by a strong wind, had died, with the unaccountable exception of the African violets, which somehow remained outwardly unaffected. The control group, allowed to grow in peace, flourished.

When she reported these results to her biology professor, Francis F. Broman, and asked if she could do a more elaborately controlled experiment for credit in his course, he reluctantly consented. "The idea made me groan a little," said Broman afterward, "but it was novel and I decided to okay it, even though most of the other students laughed out loud." Broman made available to Dorothy Retallack three new Biotronic Mark III Environmental Chambers fifty-six feet long, twenty-six feet high, and eighteen feet deep, recently purchased by his department, similar in shape but much larger than home fish aquariums, which allowed for precise control of light, temperature, and humidity.

Allotting one chamber for a control group, Mrs. Retallack used the same plants, with the exception of the violets, as in the first experiment, setting them in identical soil and affording them equal amounts of water on schedule. Trying to pinpoint the musical note most conducive to survival, each day she tried an F note, played unremittingly for eight hours in one chamber and three hours intermittently in another. In the first chamber her plants were stone dead within two weeks. In the second chamber, the plants were much healthier than controls left in silence.

Mrs. Retallack and Professor Broman were nonplused by these results; for they had no idea what could be causing the disparate reactions, and could not help wondering whether the plants had succumbed to fatigue or boredom or had simply been "driven out of their minds." The clearcut experiments aroused a spate of controversy in the biology department, with both students and professors either dismissing the whole effort as spurious, or intrigued by the inexplicable outcome. Two students, following Mrs. Retallack's lead, ran an eight-week experiment on summer squashes, broadcasting music from two Denver radio stations into their chambers, one specializing in heavily accented rock, the other in classical music.

The cucurbits were hardly indifferent to the two musical forms: those exposed to Haydn, Beethoven, Brahms, Schubert, and other eighteenth- and nineteenth-century European scores grew *toward* the transistor radio, one of them even twining itself lovingly around it. The other squashes grew away from the rock broadcasts and even tried to climb the slippery walls of their glass cage.

Impressed with her friends' success, Mrs. Retallack ran a series of similar trials early in 1969 with corn, squash, petunias, zinnias, and marigolds; she noticed the same effect. The rock music caused some of the plants first to grow either abnormally tall and put out excessively small leaves, or remain stunted. Within a fortnight all the marigolds had died, but only six feet away identical marigolds, enjoying the classical strains, were flowering. More interestingly, Mrs. Retallack found that even during the first week the rock-stimulated plants were using much more water than the classically entertained vegetation, but apparently enjoying it less, since examination of the roots on the eighteenth day revealed that soil growth was sparse in the first group, averaging only about an inch, whereas in the second it was thick, tangled, and about four times as long.

At this point, various critics sourly suggested that the experiments were invalid because such variables as sixty-cycle hum, the "white sound" heard from a radio tuned to a frequency not occupied by a radio transmitter, or the announcers' voices emitted by the radio sets had not been taken into account. To satisfy these cavils, Mrs. Retallack taped rock music from records. She selected the extremely percussive rock renditions of Led Zeppelin, Vanilla Fudge, and Jimi Hendrix. When plants leaned away from this cacophony, Mrs. Retallack rotated all the pots 180 degrees, only to see the plants lean in the opposite direction. This convinced the majority of critics that the plants were definitely reacting to the sounds of rock music.

Trying to determine what it was about rock that so jarred her plants, Mrs. Retallack guessed that it might be the percussive component in the music and started yet another experiment in the fall. Selecting the familiar Spanish tune "La Paloma," she played one version of it performed on steel drums to one chamber of plants and another version played on strings to a second. The percussion caused a lean ten degrees *away* from the vertical in Mrs. Retallack's plants, but nothing compared to the rock. The plants listening to the fiddles leaned fifteen degrees *toward* the source of the music. An eighteen-day repeat of the same experiment using twenty-five plants per chamber including squash from seed and flowering and leaf-type plants from greenhouses produced largely similar results.

Now Mrs. Retallack wondered how the effects of what she called "intellectual mathematically sophisticated music of both East and West" would appeal to plants. As program director for the American Guild of Organists, she chose choral preludes from Johann Sebastian Bach's *Orgelbüchlein* and the classical strains of the *sitar*, a less-complicated Hindustani version of the south Indian *veena*, played by Ravi Shankar, the Bengali Brahmin.

The plants gave positive evidence of liking Bach, since they leaned an unprecedented thirty-five degrees *toward* the preludes. But even this affirmation was far exceeded by their reaction to Shankar: in their straining to reach the source of the classical Indian music they bent more than halfway to the horizontal, at angles in excess of sixty degrees, the nearest one almost embracing the speaker.

In order not to be swayed by her own special taste for the classical music of both hemispheres Mrs. Retallack, at the behest of hundreds of young people, followed Bach and Shankar with trials of folk and "country-western" music. Her plants seemed to produce no more reaction than those in the silent chamber. Perplexed, Mrs. Retallack could only ask: "Were the plants in complete harmony with this kind of earthy music or didn't they care one way or the other?"

Jazz caused her a real surprise. When her plants heard recordings as varied as Duke Ellington's "Soul Call" and two discs by Louis Armstrong, 55 percent of the plants leaned fifteen to twenty degrees *toward* the speaker, and growth was more abundant than in the silent chamber. Mrs. Retallack also determined that these different musical styles markedly affected the evaporation rate of distilled water inside the chambers. From full beakers, fourteen to seventeen milliliters evaporated over a given time period in the silent chambers, twenty to twenty-five milliliters vaporized under the influence of Bach, Shankar, and jazz; but, with rock, the disappearance was fifty-five to fifty-nine milliliters.

When the office of public information at Temple Buell got wind that Mrs. Retallack was the first grandmother ever to be graduated from its college, it informed Olga Curtis, a reporter on the Denver *Post*, about her extraordinary doings with plants. Mrs. Retallack set up a brand-new experiment for Curtis in which she compared the effects of rock with that of string quartets by such twentieth-century composers as Schoenberg, Webern, and Berg. The point of choosing the largely twelve-tone music of these neo-classicists was to see whether its dissonances, like those of rock, would also cause the plants to cringe. They did not. Root examination showed that the specimens in the rock chamber were scrawny, whereas those subjected to the avant-garde music were comparable to control plants.

On June 21, 1970, the *Post*'s weekend supplement *Empire Magazine* came out with a color-illustrated four-page spread entitled "Music That Kills Plants," which won for Curtis an annual award by the National Federation of Press Women. Syndicated by Metro Sunday Newspapers, the piece appeared all over the United States, spawning a new generation of articles with such titles as "Bach or Rock: Ask Your Flowers," "Mother Is Knitting Earmuffs for Our Petunias," and more alarmingly, "It Shouldn't Happen to Teenagers." Tying rock music to the proliferation of drugs among American youth, one writer for the popular right-wing *Christian Crusade Weekly* sanctimoniously wrote: "The Scripture admonishes the sluggard to go to the ant! Perhaps the druggard should go to the plant!"

From an avalanche of mail Mrs. Retallack learned that her experiments had elicited the interest of hundreds of readers, including a passel of professors who asked for her published scientific works. Spurred by the unsolicited interest, Retallack, together with Professor Broman, prepared a nine-page scientific paper, "Response of Growing Plants to a Manipulation of Their Sonic Environment," and sent it in to *BioScience Magazine*, published by the American Institute of Biological Sciences. They received a turndown, in the form of a review by Dr. Robert S. Leisner, stating that though one could draw a "highly tentative" conclusion that sound affects plant growth, the Retallack-Broman conclusions were hardly novel in light of the earlier work of Weinberger and Measures in Ottawa.

Meanwhile, Mrs. Retallack was called by CBS television and asked to set up a Rock-versus-Shankar experiment for filming with time-lapse cameras. Almost sick with nervousness lest her charges not deliver their message for the CBS technicians, Mrs. Retallack was relieved when the plants performed as if they knew they were scheduled for a nationwide broadcast. Aired on Walter Cronkite's newscast on October 16, 1970, the program added another enormous pile to her correspondence, which included a number of reports which researchers around the country wanted to share with her.

From them Dorothy Retallack learned that two North Carolina State University professors, L. H. Royster, of the Department of Mechanical and Aerospace Engineering, and B. H. Huang, of the Department of

Biological Engineering, had teamed with C. B. Woodlief, a researcher at Fiber Industries in the town of Shelby, to perform an experiment written up in the *Journal of the Acoustical Society of America* as "Effect of Random Noise on Plant Growth." The threesome, who realized that the effects of proliferating noise pollution on animals and man had been studied but that similar effects on plant systems had been overlooked, put twelve male sterile tobacco plants into an environmental control chamber with constant soil and temperature conditions. From a Bruel and Kraer random-noise generator they harried the plants with noise frequencies ranging from 31.5 to 20,000 cycles per second and concluded that growth rate in each plant decreased 40 percent.

Another correspondent was Dr. George Milstein, of Long Island City, New York, a retired dental surgeon turned teacher of horticulture at the New York Botanical Garden. After some of his patients had presented him with exotic plants the names of which no florist could be sure of, Milstein had dipped into botanical sources, become fascinated with the vegetal world, and begun growing exotic and colorful Bromeliads, an extended plant family which includes specimens as diverse as the pineapple and Spanish moss.

Learning of the Canadian research on wheat, he decided to see how sonics would affect other plants. Selecting a wide variety of house plants and two bananas, he subjected them to sonic vibrations delivered directly through the air or transduced through the soil of their pots or through their stems. Assisted by an NBC sound engineer, Milstein found that a continuous low hum at 3,000 cycles per second accelerated the growth of most of his subjects and even caused some of them to bloom six full months ahead of their normal schedule.

When Pip Records, a division of Pickwick International, Inc., asked him to make a record of stimulatory sounds for plants, it insisted that the record also contain music. Milstein accordingly embedded the stimulating hum in the record's musical selections. In an insert in the disc's jacket, "Growing Plants Successfully in the Home," Milstein, after giving precise information on the best kind of light, humidity, ventilation, temperature, watering, fertilizer, and pots, stated that just as all plant growth and flower development are stimulated by light vibrations, so it is logical to assume that the vibrations of sound energy can also exert a beneficial influence on horticulture. Milstein recommended that for best results the record be played daily.

When the record attracted attention in the United States and other countries, Milstein was pestered in the mail and over the telephone by hundreds of persons who wanted to know what kind of music best suited plants, and whether his research accorded with that of Dorothy Retallack and tied in with that of Cleve Backster. Milstein blew up. Mrs. Retallack's experiments, he says, have nothing to do with science, since "plants can't hear." Appalled at what he calls the total fakery of comparing plants to people, and disgusted at the "dishonesty" on the part of those promoting the record, he says he is tired of the repeated allegations that he used *music* to enhance plant growth.

Asked to comment on Cleve Backster's work, the dentist turned horticulturist said: "Backster must be, at best, self-deluded since no one who has studied botany or physiology could ever agree that plants, whose tissues differ completely from those of animals and man, have minds or emotions and can be frightened by a mental threat."

As secretary of the Society of American Magicians, Milstein, who performed magic to work his way through college, said he had investigated hundreds of so-called "psychic phenomena" and never found a case in which the person claiming a given psychic power could perform under test conditions. "At least Backster isn't collecting money the way some other charlatans are," said Milstein, "but I don't want any part of his research because everything he says he has discovered can be disproved."

Milstein's dogmatic statement was paralleled by those of various professors at Temple Buell. The *New York Times*, which published a feature article on Mrs. Retallack's work on February 21, 1971, stated that the academicians seemed to "cringe and die" quite as much as Dorothy Retallack's acid-rock-exposed plants when it was suggested to them that Backster could be serious. "They find the whole thing an excruciating embarrassment," the *Times* stated, then quoted one of the college's own biologists as saying, "We have been ridiculed professionally." Dr. Cleon Ross, a plant physiologist at Colorado State University, though he reluctantly agreed to discuss the subject of the effect of sonic energy on plants with the *Times* reporter, Anthony Ripley, when asked to comment on Backster's discovery that plants respond to human thought, only blurted out: "Pure garbage!"

At Utah State University, Dr. Frank B. Salisbury of the Plant Science Department was a bit kinder. "I don't know what to make of it all," protested the professor about the effect of music on plants. "It's been going on since 1950. There was a report at the 1954 International Botanical Congress by a man from India who played violins to plants. I hate to just out-and-out say it's all baloney, but there's been an awful lot of pseudo-science in this field for years. Most of this stuff just doesn't have the right kind of experimentation. Until that comes along I don't believe any of it."

Her own unequivocal results caused Mrs. Retallack to wonder whether the nationwide craze for acid rock among the younger generation might not be deleterious to their development. Her doubts about the effects of rock increased when she read an article in the Napa, California, *Register* stating that two doctors had reported to the California Medical Association that of forty-three musicians playing amplified hard-rock music forty-one had suffered permanent hearing loss.

Some of Denver's rock buffs also seemed deeply impressed by Mrs. Retallack's experiments. One long-haired musician, peering into the rock-suffused biotronic chamber, said to her: "If rock is doing *that* to plants, man, I wonder what it's doing to me?" Mrs. Retallack wants to continue her experiments in order to collect enough scientific data to give the young musician a reasoned answer. One test she envisions will involve playing musical tapes backward to see if they produce effects similar to or different from the same tapes played in the normal direction.

When she began writing a short book on her experiments, *The Sound of Music and Plants,* published in early 1973, Mrs. Retallack was inspired with a line from Oscar Hammerstein she had sung years before as the star of *The Sound of Music* in Denver's summer opera: "The hills are alive with the sound of music, with songs they have sung for a thousand years."

Delving in libraries to find material with which to give a philosophical underpinning to her experimental work, she came across a declaration in the *Book of the Secrets of Enoch* that everything in the universe, from the herbs of the field to the stars of the heavens, had its individual spirit or angel, and noted that Hermes Trismegistus was reputed to have stated that plants had lives, minds, and souls, even as did animals, men, and higher beings. Hermes, named "thrice greatest" by the Greeks and from whose name the word "hermetic" is derived, was regarded as the originator of Egyptian art, science, magic, alchemy, and religion.

That musical sound lies within the very hearts of atoms is the contention of a professor of chemistry, now retired after a long career at Johns Hopkins University, Donald Hatch Andrews. In his book, *The Symphony of Life*, Andrews invites readers to join him on an imaginary journey inside a magnified calcium atom taken from the bone beneath the tip of his forefinger. Inside the atom, says Andrews, there are shrill tones dozens of octaves above the highest tones of a violin, the music of the atomic nucleus, the tiny particle at the center of the atom. If one listens closely, he continues, one is aware that this music is far more complex than familiar church music. There are many dissonant chords like those found in the music of today's modern composers.

The whole purpose of dissonant music, according to Cyril Meir Scott, the English composer and theosophist, was to break up thought forms, which, settling over whole countries and people, turn them stagnant with lethargy or rampant with madness. It is an occult musical fact, says Scott, that discord—used in its moral sense—can alone be destroyed by discord, the reason for this being that the vibrations of intrinsically beautiful music are too rarefied to touch the comparatively coarse vibrations of all that pertains to a much lower plane.

So far, no researcher with the exception of Hans Kayser, the German author of *Harmonia Plantarum* and other mathematically learned books on the relation of sound intervals to the growth of plants, seems to have become interested in the octaval correspondences between the shapes of plants and musical notes. Kayser observed that if one projects all tones within the space of one octave—in the same manner that the astronomer and astrologer Johannes Kepler worked out in his *Harmonice Mundi* for the solar planetary system—and sketches their angles in a specific way, one obtains the prototype of leaf form. The interval of the octave, the basis for music making and indeed all sensation, thus contains within itself the form of the leaf.

Not only does this observation lend new "psychological" support to Goethe's metamorphosis of plants, which derive their development from the leaf form, but it casts new light on the ingenious classificatory system developed by Linnaeus. When one considers, says Kayser, that a passion flower contains two ratios, a *five*-part petal and stamen arrangement and a *three*-part pistil, even if one rejects a logically reasoning intelligence, one must admit that in the soul of plants are certain form-carrying prototypes—in the passion flower's case musical thirds and fifths—which work, as in music, to shape the blossom forms as intervals. It is from this point of view that Linnaeus' system acquires a "psychic" rehabilitation, concludes Kayser, for, with his "sexual" classification scheme, the famous Swedish botanist hit on the psychic nerve of plants.

What humans are able to perceive consciously with their limited senses is but a minute fraction of what vibrationally affects them. The so-called scentless daisy may be as sweet-smelling as the rose—if people had the olfactory ability to detect the particles the daisy throws off. Efforts to prove that a given sonic vibration will affect plants or man may, far from resolving the interaction of music and life, be only unraveling a wondrously resonating tapestry of influences into its separate, unrelated threads.

CHAPTER 11

Plants and Electromagnetism

Just as plants respond to the wavelengths of music, so also are they continually being affected by wavelengths of the electromagnetic spectrum, from earth, moon, planets, cosmos and from a proliferation of man-made devices; only it remains to be established exactly which are beneficial and which are harmful.

One evening in the late 1720s a French writer and astronomer, Jean-Jacques Dertous de Mairan, was watering a series of pet *Mimosa pudica* in his Paris drawing room when he noticed to his surprise that the disappearance of the sun appeared to be causing the sensitive plants to fold their leaves just as they did when touched by his hand. A true searcher, esteemed by his contemporary Voltaire, Mairan did not instantly conclude that his plants were "simply going to sleep" as darkness fell. Instead he waited for the sun to rise again and put two of the mimosas in a pitch-dark closet. At noon he noticed that their leaves remained wide open; but at sunset they shut just as promptly as the ones on the drawing-room table. The plants, concluded Mairan, must be able to "sense" the sun without "seeing" it.

As to the cause of this effect, Mairan—whose scientific investigations ranged from the rotational movement of the moon and the physical properties of the aurora borealis to the reason for light in phosphors and the peculiarities of the number 9—could offer no solution. In his report to the French Academy he lamely suggested that his plants must be under the influence of an unknown factor in the universe, and that because hospitalized patients seemed to get extremely weak at certain times they too might be subject to the same force.

Some two and a half centuries later, Dr. John Ott, who runs the Environmental Health and Light Research Institute at Sarasota, Florida, was struck by Mairan's observations, which he was able to confirm, and wondered if this "unknown energy" could penetrate a massive amount of earth, the only shield known to be able to block so-called "cosmic radiation."

Ott took six mimosa plants down a mine shaft at noon to a point 650 feet beneath the earth's surface. Unlike those in the dark of Mairan's closet, Ott's subterranean specimens immediately closed their leaves without waiting for sunset; they did so even when incandescent bulbs were lit all around them. Except for the fact that he related the phenomenon to electromagnetism, of which little was known in Mairan's time, Ott was as much in the dark about the cause of it as had been his eighteenth-century French predecessor.

Mairan's contemporaries had known about electricity only what the Hellenes had passed on to them concerning the properties of amber, or *electron*, as they called it, which when vigorously rubbed attracted a feather or a piece of straw. Before Aristotle, it had been known that lodestone, a black ferrous oxide, could also exert an equally inexplicable attraction on iron filings. Since this material was found in liberal quantities in a region of Asia Minor called Magnesia, it was dubbed *magnes lithos,* or magnesian stone, a term shortened to *magnes* in Latin and to *magnet* in English.

First to link electricity and magnetism was the sixteenth-century savant William Gilbert, whose medical skill and philosophical erudition won him appointment as personal physician to Queen Elizabeth I. Announcing that the planet itself was a globular magnet, Gilbert attributed to the lodestone a "soul," since it was "part and choice offspring of its animate mother, the earth." Gilbert also discovered that materials other than amber could be caused to attract light objects if friction was applied to them. He designated them "electrics" and coined the term "electric force."

For centuries the attractive forces in amber and lodestone were thought to be "penetrating etheric fluids" (whatever *they* might be), emitted by the substances. Even fifty years after Mairan's experiments, Joseph Priestley, known principally as the discoverer of oxygen, wrote in his popular textbook on electricity:

> The earth and all the bodies we are acquainted with, without exception, are supposed to contain a certain quantity of an exceedingly elastic and subtle fluid which philosophers have agreed to term electric. The moment any body becomes possessed of more or less than its natural quantity, very remarkable effects arise from it. The body is said to be electrified and is capable of exhibiting appearances which are ascribed to the power of electricity.

By the twentieth century real knowledge about magnetism had progressed very little. As Professor Silvanus Thompson stated in his Robert Boyle lecture just before World War I, "Those occult qualities of magnetism which for centuries have excited the admiration of mankind are still *occult,* not in the sense only that they need to be investigated by experiment, but that their ultimate cause still remains unexplained." In a text published right after World War II by Chicago's Museum of Science and Industry, it is stated that human beings still do not know why the earth is a magnet, how magnetic materials can be mechanically affected by other magnets at a distance from them, why electric currents have magnetic fields about them, or even why tiny atoms of matter, small as they are, occupy such empty but prodigious volumes of energy-packed space.

In the three and one half centuries since Gilbert's famous work *De Magnete* was published, many theories have been proposed to explain the origin of geomagnetism but none is satisfactory.

The same can be said for contemporary physics, which has substituted for the idea of an "etheric fluid" a spectrum of undulating radiations called "electromagnetic radiations," ranging from enormous macropulsations, lasting several hundred thousand years each, with wavelengths millions of miles long, to super-rapid energy pulses alternating 10,000,000,000,000,000,000,000,000 times a second, with wavelengths measuring an infinitesimal ten billionths of a centimeter. The first type are associated with such phenomena as the reversal of the earth's magnetic field, the second with the collision of atoms, usually those of helium and hydrogen, moving at incredibly high speeds and converted to radiant energy termed "cosmic rays." In between lie countless bands of energy waves, including gamma rays, originating in the nuclei of atoms; X-rays, originating in their shells; a collection of frequencies which because they can be perceived with the eye are called light; those used in radio, TV, radar, and a growing multitude of applications from space research to electronic cooking.

The electromagnetic waves differ from sound waves in that they can travel not only through matter but through "nothing," racing at a speed of 186 million miles per second through vast regions of the cosmos which previously was thought to contain a medium called "ether" but is now held to be almost a perfect vacuum. But no one has yet explained exactly how they travel. As one eniment physicist complained to the authors, "We just don't know the mechanism for the damn thing."

In 1747, Jean Antoine Nollet, a French abbot and physics tutor to the dauphin, was informed by a German physicist in Wittenberg that water, which normally issued drop by drop from a capillary tube, would run out in a constant stream if the tube was electrified. After repeating the German's experiments and adding some of his own, Nollet, as he later put it, "began to believe that this electrical virtue employed in a certain manner might have some remarkable effect on organized bodies which can be looked upon, in some way, as hydraulic machines prepared by nature itself." Nollet put several plants in metallic pots next to a conductor and was intrigued to note that the rate of their transpiration increased. In a long series of experiments, Nollet carefully weighed not only daffodils but sparrows, pigeons, and cats and found they lost weight faster if electrified.

Wondering how electrical phenomena might influence seeds, Nollet planted several dozen mustard grains in two tin containers and electrified one of them from 7 to 10 A.M. and from 3 to 8 P.M. seven days running. At the end of the week, every grain in the electrified container had sprouted and grown to an average height of 15 to 16 French *lignes;* the *ligne* is an old French measure, the twelfth part of an inch, or about 2.25 millimeters. Of the nonelectrified seeds the three which had broken ground were only 2 to 3 *lignes* tall. Though he had no idea why, Nollet could only suggest in his book-long report to the French Academy that electricity somehow had profound effects on the growth functions of life forms.

Nollet's conclusion was formulated a few years before the announcement rocked Europe that Benjamin Franklin had been able to collect a charge of electricity from lightning by flying a kite during stormy weather outside Philadelphia. When the bolt struck a metal point on the kite's frame, it had run down the kite's wet string into a Leyden bottle, a device developed in 1746 at the University of Leyden, whereby electricity could be stored in water and discharged in a single sudden burst. Theretofore, only static electricity obtained with an electrostatic generator had been storable in a Leyden jar.

As Franklin was now collecting electricity from clouds, the brilliant astronomer Pierre Charles Lemonnier, who was admitted to the French Academy at twenty-one and later acclaimed for his discovery of the obliquity of the ecliptic, determined that a permanent state of electrical activity exists in the earth's atmosphere even on a clear and sunny day, but exactly how the omnipresent charges interact with plants remained veiled in mystery.

The next efforts to adapt atmospheric electricity to the fructification of plants came in Italy. In 1770 a Professor Gardini stretched a number of wires above a productive monastery garden in Turin. Within a short time, many of the plants began to wither and die. When the monks dismantled the wires, the garden revived. Gardini hypothesized that either the plants had been deprived of a natural supply of electricity necessary to their growth or that they had received an overdose. When Gardini heard from France that the brothers Joseph-Michel and Jacques-Etienne Montgolfier had sent aloft an enormous balloon filled with heated air to carry two passengers on a ten-kilometer, twenty-five-minute trip over Paris, he recommended that this new invention be practically applied to horticulture by attaching a long wire to it along which electricity could be conducted from great heights into fields and gardens below.

These French and Italian reports caused little stir among the scientific pundits of the day, who, even then, were beginning to pay more attention to the effects of electricity on inert, rather than on living, bodies. Nor were they impressed when yet another clergyman, Abbé Bertholon, came out in 1783 with a full-scale treatise, *De l'Electricité des Végétaux*. A professor of experimental physics at French and Spanish universities, Bertholon gave strong support to Nollet's idea that by altering the viscosity, or flow resistance, of fluids in living organisms electricity could change their growth functions. He cited the report of an Italian physicist, Giuseppe Toaldo, that in a row of jasmine bushes the two which were next to a lightning conductor grew thirty feet tall whereas all the others attained only four feet.

Bertholon, who was considered something of a sorcerer, had a gardener stand on a slab of insulating material and sprinkle vegetables from an electrified watering can. He reported that his salads grew to an extraordinary size. He also invented what he called an "electrovegetometer" to collect atmospheric electricity by means of an antenna, and pass it through plants growing in a field. "This instrument," he wrote, "is applicable to all kinds of vegetal production, everywhere, in all weather; and its utility and efficacy cannot be ignored or doubted except by timid souls who are not inspired by discoveries and who will never push back the barriers of the sciences but will remain eternally within the narrow confines of a cowardly pusillanimity which, to palliate it, is too often given the name of prudence." In his conclusion, the abbot boldly suggested that one day the best fertilizer for plants would come in electrical form "free from the sky."

The exciting notion that living things interacted and indeed were imbued with electricity advanced a giant step in November, 1780, when the wife of a Bolognese scientist, Luigi Galvani, accidentally discovered that a machine used to generate static electricity caused the severed leg of a frog to jump spasmodically. When his attention was called to it, Galvani was surprised and instantly wondered whether electricity was not in fact a manifestation of life. Deciding on Christmas Day that it was, he wrote in his workbook: "The electrical fluid should be considered a means to excite nervo-muscular force."

For the next six years Galvani worked on the effects on muscular motion of electricity until he happened accidentally to discover that his frogs' legs would twitch just as well without the application of an electric charge if the copper wires they hung from were blown by the wind against an iron railing. Realizing that the electricity in the three-part circuit had to be coming from the legs or the metals, Galvani, who believed it to be a living rather than a dead force, decided it was associated with the animal tissue and ascribed the reaction to a vital fluid or energy in the frogs' bodies which he termed "animal electricity."

Galvani's findings at first received warm support from his compatriot Alessandro Volta, a physicist at the University of Pavia in the Duchy of Milan. But when Volta repeated Galvani's experiments and found he could elicit the electrical effect only when two different metals were used, he wrote to Abbot Tommaselli that it was obvious that the electricity came, not from the frog's legs, but from "the simple application of two metals of different quality." Concentrating on the electrical properties of metals, Volta was led in 1800 to the invention of a pile of alternating zinc and copper discs with a piece of wet paper sandwiched between each two layers. Instantly chargeable, it could be used to produce electric current at will, not only once, like the Leyden jar, but thousands of times, and thus for the first time researchers were freed from their dependence on static or natural electricity. This first ancestor of our electric storage cell disclosed an artificial dynamic or kinetic electricity, which all but obliterated Galvani's notion of a special vital energy in living tissues.

Though at first Volta had accepted Galvani's findings, he later wrote: "If we deprive animal organs of any electrical activity of their own and abandon this attractive idea which Galvani's beautiful experiments suggested, these organs can be regarded simply as electrometers of a new kind and of a marvelous sensitivity." Despite Galvani's prophetic assertion, just before his death, that one day the analysis of all the necessary physiological aspects of his experiments "would provide better knowledge of the nature of the life forces, their different duration, according to variations in sex, age, temperament, illnesses, and even the very constitution of the atmosphere," scientists neglected his theories and denied them in practice.

A few years earlier, unknown to Galvani, the Hungarian Jesuit Maximilian Hell had revived Gilbert's idea of "soul-like" characteristics in the lodestone being transmitted to ferrous metals; and with this idea had invented a singular arrangement of magnetized steel plates to cure his own persistent rheumatism. His friend the Viennese physician Franz Anton Mesmer, who picked up an interest in magnetism by reading Paracelsus, was impressed with Hell's subsequent cures of a variety of afflictions in others, and embarked on a long series of experiments to check them. In so doing Mesmer became convinced that living matter had a property susceptible to being acted upon by "earthly and celestial magnetic forces," which in 1779 he called "animal magnetism" and to which he devoted a doctoral thesis entitled "The Influence of the Planets on the Human Body." Learning that a Swiss priest, J. J. Gassner, was healing patients by touch, Mesmer successfully adopted Gassner's technique and proclaimed that some people, himself included, were better endowed with the "magnetic" force than others.

Though it seemed that these startling discoveries of bioelectrical and biomagnetic energy might open the door to a new age of research which could unite physics with medicine and physiology, the door was again slammed shut for more than a century. Mesmer's success in treating cases, where others had failed, provoked his Viennese medical colleagues to jealousy. Attributing his cures to witchcraft and the devil, they organized a commission to investigate his claims. When the commission reported unfavorably, Mesmer was expelled from the medical faculty and told to give up his practice.

Moving in 1778 to Paris, where he found "people more enlightened and less indifferent to new discoveries," he made a powerful convert to his new methods of Charles D'Eslon, first physician to the court of the brother of Louis XVI, who introduced Mesmer to influential circles. It was not long before the French physicians grew as angry and jealous as had their Austrian counterparts. Their clamor forced the king to appoint a royal commission to investigate Mesmer's claims, despite the fact that D'Eslon at a meeting of the medical faculty of the University of Paris had championed Mesmer's scientific contribution as "one of the most important of our age." When the commission, whose members included the director of the French Academy of Sciences—which in 1772 had solemnly ruled that meteorites did not exist—and whose chairman was the American ambassador, Benjamin Franklin, returned a verdict that "animal magnetism is nonexistent and can have no salubrious effect," Mesmer's great popularity, held up to public ridicule, began to wane. Retiring to Switzerland, he completed, one year before his death in 1815, his most important work: *Mesmerism or the System of Reciprocal Influences; or The Theory and Practice of Animal Magnetism.*

In 1820, Hans Christian Oersted, a Danish scientist, found that a compass needle placed near a current-carrying wire always turned so that the needle became perpendicular to the wire. When the current was reversed, the compass needle pointed in the opposite direction. The fact that a force could act on the compass needle indicated that a magnetic field existed in the space around the wire. This led to one of the most profitable discoveries in the history of science when Michael Faraday in England and Joseph Henry in the United States independently realized the opposite phenomenon was equally valid, that a magnetic field could induce an electric current if the wire were moved through it. Thus the "generator" was invented, and with it a whole new world of electrical appliances.

Today, books on what man can *do* with electricity fill seventeen 100-foot shelves of stacks in the Library of Congress, but what electricity *is* and why it functions are as much a mystery as they were in Priestley's day. Modern scientists still have no idea of the composition of electromagnetic waves. They simply use them for radio, radar, television and toasters.

Because of such a lopsided concentration on the mechanical properties of electromagnetism, only a corporal's guard of individuals has paid attention over the years to how and why electromagnetism might affect living things. A notable exception was Baron Karl von Reichenbach, a German scientist from Tübingen who in 1845 had discovered wood-tar products, including creosote, used for the preservation of above-ground fencing and underwater pilings. He became aware that specially gifted persons whom he termed "sensitives" could actually see a strange energy emanating from all living things and even from the ends of bar magnets; this energy he called *Odyle* or *Od.* But, though his works were translated into English by a distinguished medical doctor, William Gregory, appointed professor of chemistry at the University of Edinburgh in 1844, as *Researches into the Forces of Magnetism, Electricity, Heat and Light in Relation to the Force of Life,* his attempts to prove its existence to his physicist contemporaries in England and on the continent were rejected out of hand.

Reichenbach indicated the reason why his "odic force" was spurned when he wrote: "Whenever I began to touch on the subject, I felt at once that I was harping on a string of an unpleasant tone. They coupled Od and sensitivity in their minds with so-called 'animal magnetism' and 'Mesmerism' and with that all sympathy was at an end." The coupling was entirely unjustified, in that Reichenbach had clearly stated that though the mysterious odic force might resemble animal magnetism and was associated with it, it also could exist quite independently.

Years later, Wilhelm Reich contended that "the energy with which the ancient Greeks and the moderns since Gilbert were dealing was a basically different energy from that with which the physicists are dealing since Volta and Faraday, one obtained by the movement of wires in magnetic fields; different not only with regard to the principle of its production, but *fundamentally* different."

Reich believed that the ancient Greeks, with the principle of friction, had discovered the mysterious energy to which he gave the name "orgone," so similar to Reichenbach's Od and to the ether of the ancients. Reich claimed that orgone is the medium in which light moves, and the medium for electromagnetic and gravitational activity, that it fills all space, though in different degrees and concentration, and is even present in vacuums. He considered it the basic link between inorganic and organic matter. By the 1960s, shortly after Reich's death, the evidence for the electrical basis of organisms was becoming overwhelming. As D. S. Halacy, a writer on orthodox science, praided it simply: "The flow of electrons is basic to practically all life processes."

The difficulties encountered in the period between Reichenbach and Reich stemmed partly from the vogue in science for taking things apart, rather than studying them as functioning wholes. Simultaneously the gulf widened between workers in what came to be known as the "life sciences" and physicists who more and more would believe only what they could see or instrumentally measure. In between, chemistry concentrated on increasingly varied and smaller separate entities, which in their artificial recombination offered a cornucopia of fascinating new products.

The first artificial synthesis in the laboratory of an organic substance, urea, in 1828, seemed to destroy the idea that there was a special "vital" aspect in living things. The discovery of cells, the purported biological counterparts of the atoms of classical Greek philosophy, suggested that plants, animals, and man himself were merely different associations of these building blocks or chemical aggregates. In this new climate, few took initiative to delve deeper into the effects of electromagnetism on life. Nevertheless, individualistic mavericks occasionally brought forward an idea on how plants might respond to external cosmic forces and thus kept the findings of Nollet and Bertholon from expiring.

Across the Atlantic in North America, William Ross, testing claims of the Marquis of Anglesey that seeds sprouted faster when electrified, planted cucumbers in a mixture of black manganese oxide, table salt, and clean sand, watered with dilute sulphuric acid. When he applied an electric current to the mixture, the seeds sprouted well ahead of those in a similar but nonelectrified mixture. A year later, in 1845, the first issue of the London *Journal of the Horticultural Society* published a long account of the "Influence of Electricity on Vegetation" by an agronomist, Edward Solly, who, like Gardini, suspended wires in the air over garden plots, and, like Ross, tried burying them under the soil. But of Solly's seventy experiments with various grains, vegetables, and flowers, only nineteen were of any benefit, and nearly as many were harmful.

The conflicting results of these researchers made it obvious that the amount, quality, and duration of electrical stimulation was of crucial importance to each form of vegetal life. But since physicists lacked instrumentation to measure its specific effects, and still knew little about how electricity, artificial or atmospheric, actually operated on plants, the experimental field was left to persistently curious horticulturalists or out-and-out cranks. Still, various observations showing that vegetation had an electric quality continued to be recorded.

In 1859 an issue of the London *Gardeners' Chronicle* published a report of light flashes passing from one scarlet verbena to another and noted that the phenomenon could best be seen during crepuscular periods when a thunderstorm approached after a long spell of dry weather. This validated an observation of Goethe's that the flowers of oriental poppies could be seen flashing at dusk.

It was not until the latter part of the century that new vistas were opened in Germany onto the exact nature of the electricity in the air which Lemonnier had discovered. Julius Elster and Hans Geitel, who specialized in the spontaneous emission of radiation from inorganic substances which was coming to be called "radioactivity," began a vast study of atmospheric electricity. This disclosed that the soil of the earth continually emits electrically charged particles into the air. Called *ions* from the neuter present participle of the Greek verb, *ienai,* meaning "to go," these particles were either atoms, groups of atoms, or molecules regarded as having a net positive or negative charge after gaining or losing electrons. Lemonnier's observation that the atmosphere was continually filled with electricity at last had some kind of material explanation.

Since on a clear day in good weather the earth has a negative electrical charge while the atmosphere is positive, electrons stream skyward from the soil and plants. During storms the polarity is reversed, the earth becoming positive and the base of the cloud layer negative. Because there are at any time an estimated three to four thousand "electrical" storms raging over the surface of the globe, the charges lost by the earth in those areas favored by balmy weather are thus replaced, and a seesawing balance of electrical gradients maintained.

As a result of the ever-present flow of electricity, the voltage, or electric pressure, increases at higher altitudes. Between the head of a six-foot man and the ground he stands on, it is 200 volts; from the top of the Empire State Building to the sidewalks around it, 40,000 volts; in the interval between the lowest layers of the ionosphere and the earth's surface, 360,000 volts. Though this sounds dangerous, not much shocking power can be generated because there is little current flow. The chief difficulty in harnessing this vast reservoir of energy and putting it to work is lack of precise knowledge of exactly how it functions and of the laws which govern its operations.

A new attack on the application of atmospheric electricity to the growth of plants began when a Finnish scientist of eclectic interests, Selim Lemström, made four expeditions to the subpolar regions of Spitsbergen, northern Norway, and Lapland from 1868 to 1884. An expert on polar light and earth magnetism, Lemström theorized that the luxuriant vegetation in those latitudes, which popular opinion ascribed to the lengthened days of their summers, was actually attributable to what he called "that violent electrical manifestation, the aurora borealis."

As it had been known from the time of Franklin that sharp points were especially attractive to atmospheric electricity—an observation which led to the development of the lightning rod—Lemström reasoned that "the sharp points of plants acted like lightning rods to collect atmospheric electricity and facilitate the exchange of charges of the air and the ground." Lemström conducted studies on the rings in cross-sections of fir-tree trunks and found that the annual growth fully correlated with periods of high aurora and sunspot activity, the effects being most pronounced as one traveled north.

When he came home to verify these observations by experimentation,

Lemström connected a series of flowers in metal pots to a static generator by an overhead network of wires sixteen inches above them and a pole set into the soil as a ground. Other pots he "left to nature." After eight weeks, the electrified plants showed gains in weight of nearly 50 percent over their electrically deprived neighbors. When he transferred his apparatus into a garden he not only more than doubled the yield of strawberries but found them to be much sweeter; his harvest from barley plants increased by one-third.

In a long series of experiments conducted as far south as Burgundy, Lemström's results varied not only with specific vegetables, fruits, and cereals but also with temperature, moisture, and the natural fertility and manuring of the soil. Lemström reported his success in 1902 in a book *Electro Cultur*, published in Berlin, and the term was included in Liberty Hyde Bailey's *Standard Cyclopedia of Horticulture*.

The English translation of Lemström's book, entitled *Electricity in Agriculture and Horticulture*, which appeared in London two years after the German original, acerbically, yet truthfully, as it turned out, warned in its introduction that, since the whole complicated subject was connected with no less than three separate sciences, physics, botany, and agronomy, it might not seem "particularly attractive" to scientists. This caveat was not needed for one of his readers, Sir Oliver Lodge. After achieving singular distinction in the field of physics, Lodge went on to demonstrate his open-mindedness by joining the London Society for Psychical Research and brought out a dozen books which advanced his conviction that whole worlds lay beyond the physical.

Lodge determined to obviate Lemström's time-consuming difficulties in moving his wire network upward as his plants grew; to allow the movement of people, animals, and farm equipment through his electrified fields, he suspended his grid on insulators attached to high poles. During one growing season Lodge was able to increase the per-acre yield of Canadian Red Fife wheat by 40 percent and was pleased that the bakers who used flour ground from it claimed it produced bread of a far better quality than that made from the wheat they were normally furnished.

After working with Lodge, his collaborator, John Newman, adapted the system to achieve over 20 percent increase in wheat yields in Evesham, England, and in potatoes dug at Dumfries, Scotland. Newman's strawberries were not only vastly more productive than nonelectrified equivalents but, like Lemström's, were more succulent and sweet; his sugar beets tested out as having greater than normal sugar content. Of passing interest, Newman published his report, not in a botanical journal, but in the fifth edition of the *Standard Handbook for Electrical Engineers*, brought out by McGraw-Hill in New York. Ever since, it has been more the engineering fraternity than the plant men who have assiduously pursued electrocultural efforts.

CHAPTER 12

Force Fields,
Humans and Plants

Because their profession calls upon them for practical solutions to problems no matter how difficult they appear at first glance, engineers, unlike researchers in pure science, are less concerned with *why* or *how* something works than with *whether* it will work. This attitude frees them from the shackles of theory, which in the history of science has often caused pedants to disregard the brilliant new findings of geniuses because there was no theoretical basis to support them.

When an ingenious Hungarian refugee, Joseph Molitorisz, who escaped from his Soviet-occupied homeland and took an engineering degree, came across Abbé Nollet's ideas about electro-osmosis, he started thinking about how the Frenchman's efforts could be applied to agricultural problems. It seemed strange to Molitorisz that a redwood can raise its sap more than three hundred feet whereas the best man-designed suction pump can pull water up less than a tenth of that distance. There was evidently something about trees and electricity that defied laws of hydrodynamics in standard engineering. At an agricultural research station run by the U.S. Government near Riverside, California, Molitorisz decided to adapt what he had learned from Nollet's insights to citrus orchards. In an early experiment, he ran current through citrus seedlings. When the current flowed in one direction, the growth of the tiny trees was speeded up; when the direction was reversed, the seedlings shriveled. Evidently, the electricity somehow abetted the natural flow of electric current present in the plants or, when severed, blocked it. In another experiment, partly inspired by his reading of Abbé Bertholon, Molitorisz applied a fifty-eight-volt current to six branches of an orange tree but left another six branches untouched, only to discover that within eighteen hours sap was freely circulating in the "powered" branches while in the untouched branches there was very little sap flow.

One of the problems of harvesting oranges is the fact that their fruit does not all ripen simultaneously and must be laboriously hand-picked over many days if it is not to rot on the branches. Molitorisz theorized that picking costs might be reduced if he could get a tree to drop its ripe fruit through electrical stimulation. By wiring one orange tree to a source of direct current, he got it to drop its ripe fruit but retain the still-green oranges on its branches. Even with this success he could not get funds for additional experimentation; but Molitorisz, who has also invented an "electrical flower pot" which can keep flowers alive much longer than is normally possible, believes that one day it will be easy to harvest electrically the fruit of an entire citrus orchard and obviate the necessity of raising pickers into the trees.

While Molitorisz was working on the West Coast, another engineer, Dr. Larry E. Murr, of the Materials Research Laboratory at the Pennsylvania State University, became the first to simulate artificially in the laboratory the electrical conditions of short thunderstorms and long periods of rainy weather. After seven years of work in his man-made "mini-climate," he was able to get significant increases in plant growth by carefully regulating the voltage field strength over plants in lucite pots set on an aluminum plate to serve as one electrode, the other supplied by an aluminum wire mesh hung from insulating poles. Other voltages, he found, severely damaged the leaves of plants. Murr reached the conclusion that "whether or not we can augment acreage yield by maintaining artificially devised electric fields over crop areas is still a matter for speculation. The cost of achieving such gains by large-scale outdoor installations might be much more than they are worth. Nevertheless, the possibility exists."

Dr. George Starr White, who published a book entitled *Cosmoelectric Culture*, discovered that metals like iron and tin could facilitate plant growth if bright pieces were dangled from fruit trees. His evidence was corroborated by Randall Groves Hay, an industrial engineer from Jenkintown, New Jersey. Where Hay attached metallic Christmas tree balls to tomato plants, they would bear their fruits earlier than normal. In his own words: "At first, my wife would not let me hang the balls on the plants because she said it would look just too ridiculous. But when fifteen potted tomatoes hung with balls started to ripen in cold, inclement weather long before those of any other grower, she allowed me to continue."

The experiments of James Lee Scribner, an electronic engineer in Greenville, South Carolina, who worked thirty years in radio with electronic bathing of seeds, have resulted in a rival to Jack's beanstalk. Scribner wired an aluminum pot to an ordinary electric outlet. Spread between the electrodes was a wet metallic mix made up of millions of zinc and copper particles, which, when dried, allowed electricity to filter between the electrode strips. A butterbean planted in the pot grew to the amazing height of twenty-two feet, though similar beans normally never exceed two feet. At maturity it produced *two bushels* of delicious beans. Scribner believes that

it is the electron that is responsible before the photosynthesis can take place, for it is the electron that magnetizes the chlorophyll in the plant cell that makes it possible for the photon to assert itself and become a part of the plant in the form of solar energy. It is also this magnetism that draws the molecules of oxygen into the ever expanding chlorophyll cells of the plant, and so we must assume that moisture is in no way integrated into the plant through any absorption process whatsoever, for the integration of moisture is purely an electronic one. The so-called root pressure (moisture droplets) appearing on plant surfaces is not root pressure at all, but an abundance of electrons working with the rather excessive water energy in the bed.

Scribner's findings on seeds had apparently been anticipated in the 1930s, when the Italian Bindo Riccioni developed his own system for electrically treating seeds at the rate of five tons per day by allowing them to flow through parallel plate capacitors at about five meters per second. From the treated seeds Riccioni reported harvests from 2 to 37 percent greater than the national average, depending on soil and weather conditions. His work was interrupted by World War II, and his 127-page book, translated into English only in 1960, does not thus far seem to have stimulated further experimentation in the United States or Western Europe.

In the Soviet Union, however, a commercial processing plant to treat seeds with electrical energy, with a 2-ton-per-hour capacity, was reported in 1963. Results indicated that yields for the green mass of corn jumped 15 to 20 percent over the average, oats and barley 10 to 15 percent, peas 13 percent, and buckwheat 8 to 10 percent. What promise this pilot project might hold to relieve Russia's persistent grain shortages was not mentioned. To an agricultural industry which has relied almost wholly on artificially produced chemicals not only to fertilize its soil but to rid its crops of marauding pests, the electrocultural horizons being opened up afresh by engineers seem either unnecessary or a threat. This explains why almost no money has been made available for more investigation.

A former director of the United States Department of Agriculture's Division of Agricultural Engineering Research, E. G. McKibben, complained as far back as 1962 that this policy was extremely short-sighted. In an address to the American Society of Agricultural Engineers McKibben said: "The importance and the possibilities of the application of electromagnetic energy in its many forms to agriculture are limited only by the creative imagination and physical resources available. Electromagnetic energy is probably the most basic form. It, or something closely related to it, appears to be the basic substance of all energy and all matter and the essential fabric of all plant and animal life." McKibben stressed that as yet undreamed-of developments and accomplishments might be reasonably attained if only much more support was put behind electrocultural efforts; but his plea has thus far fallen on deaf ears.

Even before McKibben made his appeal, brand-new discoveries about the influence of magnetism on vegetation were coming to light. In 1960 L. J. Audus, a professor of botany at London University's Bedford College, while trying to find out exactly how plants respond to gravity, stumbled onto the fact that their roots are sensitive to magnetic fields and published a pioneering paper, "Magnetotropism, a New Plant Growth Response," in *Nature*. Nearly simultaneously, two Russians, A. V. Krylov and G. A. Tarakanova, issued their report in Moscow, showing that tomatoes ripen inexplicably faster nearer the south than the north pole of a magnet.

In Canada, Dr. U. J. Pittman, of the Agricultural Research Station in Lethbridge, Alberta, had observed all across the North American continent that the roots of various domestic and wild cereal grains, as well as those of a number of species of weeds, consistently aligned themselves in a north-south plane parallel to the horizontal force of the earth's magnetic field. He found that the earth's magnetism speeded up the germination of Chinook and Kharkov wheat, Compana barley, Eagle oats, Redwood flax, and common fall rye if the long axes of the seeds and embryo ends were oriented toward the north magnetic pole. "When Granny insisted that her pumpkin seeds be planted pointing north," wrote Pittman in *Crops and Soils Magazine*, "she may have been dead right!"

In the United States, the possibility of large-scale application of the occult force of magnetism to agriculture arose when in Denver, Colorado, still another engineer, Dr. H. Len Cox, chanced to read an article in a 1968 issue of *Aviation Week and Space Technology* which reported that infrared photos taken from NASA satellites seemed to indicate that wheat plants attacked by pests, or otherwise incapacitated, had an entirely different "electromagnetic signature" from those in a field expected to produce a bumper crop. Intrigued by a phenomenon for which he had no explanation, Cox, a space scientist, after dipping into the electrocultural literature, asked a metallurgist friend whether he knew of any magnetizable substance which could make plants grow faster and more fruitfully.

When the metallurgist suggested that deposits of a useless ferrous ore, magnetite, totaling billions of tons, were easily accessible in nearby Wyoming, Cox brought back a truckload and ground it into powder. After charging it in a magnetic field of undisclosed strength and mixing it with trace minerals, he sifted it into the soil of a garden plot where it could come into contact with the roots of red and white radishes. Though the green tops of the maturing plants seemed no different from similar radishes allowed to grow normally in a neighboring plot, when Cox pulled his "activated" vegetables from the ground, he saw results beyond his wildest expectations. Not only were the activated radishes on an average twice as large as the controls, but the fact that their tap roots were three to four times as long indicated that root stimulation seemed to have produced the increased growth. The remarkable effect on radishes was also obtained for other root vegetables, such as rutabagas, turnips, and carrots, and also for green plants such as beans, lettuce, broccoli, and oyster plant.

When Cox's Electroculture Corporation began selling the new product in ten-pound cans in 1970, users reported not only that they got much larger yields but that the vegetables produced had a far better flavor, corroborating Lemström's report on his strawberries and Sir Oliver Lodge's bakers' comments on their bread. Others reported that irises doubled the number of blossoms on a single stalk no matter whether they were planted with or without fertilizer, and a plastic surgeon told Cox that when he had put the magnetized ore among the roots of one of two ponderosa pine seedlings in his lawn, the little tree had grown in one summer four times as high as its neighbor.

Asked how the "activator" works Cox replied: "It is still a mystery. No one knows how it functions any more than doctors know why aspirin has its effect. Disappointing to nurserymen and city-dwelling plant lovers is the odd fact that the magnetized powder produces no results when shaken into flower pots or greenhouse flats. To work it has to go into the soil of the earth itself." One explanation for this anomaly is that the ferrous oxide—which when magnetized is called lodestone—radiates its power only when in contact with what Gilbert, in his day, called "its animate mother."

Whatever the ultimate solution to the problem, in the two decades following World War I startling new discoveries were coming to light in laboratories suggesting that mysterious radiations in the natural environment might be far more crucial to the well-being of plants and animals than had hitherto been suspected.

In the early 1920s Georges Lakhovsky, a Russian-born engineer living in Paris, had begun a series of books which suggested that the basis of life was not matter but immaterial vibrations associated with it. "Every living thing emits radiations," stressed Lakhovsky, and advanced the revolutionary new theory that cells, the essential organic units of all living things, were electromagnetic radiators capable, like wireless sets, of emitting and absorbing high-frequency waves.

The essence of Lakhovsky's theory was that cells are microscopic oscillating circuits. In electrical parlance such an oscillating circuit requires two basic elements: a capacitor, or source of stored electric charge, and a coil of wire. As the current from the capacitor flows back and forth between one end of the wire and the other, it creates a magnetic field which oscillates at a certain frequency, or so many times per second. If such a circuit is greatly reduced in size, very high frequencies are obtained; Lakhovsky believed this to be what occurs in the microscopically tiny nuclei of living cells. In the small twisted filaments within cellular nuclei Lakhovsky descried the analogs to electrical circuits.

In his *L'Origine de la Vie*, published in 1925, Lakhovsky set forth a number of startling experiments upholding the idea that disease is a matter of disequilibrium in cellular oscillation, that the fight between healthy cells and pathogens, such as bacteria or viruses, is a "war of radiations." If the radiations of the microbes are stronger, cells begin to oscillate aperiodically and became "diseased." When they cease to oscillate, they die. If the cellular radiations gain ascendance, the microbes are killed. In order that a diseased cell be restored to health, Lakhovsky felt it should be treated by means of a radiation of appropriate frequency.

In 1923, Lakhovsky designed an electrical apparatus emitting very short waves (with lengths of two to ten meters) which he called a "radio-cellulo-oscillator." In the surgical clinic of the famous Salpêtrière hospital in Paris he inoculated geraniums with cancer-producing bacteria. When the plants had developed tumors the size of cherry stones, one of them was exposed to radiation from the oscillator. During the first days the tumor grew rapidly, but after two weeks it suddenly began to shrink and die; after a second two-week period it fell off the afflicted plant. Other geraniums treated over different time periods also shed their cancers under the effect of oscillator radiations.

Lakhovsky saw these cures as supporting his theory. The cancer had been overcome by the *enhancement* of the normal oscillations of healthy cells in the geraniums. This was quite opposite to the approach of the radium specialists, who proposed that the cancer cells be destroyed by external radiation.

In the development of his theory Lakhovsky was faced with the problem of the origin of the energy necessary for the normal production and maintenance of cellular oscillations. It did not seem probable to Lakhovsky that the energy is produced within cells any more than the energy in an electric battery or a steam engine is internally produced. He therefore came to the conclusion that the energy is externally derived from cosmic radiation.

To try to establish the cosmic origin of the energy, Lakhovsky decided to dispense with the device he had dreamed up to produce artificial rays and tap natural energy from space. In January, 1925, he picked one of a series of geraniums previously inoculated with cancer and surrounded it with a circular copper spiral thirty centimeters in diameter, its two unjoined ends fixed in an ebonite support. After several weeks he found that whereas all the control geraniums inoculated with cancer had died and dried up, the plant ringed with the copper spiral was not only radiantly healthy but had grown twice as high as uninoculated controls.

These spectacular results led Lakhovsky into a complex theory as to how the geranium had been able to pick up from the vast field of waves in the external atmosphere the exact frequencies which enabled its cells to oscillate normally and so powerfully that the cancer-afflicted cells were destroyed.

To the multitude of radiations of all frequencies emanating from space and unceasingly traversing the atmosphere Lakhovsky gave the generic name "universion." He concluded that some of them, filtered by the spiral, were brought specifically into action to restore the degenerating cells of the diseased geranium to healthy activity.

The universion, or collectivity of universal radiation, was not, in Lakhovsky's mind, to be associated with the notion of a complete vacuum in space with which physicists had replaced the ether of the nineteenth century. To Lakhovsky the ether was not the negation of all matter but a synthesis of radiation forces, the universal plexus of all cosmic rays. It was a ubiquitous and all-pervading medium, into which disintegrated elements were consigned and transformed into electrical particles. Lakhovsky believed that with the recognition of this new concept the bounds of science could be extended and a basis laid for an attack on the most absorbing problems of life, including telepathy, the transmission of thought, and, by inference, man's communication with plants.

In March of 1927 Lakhovsky wrote a communication, "Influence of Astral Waves on Oscillations of Living Cells," which was presented to the French Academy by his friend the eminent biophysicist and discoverer of diathermy, Professor Jacques Arsène d'Arsonval.

By March of 1928, the geranium with the spiral around it had attained the abnormal height of four and one-half feet and was flourishing even in winter. Sure that by his work on plants he had stumbled on a new therapy of unimaginable importance to medicine, Lakhovsky went on to develop a sophisticated therapeutic device for human beings which he called a "multi-wave oscillator." It was successfully used in French, Swedish, and Italian clinics to cure cancerous growths and lesions brought about by radium burns; goiters; and a variety of diseases regarded as incurable. When Lakhovsky, fleeing the Germans who had occupied Paris and were seeking him out as a prominent anti-Nazi, came to New York in 1941, the physiotherapy department of a large New York hospital employed his multi-wave oscillator successfully to treat arthritis, chronic bronchitis, congenital hip dislocation, and other ills, and a Brooklyn urologist and surgeon, though he would not reveal his name, stated that he had used it on hundreds of patients to arrest bodily disturbances unamenable to other treatment. When Lakhovsky died in 1943, his astonishing findings, which laid the basis for radiobiology, were left unpursued by the medical profession, and today use of the multi-wave oscillator for medical treatment is officially banned by U.S. health authorities.

While Lakhovsky was working in Paris, at the Texas State University a team headed by Professor E. J. Lund devised a way to measure electrical potentials in plants. In a series of experiments lasting more than ten years, Lund showed that plant cells produce electric fields, currents, or impulses which, as Bose had implied, could serve as "nervous systems." Lund further demonstrated that the growth of plants is triggered by these electrical nervous systems rather than by growth hormones, or auxins, as was previously believed, and that the auxins are summoned and even transported by the cell-generated electric fields to the place where growth is known to occur.

In an important but little-known book, *Bioelectric Fields and Growth*, Lund put forward the revolutionary finding that the electric pattern in plant cells changes nearly a half hour before the diffusion of hormones in them can be effective and growth detected.

Meanwhile, the research of the Russian Alexander Gurwitsch, which inspired L. George Lawrence to begin his study of the potentialities of biocommunication, despite its rejection by the U.S. Academy of Sciences, began to get a new lease on life. The distinguished bacteriologist at Cornell University, Professor Otto Rahn, was amazed to find that whenever any of his laboratory workers fell ill they appeared to cause the death of yeast cells with which they were experimenting. A few minutes' exposure to their fingertips even at a distance would kill vigorous cells of this carbohydrate-fermenting fungus. Further investigation showed that a chemical compound excreted from the hands and face of the sick technicians was responsible; but exactly how it acted at a distance was a mystery. Rahn went on to prove that the continually renewed tissue of the cornea of the eye, as well as most wounds and cancer tumors, emit radiation; he set these and other findings down in a book, *Invisible Radiation of Organisms*, which, on the whole, was ignored by his colleagues.

Because most physicists still had no better means of detecting all this new and strange radiation than they did Mesmer's "animal magnetism" or Reichenbach's "odic force," the idea that living tissue could emit or respond to vibrations of energy was greeted with skepticism. The questioning light thrown on discoveries such as Lakhovsky's, Gurwitsch's, and Rahn's was also focused on those of a surgeon, George Washington Crile, founder of the Cleveland Clinic Foundation, who published *The Phenomena of Life: A Radio-Electrical Interpretation* in 1936. The result of a lifetime of research, it offered evidence that the living organism is specifically adapted to the formation, storage, and use of electrical energy, the genesis of which was, according to Crile, ultra-microscopic units or furnaces in protoplasm which Crile called radiogens.

Three years before his book appeared, Crile pointed out in an address to the Congress of the American College of Surgeons that it would be possible for future skilled radio-diagnosticians to detect the presence of disease before it became outwardly apparent. For his efforts Crile was ridiculed by both his medical colleagues and by cellular biologists, who accused him of having no solid grasp of the literature.

The effects of electromagnetic energy on living cells, both healthy and diseased, which most doctors and medical researchers, including cancer specialists, have yet honestly to confront, were finally to be revealed by the magic of time-lapse photography. Because most plants grow very slowly they look as unchanging to the human eye as if petrified. Only by looking away from plants for several hours or, better, for several days, can one notice that they are different from the plastic flowers and shrubs which are supplanting living plants in florist shops across the world.

In 1927, an Illinois teen-ager, staring at the buds on a large apple tree in his front yard, wondering when they would open into flowers, realized that if he could take pictures of them in regular sequence he would be able to watch the buds unfold before his eyes.

Thus began the career of John Nash Ott, whose pioneering interest in time-lapse photography led him to unveil new mysteries in the kingdom of plants.

To experiment with exotic varieties of plants Ott built a small greenhouse, where he found that each variety of plant presented to him as many problems as would a different tribe to an anthropologist. Many of his charges seemed to act like temperamental prima donnas with deep psychological disturbances. As he consulted with university botanists and research scientists on the staffs of large companies, little by little the basic biological causes for his plants' misbehavior became clear: they were extremely sensitive not only to light and temperature but to ultraviolet, TV and X-rays.

Ott's discoveries about light and temperature may lead to the explanation of many botanical mysteries, not the least of which is the tremendous size of plants growing high in the mountains of central Africa.

Over thirty years ago the English author Patrick Synge in his book *Plants with Personality* suggested that though no one had been able to produce a satisfactory theory on the origin of giantism in plants, it perhaps might happen on account of a complement of peculiar environmental conditions, namely, a low but moderately constant temperature, a consistently high humidity, and a strong intensity of ultraviolet light due both to the altitude and to the equatorial location.

In the European Alps vegetation growing high up tends toward dwarfism, but in the Mountains of the Moon, or Ruwenzori as the Africans call them, Synge encountered heathers "as mighty as great trees" and found shell-pink impatiens with flowers two inches across.

On the extinct volcano Mount Elgon, rising fourteen thousand feet on the Kenya-Uganda border, Synge found lobelias, which in England are tiny blue-flowered plants, growing nearly thirty feet tall, "like gigantic blue and green obelisks." He photographed them half covered with snow and with icicles hanging from the tips of their leaves. But when the same plants were brought back to England, they could not survive outdoors even in the mild winters of Surrey.

Synge's idea accorded with the hypothesis of the French chemist Pierre Berthelot, that it is the continuous presence of electricity high in the Alpine ranges that accounts for the luscious growth of plants in very poor soil. If the conditions enumerated by Synge are someday simulated by researchers, perhaps these giant plants will be successfully grown at sea level.

Ott's experiments in time-lapse photography were to lead him to the discovery that different wave lengths of light have a fundamental effect on photosynthesis, the process by which green plants convert light to chemical energy and by means of it synthesize organic compounds from inorganic ones, turning carbon dioxide and water into carbohydrates, with a release of oxygen. To attack this problem, he spent months building equipment which would allow him to take microscopic pictures of the streaming of protoplasm in the cells of Elodea grass while it was stimulated by direct unfiltered natural sunlight. Exposed to the sun's rays, the chlorophyll-containing bodies, called chloroplasts, which are the principal agents of photosynthesis, streamed in an orderly fashion around the edges of the obloid cells. But when the ultraviolet light in the sunlight was filtered out, some of the chloroplasts would drop out of the streaming pattern and huddle, immobile, in the corners. Cutting out the colors from the blue end of the spectrum toward the red increasingly slowed the chloroplast action.

Particularly fascinating to Ott was the fact that, at the day's end, all the chloroplasts slowed down and stopped no matter how intensely they were subjected to artificial light. Only when the sun rose the next day would they resume the normal streaming pattern.

Ott realized that if the basic principles of photochemistry, as they applied to plant photosynthesis, had analogs in the animal world then, as the proponents of color-therapy have long maintained, various frequencies of light might affect the physical well-being of humans by acting on the body chemistry in a way similar to the action of certain drugs on nervous and mental disorders.

In 1964 an article in *Time* magazine spurred Ott to research the effect of TV radiation on plants and humans. The story suggested that symptoms of nervousness, continuous fatigue, headaches, loss of sleep, and vomiting in thirty children under study by two U.S. Air Force physicians were somehow related to the fact that all of these children were watching TV from three to six hours on weekdays and from twelve to twenty hours on weekends. Though the doctors had concluded that the children were afflicted by prolonged idleness in front of the set, Ott wondered if some sort of radiation might not be at issue, particularly that of X-rays, which lie beyond ultraviolet in the energy spectrum.

To test this idea, Ott covered half of the picture tube of a color TV set with a sixteenth of an inch of lead shielding, normally used to block out X-rays. The other half he covered with heavy black photographic paper capable of stopping visible and ultraviolet light, but allowing other electromagnetic frequencies to penetrate.

Ott placed six pots of bean sprouts in front of each half of the TV tube, a pair at three different levels from top to bottom. As a control, six more pots, each with its three bean sprouts, were placed outdoors, fifty feet from the greenhouse where the TV set was located.

At the end of three weeks, both the lead-shielded beans and those growing outdoors had risen to a height of six inches and appeared healthy and normal. The beans shielded from the TV only by the photographic paper had been distorted by toxic radiations into a vine-type growth. In some cases the roots appeared to have grown incongruously upward out of the soil. If TV radiation could make monsters of bean plants what might it do to children?

Several years later, when Ott was discussing the distortion of the beans with space scientists, he was told that the root growth of his bean plants exposed to radiation resembled that of wheat seedlings in a bio-capsule in outer space, where it was thought to be due to the weightless condition from lack of gravity. Some of the scientists seemed intrigued by his idea that not weightlessness but a general background radiation of an unspecified energy might cause the eccentric root growth.

Since general background radiation coming from the zenith, or the point directly overhead, penetrates through less of the earth's atmosphere and is therefore more powerful than that coming in at any other angle, Ott thinks that roots of plants grow downward to get away from the radiation directly above them.

Similar experiments showed that white rats exposed to the same radiation which caused the wild growth in the beans became increasingly hyperactive and aggressive, then progressively lethargic, to a point where it was necessary to push them to make them move in their cages.

Ott noticed further that after he set up his TV in the greenhouse, rats in an animal-breeding room fifteen feet away produced litters of only one or two babies, as against a norm of eight to twelve, even though two building partitions intervened between the TV set and the pregnant mothers. When the TV set was removed, it took six months for the breeding to return to normal.

Because of increasing difficulty in maintaining discipline in schools, children who are hyperactive or have difficulty concentrating have over recent years been administered so-called behavioral modification drugs or "peace pills." This practice has aroused a storm of controversy among parents, doctors, government officials and even Congressmen. Though it has not been publicly suggested, Ott wonders whether this hyperactivity—and increasingly reported forms of lethargy including prolonged sleep—may be a result of exposure to radiation from TV sets. When Ott offered to repeat his experiments cost-free for technicians at RCA's Bio-Analytical Laboratory, the director of research not only hastily declined but was later quoted as saying, "It is utterly impossible for any TV set today to give off harmful rays."

Ott knew, however, that since the radiation from a TV tube is contained in an extremely narrow band on the electromagnetic spectrum, biological systems sensitive to this narrow spike of energy could be as overstimulated by it as they would be by light focused through a magnifying glass. The only difference is that, whereas the magnifier concentrates the light in one direction, the specific energy emitted from the TV can travel in any direction where it meets no obstruction. "If one-half of a milli-roentgen doesn't appear to be a cause for worry," says Ott, "then it can be pointed out that a pound of gold can also be called one-half of a thousandth of a ton. And it is easy to juggle the decimal point in infinitesimal amounts without realizing the true relationships involved. Eighty degrees Fahrenheit is a comfortable temperature level but one has only to double this figure to reach a point where most forms of life on earth could no longer exist."

Ott's belief that electromagnetic radiation affects plants and animals in many unsuspected ways increased when he was called by Paramount

Pictures in Hollywood to make time-lapse photos of flowers for a new picture, starring Barbra Streisand, based on the Broadway musical hit *On a Clear Day You Can See Forever*. In the story the heroine numbers among her extrasensory abilities that of making flowers grow as she sings to them. The studio wanted Ott to begin work immediately on geraniums, roses, irises, hyacinths, tulips, and daffodils for inclusion in this part of the film.

To duplicate as nearly as possible natural rays of outdoor sunlight, Ott had developed a new full-spectrum fluorescent tube, with added ultraviolet. Because he had a tight deadline, he knew that only if the flowers would grow under the new lights could he hope for success. To his relief, all the flowers grew well. But Ott noticed that the best results came when the flowers were placed under the center, rather than the ends, of the fluorescent tubes. He knew that the tubes worked on the same principle as the cathode guns in TV sets or in X-ray machines, but at much lower voltages, so low in fact that textbooks stated they could not produce harmful radiation. Suspecting the textbooks might be wrong, Ott placed two sets of ten parallel tubes end to end so that there were twenty cathodes in close proximity. When he sprouted the same kind of potted beans used in the TV experiments, he was startled to see that the ones close to the cathodes were stunted whereas those both at the center of the tubes and ten feet away from them appeared normal.

After many more experiments with beans, Ott became certain that they are far more sensitive to trace amounts of radiation than the standard radiation-measuring equipment presently available. This, he thinks, is because whereas the instruments pick up only a single reading of energy the biological systems are exposed to its cumulative effects.

Ott was next confronted with the possibility that light frequencies could affect the development and growth of cancer.

His initial clue that there was a connection between light frequencies and cancer came when a physician in charge of cancer research at one of New York's largest hospitals agreed to ask fifteen human cancer patients to spend as much time as possible outdoors in natural sunlight without their glasses and avoid artificial light sources, including television.

By the end of the summer the doctor told Ott that it was the consensus of all those assisting in the project that fourteen of the patients had shown no further advancement in tumor development.

In the meantime, Ott had aroused the interest of a leading Florida ophthalmologist, who explained to him that a layer of cells in the retina of the eye, with no function in vision, showed abnormal response to tranquilizing drugs and asked if he would run toxicity tests of the drugs by utilizing microscopic time-lapse photography. Ott used a phase-contrast microscope equipped with a complete set of colored filters, which permit the outline and details of cell structure to be clearly seen without killing them with stain as was previously necessary. This technique revealed that exposure to the wavelengths of blue light elicited abnormal pseudopodical activity in the pigment of the retinal cells whereas red light caused the cell walls to rupture. Even more interesting was the fact that when the cells were fed, by adding fresh media to the slide chambers, cell division was not encouraged at constant temperature, but if the temperature was lowered during the feeding accelerated division would take place within sixteen hours.

During their work the researchers also noticed that just before sunset the activity of the pigment granules within the cells would slow down and would return to normal only the next morning. It seemed to Ott that they were behaving just like the chloroplasts in the cells of Elodea grass. Perhaps plants and animals had more similarities in their basic functioning than had hitherto been suspected.

Ott suggests that the responses of chloroplasts and the pigment granules in retinal epithelial cells may be "tuned" to the natural light spectrum of sunlight, under which all life on this earth has evolved. "It would thus appear," he says, "that the basic principles of photosynthesis in plants, where light energy is recognized as a principal growth-regulating factor, might carry over from plant life and be equally important as a growth-regulating factor in animal life through control of the chemical or hormonal activity."

Other studies of cellular behavior have led Ott to conclude that malillumination or malradiation may be as important as malnutrition in the initiation of disease.

At the 1970 meeting of the American Association for the Advancement of Science, Dr. Lewis W. Mayron, in his discussion of Ott's research with bean plants and rats exposed to TV radiation, concluded that "the radiation has a physiological effect both on plants and animals which appears to be chemically mediated." Mayron also commented on Ott's experiments with the effects of fluorescent tubes on beans, stating: "The implications for human health are enormous when one considers the magnitude of the use of fluorescent lighting in stores, offices, factories, schools and homes."

With generous support from the Evelyn Wood Foundation, Ott has carried on studies on what effects TV sets might have on children with behavioral problems. With the cooperation of Mrs. Arnold C. Tackett, principal of a school which devotes itself to such children in Sarasota, Florida, Ott made checks of home TV sets watched by the youngsters and found measurable amounts of X-ray radiation in most of them, especially those which had run for long hours without overhaul. The parents agreed to get the children to spend much more time playing outdoors during the summer vacation and to sit far back from the TV while watching it.

By November of the new school year, Mrs. Tackett was able to report that the behavioral problems of children so treated were markedly diminished.

By the late 1960s the U.S. Congress had passed a Radiation Control Act by a vote of 381 to 0. Florida Representative Paul Ropes, co-author of the act, credited Ott with "getting us all started on the road toward control of radiation from electronic products." Ott credits his plants with showing him the way to the light.

Since the work of Gurwitsch, Rahn, Crile, and the proponents of electroculture all supported the earlier contentions of Galvani and Mesmer that living things have electrical or magnetic properties, it was strange that no one had suggested that they must also have about them the same electromagnetic fields as those accepted in the world of particle physics. This was exactly the theory boldly advanced by two Yale University professors, one a philosopher, F. S. C. Northrop, the other, like Galvani, a medical doctor and anatomist, Harold Saxton Burr.

By asserting that electrical fields are the very organizers of life systems,

Northrop and Burr offered chemists a new basis on which to explain how the thousands of separate constituents they had uncovered might be put together. They suggested to the biologists that their long hunt might be over for the "mechanism" which assures that all the cells of the human body, replaced every six months, are properly aligned. This appeared to revitalize the rejected theories of Mesmer's animal magnetism and Galvani's animal electricity and provide a seemingly tangible underpinning for the airy "élan vital" of the French philosopher Henri Bergson, and the "entelechy" of the German biochemist Hans Driesch.

To prove their theory, Burr and his laboratory colleagues constructed a voltmeter of a new design, which drew no current from life forms to be studied and thus could not disrupt the total fields around them. Twenty years of research with this device and its more sophisticated descendants revealed to Burr and several of his associates astonishing things about the vegetal and animal world. Dr. Louis Langman, an obstetrician and gynecologist who worked with Burr's technique, found for example that the precise moment of a woman's ovulation can be measured with great accuracy and that some women ovulate over the entire menstrual cycle, in some cases without menstruation. Though the detection procedure is extremely simple, and in no way counters the rhythm method of birth control of the Catholic Church, it has yet to filter down to millions of women who would like to learn better how, or how not, to have children.

Burr himself determined that malignancies could be detected in certain organs before any clinical signs could be observed, and that the rate of healing in wounds could be reliably measured. The future location of a chick's head could be found and pinpointed in the egg from which it would hatch, without breaking it, during the first day of its incubation.

Turning to the world of plants, Burr measured what he came to call "life-fields" around seeds, and found that profound changes in the voltage patterns were caused by the alteration of a single gene in the parent stock. Even more potentially interesting to plant breeders was his discovery that it is possible to predict how strong and healthy a future plant will be from the electrical diagnosis of the seed which produces it.

Because, of all living things, they seemed the most enduring and the least motile, Burr charted the life fields of trees on the Yale campus and at his laboratory in Old Lyme, Connecticut, over nearly two decades. He found that recordings related not only to the lunar cycle and to sunspots, which flare up at intervals with many years between them, but revealed cycles recurring every three and six months that were beyond his explanation. His conclusions seemed to make less suspect the long-mocked practices of generations of gardeners who claimed that their crops should be planted according to the phases of the moon.

One of Burr's students, Leonard J. Ravitz, Jr., who was to become a psychiatrist, was able to measure depths of hypnosis with the Burr-discovered techniques as far back as 1948. He went on to the not surprising conclusion that all humans are in hypnotic states most of the time, even when wide awake.

The continuous charting of life fields in people indicates a cyclic rise and fall of voltage, the peaks and valleys of which correlate to the periods when they feel good or bad, "up" or "down." By plotting the curves in advance it is possible to predict highs and lows weeks in advance, as the students of bio-rhythms have proposed, going back to the time when they were first theorized by Dr. Wilhelm Fliess, whose letters were so encouraging to Sigmund Freud during the years of Freud's self-analysis.

Burr's life work, as further developed by Ravitz, indicates that the organizing field around the "bodies" of living things *anticipates* the physical events within them and suggests that the mind itself, as Marcel Vogel maintains, can, by modulating the field, affect positively or deleteriously the matter with which it is held to be associated. But these signposts had yet to be read by the leaders of organized medicine, and Burr's work has only recently begun to be seriously considered.

Medical pundits are now in for a further shock due to a startling discovery in 1972 at the Institute of Clinical and Experimental Medicine in Novosibirsk, a burgeoning industrial city of over a million people on the banks of Siberia's mighty river Ob, which strongly supports the findings of Gurwitsch, Rahn and Crile.

S. P. Shchurin and two colleagues from the Institute of Automation and Electrometry have been awarded a special diploma by the USSR

State Committee for Inventions and Discoveries for discovering that cells can "converse" by coding their messages in the form of a special electromagnetic ray.

The experimenters placed identical tissue cultures in two hermetically sealed vessels separated by a wall of glass, then introduced a lethal virus in one of the chambers which killed the colony of cells inside it. The second colony remained wholly unaffected. However, when they replaced the glass divider with a sheet of quartz glass and again introduced killing viruses to one of the colonies, the Soviet scientists were astonished to see that the second colony also met the same fate as the first, even though the viruses could not possibly have penetrated the barrier. Other first and second colonies of cells, separated by the quartz glass, both perished when only the first colony was murdered with chemical poisons or lethal radiation and the second left unexposed. What killed the second colony in each case?

Since ordinary glass does not permit ultraviolet rays to pass but quartz glass does, it seemed to the Soviet scientists that here was a key to the mystery. They recalled that Gurwitsch had theorized that onion cells could emit ultraviolet rays, and they resurrected his ideas from the limbo to which they had been consigned in the 1930s. Working with an electronic eye amplified by a photomultiplier and registered by a self-recorder which traced a graph marking the energy levels on a moving tape, they found that when life processes in the tissue cultures remained *normal*, the ultraviolet glow, invisible to the human eye but detectable as oscillations on the tape, remained *stable*. As soon as the affected colony began to battle against its infection, the radiation intensified.

Reports on this work in Moscow newspapers disclosed that, however fantastic it might seem, the ultraviolet radiation from the afflicted cells *carried information* encoded in the fluctuation in intensity which was somehow received by the second colony, just as words are transmitted and received in dots and dashes in the Morse code.

Since the second colony seemed in each case to die in exactly the same way as the first, the Soviets realized that it was as dangerous for healthy cells to be exposed to the transmitted signal of dying cells as it was for them to be exposed to viruses, poisons, and lethal radiation. It appeared that the second colony upon receiving the alarm signal from the dying first colony began to mobilize for resistance and that its very "restructuring for war" against a nonexistent enemy proved as fatal as if it had indeed been attacked.

Moscow newspapers suggested that the Novosibirsk work may help to pinpoint what inner reserves the human body possesses to resist disease and quoted Shchurin on how it may help to open new horizons in diagnosis: "We are convinced that the radiation is capable of giving the first warning about the beginning of malignant regeneration and of revealing the presence of particular viruses. At the present time the early identification of many ailments, for instance the numerous forms of hepatitis, presents major difficulties."

Thus, fifty years after his work, his countrymen have finally brought recognition to Gurwitsch's brilliant research. Coincidentally they have also validated the work of another obscure compatriot, Semyon Kirlian, who has managed to capture on film extraordinary pictures of the force fields around humans and plants so accurately described and measured by Burr and Ravitz.

CHAPTER 13

The Mystery
of Plant and Human Auras

The long train was on the last leg of its journey from Moscow to Krasnodar, a south Russian inland port on the Kuban River, two hundred miles northwest of the volcanic Elbrus, Europe's highest mountain peak in the Greater Caucasus range.

In one of its "soft" cushioned cars reserved for Soviet officials, a plant specialist, bored with watching the flat countryside, still only partly recovered in 1950 from the Nazi ravages of the "Great Patriotic War," reopened his satchel to check the condition of two similar leaves which he had plucked in a greenhouse before leaving the Soviet capital. Relieved to see that the leaves were still sparkling fresh and green in their bedding of moist cotton wool, he sat back in his fauteuil to admire the approach of the Caucasian piedmont.

Late that evening in a small Krasnodar apartment, a corner of which was fitted out as a miniature laboratory, Semyon Davidovich Kirlian, an electrician and amateur photographer, and his wife, Valentina, were making some adjustments to equipment they had begun building two years before the Nazi attack on their country.

With their new invention they had discovered they could photographically reproduce—without lens or camera—a strange luminescence which seemed to issue from all living things but was unapprehensible by the human eye.

A knock on the door surprised them, as no visitor was likely to call at that time of evening; they were even more surprised when a total stranger announced he had come all the way from Moscow to see if they could make for him photographs of the strange energy which he had heard they alone could make visible on film. From his brief case the stranger pulled the two identical leaves and handed them to the Kirlians.

Excited at the prospect that their discovery was to be put to an official test, the Kirlians stayed up till after midnight, but were disappointed to note that while they could make excellent pictures of energy flares from one of the leaves, they could get only a weak facsimile from the other. They worked on through the night, trying to get photos of the luminescence as similar as the leaves themselves, but were wholly unsuccessful.

In the morning, crestfallen, they showed their results to the scientist, who shouted in amazement: "But you've found it! You've proven it photographically!" He explained that one leaf had been plucked from a healthy plant, the other from a diseased specimen. Although the two leaves appeared identical to the human eye, the pictures plainly differentiated between them. Illness was evidently manifest in a plant's energy field before becoming visible as a symptom in its physical body.

That plants, as well as animals and human beings, have fields of fine sheaths of subatomic or protoplasmic energy which permeate the solid physical bodies of molecules and atoms was a centuries-old allegation by seers and philosophers. This extra dimension or "aura" depicted in ancient iconography around the bodies of saints, with golden halos around the heads, has been referred to by persons gifted with extrasensory perception since the beginnings of recorded history. By laying film or plate in contact with an object to be photographed and passing through the object an electric current from a high-frequency spark generator which put out 75,000 to 200,000 electrical pulses per second, the Kirlians had come across a way of photographing this "aura"—or something akin to it.

Leaves from plants, sandwiched with film between the electrodes of their device, revealed a phantasmagoria hitherto restricted to clairvoyants, a micro-universe of tiny starry points of light. White, blue, and even red and yellow flares were pictured surging out of what seemed to be channels in the leaves. These emanations, or force fields round a leaf, became distorted if the leaf was mutilated, gradually diminishing and disappearing as the leaf was allowed to die. The Kirlians were next able to magnify this luminescence by adapting their photographic processes to optical instruments and microscopes. Rays of energy and whirling fireballs of light appeared to shoot out of plants into space.

The Kirlians also examined all kinds of "inanimate" substances, including metal coins. Each had a different luminating pattern. Most interesting was the fact that while a two-kopeck coin showed only a constant glow around its edges, human fingertips seemed to shoot forth flaming energy in bursts like miniature volcanoes.

After their photographic demonstration of pathology in the leaf from the sick plant for the Muscovite visitor, it was another ten years before the Kirlians began to emerge from obscurity in the USSR.

In the early 1960s Dr. Lev Fedorov of the USSR's Ministry of Public Health, struck by the possibilities of the new photography for medical diagnosis, awarded the Kirlians a first research grant but when Fedorov died soon thereafter, official funding from Moscow began to dwindle and academic skeptics were once more in control.

It was only when a journalist took up the Kirlians' story that interest was again aroused. "This situation," wrote I. Belov, "is as bad as before the revolution, when the evil hand of Tsarist bureaucrats determined there was too much uncertainty in novelty. *Twenty-five years have passed* since the Kirlians made their discovery, yet the Ministries in charge still haven't released the funds."

Belov's effort had its effects. In 1966, a conference bringing together many scientists interested in all aspects of what was coming to be called "biological energy" was held in Alma Ata, capital of the Kazakh Republic. In proceedings of the conference, entitled *Problems in Bioenergetics*, a Moscow biophysicist, Viktor Adamenko, joined with the Kirlians to author a seminal paper "On Research of Biological Objects in High-Frequency Electrical Fields." The paper stressed the enormous difficulties of studying the spectrum of "electrobioluminescence" but added that when these are overcome, "we will be able to obtain important information about bioenergetic processes in a living organism."

For all the mounting Soviet interest, it was another three to four years before American science—which had branded as fake Wilhelm Reich's 1939 discovery of a life energy in plants and humans which he called orgone—paid attention to the new developments. What attracted this attention was not the Soviet scientific publications but a book, *Psychic Discoveries Behind the Iron Curtain*, by two North American journalists, Sheila Ostrander and Lynn Schroeder, which appeared in the summer of 1970.

Excited by what she had read in the Ostrander-Schroeder volume, a former Broadway actress, now professor at the Neuropsychiatric Institute of the University of California at Los Angeles, Thelma Moss, Ph.D., wrote to Russia and received an invitation to visit Professor Vladimir Inyushin at Alma Ata.

Working with several colleagues, Inyushin had written up his research into the Kirlians' work in 1968 in a book-long scientific paper: *The Biological Essence of the Kirlian Effect*. Though Kirlian himself had maintained that the strange energy in his pictures was caused by "changing the nonelectrical properties of bodies into electrical properties which are transferred to film," Inyushin and his collaborators went several steps further. They declared that the bioluminescence visible in Kirlian pictures was caused not by the electrical state of the organism but by a "biological plasma body" which seemed to be only a new word for the "etheric" or "astral" body of the ancients.

In physics plasma is defined today as an electrically neutral, highly ionized gas composed of ions, electrons, and neutral particles which has been called the "Fourth State of Matter" (after solids, liquids, gases).

As far back as 1944, as the Allied armies were storming "Fortress Europe," a book by the Russian V. S. Grishchenko, *The Fourth State of Matter,* appeared in French in Paris. Credit for coining the term bioplasma may thus belong to Grishchenko. The same year the discoverer of "mitogenetic radiation," A. G. Gurwitsch, published his book in Moscow entitled *The Theory of a Biological Field,* summing up twenty years of work.

Inside the "bioplasmic" body, said Inyushin, processes have their own labyrinthine motion, different from the energy pattern in the physical body, yet the bioplasmic body is not a chaotic, but a whole unified organism which acts as a unit, is polarized, gives off its own electromagnetic fields, and is the basis for "biological" fields.

When Thelma Moss arrived on an evening flight in Alma Ata, she was invited by Inyushin to visit his laboratory and lecture to his students. Elated, she went to sleep sure that she would be the first American scientist to visit a Soviet institution engaged in studying Kirlian photography. The following morning when Inyushin came to pick her up at her hotel, he regretfully told her that "permission for the visit had not come from Moscow."

Moss was nevertheless able to learn from Inyushin that during six years of research with Kirlian photography he had been able to note that specific areas of the human body revealed characteristic colors which might prove significant in medical diagnoses. The clearest photos, he told Moss, were those taken at four o'clock in the afternoon, the worst at midnight. When Moss asked Inyushin point-blank if his "bioplasma" body was what occult Western literature refers to as the "aura" or the "astral" body, he said: "Yes!"

In ancient philosophies and in Eastern and Theosophical teaching, the energy body which duplicates the human body is also called the etheric body, fluidic body, or prephysical body. It is believed to be the unifying agent for the material body, a magnetic area where immaterial or subatomic vortices of the cosmos are transformed into the individual, the channel through which life communicates with the physical body, the medium for telepathic and clairvoyant projection. For decades scientists have been trying to find a way to make this body visible.

While Moss was in Alma Ata, the eminent American psychiatrist Montague Ullman, director of the department of psychiatry at the Maimonides Medical Center in New York City, was simultaneously interviewing Viktor Adamenko in Moscow.

Ullman was informed, somewhat to his surprise, that Adamenko and other Soviet scientists had been able to determine that the "bioplasma" not only undergoes a drastic shift when placed in a magnetic field but is concentrated at hundreds of points in the human body which seem to correspond to the ancient Chinese system of acupuncture points.

Thousands of years ago the Chinese mapped seven hundred points on the human skin as paths along which they believed a life force or vital energy to circulate. The Chinese insert needles at these points to correct imbalances in the energy flow, and to cure disease. Spots where the Kirlian lights flared most brilliantly on a human body appeared to match the acupuncture points mapped by the Chinese.

Adamenko is still unsure about Inyushin's attribution of the phenomena to a "bioplasma body," because there is as yet no "rigorous proof" of its existence, and therefore prefers to define the visible emanations as "a cold emission of electrons from the live object into the atmosphere."

In the United States this "cold emission of electrons" is almost universally translated as a "corona discharge," which is compared to the static electricity emitted by a person after walking across a carpet and touching a grounded metal. The name is derived from the faintly colored luminous ring which surrounds celestial bodies and is visible through a haze or thin cloud or the luminous irregular envelope of highly ionized gas outside the chromosphere of the sun. But giving it an academic name has explained neither its substance nor its function.

As president of the American Society for Psychical Research, Ullman found it extremely interesting that Dr. Anatoli Podshibyakin, a Kiev electrophysiologist, had discovered that bioplasma, if that is what it is, *instantly* reacts to changes on the surface of the sun even though cosmic particles, ejected by the sun, take about two days to reach the earth.

Many parapsychologists view man as an enmeshed, integral part of life on earth and in the universe. They maintain he is linked to the cosmos via his bioplasmic body, and reacts to changes in the planets as well as to the moods and illnesses of others, to thought, emotion, sound, light, color, magnetic fields, the seasons, cycles of the moon, tides, thunderstorms, strong winds and even levels of noise. If there is a change in the universe and environment, say the parapsychologists, a resonance is produced in the vital energy of the human body which in turn affects the physical body. It is through his bioplasmic body that parapsychologists believe a man can be in direct contact with a living plant.

Still another U.S. parapsychological researcher, Dr. Stanley Krippner, director of the extraordinary Dream Laboratory at the Maimonides Medical Center in New York—where pictures have been successfully directed at sleepers in order to produce in their minds desired dreams—trekked to Russia in the summer of 1971. While in Moscow, Krippner was the first American invited to give an address on parapsychology to the Institute of Psychology in the Academy of Pedagogical Sciences. The lecture was attended by some two hundred psychiatrists, physicists, engineers, space scientists, and cosmonauts in training.

Krippner found out that Genady Sergeyev, a neurophysiologist working at the Ukhtomskii Military Institute in Leningrad, had made Kirlian photographs of Nina Kulagina, a sensitive who can, by simply passing her hand over but not touching them, move paper clips, matches, cigarettes, and other objects on a table top.

Sergeyev's photographs revealed that while Kulagina performs these psychokinetic feats, the "bioplasmic field" around her body expands and pulses rhythmically and *a ray of luminescence seems to shoot out of her eyes.*

In the fall of 1971, William A. Tiller, chief of the Materials Science Department at Stanford University (Palo Alto, California) and one of the world's experts on crystals, was the first American physicist invited by Edward Naumov, chief coordinator for Technical Parapsychology in Moscow, to investigate Kirlian photography in the USSR.

Although, like Moss and Ullman, Tiller was not permitted to visit Soviet laboratories, he was able to spend several days with Adamenko. When he returned to the United States, Tiller recommended in a highly technical report that the Kirlian method and devices, among others, were "so important to parapsychological and medical investigations that attention should be focused on immediate construction of such devices and the duplication of the Soviet results."

Tiller, who like Adamenko does not see the need for postulating any new "bioplasma," and substitutes for it the "cold emission of electrons," has been building extremely sophisticated equipment for taking Kirlian photographs in his Palo Alto laboratory.

One of the first actually to make Kirlian-type pictures in the United States was Thelma Moss, who worked on the project with one of her students, Kendall Johnson. With their apparatus, Moss and Johnson were the first Americans to take color photos of leaves and pick up almost every region of the visible spectrum. American coins, appropriately enough, come out in red-white-and-blue, as do photos of the energy from the fingertips of the human hand.

Henry C. Monteith, an electrical engineer in Albuquerque, New Mexico, working at home, put together an apparatus consisting of two 6-volt batteries, a vibrator used to power automobile radios, and an ignition coil sold at all auto-supply stores. Like the Russians, Monteith found that a live leaf gave beautiful and varied self-emissions that cannot be adequately explained by conventional theory. He was further mystified when he discovered that a dead leaf gave, at most, only a uniform glow. Exposed to only 30,000 volts, the dead leaf did not reveal anything at all on film, even when bathed in water, but the live leaf shimmered in a radiance of self-emissions.

As the potential implications of a photographic process in existence for more than thirty years—which seemingly gave substance to the notion of the existence of an *aura*, a subject considered by most Western scientists to be on the "lunatic fringe" of investigatory effort—began to be realized in the United States, demand mounted for more hard information. Stanley Krippner enlisted the cooperation of several financial backers and organized the First Western Conference on Kirlian Photography and the Human Aura in the spring of 1972 at Manhattan's United Engineering Center, where a crowd of doctors, psychiatrists, psychoanalysts, psychologists, parapsychologists, biologists, engineers and photographers packed the ground-floor auditorium to overflowing. At the conference startling pictures by Moss and Johnson were shown of a leaf before and after being pricked. Done with Kirlian techniques, the photo of the wounded leaf revealed an enormous blood-red pond of energy in its center which took the place of the bright azure and pinkish hue which showed up before the pricking.

The mystery of the link between human emotional or psychic states and emanations radiating from the fingertips is deepened by Moss's further finding that pictures of both her own and Kendall Johnson's fingers differ from day to day and hour to hour.

Since the photos of leaves change with variations in parameters, Moss conjectures that "at whatever frequency we take a picture, we are resonating, or vibrating at the same frequency, *with one particular aspect of the material;* thus, not a whole picture, but different pieces of information are picked up."

Tiller speculated that the radiation or energy coming out of a leaf or a human fingertip actually might be coming from whatever is present *prior to the formation of solid matter.* This, says Tiller, "may be another level of substance, producing a hologram, a coherent energy pattern of a leaf which is a force-field for organizing matter to building itself into this kind of physical network."

Tiller thinks that even if part of the network were cut away, the forming hologram would still be there. Apparently this is just what the Russians have been able to prove with a plant leaf. A picture printed in the *Journal of Paraphysics* (published in Downton, Wiltshire, England) shows a Russian Kirlian photograph of a leaf with one part cut away. Yet, where nothing would show ordinarily, the outline of the missing part of the leaf remains.

That this was not just Russian subterfuge was strikingly confirmed when Douglas Dean made photos of the fingertip of a New Jersey healer, Ethel de Loach, whose files bulge with successful case histories. One picture, taken while the healer was at rest, showed only a dark blue radiation streaming out of the skin and revealing the tip of the long nail. A second picture, shot when she was asked to heal, revealed in addition to the blue radiation an enormous orange and red flare leaping out of a point below the actual fingerprint. Both pictures were subsequently published on the cover of the medical journal *Osteopathic Physician*. Kirlian photos of faith healers reveal a smaller glow after healing, while those healed have greater emanations, indicating some sort of energy flow from the hands of the healer into the body of the patient, giving substance to Galvani's and Mesmer's theory of "animal magnetism."

At the Human Dimensions Institute at Rosary Hill College in Buffalo, New York, one of the professors, Sister M. Justa Smith, a Catholic nun and biochemist, began thinking that healing energy coming from or through a healer's hands would have to affect the enzyme system *before* diseased cells could change to a state of health. Sister Justa —who had finished a doctoral dissertation proving that magnetic fields increase, while ultraviolet light decreases, enzyme activity—after engaging the cooperation of a healer, found that when he was in an "optimum psychological state," or good mood, the energy coming from his hands could activate the pancreatic enzyme trypsin in a way which compared to the effects of a magnetic field measuring from 8,000 to 13,000 gauss. (Human beings normally live in a magnetic field of 0.5 gauss.) Sister Justa is continuing experimentation to find out whether a healer can activate other enzymes in the body and whether this activation can be of help to the maintenance of health.

How magnetic fields affect life and how they might be related to the energy of the "aura" is a mystery only beginning to be unveiled. In recent years scientists have found, for instance, that snails perceive extremely weak magnetic fields and, since they can also distinguish their direction, could be said to incorporate structures which behave like navigational compasses.

Jan Merta, whose own projections of what he terms "auric energy" have not only turned dowsing devices held in a doctor's hands against the doctor's will and efforts to prevent it, but also so disturbed the magnetic components of the video tape recording the procedure that the film blacked out while supposedly recording a crucial sequence, has developed a whole theory about auras, part of which suggests that magnetic fields might significantly affect a learning process. Merta took thirty mice and housed them in small cages made of transparent plastic. Ten of them were exposed to the south pole, ten to the north pole, with field strength of 5–10 gauss of a bar magnet. The third ten were left untreated. With an ingenious learning device Merta was able to establish that those mice which had lived under the influence of a magnetic field were not only more active than the nonmagnetized mice, but somehow were able to learn quicker.

It would seem that some correlation exists between the activity of the "bioplasmic" or "auric" fields—if that is what they are—around living things and their subjection to various types of radiation. Certainly there is no doubt, in light of the pioneering Soviet work and its American confirmation, that the health, physical or emotional, of plants and animals can be objectified with the Kirlian technique.

The main strength of the Russian research, according to Professor Tiller, is that "it has been able to provide us with detectors and devices with which we can begin to show cause-effect relationships between psycho-energetic phenomena and the kind of read-outs which our colleagues find acceptable and that our logical system has come to accept as proof. We're *at that stage of naïveté* that we need this proof."

The first Kirlian conference was so successful that a second meeting was held in New York's Town Hall in February 1973. One of the most striking presentations was that of Dr. John Pierrakos, a Greek-born psychiatrist who showed detailed drawings of auras which he can visually perceive around plants, animals and human beings and which he is able to monitor in continual movement around neurotically and psychotically disturbed patients. In her book *Breakthrough to Creativity*, published in 1967, Shafica Karagulla, M.D., reported how many physicians use their observations of the human energy field in their diagnostic work. Because they were guarded about discussing their unusual abilities outside their own circle, Karagulla did not refer to any of them by name. Pierrakos is perhaps the first physician publicly to state that his perceptions of the human aura assist him in his diagnoses.

"Man is an eternal pendulum of movement and vibration," Pierrakos told the Town Hall audience. "His spirit is captured in a body in which forces throb and pulsate like the beat of a heart. Often, they thunder and quake in his body with strong emotions that shake the very foundations of his physical being. Life goes on, rhythmically and quietly pulsating with the warm feeling of love or cascading with avalanches of violent emotion, for movement and pulsation is life. When movement diminishes, the person becomes ill, and when the movement stops, the person is dying."

Pierrakos likened human bodies to time capsules in which biological functions are performed "for a century or so" after which the capsule changes the shape of its existence. "During this time, like the flower that brings the blossom and the seed that brings the flower and the fruit, man's time capsule has to become aware of what is going on within and without." To do so, asserted Pierrakos, we must describe and understand, fuse and integrate two attributes: *life energy* and *consciousness* —the former seen as the aura around the body with gradations similar to that of the atmosphere which thins as it proceeds outward from the earth. Though to his Hellenic ancestors energy was "something producing movement," Pierrakos holds that this nebulous definition should be made more precise. "Energy is a living force emanated by consciousness," he suggests. "By observing the energetic field emanating from the body—not unlike the steam over boiling water which, correctly observed, gives an idea of the water's nature—I get an idea of what is happening in the body," Pierrakos said.

In his pictures, Pierrakos illustrated the three layers he sees around most of his patients. The first, a dark band no more than one-sixteenth to one-eighth of an inch thick, lies close to the skin and looks like a transparent crystalline structure. The second, a broader dark blue layer, reminiscent of a cluster of iron filings, forms an ovoid envelope around the body when seen from the front. The third is a lightish blue haze of radiant energy which, when the patient is in good health, extends several feet away from the body and accounts for why we describe happy zestful persons as "radiant."

Pierrakos also showed how in patients with disturbances there are interruptions in these layers and changes in their colors of which he can see only the grosser aspects. When a psychotic patient told Pierrakos that she was "secure" because another person stood next to her constantly "on guard," he asked her to let him see this other person. All at once he noticed a mass of light blue-gray energy in the shape of a human body next to his patient.

The energy field of plants can also be severely affected by disturbed patients, says Pierrakos. "In some experiments with plants conducted in my office with Dr. Wesley Thomas, we found that a chrysanthemum's field contracts markedly when a person shouts at it from a distance of five feet, and loses its blue-azure color, while its pulsation diminishes to one third. In repeated trials, keeping live plants more than two hours daily near the heads of screaming patients (a distance of three feet away), the lower leaves started falling down and the plant withered within three days and died."

Pierrakos related that the number of pulsations the energy field emits per minute is also an indication of the internal state of a human being. The pulsations are much slower in older persons than in children, and in sleep than in wakefulness.

Since the direction of the flow of energy on the front of the body starts in the midriff and proceeds downward in a sort of curving L toward one of the legs and upward in an inverted L to the opposite shoulder, then reverses this flow on the back side of the body, the whole energy pattern around the body forms a figure 8. Put together in symbolic form, the two pairs of L shapes, front and back, have from time immemorial been represented in cultures throughout the world as the *swastika*, a Sanskrit word for "well-being."

The same kind of energy field observable in humans is seen by Pierrakos macrocosmically over the ocean with miles-high fountains of radiation bursting forth from narrower bands of pulsation below. Since the amount of activity in this earthly aura plotted by Pierrakos against the time of day reveals the lowest ebb just after midnight and the highest shortly following noon, this directly correlates with Rudolph Steiner's account of how the chemical ether is exhaled and inhaled by our planet.

A research team of physicists and electronics specialists is currently seeking to objectify Pierrakos' "sensitive" sight. Under the auspices of the Center for Bio-Energetic Analysis they are developing a means of detecting the radiations of the human animal and plant auras with a sensitive photomultiplier tube, an instrument which measures photons or light energy from the "etheric" field around a body. In a preliminary report they stated in Town Hall that, to date, their work indicates strongly that human beings radiate a strange field, detectable by the tube, the properties of which remain to be analyzed and explained.

Pierrakos, who can also see the energy pumping forth from plants and trees, warns of the danger of comparing the phenomena revealed by Kirlian photography to known radiations such as X-rays. "The study of the aura could become completely mechanized and objectified without reference to the great phenomena of life within the entity," he says.

In this observation Pierrakos is not far from the philosopher-mathematician Arthur M. Young, inventor of the Bell helicopter, who stresses that in back of the whole hierarchy of active energies, known or unknown, may lie *intent.* "Content requires substance," says Young, "whether by reference to actual physical objects or to human feelings or emotion. Substance is indeed what the work connotes, that which stands under—*sub stance*—the interactions of the physical world. To the physicist this is *energy.* To the human being it is *motivation.*"

Through *motivation* or *intent,* or some other agency of will, is it possible for living forms to effect changes in their own physical systems? Is it possible for plants and men—which materialists assert are only renderable at death into so much compost, soap, or chemicals—to grow the way they want?

In the Soviet Union, a country which was originally founded on the most materialist of philosophies, the developments resulting from Kirlian photography have raised certain profound questions about the true nature of life—vegetal, animal and human—about mind and body, about form and substance. Thelma Moss believes that research in the field has actually become of such great scientific importance to both the Russian and U.S. governments that they are keeping their official efforts strictly secret. Nevertheless, a spirit of friendly rivalry and of cooperation has arisen between groups, thus far small, of Russian and American scientists.

As Semyon Kirlian put it in a letter to the First Western Conference to take up the implications of his work, "the new research will have such enormous significance that an impartial assessment of the methods will be carried out only by minds in succeeding generations. The possibilities are immense; indeed, they are practically inexhaustible."

PART IV

CHILDREN OF THE SOIL

CHAPTER 14

Soil: The Staff of Life

Despite Carver's prescient observations on how to bring life back to the cotton-debased soils of Alabama by rotating crops and fertilizing the soil with natural humus, the farmers of that state—and those in every other state of the Union—have since Carver's death been lured by the promise of large profits to deal with the land, not in a natural, but in an artificial way in order to force from it every ounce of productivity. Instead of exerting patient and tender efforts to keep their soils in natural balance they have been seeking to subjugate nature rather than cooperate with her. Everywhere there are indications that in the process of being raped rather than loved, nature is protesting. If the process goes on, the victim may die of bitterness and indignation, and with her all that she nurtures.

An example—one among thousands—is Decatur, Illinois, a farming community in the heart of the United States cornbelt. As the summer of 1966 was drawing to a close, steamingly hot and sultry, the corn stood in the fields as high as an elephant's eye, promising a bumper crop in every direction, perhaps eighty to a hundred bushels to the acre. In the twenty years since World War II the farmers had almost doubled the land's yield in corn by the use of nitrate fertilizers, unaware of the deadly danger they were courting.

The following spring one of Decatur's seventy-eight thousand townsmen—whose living depended indirectly on the success of the corn harvest—noticed that a cup of drinking water from his kitchen faucet tasted funny. As the water was supplied directly from Lake Decatur, an impoundment of the Sangamon River, he took a sample to the Decatur Health Department for testing. Dr. Leo Michl, a Decatur health official, was alarmed to find that concentrations of nitrate in the waters of Lake Decatur and the Sangamon River itself were not only excessive but potentially lethal.

Nitrate, in itself innocuous to the human physical constitution, can become deadly when converted by intestinal bacteria; these combine nitrate with the blood's hemoglobin into methemoglobin, which prevents the natural transport of oxygen in the bloodstream. This can cause a disease known as methemoglobinemia, which kills by asphyxiation; infants are particularly susceptible to it. Many cases of the mysterious epidemics of "crib death" are now attributed to it.

When a Decatur newspaper ran a feature suggesting that the city's water supply had become polluted with excessive nitrate and that fertilizers being poured on the surrounding cornfields might be the source of the trouble, the story exploded like a bombshell in the cornbelt communities. At the time of the water analysis, farmers were resorting almost exclusively to nitrogen fertilizer as the cheapest, and indeed the only, means to produce over eighty bushels of corn to the acre, an amount dictated by the economics of corn production as necessary to realize a profit. Corn, or maize as it is known in the English-speaking world outside North America, is a heavy consumer of nitrogen, which, under *natural* conditions, is stored in the soil as a part of its humus, a brown-black material composed almost wholly of decayed vegetable matter.

For countless ages before man began to till the soil, humus was accumulated by return to the soil of vegetation which died and rotted. When man began to harvest crops he saw to it that humus, rich in nitrogen and other elements upon which plants depend, was replaced in the form of animal wastes and straw, the components of barnyard manure. In many countries of the Far East, man's own excrement, euphemistically termed "night soil" by Westerners, is applied to the land instead of being allowed to float away through sewage systems into rivers.

An almost inexhaustible supply of such a natural manure is still available to Decatur in nearby Sioux City, Iowa, America's heartland city on the Missouri River, where millions of animals have been fed and slaughtered and from which they have been shipped to the nation's retail markets for over half a century. A pile of steer manure has accumulated longer than a football field. This mountain of organic waste, which poses a headsplitting disposal problem to the city fathers, could easily be processed into natural soil-enlivening products were anyone interested in saving the soil. Nor is the Sioux City manure pile an exception. Dr. T. C. Byerly, leader of the USDA's waste-disposal programs, states that wastes from livestock operations in the United States are presently equal to those produced by the entire U.S. population and that by 1980 they will double in size.

Instead of returning this natural humus-nitrogen to the soil, the farmers chose to apply artificial nitrogen fertilizers. In Illinois alone the consumption rose from ten thousand tons in 1945 to well over half a million tons in 1966, and is rising constantly. Since the amount of nitrogen applied is more than the corn can naturally take up, the excess washes out of the soil into the local rivers: in the case of Decatur, all the way into the drinking cups of citizens.

Joe Nichols, a physician and surgeon who founded the Natural Food Associates in Atlanta, Texas, reported that a survey on farms throughout the Middle West disclosed that the corn growth was so heavily fertilized with synthetic nitrogen that it was unable to convert carotene into vitamin A and that the cattle feed produced from it was also deficient in vitamins D and E. Not only were the cattle not gaining weight but they were not even reproducing as well as they should have, and, as a result, the farmers were losing money. When certain strains of corn were cut for silage, the nitrate content was so high the silos blew up and the juice that ran out killed every cow, duck, and chicken unfortunate enough to drink it. Even when silos did not explode, the nitrogen-laden corn in them became lethal, in the form of nitrous oxide fumes sufficient to kill a man unsuspectingly breathing it.

The swirl of controversy which broke upon the Illinois cornbelt when the truth became public had already arisen in scientific circles when Dr. Barry Commoner, director of the Center for the Biology of Natural Systems at Washington University in St. Louis, Missouri, presented a prophetic paper on the relation between nitrogen fertilizer and the nitrate level in Midwestern rivers at the annual meeting of the American Association for the Advancement of Science. Two weeks later, a vice-president of the National Plant Food Institute, a lobby whose goal is to protect the interests of the $2-billion American fertilizer industry, sent copies of Commoner's paper for rebuttal to soil experts at nine major universities. Because they had spent most of their careers advising farmers that the best way to insure bountiful crops is to apply artificial fertilizers to the land, many scientists in these centers of academic learning were as irritated at Commoner's allegations as were the fertilizer-lobby officials and rushed to take up cudgels in the lobby's and their own defense.

An exception was Washington University's Dr. Daniel H. Kohl, an expert in the process of photosynthesis, who concluded that the problem was so serious the fate of the planet might be at stake. When he joined Dr. Commoner to ascertain, by isotopic analysis, exactly what was happening to the excess nitrogen fertilizer in Illinois soils, his efforts were immediately and viciously attacked by his departmental colleagues on the grounds that such work was not a proper part of the department's goal of pure research.

Dr. Commoner in his book *The Closing Circle* challenged his academic colleagues by pointing out that the new technology allowing more corn to be produced on less acreage than before might be a success economically but was ecologically a disaster. Commoner characterized the nitrogen-fertilizer industry in its hurtling dash for profits as one of the "cleverest business operations of all time." Evidence suggests that in the presence of artificial nitrogen, the natural fixation of nitrogen from the air by soil bacteria stops and, as a result, it is increasingly difficult for farmers to give up the use of the artificial product. Like addictive drugs, fertilizer nitrogen creates its own demand, the buyers having been "hooked" on the product.

Dr. William Albrecht, a professor of soil science at the University of Missouri, who, more than a quarter of a century ago was almost single-handedly struggling to stress the importance of healthy soil to crops, animals, and men, states that, with respect to analyzing fodder, cows are more intelligent than people. Regardless of how tall and green forage looks to the eye when grown with an excess of artificial nitrogen, says Albrecht, the cow will refuse it and will eat the surrounding grass shorter and shorter. "Though the cow cannot classify forage crops by variety name, or by tonnage yield per acre, she is more expert than any biochemist at assessing their nutritional value."

Albrecht's years of research were admired by the director of studies of France's National Veterinary School at Alfort, near Paris, Dr. André Voisin. In 1959 Dr. Voisin produced a book, *Soil, Grass and Cancer,* which was translated into English by the secretary of the Irish Agricultural Organization Society and published by New York's Philosophical Library. The thrust of Voisin's important work is that man, in his effort to produce food for an exploding world population, has forgotten that his body comes from soil or, as the Bible put it, "dust and ashes."

Voisin's realization that plants and animals are intimately associated with the soil where they are born was strengthened when he visited the Ukraine and saw that, within a few generations, the giant dappled Percheron draft horses, developed on the soils of a French district south of Normandy, had dwindled to the size of Cossack horses, though their bloodlines had been kept pure by the Soviets and their conformation remained the same, though miniaturized. This should remind us, says

Voisin, that all living things are biochemical photographs of their environment. Our ancestors, he says, were well aware of the fact that the dust of the soil itself is what finally determines vigor and health.

Developing his theme that the soil makes the plant, the animal, and man, Voisin exposed his readers to a fascinating panoply of data which illustrates that animals and plants on the land, not chemists in laboratories, are the supreme judges of agronomic methods. Voisin also provided copious examples to prove that, by itself, chemical analysis of foodstuffs, plants, and soil is wholly insufficient to the evaluation of their essence. Voisin points out that chemists work mainly on "analytical groups," which can be said to be "mere creations of their minds." Noting that farmers have long been given advice on the nutrition of their animals on the basis of certain tests for nitrogen content, Voisin quotes the 1952 Nobel Prize winner in chemistry, R. L. M. Synge, who stated that it was wholly presumptuous in this way to conclude anything about the real nutritive qualities of grass, or human food.

The dean of agriculture at the University of Durham in England was so impressed with Voisin's lecture to the British Society of Animal Production in 1957 that he summed it up for the assembled audience, saying: "As Monsieur Voisin has forcibly explained to us, a herbage which appears ideal to the chemist as judged by his analysis is not necessarily ideal for the cow."

While Voisin was in England, he visited one farm on which the incidence of a disease known as grass tetany afflicting a 150-head herd of cattle was particularly high. Voisin learned from the farm owner that his livestock had been foraging, not on seasoned pastureland, but on new sowings of young grass to which enormous applications of industrial fertilizer, particularly potash, had been applied. Voisin told the farmer that when potash is applied to grass and other forage plants, the plants gorge themselves immediately and indulge in "luxury consumption." This results in an enormous increase of the potash content of the plants in a very short time and diminishes the quantity of other elements absorbed, such as magnesium, the lack of which leads directly to tetany.

When a local veterinary arrived at the farm to care for some of the stricken animals, Voisin asked him whether he knew to what extent his client had employed potash to fertilize his grazing land. The animal doctor, who had no idea that he was talking to one of the most distinguished French representatives of veterinary science, curtly replied: "This question concerns the farmer. My role is to care for sick animals and to cure them." Voisin was aghast at this stock reply. "I think," he wrote, "that it is not merely a question of healing the animal or man stricken by disease, it is necessary to heal the soil so as not to have to heal the animal or man."

To Voisin it appears that the rise of the artificial fertilizer industry has caused man mechanically and unthinkingly to rely to such an extent on its products that he has forgotten his intimate relationship with the soil as nature made it, that his adulteration of the dust from which he springs may be sealing his destiny on planet earth. Though this predicament is hardly a century old, its progression has been geometric in the proliferation of degenerative diseases in both animal and man consequent on the overuse of artificial fertilizers.

It all started with Baron Justus von Liebig, a famous German chemist who published an essay in 1840, interestingly entitled *Chemistry in Its Application to Agriculture and Physiology.* In this essay he appeared to indicate that everything required by living plants was to be found in the mineral salts present in their ashes once the plants had been incinerated to destroy all the organic matter they contained. Though this theory ran directly counter to centuries of agricultural practice, and indeed to common sense, the visual results of the application of artificial fertilizers composed of nitrogen, phosphates, and potash, together with calcium oxide, or lime, seemed to prove Liebig's theory, and later resulted in the skyrocketing climb of fertilizer production by the chemical industry, of which the figures for Illinois are but one example among thousands.

Dr. Albrecht of the University of Missouri terms this sudden blind dependence upon nitrogen, phosphorus, and potassium, the main constituents of artificial fertilizers, or NPK—as they are known in chemistry —an "ash mentality," since ashes suggest the idea of *death* rather than life. Like a senile yet undeposable king, the ash theory still rules the world's agricultural realms, despite the attack on it by a far-seeing minority of individuals, a group collectively called "organic agriculturalists," who have seized upon Justus von Liebig as the progenitor of what they see as a worldwide cataclysm.

Already at the turn of the century, as the fertilizer industry was getting into stride, a British doctor and medical researcher, Robert McCarrison, later knighted for his thirty years' service as head of the Nutrition Research Agency for the Imperial Government of India, and director of its Pasteur Institute at Coonoor, had come up with a contrary conclusion after spending a period of time working among the peoples of the remote Gilgit Agency, a rugged, mountainous area south of the Wakhand Valley, which is Afghanistan's "tail."

McCarrison was struck by the fact that the Hunzas, an ancient people claiming descent directly from the soldiers of Alexander the Great, not only could walk 120 miles at a stretch in the roughest mountain country in the world, or cut two holes in a winter lake and swim from one to the other under the ice for the fun of it, but, with the exception of an occasional eye inflammation due to badly ventilated fires in their huts, were wholly free of disease and lived to a great age. McCarrison also found the Hunzas' health to be matched by their superior intelligence, wit, and urbanity; though they were numerically few and their neighbors warlike, they were rarely attacked—because they always won.

As neighboring people living in the same climate and geographical conditions were afflicted with many diseases which never appeared among the Hunzas, McCarrison began a comparative study of the dietary practices of Gilgit Agency peoples which he extended to various races all over India. By feeding diverse Indian diets to rats—foolish enough to eat whatever humans will eat—McCarrison found that his rats reflected the conditions of growth, physique, and health of the people eating the same foods. The rats which ate the diets of the peoples such as the Pathans and Sikhs increased their body weight much faster and were much healthier than those ingesting the daily fare of peoples like Kanarese and Bengalis. When offered the food of the Hunzas, which was limited to grain, vegetables, and fruits, along with unpasteurized goat milk and the butter made from it, the rodents appeared to McCarrison the healthiest ever raised in his laboratory. They grew rapidly, were apparently never ill, mated with enthusiasm, and had healthy offspring.

When they were killed and autopsied at twenty-seven months—the equivalent of fifty-five years in humans—nothing whatsoever was wrong with their organs. Most amazing to McCarrison was the fact that throughout their lifetimes they were gentle, affectionate, and playful.

Contrasted to these "Hunza rats" others contracted precisely the diseases of the people whose diets they were being fed and even seemed to adopt certain of their behavioral characteristics. Illnesses revealed at autopsy filled a whole page. All parts of their bodies, from womb and ovary to skin, hair, and blood, and respiratory, urinary, digestive, nervous and cardiovascular systems, were afflicted. Moreover, many of them, snarling and vicious, had to be kept apart if they were not to kill each other.

In laboratory work based on the newly discovered accessory food factors, named *vitamins* in 1921 by the Polish-born American biochemist Casimir Funk, McCarrison was able to prove that pigeons given a diet which in people produces goiter developed polyneuritis. What was surprising to McCarrison was that other healthy birds fed on normal diets harbored the same microbes but did not get ill. McCarrison believed it was the faulty diet which led to the microbic triumph, not the presence of the microbes themselves.

During a lecture to the British College of Surgeons McCarrison described how, in the course of more than two years, his rats fed on the diets of the more vigorous and well-developed Indian races never fell ill. But the *British Medical Journal,* in a leading article on McCarrison's address, concentrated only on the diseases which diet would help to prevent and completely overlooked the astonishing fact that the radiant health of a group of people could be transferred dietarily to a group of rats, simply by diet. Doctors, used to textbook explanations that pneumonia was due to exhaustion, chills, a blow on the chest, the pneumococcus microbe itself, weakness in old age, or other illnesses, were unimpressed with McCarrison's finding that, in every case, his Coonoor laboratory rats had fallen ill with pneumonia because of faulty food. The same was true for diseases of the middle ear, peptic ulcers, and other afflictions.

American medical circles were no more receptive to the basic truth which McCarrison was propounding than their British colleagues. During a Mellon lecture delivered before the Society for Biological Research at the University of Pittsburgh, where McCarrison spoke on "Faulty Food in Relation to Gastro-Intestinal Disorders," they listened impassively as he said of the Hunzas: "Indeed their buoyant abdominal health has, since my return to the West, provided a remarkable contrast with the dyspeptic and colonic lamentations of our highly civilized communities." Then as now, the weight of McCarrison's evidence that Hunzas enjoy a remarkably disease-free and long life failed to mobilize any medical-research expedition to Hunza land. His stunning data were buried in the *Indian Journal of Medical Research.*

Only when a British doctor, G. T. Wrench, brought out a book, *The Wheel of Health,* in 1938 was McCarrison's evidence given broad public exposure. In the introduction to his work Wrench asked thought-provokingly why, as students, young doctor aspirants were always presented with sick or convalescent people for their teaching and never with the ultrahealthy. It was abhorrent to Wrench that medical schools—presuming that knowledge about health in its fullness was picked up by a baby at its birth—taught only disease. "Moreover," wrote Wrench, "the basis of our teaching upon disease is pathology, namely the appearance of that which is dead from disease." Then, as today, it seems the emphasis was on *pathology,* not natural health. Neither Wrench's admonition nor the startling evidence of McCarrison—who after retiring as a major general became physician to King George V—seemed to have any effect on the health authorities of the United States and other countries. In 1949 Dr. Elmer Nelson, in charge of nutrition at the U.S. Food and Drug Administration, was reported by the Washington *Post* to have declared in court: "It is wholly unscientific to state that a well-fed body is more able to resist disease than a less well-fed body. My overall opinion is that there has not been enough experimentation to prove that dietary deficiencies make one more susceptible to disease."

Some time before McCarrison arrived in the Gilgit Agency, Albert Howard, a young mycologist and agricultural lecturer to the Imperial Department of Agriculture at Barbados in the West Indies, concentrating on fungus diseases of sugar cane, came to the conclusion that the true cause for plant diseases would never be found by researchers sequestered in small laboratories and greenhouses full of flowerpots. As he put it: "In Barbados I was a laboratory hermit, a specialist of specialists, intent on learning more and more about less and less." Because another part of his job was to tour the Windward and Leeward Islands and advise people on how to grow cacao, arrowroot, peanuts, bananas, citrus fruits, nutmegs, and a host of other plants, Howard found that he learned much more from men in actual contact with the land and its abundance than he ever had in his botany classes.

He began to detect a fundamental weakness in the organization of the research into plant pathology. "I was an investigator of plant diseases," he wrote, "but I had myself no crops on which I could try out the remedies I advocated. It was borne in on me that there was a wide chasm between science in the laboratory and practice in the field."

Howard's first big chance to combine theory and practice came in 1905, when he was appointed imperial botanist to the Government of India. In the Bengali town of Pusa, site of the agricultural research station about to be founded by Lord Curzon, then Viceroy to India, Howard decided to see whether he could create, on a seventy-five-acre holding, plants with such health that they would not require poison sprays to resist disease. Howard took as his teachers, not learned plant pathologists, but the natives of the region. He felt that, since the crops grown by cultivators around Pusa were remarkably free of pests, he would make an in-depth study of Indian agricultural practices. As he put it, he "speedily found my reward."

By following the practices of the Indians, who used no pesticides or artificial fertilizers but returned to the land carefully accumulated animal and vegetal wastes, Howard was so successful that by 1919 he had learned "how to grow healthy crops, practically free from disease, without the slightest help from mycologists, entomologists, bacteriologists, agricultural chemists, statisticians, clearing-houses of information, artificial manures, spraying machines, insecticides, fungicides, germicides, and all the other expensive paraphernalia of the modern experimental station."

Howard was further astonished that his herd of work oxen, the ordinary power unit of Indian agriculture, when fed only the produce from his fertile land, never came down with foot-and-mouth disease, rinderpest, septicemia, and other cattle diseases, which frequently devastated herds of the modern experimental stations. "None of my animals were segregated," he wrote; "none were inoculated; they frequently came into contact with diseased stock. As my small farmyard at Pusa was only separated by a low hedge from one of the large cattle-sheds on the Pusa estate, in which outbreaks of foot-and-mouth disease often occurred, I have several times seen my oxen rubbing noses with foot-and-mouth cases. Nothing happened. The healthy, well-fed animals failed to react to this disease exactly as suitable varieties of crops, when properly grown, did to insect and fungous pests—no infection took place."

Howard recognized that the entire basis for eliminating disease in plants and animals was the fertility of the soil and that the first prerequisite for all subsequent work was the bringing of the whole Pusa experiment station to the highest state of fertility. To do this he determined to copy the age-long practices of China and build a large-scale system for utilizing farm wastes to turn them into humus.

Unfortunately, while the idea was taking shape in his mind, the Pusa agricultural research organization had developed to the point where, as Howard saw it,

> A series of watertight compartments—plant breeding, mycology, entomology, bacteriology, agricultural chemistry and practical agriculture—had become firmly established. Vested interests were created which regarded the organization as more important than its purpose. There was no room in it for a comprehensive study of soil fertility and its many implications by one member of the staff with complete freedom of action. My proposals involved "overlapping," a defect which was anathema both to the official mind (which controlled finance) and to a research institute subdivided as Pusa always had been.

Howard therefore laboriously collected funds to found a new center, the Institute of Plant Industry, at Indore, three hundred miles northeast of Bombay, where he had complete freedom of action. Since the fundamental prerequisite for growing cotton, the principal commercial crop around Indore, was raising soil fertility, Howard was in his element. He accordingly developed what came to be known as the "Indore process" of humus production. Within a short time he found not only that the yields of his cotton were three times those of the surrounding countryside but that the cotton was remarkably free of diseases. "These results," Howard later wrote, "were progressive confirmation of the principle I was working out—the connection between land in good heart and disease-free crops; they were proof that as soon as land drops below par, disease may set in." Howard was firmly convinced that the two most important goals were to keep the texture of his soils right and not to overwork his land beyond a volume of operations for which it had sufficient natural reserves.

Based on his findings, Howard wrote a book, *The Waste Products of Agriculture: Their Utilization as Humus,* which was greeted with favorable and even enthusiastic reviews around the world. But, when the book was circulated to agricultural scientists working on cotton problems in research stations all over the British Empire, the reception was hostile and even obstructive. This was because Howard's successful methodology challenged the ingrained beliefs that *breeding methods alone* could improve cotton yields and the quality of plant fibers, and disease was to be reduced by *direct assault with pesticides.*

Furthermore, the time factor was ridiculed. How could one possibly waste several years bringing the land back into what Howard called "good heart"? This would demand the abandonment of chemical fertilizers and the time-consuming production of Indore compost, a mixture of decaying animal and plant matter at a ratio of three to one. Howard clearly saw the threat he posed to the established order: "The production of compost on a large scale might prove to be revolutionary and a positive danger to the structure and perhaps to the very existence of a research organization based on the piecemeal application of the separate sciences to a complex and many sided biological problem like the production of cotton."

Research workers on many other crops throughout the Empire took the same dour view as that of the cotton specialists and they were strongly supported by the moguls of the burgeoning artificial fertilizer and pesticide industries.

When Howard went home to England at the end of 1935, he was invited by the students of the School of Agriculture at Cambridge University to address them on "The Manufacture of Humus by the Indore Method." Because he had distributed printed copies of his remarks beforehand in order to insure that a lively discussion would follow his lecture, practically the whole staff of the school was present when he mounted the lecture platform. But since he had been so consistently attacked by plant specialists in England, India, and other parts of the world, it was no surprise to Howard that nearly all of the school's faculty from chemists to plant breeders to pathologists heatedly opposed his remarks. Only the student body seemed enthusiastic and, as Howard recalled, vastly amused at finding their teachers on the defensive and vainly endeavoring to bolster up the tottering pillars supporting their temple. "Here again I was amazed by the limited knowledge and experience of the world's agriculturists disclosed by this debate. I felt I was dealing with beginners and that some of the arguments put forward could almost be described as the impertinences of ignorance." It was obvious from this meeting that little or no support for organic farming would be obtained from the agricultural colleges and research institutes of Great Britain.

Howard was correct. When later he read to the British Farmers' Club a paper on "The Restoration and Maintenance of Fertility," representatives of experimental stations and of the fertilizer industry in the audience poured ridicule on his ideas. To their protestations Howard replied that he would shortly have his answer "written onto the land itself." Two years later Sir Bernard Greenwell, who had meticulously followed Howard's directions on his two estates, gave an account to the club which more than bore out Howard's findings. But the scientists and the fertilizer salesmen, knowing that success was the one unanswerable argument in favor of organic farming, failed to attend the lecture.

Despite the truculence of these vested interests, Howard, like McCarrison, was knighted by the British Crown for his achievements. Yet only a few sensible individuals began to follow his lead. One of these was Lady Eve Balfour, who since childhood had suffered bad bouts of rheumatism and continual head colds each winter from November to April. Learning of Howard's research just before World War II, she initiated an Indore-type operation on her own farm at Haughley in Suffolk. Instead of bakers' loaves she ate bread made only from whole-grain flour ground from her own compost-benefited wheat. During the winter following the change in her overall diet, she was entirely free from colds for the first time in her life and was no longer bothered with rheumatic pains in prolonged periods of cold, damp weather.

During the war, Lady Eve's book *The Living Soil* appeared in heavily rationed England. The result of long detective work in libraries and interviews with health specialists who were convinced of the soundness of Howard's and McCarrison's views, it amassed a compendium of scattered data on the links between humus-grown plants and the health of animals and humans fed upon them. Lady Eve compared man's prideful "conquest of nature" with the conquest of Europe taking place under the Nazis. "As Europe is in revolt against the tyrant," she wrote, "so is nature in revolt against the exploitation of man."

Lady Eve soon discovered that her piglets, attacked at the age of one month by a disease called white scour, which the textbooks explained was due to iron deficiency, and for which accordingly they recommended doses of chickweed or other plants rich in that element, could be cured equally effectively by being fed actual soil from fields rich in humus to which no chemical fertilizers had been applied, whereas soil from land "exhausted" from the application of fertilizers had no effect upon the disease's progress.

About the same time Friend Sykes, a British farmer and breeder of thoroughbred horses, attracted by Howard's ideas, bought a 750-acre derelict farm in Wiltshire at nearly one thousand feet altitude, overlooking the Salisbury Plain, on which the land had been completely farmed out. Sykes's previous experience as an agricultural consultant had taught him that specialized farms, on which only certain crops or one variety of animals were raised, resulted in the inevitable weakening of stock and plants by disease. He came to see that outbreaks of disease could be completely eradicated by an "enlightened practice of good husbandry," particularly the introduction of mixed agriculture.

A student of ecology long before the subject became a household word, and an opponent of DDT more than ten years before Rachel Carson shocked the world with her *Silent Spring,* Sykes wrote in his *Food, Farming and the Future,* published in 1951: "The first thing that Nature does when she has been treated with poison is to battle against it and try to breed a resistant strain of the form of life that is being attacked. If the chemist persists in his poisonous methods, he often has to invent more and stronger poisons to deal with the resistance that Nature sets up against him. In this way, a vicious cycle is created. For, as a result of the conflict, pests of a hardier nature and poisons still more powerful are evolved; and who is to say that, in this protracted struggle, man himself may not ultimately be involved and overwhelmed?"

Sykes's experience with his crops, based on his intuition that the soil had a *latent fertility* which could be brought out simply by being tended, and without the application of any fertilizer whatsoever, was little short of fantastic. Sykes had the soil on one twenty-six-acre field analyzed. The laboratory report indicated severe deficiencies of lime, phosphate, and potash and appended a recipe of artificial fertilizers to correct the condition.

Ignoring the report, Sykes simply plowed and harrowed his field and, *without adding any fertilizer,* sowed oats. To the amazement of his neighbors he got a crop yielding ninety-two bushels per acre, which was followed by an equally successful crop of wheat. After tilling the soil again throughout the summer, he again sent a sample of it to the laboratory and found that only a deficiency of phosphorus remained, the lime and potash having been completely restored. In spite of the unanimous views of experts that cereal crops could not be successfully grown without a heavy dressing of phosphates, Sykes merely subsoil plowed the acreage and achieved a harvest of wheat larger than the first one. Subsoil plowing digs deeper into the ground and aerates this otherwise packed and useless earth. When Sykes ordered his subsoiler plow in Chantry, the agent who took his order said: "What on earth do you want a tool like that for in this God-forsaken country? My firm has been in business over a hundred years and has never supplied such an implement before." Sykes's wheat crop, which had been undersown with rye grasses and clover, produced two and a half tons of hay to the acre in one cut the following year. Sykes then replowed his land, planted it to oats, and was rewarded with a crop yielding over one hundred bushels to the acre. A third laboratory analysis of his soil showed no deficiencies whatsoever.

Sykes described this procedure in an essay, "Farming for Profit with Organic Manures as the Sole Medium of Re-Fertilization," in which he concluded that he had made his livestock healthy, his plants disease free without poison sprays, and had been able to plant the same varieties of wheat, barley, and oats from their seeds six consecutive years in a row although other farmers had had to make changes.

Having achieved among his other successes a reversal of the trend in seed degeneration which has led to increasing dependence by farmers on hybrid varieties that are of questionable nutritional value, Sykes teamed with Lady Eve Balfour and others to form the Soil Association, the principal object of which was to unite people, of whatever country, working for a fuller understanding of the vital relationships among the soil, plants, animals, and man. Its philosophy centered on the idea that, when quality is sacrificed to quantity, total food supply diminishes.

The Soil Association began a research project on land donated in Suffolk, the referees for which stated:

> Humanity has been badly frightened by the invention of the atomic bomb. Yet the slower but more widespread devastation wrought by exhausting the soil upon which we depend for subsistence, is ignored by the majority of people, who think of calamity only in terms of disaster or war. Wasteful exploitation of the soil's fertility is due in part to the desire for quick cash returns, but in a greater degree to ignorance. Many scientists and agriculturalists now realize that their knowledge of the natural processes underlying soil fertility is incomplete. They recognize that these processes are only partly explicable in terms of agricultural chemistry and that the purely inorganic approach to the study of soil science is a line of thought as dead as the mechanical determination of nineteenth-century physics. "Dead" is the appropriate word; for the missing factor is that of life itself.

Shortly before the organization of the Soil Association in Britain, J. I. Rodale, editor of a health magazine in Pennsylvania, also came across the work of Sir Albert Howard. "To say I was stunned," wrote Rodale afterward, "would be a definite understatement. Surely the way food is grown has something to do with its nutritional quality. Yet this theory had not found its way into the articles of any of the health magazines I was reading. To physicians and nutrition specialists carrots were carrots were carrots." In 1942 Rodale bought a farm of his own in Emmaus, Pennsylvania, and set about publishing Sir Albert Howard's book, *An Agricultural Testament.* He then launched a journal, *Organic Gardening and Farming,* which today, after three decades of growth, has some 850,000 subscribers. A companion magazine to enlighten the public on the links between health and organically grown foods, called *Prevention,* was started by Rodale in 1950 and now circulates to over one million readers increasingly anxious about the quality of American food.

For his efforts in fighting for integrity in foods Rodale was harassed by the U.S. Federal Trade Commission, which sought to stop the sale of his book *The Health Finder* because it was advertised as being able to "help the average person to remain comparatively free of many terrible diseases." Rodale fought the case in court in a battle which cost him nearly a quarter of a million dollars. He won hands down but was not able to sue the government to recoup his losses.

Rodale's campaign began to challenge the usual view of people living in the cities and suburbs of the United States—and this is the vast majority—that soil is a static, inert substance. He challenged the use of the word *dirt* as a synonym in English for *soil.* The former is used to mean something mean, contemptible, or vile, whereas soil is alive and clean.

Below its surface the earth teems with organisms. Earthworms, called *Annelida* after the Latin word for rings, because they are made of one hundred to two hundred ringlike segments, each an independent miniature body, burrow in the ground to depths of more than the height of a tall man, acting as nature's plow, eating the soil as they move, ejecting it again as castings to produce rich topsoil. Called by Aristotle the "intestines of the soil," they could also be considered its vascular system, since, when they are lacking, soils get hard-packed as if their arteries had hardened.

In 1881, a year before his death, Charles Darwin brought out a book, *The Formation of Vegetable Mould through the Action of Worms,* in which he made the statement that, without worms, vegetation would degenerate to the vanishing point. He estimated that in a single year more than *ten tons* of dry earth per acre passed through the digestive systems of earthworms and that in a field well populated with them *one inch* of topsoil would be created *every five years*. Darwin's earthworm book moldered on the shelf for fifty years before it was re-examined; even then his ideas did not penetrate into the curricula of the agricultural schools, and it is not realized that with heavy application of chemical fertilizers and pesticides, a field can lose its entire earthworm population, so important for keeping it in a state of health necessary to the production of nutritious crops.

The favorable action of earthworms is often mocked, though in an experiment run about 1950 their ability to improve poor soil was definitely demonstrated. Twenty barrels were filled with impoverished soil and planted with grass. Half the barrels contained live, the other half dead, worms so that all shared identical amounts of organic matter. Each barrel was treated with an equal amount of organic fertilizer. The barrels with the live worms produced four times as much grass.

Just after World War I, Dr. William Beebe, first to explore the ocean in a bathysphere, decided after a bird-collecting expedition in Brazil that he needed something to do on the sea journey back to New York: so he decided to examine jungle soil. Working on shipboard with a magnifying glass and an old bag of earth mold and decaying leaves, Beebe found himself plunged into a strange world of miracles. By the time he reached New York Harbor Beebe had discovered in his soil over five hundred separate specimens of life; he believed that more than twice as many remained to be identified.

If Beebe had resorted to the microscope, and thus come across bacteria, he would have been helpless to count them. Sir E. John Russell, in his book *Soil Conditions and Plant Growth*, says that in one tiny gram of soil treated with farmyard manure there are some twenty-nine million bacteria; however, where chemical fertilizers were used, the number was cut almost in half. In an acre of rich earth, bacteria are estimated to weigh more than a quarter of a ton; as they die, their bodies become converted to humus, enriching the soil in a natural way.

In addition to bacteria are myriads of other microscopic organisms:

actinomycetes, filamentous forms resembling both bacteria and fungi; tiny algae, related to seaweeds; protozoa, animals made up of a single cell apiece; and the strange chlorophyll-less fungi themselves, ranging from one-celled forms to branched bodies, including yeasts, molds, and mushrooms.

The vegetative part of one kind of fungus associates with the roots of many green plants in a way beneficial to both that is still mysterious. Though it seems to have escaped the attention of many agricultural scientists, these fungi, called "mycorrhizae," were discovered by Dr. M. C. Rayner in England to have their threads consumed by tree roots with which they were associated. Traveling in France, Sir Albert Howard found that the roots of the healthiest vines for wine grapes were rich in mycorrhizae. No artificial fertilizers had ever been used on the vines, yet they were noted for the high quality of their wines.

Another great advantage of natural agriculture, well known to yesterday's farmer, has been forgotten in the highly specialized mono-crop agriculture of today: the advantage of symbiosis in plants. As the Russian essayist Vladimir Soloukhin has pointed out in *Grass*, modern Soviet agronomy has lost all feeling for the benefits of plant companionships. Though the specialists mock the idea that cornflowers growing in a field of waving rye have a salubrious effect on this cereal crop and consider the blue-blossomed plants—known to Americans as bachelor's buttons —as only noxious weeds, Soloukhin asks: "If the cornflower were an evil weed, would not the farmers of the world have grown to hate it before the appearance of the learned agronomists?"

How many botanists, asks Soloukhin, realize that the first sheaf of rye harvest was lovingly decorated with a cornflower wreath and placed in front of an icon, or that cornflowers were held by country folk to supply bees with abundant nectar for honey even in the driest weather? Suspecting that all this folk wisdom had a solid basis in fact, Soloukhin checked in scientific literature and found evidence supporting the accuracy of peasant intuition. He read that if a hundred wheat grains are mixed with twenty seeds from the ox-eye daisy the sprouting wheat will be overwhelmed, but that if only one daisy seed is added, the wheat will grow better than if no daisies come up in its field. The same is true for rye and cornflowers.

Soloukhin's view on plant symbiosis supports that of an American professor of botany and conservation, Dr. Joseph A. Cocannouer who, while Sir Albert Howard was working in India, ran the Department of Soils and Horticulture at the University of the Philippines for a decade and set up an extensive research station in Cavite province. In his book *Weeds: Guardians of the Soil,* published nearly a quarter of a century ago, Cocannouer sets forth the thesis that, far from being harmful, plants usually considered noxious and troublesome, such as ragweed, pigweeds, purslane, and nettles, bring up minerals from the subsoil, especially those which have been depleted from the topsoil, and are excellent indicators of soil conditions. As companion crops they help domesticated plants to get their roots down to food which would otherwise be beyond their reach.

Writing of the "law of togetherness of all things," Cocannouer warned that the whole of world agriculture was beginning to ignore it. "In America," he wrote, "in our frenzied efforts to take advantage of high prices for agricultural products, we are mining our soils instead of farming them." The same was beginning to be true of Europe, he added, where, since World War II, few farmers have been practicing the *law of return.*

Farmers are becoming more and more mechanical-minded, says Cocannouer, one of whose best friends told him: "You and your Nature stuff! That's all very well in theory . . . but starving people are looking to America for food. We've got to feed 'em. We've got to mechanize our agriculture and make our land produce to its limit!"

Today, Americans live in a country where food production is supposed to be the world's most efficient. Yet food prices have continued to rise. The cliché holds that back in 1900 one U.S. farmer could feed only five people besides himself and that today he can feed thirty. But Michigan University food scientist Georg Borgstrom says these mathematics are illusory. At the turn of the century farmers, in addition to working their land and raising livestock, delivered their own milk, butchered their own animals, churned fresh farm butter, salted meat, baked bread, and farmed with draft animals for which they produced feed. Now these draft requirements are fulfilled by expensive machinery using increasingly costly and depletable fossil fuels, and the husbandman's arts have been taken over by factories. In less than twenty-five years several million poultry raisers, whose chickens roamed the land ingesting all sorts of natural vegetable and mineral products as well as insects, have disappeared, to be replaced by some six thousand semiautomated outlets where broilers, packed wing to wing in cages, are fed diets full of artificial supplements.

All these off-farm activities figure in the high cost and dubious quality of food. In fact, if one divides the twenty-two million workers building farm machinery and farm-to-market roads, delivering and processing farm produce and engaged in other food-production tasks, it becomes clear that it takes about the same number of people to feed Americans today as it did in 1900.

Cocannouer nevertheless realized that the views of his nature-scoffing friend were bound to prevail. He was in despair that no publicity had been given Luther Burbank's firm belief that all agricultural learning should begin with a study of nature.

Now there are signs that the agricultural worm may at last be turning and that university scientists are beginning to wake up to the views propounded long ago by McCarrison, Howard, and Rodale. As if they were discovering something new, Drs. Robert F. Keefer and Rabindar N. Singh, agricultural researchers at West Virginia University in Morgantown, issued a press release on March 4, 1973, to the effect that "what man eats is determined partly by the fertilizer that farmers put on their crops." In their experiments the two professors say that they have determined that the amounts of trace elements in sweet and fodder corn, so important in the diets of animals and humans, are dropping dramatically owing to the kinds and amounts of fertilizers grown in some soils.

Their somewhat belated rediscovery of this basic truth has also reinforced a survey conducted in eleven Midwestern states, where it was found that the iron, copper, zinc, and manganese content in corn has fallen off severely in the past four years. The application of huge doses of nitrogen fertilizer such as that which has alarmed the citizens of Illinois, may, says Singh, "have far-reaching effects on the health of animals and men." He adds that work of another of his West Virginia colleagues shows that fertilization of pastures with high rates of nitrogen may produce changes in the milk of grazing animals, as revealed by feeding it to rats.

In light of the findings of such pioneers as McCarrison, Howard, Albrecht, Voisin, Sykes, and Lady Eve Balfour, the West Virginia professors' research comes very late in the day, and their caution seems somewhat ludicrous in the face of mounting rates for degenerative diseases in the United States.

It is a strange fact that U.S. medical schools, concerned mainly with the study of diseased tissues and bodily systems and organs rather than with healthy people, do not even have a single fundamental course on nutrition in their curricula.

CHAPTER 15

Chemicals, Plants and Man

In the early nineteenth century an American of English descent named Nichols cleared hundreds of acres of rich virgin land in South Carolina, on which he grew crops of cotton, tobacco, and corn so abundant that with the revenue he built a big house and educated a large family. Not once in his lifetime did he add anything to the soil. When it became depleted and his crops dwindled, he cleared more land and continued his exploitation. When there was no more land to be cleared the family fortunes declined.

Nichols' son, grown to manhood, looked at the poverty-stricken acreage, took Horace Greeley's advice and moved west to Tennessee, where he cleared two thousand acres of virgin land; like his father he planted cotton, corn, and tobacco. When his own son was grown to manhood, the land was once more so depleted from having living things taken from it and none returned that he moved on to Horse Creek in Marengo County, Alabama, there to purchase another two thousand acres of fertile soil and raise a family of twelve children on the proceeds; the town became Nicholsville; Nichols became the owner of a sawmill, a general store, and a gristmill. This man's son also grew up to see devastation where his father had grown rich. He decided to move further west and settled in Parkdale, Arkansas, where he bought one thousand acres of good land on the bayou.

Four moves in four generations. Multiplied by thousands, this is the story of how Americans raised food on a continent which was there for the taking. The great-grandson of the original Nichols, together with thousands of other farmers, inaugurated a new era. After World War I he began by farming his new acreage, instead of just mining it, adopting the new government-recommended artificial fertilizers. For a time his cotton crops prospered, but soon he noticed that his pest population was much worse than it had been. When the bottom fell out of the cotton market his son Joe decided that medicine, not farming, was to be his career.

At the age of thirty-seven Joe Nichols was a full-fledged physician and surgeon in Atlanta, Texas, when he suffered a massive heart attack which nearly killed him. He was so frightened that for weeks he gave up his practice to consider his situation. All he had been taught in medical school, plus the opinions of his colleagues, suggested his prognosis was extremely doubtful. There was no answer for his affliction beyond nitroglycerin pills, which alleviated his chest pains but caused equally painful headaches. With nothing better to do than to leaf through the ads of a farming magazine, Nichols casually came across the line "People who eat natural food grown in fertile soil don't get heart disease."

"Pure quackery! Quackery of the worst sort," said Nichols of the magazine, which was *Organic Gardening and Farming,* edited by J. I. Rodale. "He isn't even a doctor!"

Nichols remembered that for lunch on the day of his massive heart attack he had consumed ham, barbecue meat, beans, white bread, and pie, which he considered a healthy meal. As a doctor he had advised hundreds of patients on diet. But a line in the magazine nagged him: What *was* natural food? What *was* fertile soil?

At the local library the librarians were helpful in bringing Nichols books on nutrition. He also scoured the medical literature, but could find no answer to what constituted natural food.

"I had an A.B. and an M.D. degree," says Nichols, "was fairly intelligent, had read a lot, owned a farm, but I didn't know what was natural food. Like many another American who hadn't really investigated the subject, I thought natural food meant wheat germ and black molasses, and that all natural-food addicts were faddists, quacks, and nuts. I thought you made land fertile by dumping commercial fertilizer on it."

Now, more than thirty years later, Joe Nichols' thousand-acre farm near Atlanta, Texas, is one of the showplaces of the state; he has never again been afflicted with a heart attack. He ascribes both successes to the advice which he took from Sir Albert Howard's book *Agricultural Testament* and Sir Robert McCarrison's *Nutritional and Natural Health*. On his farm, not another ounce of chemical fertilizer went into the land, nothing but natural compost.

Nichols realized that all his life he had been eating "junk food," food produced from poisoned land, food that had led straight to a massive heart attack. A third book, *Nutrition and the Soil* by Sir Lionel J. Picton, convinced him that the answer to metabolic disease, whether it was heart trouble, cancer, or diabetes, was indeed natural, poison-free food grown on fertile soil.

The food we eat is digested and absorbed from the intestine into the bloodstream. Essential nutrients are carried to the individual cells all over the body, where repair work is done by metabolism, the process by which stable nonliving matter is built up into complex and unstable living material, or protoplasm. The cell has an amazing capacity to repair itself provided it gets proper ingredients through proper nutrition; otherwise it becomes stunted or goes out of control. The cell, or basic unit of life where metabolism occurs, needs essential amino acids, natural vitamins, organic minerals, essential fatty acids, unrefined carbohydrates, and several more as yet unknown, but presumably natural, factors.

Organic minerals, like vitamins, are found in balanced proportions in natural food. The vitamins themselves are not nutrients, but substances without which the body cannot make use of nutrients. They are parts of an extremely complex, intricately interrelated whole.

In "balance" means that all the nutrients used by the tissues must be available to the cell simultaneously. Furthermore the vitamins essential to proper nutrition and good health must be natural. There is a great difference between natural and synthetic vitamins, not a chemical but a biological difference. There is something missing in the artificial that is of biological or life-enhancing value. Not yet widely accepted, this fact has been unequivocally established by the work of Dr. Ehrenfried Pfeiffer, a biochemist and follower of the great natural scientist and clairvoyant Rudolf Steiner. Dr. Nichols thinks the Pfeiffer techniques can reveal exactly why natural foods or those containing natural vitamins and minerals and enzymes—another chemical compound, of vegetable or animal origin, which causes chemical transformation—are superior to those grown and preserved with chemicals.

When Pfeiffer came to the United States at the outbreak of World War II, and settled at Three-Fold Farm in Spring Valley, New York, he worked out Steiner's "Biodynamic" system for making composts and for treating the land, and set up a laboratory to investigate living things without breaking them into chemical constituents.

Before his arrival in the United States Pfeiffer had developed in his native Switzerland a "sensitivity crystallization method" to test finer dynamic forces and qualities in plants, animals, and humans than had thus far been detectable in laboratories. Dr. Steiner, who had given a series of esoteric lectures at the Silesian estate of Count Keyserling in the 1920s for agronomists concerned about the falling productivity of their crops, had asked Pfeiffer to find a reagent which would reveal what Steiner called "etheric formative forces" in living matter. After months of tests with Glauber's salt, or sodium sulfate, and many other chemicals, Pfeiffer discovered that if a solution of copper chloride to which extracts of living matter had been added was allowed to evaporate slowly over fourteen to seventeen hours it would produce a crystallization pattern determined not only by the nature but by the quality of the plant from which the extract was taken. According to Pfeiffer, the same *formative forces* inherent in the plant and acting to bring about its form and shape would combine with living growth forces to form the pattern of crystal arrangement.

Dr. Erica Sabarth, current director of the Pfeiffer-established laboratory in Spring Valley, showed the authors rows of beautiful crystallizations, looking like exotic undersea corals. She pointed out how a strong, vigorous plant produces a beautiful, harmonious, and clearly formed crystal arrangement radiating through to the outer edge. The same crystallization made from a weak or sick plant results in an uneven picture showing thickening or incrustation.

Pfeiffer's method, says Sabarth, can be applied to determine the inherent quality of all sorts of living organisms. When a forester sent Pfeiffer two seeds taken from different pine trees, and asked if he could detect any difference in the trees themselves, Pfeiffer submitted the seeds to his crystallization tests and found that, whereas one crystal picture was an example of harmonious perfection, the other was distorted and ugly. He wrote to the forester that one of the trees should be a fine specimen, the other must have a serious defect. By return mail the forester sent Pfeiffer enlarged photographs of two grown trees: the trunk of one was mast straight; the other was so crooked it was useless for lumber.

At Spring Valley Pfeiffer developed an even simpler and less time-consuming method to demonstrate how life veritably pulsates from living soils, plants, and foods, but not from inorganic minerals, chemicals, and synthetic vitamins, which are dead. Requiring none of the complex equipment of the standard chemical laboratory, it uses circular filter-paper discs fifteen centimeters in diameter, provided with a small hole in the center for insertion of a wick. The discs are laid in open petri dishes in which stand small crucibles containing a 0.05 silver-nitrate solution. This solution climbs up through the wick and spreads over the discs until it has expanded about four centimeters from the center.

From the brilliant-colored concentric patterns Pfeiffer has been able

244 CHILDREN OF THE SOIL

to disclose new secrets of life. Testing natural vitamin C taken from such products as rose hips, he established that the pattern of vitality was far stronger than from artificial vitamin C, or ascorbic acid. Rudolf Hauschka, a follower of Rudolf Steiner, suggests that vitamins are not chemical compounds that can be synthetically produced but "primary cosmic formative forces."

Before his death, Pfeiffer pointed out in his own booklet *Chromatography Applied to Quality Testing* that Goethe had stated a truth more than 150 years ago which is of the utmost importance with regard to the recognition of natural biological quality: *The whole is more than the sum of its parts.* "This means," wrote Pfeiffer, "that a natural organism or entity contains factors which cannot be recognised or demonstrated if one takes the original organism apart and determines its component parts by way of analysis. One can, for instance, take a seed, analyse it for protein, carbohydrates, fats, minerals, moisture and vitamins, but all this will not tell its genetic background or its biological value."

In an article, "Plant Relationships as Made Visible by Chromatography," published in the winter, 1968, issue of *Bio-Dynamics*, a periodical to further soil conservation and increase fertility in order to improve nutrition and health, Sabarth stressed that the chromatographic technique "especially reveals the quality, even the living force of the organism." She added that she plans to explore the possibilities of the method not only as it applies to seeds and fruits but with regard to the roots of plants and all the other plant parts.

In modern processed foods the vitamins, trace elements, and enzymes are arbitrarily removed, mostly so as to render the food more durable. As Nichols puts it: "They remove the life, in effect, killing it, so that it will not live and die later."

The leading culprits in the way of poisonous foods picked by Nichols are the bleached flour that goes into white bread, white sugar, refined table salt, and hydrogenated fats. One of the most innocent-looking of comestibles, the normal soda cracker eaten with soup, contains all of the above-mentioned noxious elements. "It is junk," says Nichols, "which leads straight to heart disease."

From long before the so-called dawn of history bread has been a basic nutrient for man. In mythology, the origin of domesticated grains is attributed to Attis or Osiris. In the ruins of Swiss lake dwellers remains of bread have been found which was baked at least ten thousand years ago.

A grain or berry of wheat consists basically of a hard nutty kernel called the germ at one end, a nub of solid starchy endosperm on which the kernel feeds when planted as a seed until its roots can grow, and three layers of protective husk collectively called bran. Essential enzymes, vitamins and minerals, including iron, cobalt, copper, manganese, and molybdenum are in the germ and husk. Other grains—barley, oats, rye, corn—have analogous constructions, and bread can be made from all of them. Wheat germ is one of a very few places in nature in which the entire vitamin B complex is found, hence bread was called "the staff of life." Whole wheat also contains traces of barium, a shortage of which in the human body can lead to cardiac disease, and vanadium, also essential to the health of the heart.

From time immemorial wheat berries have been ground between two circular stones. Until the advent of steam power the mills were worked by hand, the first steam mill being erected in London in 1784. In stone mills, the entire grain was ground into flour. In that process some of the husk was reduced to powder, which gives color to whole meal. In Deuteronomy 32, verse 14, man is enjoined to eat "the fat of the kidney of wheat"—meaning the germ. The development of iron rollers, by a Frenchman in the early nineteenth century, brought with it a separation of wheat germ, bran, and endosperm. Iron rollers were first used in place of stones in 1840 by the Hungarian Count Szechenyi in his mill in Pest. In 1877 a satisfactory roller mill was imported from Vienna to England. Soon they were employed in Canada. Governor Washburn of Minnesota, a miller, brought the Hungarian process to Minneapolis and began to devitalize American flour. By 1880 their use was universal.

From a commercial point of view the roller mill had three advantages over the old grinding stones. By separating the husk and germ from the starchy flour, the miller had two products for sale instead of one. The husk and germ were sold as "offal," or animal fodder. Removal of the germ made it possible to keep the flour in good condition for a much longer time, which increased the miller's profit. When the roller mill was introduced it became possible to adulterate wheat with 6 percent of added water. For this the germ had to be removed or the flour would not keep. It could then be sold separately.

In so-called "enriched" white bread, with the vitamins and minerals removed, nothing is left but raw starch, which has so little nutritive value that most bacteria won't eat it. Into this insipid starch synthetic chemicals are arbitrarily injected, which form only part of the missing vitamin B complex, and are not properly ingestible by human beings because they are not "in balance." For thirty years white flour was bleached with nitrogen trichloride, in what is known as the "agene process." This uses a poison which affects the central nervous system. It gives puppies fits, and may contribute to mental illness in humans. In 1949 millers voluntarily changed to chlorine dioxide for bleaching. This, says Nichols, is also a poison. Other chemicals used to "improve" flour include benzoyl peroxide, potassium bromate, ammonium persulfate, and even alloxan. Chlorine dioxide destroys the remaining vitamin E in flour, and causes the starch to swell, which is a boon to the baker. Researchers in England found that removal of the natural vitamin E from bread reduces the intake of a workman from about a thousand units a day to between two and three hundred.

To compound this trouble, just as white flour was being introduced into England so was margarine, the invention of another Frenchman, as a cheap substitute for butter, devoid of vitamins A and D. The general health of the country deteriorated. Men from northern England and southern Scotland, large and powerful during the Napoleonic Wars, became short and frail and unfit for military service by the time of the Boer War. A commission set up to investigate the phenomenon concluded it was caused by men moving to the cities, where they lived not on wholesome country bread but on white bread and white sugar. In 1919 when the U.S. Public Health Service announced a definite connection between overrefined flour and the diseases of beri-beri and pellagra —vitamin-deficiency diseases of which over 100,000 cases were reported in Mississippi alone—the millers went into action, not to change the flour, but to get the Public Health Service to shut up. Within six months the Public Health Service abjectly issued a "correction" to its bulletin. White bread, they said, was perfectly wholesome—if eaten in conjunction with an otherwise adequate diet of fruit, vegetables, and dairy products. As Gene Marine and Judith Allen were to remark in reporting the story in their recent book *Food Pollution:* "So is cardboard."

The next villains in this melodrama of life are white sugar and glucose, the heavy syrup fruits are packed in and the sweetener for most soft drinks. In the seventeenth century, European manufacturers developed a process by which after eight weeks of hard labor sugar could be refined to something approximating whiteness. This whiteness, at first so expensive, caused white sugar to be considered by the poor more worthy of being consumed. White sugar, says Nichols, is one of the most dangerous food items on the market. All the good part, the molasses, the vitamins, and minerals, are removed. There is nothing left but carbohydrates and calories—of which we have too many already. The refining is now done for purely commercial reasons; the sugar keeps better. White sugar can be stored in hundred-pound cloth sacks for years in dirty warehouses and still be sold for a profit.

Most table syrup, says Nichols, is nothing but cornstarch treated with sulfuric acid, then artificially colored and flavored. Unlike natural fruit sugars, honey, molasses, or maple syrup, it goes straight into the bloodstream, causing instant hyperglycemia—or too much sugar in the blood. This drowns the human cells in sugar. The pancreas, heeding the alarm, puts out too much insulin and produces a state of hypoglycemia, or *too little* sugar in the blood. This seesawing, says Nichols, is the cause of the vicious but ubiquitous coffee break: when a man begins his day with refined sugar in his coffee and glucose on his cereal or pancakes, he shoots his blood full of sugar, which triggers a pancreas reaction. By ten o'clock he has hypoglycemia; so he has sweetened coffee or a soft drink or a candy bar. This fills his blood with instant sugar. Again the pancreas reacts. By noon he is down again; and so on throughout the day. A side effect of hypoglycemia is that it causes a lowering of resistance, makes a person nervous and not mentally alert, an easier prey to viral and bacterial diseases.

One of the less-suspected poisons on the dining-room table is common refined salt or sodium chloride. Not in small doses, but over a long period, it can cause high blood pressure and heart disease. Sea salt contains trace minerals in balance, but by the time the salt hits the supermarket it has been refined to pure sodium chloride with all trace minerals removed. Furthermore it is treated under high heat with sodium silicate, a drying agent, which makes it free flowing in wet weather. This, says Nichols, disturbs the delicate balance of sodium and potassium in the cells of the heart. The delicacy of chemical combinations is such that if the two basic elements of table salt were to be taken separately in the same amounts, they would kill immediately.

The next and even more vicious cause of heart disease, says Nichols, is hydrogenated fats. These include most of the fats and oils commonly found in shortening, in store-bought peanut butter, and in practically all commercial bakery products, crackers, cookies, and breads. Much ice cream is made from mellorine, a cheap hydrogenated oil. Hydrogenation consists in using a heated nickel catalyst to force hydrogen into the gaps between the carbon atoms of linoleic acid. This prevents the resulting fatty oil from going rancid; but it also destroys essential fatty acids. These, says Nichols, not being absorbable by the body cells, have to go somewhere in the body, and end up lining the blood vessels, causing heart disease.

DDT and other pesticides also go straight to the seed oil of corn or cotton. There is no way to remove them, and they are cancer causing. Though DDT has largely been banned, its successors Dialdrin, Aldrin, and Heptaclore, are equally insidious. "Personally," says Nichols, "I wouldn't have corn oil in my kitchen." He recommends any of the cold-pressed oils, such as olive oil, or safflower oil, which yield a wonderfully clear, almost transparent, oily fluid.

Nichols points out that whereas natural rice is one of the best foods in the world, and is one of the richest sources of natural vitamin B complex, white processed rice is nothing but raw starch, an item already superfluous in the high-carbohydrate American diet. American missionary wives in the Philippines managed to kill off hundreds of prisoners in the local jails by philanthropically substituting polished rice for natural rice in the prison diets, causing beri-beri.

The peanut butter which Carver went to such pains to produce is now mostly being made from rancid peanuts, says Nichols, since the food chemists have learned to clean it up, deodorize it and decolor it so that it can be sold to unsuspecting mothers. By one means or another and with hundreds of toxic additives to choose from, chemists can fix food so that it is very difficult for the citizen to tell that the food is going or has already gone bad.

One of the most important items in human diet is protein, which provides eight essential amino acids, the building blocks of the body. There are twenty-two amino acids. Eight are called essential for the adult, ten are necessary for growing children. If those are included, the body can build the others.

Meat is the most popular source of protein in the United States; but the prime steak of today has come from beef that has been force-fed for 180 days with low-quality-protein hybrid grains sprayed with poison insecticides. These go straight into the fat of the meat, especially into the marbling, and, says Nichols, lead straight to heart disease. To put an extra 20 percent weight on cattle—and produce a multimillion-dollar profit—the cattle raisers feed their animals diethylstilbestrol (DES), which can be carcinogenic in both men and women.

Though the FDA finally banned DES in the spring of 1973, it has now been replaced by a compound called Synovex, which contains estradol benzoate, considered by many experts to be cancer-causing. Says Dr. Mortimer Lipsett, "Whatever dangers you want to attribute to DES, you can attribute to Synovex." Beef, steers, hogs, sheep, and poultry are also still getting sixteen other drugs, singly or in combination, which the FDA suspects are carcinogenic when ingested by humans. To detect excess amounts of the toxin in meat, even if the entire army were to join the federal meat inspectors of the FDA, it is unlikely they could stop the chemicals getting to your table. And a huge proportion of our meat is never inspected. Of the ten billion frankfurters eaten in one recent year in the United States, about three and a half billion were consumed within the states where they were manufactured; hence they were not inspected.

The organ meat of animals, says Nichols, is only edible if the animal has been fed organically. The livers of prime animals are confiscated much of the time because they contain abscesses and toxic substances. Commercially grown chickens have arsenic and stilbestrol in their bodies and much of it winds up in the liver. The liver is the detoxifying organ of the body, and that's where these poisons go. Store-bought eggs are mostly infertile, do not taste as good as fertile eggs, and are nowhere near as good for you, says Nichols, because there is a subtle biological difference. Hens that lay commercial eggs are cooped up where they cannot move, have seldom if ever seen a rooster, let alone been caught by one. "How," asks Nichols, "can an unhappy hen lay a good egg?"

In the pyramid of life, plants play an essential role, as man cannot ingest essential elements directly from the soil. They must be brought to him through the good graces of living plants, which likewise feed all animals, directly or indirectly. Via plant and animal our bodies grow out of the soil. Microorganisms break up the chemicals in the soil and make them acceptable to plants. Plants can synthesize carbohydrates from the air, rainfall, and sunshine. But, before the life processes can convert these carbohydrates into amino acids and proteins, they must have help from the soil fertility. Neither man nor animal can synthesize the necessary proteins from the elements. Animals can only assemble them from the amino acids, providing the necessary kinds and amounts of each can be collected or produced by plants with the help of microbes.

Protein-producing plants demand a long list of elements from the soil: nitrogen, sulfur, and phosphorus are required to make part of the protein molecule; calcium and lime are also required; and magnesium, manganese, boron, copper, zinc, molybdenum, and other elements are needed in connection with protein construction, even if only in such small amounts as are called "trace."

If the soil is not properly fertile, not teeming with microorganisms, the whole process goes out of kilter or grinds to a halt. To keep the microorganisms alive, great quantities of decaying organic matter need to be added to the earth. On the forest floor dead plant matter and dead animal matter go back into the land. Leaf mold, through decay, continues to give life to the land, returning to the soil what the tree took as nutrient.

It should be obvious that soil is vital to health. Healthy soil, properly composted, with the right bacteria, fungi, and earthworms, free from chemical fertilizers and pesticides, produces strong, healthy plants which naturally repel pests. Healthy plants make strong, healthy animals and strong, healthy human beings. Poor land grows poor food—poor in vitamins, minerals, enzymes, and proteins; this produces poor, sick people. Worn out land causes people to leave the farms and go live in the slums.

It's a strange fact, but plants grown on well-balanced, fertile soils do not have the same attraction for insects as those grown on poor soils, artificially stimulated by chemical fertilizers. Fertile soils have a natural immunity to insects and disease, just as a properly nourished body has an immunity to disease. Bugs and worms tend to gravitate toward a plant, or a field of plants, that has already been weakened by disease or improper development.

The end result of chemical farming, says Nichols, is always disease: first to the land, then to the plant, then to the animal, then to man. "Everywhere in the world where chemical farming is practiced the people are sick. The only ones to benefit are the companies that produce the chemicals."

Simultaneous with the application of fertilizers, the chemical companies began to douse the land with chemical pesticides, abetted by the government and with the tacit support of university professors. Three hundred million pounds of different chemical poisons are now produced under twenty-two thousand different brand names, which result in the destruction of wild life and essential insect and microbe life. Of mass spraying, Dr. George J. Wallace, Michigan University zoologist, went on the record to say that it "poses the greatest threat that animal life in North America has ever faced—worse than deforestation, worse than illegal shooting, worse than drainage, drought, oil pollution, possibly worse than all these decimating factors combined."

Not only wild life but fish in fresh water and even in the ocean are gradually being poisoned by a combination of insecticides and herbicides. Yet the DDT which wiped out fish and small game left its prime target, the boll weevil, flourishing. Despite the application of chemical pesticides the insects are gaining the upper hand, doing $4 billion worth of damage to crops each year. And no amount of argument appears to put over the fact that *healthy* crops are naturally pest resistant, keeping the insects at bay.

In the book *Silent Spring*, which Justice William O. Douglas called "the most important chronicle of the century for the human race," Rachel Carson made clear that the environment, which supports human life, is being stressed to the point of collapse. As Friend Sykes foresaw, doctors attribute to DDT and its more poisonous descendants the rise in leukemia, hepatitis, Hodgkin's disease, and other degenerative diseases. A correlation between the rise in the birthrate of mentally retarded children and the increase in the use of fertilizers and poisonous chemicals is stunning. Twenty thousand mentally retarded children were born in 1952. There were 60,000 by 1958; six years later the figure had risen to 126,000, and by 1968 it was well over half a million. Nowadays one child in eight is born mentally retarded in the United States, according to Dr. Roger J. Williams, discoverer of pantothenic acid and director of the Clayton Foundation Biochemical Institute in Texas, the first biochemist to be elected president of the American Chemical Society.

When Nichols realized what was happening to the country as a result of both chemical fertilization and chemical pesticides he took two steps. He went organic on his farm, and he sought other doctors and scientists who had made the same discoveries. Together they organized Natural Food Associates, of which Nichols became the first president. Their object was to start correcting the situation with a nationwide campaign to get the facts before the people, on the grounds that only an aroused public opinion could save America from poor food grown on poor soil. Nichols says he was determined to tell everyone just how to get natural food: "No matter how old you are, which sex you are, what color you are, where you live—north, south, east, or west, on an isolated farm or in a big city apartment."

By any means they could, Nichols and the NFA blasted the shibboleth that America is the best-nourished, healthiest nation on the face of the globe. "Nothing," said Nichols, "could be farther from the truth.

The truth is that America is the most fed and the worst nourished nation on earth. America today is suffering from a biological blight. We are facing metabolic disaster. We are a nation of sick people. Heart disease is rampaging through America; it is our Public Enemy number one. It is the leading cause of death among Americans. Fifty years ago coronary thrombosis was rarely seen by a physician. Today it strikes even the young. . . . Cancer, diabetes, arthritis, dental caries, and other metabolic diseases are rapidly increasing. Even children are falling victim to them."

Listing the facts, Nichols reported that sixteen hundred autopsies showed that in every one of the patients past the age of three years there was already disease in the aorta, the main artery of the body that carries blood from the left ventricle of the heart to all the organs and parts except the lungs. In every patient past the age of twenty, disease was already in the coronary artery.

"This should be evidence enough that practically everybody in the United States today has cardiovascular disease. We have an epidemic. And we have an epidemic of cancer. Cancer is now the leading cause of death, after accidents, in children under fifteen years of age. Babies are born with cancer! The American Cancer Society says cancer will eventually strike one in every four Americans now living. Can a nation call itself healthy when one of four must expect to get cancer, when three of four who get cancer will die of it?"

Almost immediately the agricultural chemical industry and the food processors attempted to discredit the NFA, calling them food faddists, quacks, and charlatans. They were accused of being "unscientific." The initial detractors were soon joined by the U.S. Department of Agriculture and the U.S. Department of Health, Education and Welfare, operating through the Food and Drug Administration, and even the American Medical Association. University professors, in search of fat grants, supported the claims of the FDA. A campaign was launched to make Americans believe that what the Natural Food Associates were saying was pure myth. Newspaper and magazine articles, even entire books, were published in a huge effort to destroy the effect of NFA and its credibility with the public.

The U.S. Department of Health, Education and Welfare put out a bulletin, "Food Facts vs. Food Fallacies," in which it called everything Nichols said a myth. To discredit Natural Food Associates and their objectives the AMA and the FDA organized a "Congress on Quackery," which toured the United States, holding seminars on food faddism and quackery. As Nichols put it, "They were really after men and women whose espousal of 'natural foods' or 'organic foods' or 'health foods' threatened to lower the profits of the food industry."

The stars of the show were Dr. Fred Spare and Dr. Jean Mayer, chairman of the Department of Nutrition at Harvard University's Medical School, who insisted that to get a proper balanced diet all an American had to do was go into the nearest grocery store and get a variety of the four food groups: fruit and vegetables; milk and dairy products; cereals; meat and eggs. The U.S. Public Health Department launched an all-out propaganda campaign, supported by the food processors and chemical trusts that make the poisonous food additives. Science editors, food editors, and medical editors in the daily newspapers joined their ranks.

When the NFA tried to tell the country that DDT was a cancer-producing chemical they were labeled quacks and faddists; their charges called a myth. In the end—after more than a decade of poisoning—the FDA itself was finally obliged to label DDT a dangerous poison, though pressure from agricultural interests caused the FDA to revoke its ban on DDT in milk, and establish a legal tolerance for the amount of DDT allowable in milk.

Although Australian investigators charged that BHT, or butyl-hydroxy-toluene, an anti-oxidant (originally used to preserve color motion-picture film), which turned up in processed foods, was teratogenic, that is, it interfered with the development of an embryo, the FDA allowed BHT as a freshness preserver. When newsmen questioned FDA about its research they were told the papers were secret. In the end it turned out there were only two reports on BHT in the FDA files—both written by members of the staff of the makers of BHT.

In 1960 the panel on food additives in President Eisenhower's Science Advisory Committee, which included members of the National

Academy of Sciences, university professors, and representatives of the Rockefeller Foundation and of cancer research institutes, stated that "Americans today are better fed and in better health than at any time in history. . . . The integrated contributions of the engineering, agricultural and chemical sciences have resulted in increasing quantities of uniformly high-quality and pure foods which have contributed demonstrably to the physical well being of the nation."

Thirteen years later FDA Commissioner Charles C. Edwards was still insisting that it was "established" that the vitamin content of food is not affected by the soil foods are grown in. "Vitamin or mineral deficiencies," he stated, "are unrelated to the great majority of symptoms like tiredness, nervousness, and rundown conditions." He then proclaimed that: "Scientifically it is inaccurate to state that the quality of soil in the United States causes abnormally low concentration of vitamins or minerals in the food supply produced in this country. . . . There is no relationship between the vitamin content of foods and the chemical composition of the soil."

But there is still hope if we get back on the track, says Nichols, if we begin to cleanse the poisons from every link of the food chain, so as to restore the country to proper nutrition and avoid the long decline that blighted North Africa and the Near East. To do so, and save the nation from metabolic disaster, says Nichols, we must change from an economy of exploitation to one of conservation. In the long run the country must give up chemical fertilizers and gradually revive the soil organically. Organic fertilizer can now be bought in a sack or packaged just like ordinary commercial fertilizer, and at no greater cost. Deposits of raw rock phosphate and potash with marine trace minerals and other deposits are readily available.

A great advantage of organic rock fertilizers is that after a few years of application they are no longer needed. Whereas the chemical farmer is obliged to put on more and more fertilizer each year, the organic farmer can put on less and less. Eventually the organic farmer will make more money, as it will cost him less to operate.

Organic farmers say it is not true that a man with extensive acreage cannot find enough organic matter. He has been told, says Nichols, that he must steal from one acre to get natural fertilizer for another acre; but in fact he can grow his own organic matter on every acre, by following a few simple rules. And the organic method can be applied to any kind of agriculture. All animal manures, garbage, perhaps even sewage sludge, can be composted and returned to the land. If we could halve the waste of these materials, says Nichols, we could double the fertility of our soils and thus double the food supply.

The restoration of soil fertility, according to organic farmers, would go a long way toward solving problems of floods and water shortages which cannot be solved until organic matter is restored to the soil. The usual 100 pounds of soil in East Texas won't hold 30 pounds of water. But 100 pounds of humus will hold 195 pounds of water like a sponge. Fertile soil is usually dark in color and soft to the touch. When it rains the water soaks into this soil.

The construction of dams on rivers will never completely solve the water problem, say the organic farmers. The underground water level will continue to fall until organic matter is restored to the topsoil. As Nichols puts it: "We must learn to trap the raindrop right where it falls, instead of washing our topsoil into the rivers." A third of the arable topsoil in the U.S. has already been washed into the sea over the years, and is still being lost faster than it can be replaced. During floods, millions of tons of rich topsoil are washed downstream. Soil erosion costs half a million acres of land a year. We live from about eight inches of topsoil, containing earthworms, bacteria, fungi, and other microscopic forms of life, that provides us with vegetation, trees, insects, and animals. The only inexhaustible wealth is a fertile soil. Topsoil is the greatest natural resource of any nation; civilizations of the past have been destroyed when their fertile soils were lost.

In the coming age of famine, says Nichols, proper nutrition from a fertile soil will be the first source of wealth. And we must stop contaminating the rest of the planet. He warns that the massive use of commercial fertilizer in the so-called underdeveloped nations of the world will bring them the same massive increase in metabolic disease that we already have in America. Yet the chemical companies keep pouring out propaganda and pressure for greater consumption of their product. Dr. Raymond Ewell, vice president for research at the State University of New York at Buffalo, who has been considered one of the world's leading chemical economists, says blithely that if "Asia, Africa and Latin America are not using quantities of fertilizer approaching 30 million tons by 1980, they are almost certain to be engulfed in widespread famine."

Nichols, on the other hand, says that if we continue to exploit and teach exploitation of the soil here and abroad, the result will inevitably be war, just as it was when Japan went into Manchuria looking for protein from the soybean. Peace in this world, says Nichols, depends on conservation of natural resources, not their exploitation.

CHAPTER 16

Live Plants or Dead Planets

Among the independent farmers of the nation still working the land, a band of hardy individuals have finally realized that the blandishments of the artificial fertilizer and pesticide salesmen are questionable and are setting about to avoid the harmful results of chemical farming before it is too late.

Hereford is not only the name of a popular breed of beef cattle developed in one of the English counties bordering on Wales, it is also a small town on the upper reaches of the Palo Duro River, which runs through the Texas Panhandle, a 170-mile-square area of the Lone Star State which, about a century ago, was a wild short-grass prairie roamed by thousands of American bison. For millennia the flat plains of Deaf Smith County, of which Hereford is the seat, produced a rich herbage and a variety of succulent weeds whose roots extended through two to four feet of clay-loam topsoil into the *calicahi*, a subsoil rich in calcium and magnesium, drawing up these elements and depositing them as they died on the surface to maintain a vital protein-rich graze for the wild bovines. The minerals in the soil were delicately balanced and the humus naturally provided by the dying vegetation along with the bovine droppings was sufficient to hold its own against the harsh climate, hot and dry in summer, bitterly cold in the snow-sparse winters. It was only half a century ago that farming began in the region; the first furrows were cut into the land by the metal moldboards of plows; golden grain was sown as far as the eye could reach. Where the land was not planted, herds of cattle replaced the buffalo.

As the years went by, the farmers realized that deep plowing was hurting rather than helping the soil. So they switched to breaking up the rich clay-loam to a depth of merely six to eight inches with chiseling tools pulled by low-horsepower tractors. At the same time they were delighted to discover that water from underground aquifers could be pumped up and applied to the soil to supplement the rainfall from thunderstorms which intermittently turned the prairie skies into a dark panoply of lightning-threaded cumulus and the creeks into "rivers a mile wide and an inch deep."

By the time the children of the first generation of farmers had grown into manhood, things had begun to go wrong in Deaf Smith County. Dissatisfied by smaller harvests obtained from depleted soil, farmers began adding artificial fertilizers to their land as recommended by agricultural research stations and academic advisers. In less than a decade disaster was in sight. The chemicals were burning up the organic material in the soil, upsetting the delicate natural balance of minerals. As a result, the soil began to dissipate. When mixed with irrigation water it coagulated into enormous clods weighing up to fifty pounds each. To break them up the farmers had to resort to huge 135-horsepower tractors capable of dragging enormous chiseling tools through the bricklike consistency of their land. Some of the farmers, appalled at the prospect of an end to irrigation farming in the Panhandle, owing to the unmindful application of the wrong kind of nutrients to the once rich land, were determined to react.

One of these, Frank Ford, after graduating from Texas Agricultural and Mechanical University, purchased an eighteen-hundred-acre farm in Hereford on which the land was badly eroded because of the prevailing agricultural practices. "There were gullies so deep you could hide a tractor in them," Ford recalls, but today they have all been filled and the land terraced and leveled smooth.

Ford committed himself to organic farming, using natural manures on his acreage and putting a complete stop to the use of pesticides, substituting in their stead ladybugs to kill brown mites and other pests. He also banished herbicides. Refusing to be persuaded, like other farmers, that his seeds should be chemically treated against wireworms and rust, he resolved that he would not plant any seeds he could not eat.

In addition to farming, Ford put capital into Arrowhead Mills, which specializes in the production of high-quality stone-ground flour with no preservatives, as well as other whole, natural foods. To assure himself a steady supply of organic products Ford had to persuade his fellow farmers to adopt organic methods. Attracted by his fair prices, a group of them have now organized the Deaf Smith County Organic Farmers Association, with the aim of not only growing healthier food but of protecting and improving the soil of West Texas.

Working with this group is Fletcher Sims, Jr., who came to the Texas Panhandle in 1949. One thing that caught Sims' attention was the fact that the first feedlots for cattle opened in the Panhandle, about 1965, were beginning to pile up tons of cattle manure which no one knew how to dispose of. Within a few years the waste from one lot two miles from his home in Canyon, Texas, downriver from Hereford, had collected into a pile over fifty feet high, covering forty acres, or more than thirty football fields, requiring a fleet of bulldozers and other equipment worth a quarter of a million dollars to pack. Sims further estimates that feedlots throughout the nation contain millions of cubic yards of manure which will eventually become worthless as fungi reduce them to minerals.

At the same time it seemed to Sims that the agricultural schools were going out of their way to misuse the cattle wastes on the land. At Texas A and M nearly one thousand tons of manure per acre was being plowed three feet under the soil, which Sims knew can do only violence to both soil and manure, since in the process topsoil is buried, subsoil exposed, and the manure prevented from becoming aerobically fermented. Another Texas college was pumping an organic slurry onto fields at concentrations that killed the crops; and an experimental station not far from Canyon was dumping raw manure at the rate of three hundred tons per acre onto soil on the premise that it is only a waste product to be disposed of. Other scientists were suggesting that building materials be made from manure, one group in the state of Washington even working on how to make livestock feed with it.

In the face of what Sims considered these sad and asinine approaches, he realized that the manure could best be turned into valuable compost. Dr. Joe Nichols introduced Sims to the compost work that had been done for years in Pfeiffer's research laboratory at Spring Valley, New York.

During several visits to Spring Valley Sims learned that compost making goes through distinct phases: one in which original starches, sugars, and other components are broken down by bacteria, fungi, and other organisms; a second in which the new materials are consumed by microorganisms to build up their own bodies. It was of the utmost importance, Sims was told, that the right kind of microfauna and microflora be present and that the second phase be timed correctly so that there would not be too much loss of organic matter.

"If compost is not worked properly," Sabarth told Sims, "the original proteins and amino acids break down into simple chemical compounds. In other words, organic matter gets lost as carbon dioxide, or as nitrogen escaping as ammonia and nitrates. Many gardeners think of their composts as being 100 percent organic because all their original materials are organic. But nature isn't that simple. Living cells have 70 to 90 percent water, only 15 to 20 percent proteins, amino acids, carbohydrates, and other carbon compounds. Only 2 to 10 percent is mineral: potash, calcium, magnesium, and the trace elements that are inorganic. The organic compounds can be preserved in the bodies of the microorganisms. They escape when they become free in some stage of the break-down. The N, P, and K concept comes into its own only when compost has been mineralized, but by then the biological values have been lost. In compost making you need to have a quick method for telling whether bacterial action is breaking down nitrogen-containing compounds too fast, which is indicated by the ammonia smell. If compost piles heat too fast they must be turned to interrupt the ammonia production so that bacteria rebuild more stable nitrogen compounds in bacterial protein."

The standard tests of the American Organization of Agricultural Chemists, Sabarth informed Sims, cannot reveal the state of matter in which organic materials are present since they rely on combustion or oxidation of compounds. The ashes give only the total amount present, but say nothing as to whether they originate from minerals or from living cells and tissues. Pfeiffer's colored chromatograms so well define the various stages of fermentation, whether decomposition, humus forma-tion, or mineralization, that after years of work the laboratory was able to develop a Biodynamic compost starter with a proper population of microorganisms for anyone's use.

Sabarth showed Sims chromatogram pictures, one of which illustrated how the material from a cranberry bog, though it contained an incred-ible 18 percent organic matter, was actually inert. Standard chemical analysis would not have revealed its biological valuelessness. A picture of adobe soil from California revealed that analysis of the minerals within it meant little because it had no well-developed microflora, and thus was infertile. When soils have only minerals but no organic matter, said Sabarth, the plants in them are like people forced to eat salty foods. They are driven to drink water and more water. Plants absorbing an excess of mineral salts take in an excess of moisture. Though they look lush to the eye, they are no longer in balance, and therefore no longer resistant to disease.

To his amazement Sims learned that with Pfeiffer's chromatograms Sabarth had been able to establish scientific proof that certain plants, beans and cucumbers, for instance, grow better if planted in conjunction with each other, and that other plants, such as beans and fennel, seem to fare badly together. Furthermore, the storage together of such crops as apples and potatoes mysteriously robs each of its most life-giving properties.

Pfeiffer came to realize that it is only our human egotistical point of view that labels a weed a weed, and that if they were viewed as a functioning part of nature, weeds would have much to teach. Pfeiffer proved that a whole group of weeds, including sorrels, docks, and horsetails, are sure indicators that the soil is becoming too acidic. Dandelions, which lawn owners so feverishly dig up, actually heal the soil by transporting minerals, especially calcium, upward from deep layers, even from underneath hardpan. The dandelion is thus warning the lawn owner that something is wrong with the life of his soil.

Pfeiffer showed that daisies play the same role, in that analyses of their incinerated ashes show them to be rich in calcium, the most important constituent of lime. Pfeiffer doubted whether the orthodox view, holding that the daisies have selectively "fixed" lime, was correct, since they could grow in limeless soil providing there is enough silicon present together with microorganisms. Pfeiffer came to the conclusion that, when soil lacks lime, silicon-loving plants such as daisies move onto it. When they die, they bring to the soil the missing calcium he had found in his analyses. But he could not answer the question "How does the calcium get into the daisies?"

Pfeiffer performed experiments on plant symbiosis to show that in some way camomile stimulates heavier growth of wheat, with fuller ears, but only when the ratio of camomile to wheat plants is no more than one to one hundred. Thus his latter-day research confirms the age-old wisdom of the Russian peasantry about cornflowers and rye.

Sims came to the realization that the prospects of Pfeiffer's unique tests seemed endless. He was fascinated that two chromatograms of wheat, one grown with inert chemicals, the other biologically, looked so different.

Sims took back with him to Texas a supply of the Biodynamic starter composed of some fifty different microorganisms, many coming from the outstanding soils of the world and each with its particular mission to fulfill, both in the compost as it is being made and in the soil onto which it is distributed. What makes the starter so inscrutable to the average scientist is the fact that there are homeopathic quantities of vital elements, enzymes, and other growth substances which work at dilutions of up to 1,000,000,000 to 1.

Applying the Biodynamic process to what may have been the first commercial compost operation using the Pfeiffer starter, Sims took raw manure which he could get free from the feedlots and treated it in such a way that microorganisms disassembled compounds in the waste and assembled them into new and beneficial ones. At the same time, disease organisms and seeds from weeds or grains are automatically destroyed and harmful chemicals are biologically degraded when the temperature in the piles reaches 140 degrees Fahrenheit. Laying out piles of compost in windrows, Sims turned them from time to time, using a machine of his own design with a capacity of six hundred tons per hour.

Within one month, his compost, having never been subjected either to grinding or screening, became a fine, dark brown, friable, earthy material, wholly devoid of manure odor. The cow dung was transformed, miraculously as it were, by *biological* action. As the farmers began to buy Sims's products and apply it to their land, startling results were not long in coming. John Wieck of nearby Umbarger, after only two years' treatment of his soil with half a ton of Biodynamic compost per acre and no other fertilizer or insecticides, and only two irrigations to supplement some three inches of rain, was able to harvest a fantastic 172½ bushels per acre of corn, or more than double the maximum crop achieved on the artificially nitrogenized lands of Illinois.

In the northern part of the Panhandle ten miles from Oklahoma's Cherokee Strip, another Texan, Don Hart, whose irrigated land had begun to tighten up from the use of commercial fertilizers, realized that he and his neighbors might soon be sitting on wasteland. Hearing of Sims's success, he not only began to compost his acres but soon started a composting business of his own to supply other farmers. Within a short time he found that his soil felt like a plush, moisture-laden carpet underfoot. A reporter visiting his acreage in late 1971 wrote that anyone who wanted to convince himself of the advantage of Biodynamic compost had only to drive along a road where from the car he could see on one side a beautiful crop of healthy corn plants coming up on Hart's field and on the other, planted two weeks before Hart's, a virtual nightmare: a few sickly plants starting out of hard-packed and cracked ground.

Southeastward across the enormous state of Texas, Warren Vincent has been encouraging farmers to grow rice organically in order to combat the rice growers' main nemesis, barnyard or water grass, on which herbicides of the kind used so devastatingly to defoliate the jungles of Vietnam have been extensively applied. Vincent encourages his neighbors to rotate rice with Bahaia grass, which turns the land back to sod, controls weeds, and makes an excellent pasturage for animals. Now that consumers are beginning to discover that organically grown brown rice is nutritionally far better than that grown with artificial fertilizer, other pioneering rice farmers have dared to go organic.

In northern California, 120 miles south of the towering Mount Shasta, which looks like Japan's Fuji, four Lundberg brothers, owners of Wewah Farm, have begun to grow brown rice organically. Though converting to organic methods involved additional costs, they remembered that their father had taught them that any farmer worth his salt has an obligation to improve the land he uses and, if possible, leave it to the next generation in a better condition than when he took it over, a philosophy which, applied worldwide, could make of this planet a Garden of Eden.

Despite generalized warnings against giving up the extended family of chemical products, the Lundberg brothers located a source of manure and composted it before working it into an initial seventy-six acres. Their first crop averaged thirty-seven hundred pounds per acre, low when compared to chemically treated rice, but high enough to be economically feasible, given the premium prices paid for organic rice. Their initial experiment convinced them to go all the way and convert the whole of Wewah's three thousand acres to organics. The Lundbergs next imported special milling equipment from Japan and established their own organic processing plant. This would not remove the rice's protective outer shell, the nutritious portion of the grain and to some the tastiest.

There are now indications from not only the public but also notables in California's government and even in its universities that the Lundbergs may be on the right trail. Floyd Allen, a reporter for *Organic Gardening and Farming,* visiting the state legislature in Sacramento, heard one assemblyman declare that the organic way was "a good mother philosophy." Allen was surprised to sit in the office of an eminent pesticide specialist at the University of California at Riverside and hear the man announce: "I wish someone would do something about the quality and taste of food. I'd like to eat a tomato that tastes like tomatoes used to taste."

The organic approach has also been adopted in the Middle West by dairy farmers who wish to sell their milk to such producers as Eldore Hanni, president of the Wisconsin River Valley Cheese company north of Wausau, who has been making organic cheese since 1962. When the Grade A raw milk arrives at the company it is pumped directly into the cheesemaking vat, completely by-passing pasteurization. No preservative or color is added and no imitation ingredients are used. To preserve the natural enzymes of raw milk, heating temperatures during manufacture of the cheese are not allowed to exceed 102 degrees Fahrenheit. Hanni's partner, Eldred Thiel, claims his cheese has the old-time flavor—"like my Dad used to make." The cheesemakers' suppliers are certified by the firm as "natural farmers," who take up to five years to make sure that no trace of chemicals remain on their land.

Among fruit growers who have seen the light is Ernest Halbleib, owner of Halbleib's Orchard and Organic Farm at McNabb, Illinois, who refutes the almost universal assertion that apple growers cannot get along without chemicals. Halbleib states that insects arrive in orchards just to point out the very mistakes that man is making. Producers who are fogging their orchards with deadly chemicals are finding that the single application sufficient ten years ago now has to be repeated many times in the growing season as bugs become resistant to instant death.

More than twenty years ago Halbleib went to Washington, where he testified to the FDA against poison sprays, poison fertilizers, and poison seed treatment, not a word of which he would take back today. Since that time, he has watched his colleagues administer over five hundred new chemicals to their trees. Today, says Halbleib, there is not one apple grower in his fruit belt that is not in distress. They have used so much poison on their soil that the manager of the USDA chemallurgical plant in Peoria, Illinois, told him that 100,000 acres in his area alone have been so toxified that they won't grow grass or even weeds and that the same is true for huge portions of once-rich potato land in the state of Maine.

"What do we want?" asks Halbleib. "To have children making their blood with poisoned food? Have you looked into the reason for such large enrollment in insane asylums and hospitals? Instead of pouring out funds to build more of them, why doesn't someone study the *cause* of disease?"

Lee Fryer, an agricultural and nutritional consultant who runs Earth Foods in Washington, D.C., states that in 1968 the figure spent on commercial fertilizers in the United States exceeded $2 billion. This sum would buy more than 100 million tons of Fletcher Sims's Biodynamic compost, which, if applied at the rate of one ton per acre would cover the whole state of California with enough left over for an area as large as the six New England states. For the cost of only a few days of the Vietnam war, the whole of the United States of America's soil could be given an annual treatment.

Fryer pointed to the successful use of seaweed as a natural fertilizer and soil improver as developed in the British Isles by a former chartered accountant, W. A. Stephenson, author of *Seaweed in Agriculture and Horticulture,* who quit his Birmingham job at forty and moved to the country, at the suggestion of a biochemist friend, to build a business which distributes seaweed fertilizer in liquid form all over the world.

One of the first to use seaweed successfully on a commercial operation in the United States is Glenn Graber of Hartville, Ohio, who farms four hundred acres of the blackest, richest peat soil to be found anywhere in the United States, on which he raises carloads of radishes; Bibb, Boston, iceberg, romaine, and leaf lettuces; and some fifty other vegetables. Six days a week for half the year an average of four huge trailer loads of produce leave Graber's farm for the market.

About 1955 Graber noticed that a destructive species of nematode or "roundworm" was appearing on his land and that "bluebottom" was wilting a large percentage of his crops as well as those of his neighbors.

Because the plague hit at a certain time of year, blame was universally put on the weather. Graber also found from analysis that his soil indicated a lack of trace minerals. Raised on the NPK concept which he had been following to the letter, Graber wondered what he could do to improve matters. He learned that marvelous things had been accomplished with seaweed at the Clemson College of Agriculture in South Carolina, where researchers had used seaweed meal and a liquid seaweed extract manufactured in Kristiansand, Norway, to achieve gains in sweet peppers, tomatoes, soya and lima beans, and peas.

On the basis of the little-heeded Clemson research, Graber decided to act, and ever since he has been applying kelp, imported from Norway in granulated form, to his land at the annual rate of two hundred pounds to the acre. Toward the end of the first season he noticed that healthy green mold was forming in the tracks of his farm equipment, his nematode infestation was dramatically reduced, and the bluebottom eradicated. Since then he has never put a pound of artificial fertilizer on his land, relying completely on seaweed, rock phosphate from Florida, and ground granite from Georgia, and on bacterial action and cover crops to produce nitrogen.

As his soil improved, Graber next realized that he was wasting money on pesticides, and abandoned their use, turning instead to a spray made of liquefied kelp applied at the rate of three gallons per acre over crops throughout the season. Graber is not sure how the liquid seaweed acts as a pesticide and says no research has yet been done to find out. Though he does not entirely escape infestations of pests from his neighbors' fields, Graber believes that when he incurs a 10 percent drop in his onion crop due to maggot flies, his neighbors are losing over half their crop, in spite of every insecticide they try. He is convinced that healthy plants on healthy soil resist pests naturally. To prove it he walked one visitor through a field of parsley swarming with leafhoppers, which brushed against their pants legs but were apparently not feasting on the best-looking and best-tasting parsley the visitor had ever tried.

Since his abandonment of commercial fertilizers, Graber has been able to give up a plow requiring two tractors to haul it. By simply cover-cropping his land with barley and rye, he not only adds humus and nutrients to the soil but allows it to be aerated by the plants' strong roots and by earthworms and microorganisms which flourish in it. The hardpan problem he once had disappeared as if by magic.

Another dividend to Graber is frost resistance. In one particularly unseasonable cold spell, when the mercury dipped to a chilly twenty degrees Fahrenheit, all of his freshly transplanted tomatoes and peppers withstood the cold with not a single loss, though he remembered that under the same conditions they all expired when artificially fertilized.

Graber thinks the problem of getting organically grown vegetables to the consumer is compounded because the present organic outlets do not have enough volume to warrant low-cost distribution in any one area. He thinks the only road to travel is to work through large food chains, which must find a means to isolate organically grown produce on their shelves from the conventional supplies.

Such an approach has recently been pioneered in West Germany by Latscha Filialbetriebe of Frankfort, a fast-growing family-owned supermarket chain of 123 stores with a bent for innovation. Latscha has introduced chickens, eggs, fruit juices, apples, and frozen green vegetables which are guaranteed to have only minimal quantities of "residuals" such as antibiotics, hormones, lead, and the full spectrum of pesticides. All plant products come from farms cultivated along organic gardening lines as developed by the German State Institution for Plant Protection in Stuttgart.

Latscha says that none of its controlled products costs more than 15 percent more than ordinary equivalents and that its juices and deep-frozen items can be offered at prices under those charged for standard brands. Though the premium it pays to a cooperative dairy to produce milk without such additives as chlorinated hydrocarbons and DDT is passed on to the customer, the certified milk has climbed to 10 percent of Latscha's sales and the chain's overall revenues have increased despite a generally falling market demand.

In Cambridge, Massachusetts, the Star Markets are beginning to act somewhat like Latscha. They take a trailerload a week of mixed vegetables that have been grown organically by Glenn Graber and market them in separate bins.

Oliver Popenoe, founder of Yes! Inc., one of the dozen natural-food outlets in the metropolitan area of Washington, D.C., applauding the Star Markets' effort, puts his finger on the reason why their example has not yet been widely followed: "The problem with most food chains is that their management and staffs lack commitment to organic principles," says Popenoe. "This makes it very difficult for them to market organically grown produce which *looks* about the same, or even worse to the eye, than chemicalized produce, and costs more. They suffer from a credibility gap. Credibility is everything when it comes to buying organic produce. There is no way I know of *knowing* it is organic unless you subject it to a gas chromatograph test for pesticide residues. Since such proof costs twenty-five to thirty dollars for each item tested, even the most purist of grocers use them sparingly. I think this is the main reason why the market for organic produce is so thin. Unless one knows one's farmer personally, or has great faith in the honesty of one's grocer, one hesitates to pay more for an uncertain benefit."

When Graber was asked how his fields compare with those of his neighbors, he replied candidly: "In ideal weather conditions they can beat me in yield and also in time but in adverse conditions it's the reverse." More important to Graber is the fact that he is confident that he is improving his soil as he goes along. Graber has recently begun to have a look at Biodynamic compost. At the beginning of the 1973 season he ordered enough of the product from Zook and Ranck in Gap, Pennsylvania, to treat his soil for vegetable crops at the rate of fifteen hundred pounds per acre. By running comparative tests over the next two years, Graber thinks he will be able to determine whether the compost will additionally help his soil and crops. What convinced him to begin trying the compost was his impression at an agricultural fair in Pennsylvania that not one of the farmers who visited Zook and Ranck's booth had an adverse comment about Biodynamic compost. All of them had good results and were full of praise. "You can well believe that if a farmer had spent his money for nothing," says Graber, "he would be raising the very devil."

In Switzerland a farmer working one hectare of land next to the Theological Faculty of the University of Fribourg grows enough vegetables during an eight-month season using the biodynamic method and the help of only one assistant to feed the two hundred theological students in the faculty's dormitories and send a large overflow to the public market. "I could teach this method to anyone," says the farmer, "as long as he has a natural or artificial supply of water. Just think what this could do for Third World countries with their rising population and food shortages."

For all their success in organic farming, some farmers like Glenn Graber feel that many organic proponents tend to be too "purist" and, as such, have alienated the chemical interests who might well change their closed thinking if met halfway. "It's about time the two camps got together to determine what's right and what's wrong," says Graber. This is also the opinion of Dr. John Whittaker, a veterinarian in Springfield, Missouri, who is animal health editor for the remarkable new monthly, *Acres USA*. Published in Kansas City by Charles Walters, Jr., the magazine calls itself a voice not for organic farming but for what Walters thinks is a better term: Eco-Agriculture.

Whittaker is nevertheless not at war with the chemists. He says that what is needed is to create common ground on which organic-minded farmers can meet with farmers who honestly have accepted the pronouncements of the chemical establishment. "On the one hand," he states, "the chemists have got to stop viewing the natural movement as a group of little old ladies working in geranium beds. The truth is there can be no sudden death of the technology now extant. There has to be a phasing down, a buffering process, a marriage. We have to learn from each other."

Asked how technology might harmonize with nature, Whittaker points to the development of metal proteinates, a process which takes minerals and "chelates" or hooks them to organic matter such as protein. One of the clearest statements about how proteinates work is that of Whittaker's fellow veterinarian, Phillip M. Hinze, who looks upon the physical body not only as a compilation of chemicals but as an electric complex as well.

"The animal body," says Hinze, "may be thought of as a very complex battery that not only receives, stores, and uses electricity for chemical purposes, but also maintains itself by assimilating vitamins, minerals, amino acids and other products. The body recognizes these substances when they come along. Every organic substance has an electromotive property which determines whether it can be assimilated. When an animal needs nutrients, a signal is sent out to capture that nutrient from food that has been ingested. If there is no sickness, and the needed ingredients are present, they will be assimilated. Unfortunately the needed ingredients don't always correspond with substances considered suitable for food. For instance, the requirements of the animal body for metals are often met by feeding rations containing inorganic forms of these metals. But it happens that inorganic forms of nutritionally essential metals have different electromotive properties than the same metals complexed with organic materials such as amino acids. A pig can't eat a nail. It needs organic iron."

So does the soil; overharvested, overirrigated and overgrazed, it no longer contains the necessary organic minerals to produce good food in the form of plants.

This truth has been recognized by Dr. Mason Rose, Director of the Pacific Institute for Advanced Studies, one of the first educational institutions in Los Angeles to break away from the standard university compartmentalization of knowledge and to teach the manufacture of soil humus and the breeding of bacteria.

Other groups, aware that man, having fouled his nest, must now clean it, have been experimenting with ecological farming techniques. A salient example is the New Alchemy Institute, which projects a host of activities, including backyard fish-farming, in climates as varied as those of the Canadian Maritime Provinces, New Mexico, California, and Costa Rica. The New Alchemists say their trio of goals are "To Restore the Lands, Protect the Seas, and Inform the Earth's Stewards." This is what the planet's vegetal covering on *terra firma* has been doing since long before the advent of man to his stewardship. In that sense, plants are the oldest alchemists.

CHAPTER 17

Alchemists in the Garden

The medieval alchemist, whose dream of transmuting one element into another was maliciously ridiculed for centuries, may now be vindicated —thanks to the efforts of living plants.

Early in this century a young Breton schoolboy who was preparing himself for a scientific career began to notice a strange fact about the hens in his father's poultry yard. As they scratched the soil they constantly seemed to be pecking at specks of mica, a siliceous material dotting the ground. No one could explain to Louis Kervran why the chickens selected the mica, or why each time a bird was killed for the family cooking pot no trace of the mica could be found in its gizzard, or why each day the flock produced eggs with calcareous shells though they apparently had not ingested any calcium from land which was entirely lacking in limestone. It took Kervran many years to establish that the chickens were transmuting one element into another.

Reading a novel by Gustave Flaubert called *Bouvard et Pécuchet*, young Kervran came across a reference to Louis Nicolas Vauquelin, a celebrated French chemist, who, "having calculated all the lime in oats fed to a hen, found still more in the shells of its eggs. Therefore, there is a creation of matter. In what way, no one knows."

It seemed to Kervran that, if the hen had somehow been able to manufacture calcium in its own body, everything he was taught in his chemistry class needed reviewing. Ever since the end of the eighteenth century, when Vauquelin's contemporary Antoine Laurent Lavoisier, known as the "father of modern chemistry," had laid down the principle that in the universe "nothing is lost, nothing is created, everything is transformed," it had been believed that elements could be shifted about in different combinations but could not be transmuted one to another; millions of experiments appeared to verify Lavoisier's contention.

The first crack in this seemingly unshatterable wall around the atom came at the start of the twentieth century with the discovery of radioactivity, which showed that some twenty elements could indeed change into something different, apparently no longer obeying the law of the conservation of matter. Radium, for instance, disintegrates into electricity, warmth, light, and various substances such as lead, helium and other elements. With the advent of nuclear physics, man was even able to create certain elements which had been missing on the famous chart drawn by the Russian peasant genius Dmitri Mendeleyev, because they were thought either to have vanished radioactively in former times or to have never existed in a natural state.

Ernest Rutherford, the British physicist who first theorized the existence of the atom's nucleus, showed in 1919 that one could transmute elements by bombarding them with alpha particles—identical to helium atoms less their electrons—a practice which has continued to the present time, with increasingly "heavier artillery." But even these breakthroughs did not shatter Lavoisier's dictum about the eighty or more nonradioactive elements. Chemists still hold that it is impossible to create another element by chemical reaction, and even maintain that all reactions occurring in living matter are solely chemical. In their view chemistry can and must explain life.

As a young graduate engineer and biologist, Kervran remembered Vauquelin's experiment and decided to repeat it. He fed a chicken on oats alone, the calcium content of which he had carefully measured. He then checked the calcium content in both the eggs and feces issuing from the chicken and found the bird had produced four times as much calcium as it had ingested. When Kervran asked his biochemist colleagues how the extra calcium originated, they replied it had come from the chicken's skeleton. This, Kervran realized, might do in an emergency, but if a chicken were required to make shells very long its skeleton would soon be reduced to pulp. In fact, a chicken deprived of calcium lays soft-shelled eggs within four or five days. However, if fed potassium, the chicken's next egg has a hard shell composed of calcium. The chicken is evidently capable of transmuting the element potassium—which is found in high concentrations in oats—into the element calcium.

Kervran also learned that about the time of Vauquelin's retirement, an Englishman, William Prout, made a systematic study of the variations in calcium in incubating chicken eggs and found that when chicks hatched they contained four times more lime than was originally present in the egg and that, furthermore, the lime content of the shell had not changed. He concluded that there had to be an endogenous formation of lime from within the egg. This was long before scientists knew anything about the atom, says Kervran, so it was too early to talk about atomistic transmutation.

One of Kervran's friends pointed out to him that as far back as 1600 a Flemish chemist, Jan Baptista Helmont, had planted a willow sapling in a clay pot containing two hundred pounds of oven-dried soils and for five years had given the tree nothing but rain or distilled water. When Helmont removed the tree and weighed it he found it had gained 164 pounds whereas the weight of the soil remained approximately the same. Helmont wondered if the plant had not been able to turn water into wood, bark, and roots.

Another vegetal anomaly which interested Kervran was that of *Tillandsia*, or Spanish moss, which can grow on copper wires without any contact with the soil. When burnt there was no copper residue in its ash, but iron oxides and other elements, all apparently supplied simply by the atmosphere.

Henri Spindler, another French scientist, became fascinated with how *Laminaria*, a variety of algae, seemed to be able to manufacture iodine. Searching for answers in half-forgotten literature on the dusty shelves of libraries, Spindler found that a German researcher by the name of Vogel had planted cress seeds in a container covered by a glass bell jar and fed them nothing but distilled water. A few months later when Vogel burned the adult plants, he found they contained twice the amount of sulfur which had been present in their seeds. Spindler also uncovered the fact that, soon after Vogel, two Britishers by the names of Lawes and Gilbert discovered at the famous Agricultural Research Institute at Rothamsted, England, that plants seemed to extract from the soil more elements than it contained.

For seventeen years the Rothamsted researchers cropped a clover field, mowing it two or three times a year, and sowing it only every fourth year, without adding any fertilizer at all. This piece of land gave cuttings so abundant that it was estimated that if one had to add what had been removed in the period between the arrival of one swarm of seventeen-year locusts and another, it would be necessary to dump on the field over 5,700 pounds of lime, 2,700 pounds of magnesia, 4,700 pounds of potash, 2,700 pounds of phosphoric acid, and 5,700 pounds of nitrogen, or more than ten tons of the products combined. Where had all these minerals come from?

Delving deeper into the mystery, Spindler came across the work of a Hanoverian baron, Albrecht von Herzeele, who, in 1873, brought out a revolutionary new book, *The Origin of Inorganic Substances*, which offered proof that, far from simply absorbing matter from the soil and the air, living plants are continuously creating matter. During his lifetime von Herzeele made hundreds of analyses indicating that, in seeds sprouting in distilled water, the original content of potash, phosphorus, magnesium, calcium, and sulfur quite inexplicably increased. Though the law of the conservation of matter held that exactly the same mineral content in plants grown in distilled water would be found as in the seeds from which they spring, von Herzeele's analyses proved also that not only mineral ash but every one of the plants' components increased, such as the nitrogen which burned off during incineration of the seeds.

Von Herzeele also discovered that plants seemed to be able to *transmute,* in alchemical fashion, phosphorus into sulfur, calcium into phosphorus, magnesium into calcium, carbonic acid into magnesium, and nitrogen into potassium.

One of the many odd facts in scientific history is that von Herzeele's writings, published between 1876 and 1883, were given the silent treatment by official academia, which was supporting the fashion that biological phenomena could be explained atomistically according to chemical laws. Indeed, most of Herzeele's works never found their way onto library shelves.

Spindler drew the attention of some of his colleagues to von Herzeele's experimentation. One of them was Pierre Baranger, a professor and director of the laboratory of organic chemistry at the famous Ecole Polytechnique in Paris, which, since its establishment in 1794, has trained the best scientific and engineering minds in France. To check von Herzeele's work, Baranger began a series of experiments which were to last the best part of a decade.

These experiments amply confirmed von Herzeele's work and indicated that atomic science might be faced with a veritable revolution.

When Baranger announced his discoveries to the scientific world in January, 1958, before a distinguished audience of chemists, biologists, physicists, and mathematicians at Switzerland's Institut Genevois, he noted that if his investigations were further developed a certain number of theories which did not seem to have the benefit of a sufficiently experimental basis might have to be modified.

This cautious approach dictated by scientific mores was made more explicit by Baranger in an interview for *Science et Vie* in 1959. "My results look impossible," said Baranger, "but there they are. I have taken every precaution. I have repeated the experiments many times. I have made thousands of analyses for years. I have had the results verified by third parties who did not know what I was about. I have used several methods. I changed my experimenters. But there's no way out; we have to submit to the evidence: plants know the old secret of the alchemists. *Every day under our very gaze they are transmuting elements.*"

By 1963 Baranger had incontestably proven that in the germinations of leguminous seeds in a manganese salt solution, manganese disappeared and iron appeared in its place. Trying to shed more light on the mechanisms involved, he discovered a whole web of complexities related to the transmutations of elements in seeds, including the time of their germination, the type of light involved, even the exact phase of the moon.

To understand the enormity of Baranger's work one has to realize that nuclear science asserts that in order to form the stability of elements such gigantic "energies of fixation" are needed that the alchemists, unable to produce and direct such energy, could never have transmuted one element into another as they claimed. Yet plants are constantly transmuting elements in a manner completely unknown to science without having to resort to enormous modern atom smashers. The tiniest blade of grass and the frailest crocus or petunia is able to achieve what modern-day alchemists known as nuclear physicists have heretofore found impossible.

In speaking of his new research, the quiet, courteous Baranger said: "I have been teaching chemistry at the Ecole Polytechnique for twenty years, and believe me, the laboratory which I direct is no den of false science. But I have never confused respect for science with the taboos imposed by intellectual conformism. For me, any meticulously performed experiment is a homage to science even if it shocks our ingrained habits. Von Herzeele's experiments were too few to be absolutely convincing. But their results inspired me to control them with all the precaution possible in a modern lab and to repeat them enough times so that they would be statistically irrefutable. That's what I've done."

Baranger established that seeds of Cerdagne vetch growing in distilled water showed no change in phosphorus or potassium content. But seeds growing in a calcium salt solution varied their phosphorus and potassium content by the enormous factor of 10 percent, and that calcium increased in both groups. "I understand perfectly well," Baranger told the science writers, who grilled him with every possible objection during the course of their interview, "that you are astonished by these results. For they are astonishing. I understand perfectly well that you are seeking the error which could make nonsense of these experiments. But so far no such error has been found. The phenomenon stands: plants can transmute elements."

As upsetting and contradictory as Baranger's experiments seemed, it was pointed out by *Science et Vie* that nuclear physics itself has reached a stage wherein its practitioners use four separate and quite contradictory theories about the atomic nucleus. Moreover, they add, the very secret of life has not yet been found, perhaps because no one has yet looked for it in the atomic nucleus. So far, they went on, life has been considered to be mainly a chemical and molecular phenomenon, but perhaps its roots are to be located in the most remote sub-basements and cellars of atomic physics.

The practical consequences of Baranger's findings cannot be overestimated. One of these is that certain plants can bring to the soil elements useful for the growth of other plants, which could lead to many changes in received doctrines about fallows, rotations, mixed crops, fertilizers, or, as Friend Sykes found out through actual trials on his Wiltshire land, the manuring of infertile soils. Moreover, as Baranger opines, nothing prevents us from thinking that certain plants are capable of producing rare elements of industrial importance. They appear to supply us with an example of subatomic transformation which we are not capable of performing in the laboratory without bringing into action particles of high energy in exactly the same way we are not capable of bringing about at ordinary temperatures the syntheses of innumerable products, either alkaloids or others, which are extracted from plants.

Kervran, a man with continuing ties to the land despite his urban academic duties, began to be fascinated by another phenomenon of a global nature which has long been known to agricultural specialists. He read in Didier Bertrand's *Magnesium and Life,* published in French in 1960, that each time wheat, maize, potatoes, or any other crop is harvested, elements in the earth used by plants in their growth process are taken out. Since virgin arable soil contains from 30 to 120 kilograms of magnesium per hectare, Bertrand stressed that most of the earth's arable land should long since have been exhausted of this element. Not only is this not the case, but in various parts of the world, such as Egypt, China, and the Po Valley in Italy, soils continue to remain highly fertile in spite of the enormous quantities of magnesium taken from them through harvests of crops over thousands of years. Is it because plant life is able to upset the periodic table of the elements, to make magnesium from calcium or carbon from nitrogen, for instance, that lands have been able to replace the products they need, wondered Kervran.

With the Celtic directness of a Breton, Kervran published his *Biological Transmutations* in 1962, the first of a series of books which offered a whole new perspective on living creatures. It made clear that those who believe in a system of farming which takes into account chemistry alone are in for a rude shock and that man and animals nourished on diets formulated by chemists will not long survive. Kervran freely accepted the notion that Lavoisier was right as far as chemical reactions were concerned. The mistake made by science, he said, is to contend that *all* reactions in living organisms are chemical in nature and that, consequently, life should be interpreted in chemical terms. Kervran suggests that the biological properties of a substance are only inadequately determined by chemical analysis.

Kervran wrote that one of the main purposes of his book was "to show that matter has a property heretofore unseen, a property which is neither in chemistry nor in nuclear physics in its present state. In other words the laws of chemistry are not on trial here. The error of numerous chemists and biochemists lies in their desire to apply the laws of chemistry at any cost, with unverified assertions in a field where chemistry is not always applicable. In the final phase the results might be chemistry, but only as a consequence of the unperceived phenomenon of transmutation."

Rudolf Hauschka in his brilliant book *The Nature of Substance* carries Kervran and Heerzele's ideas even further, saying that life cannot possibly be interpreted in chemical terms because life is not the result of the combination of elements but something which precedes the elements. Matter, says Hauschka, is the precipitate of life. "Is it not more reasonable," he asks, "to suppose that life existed long before matter and was the product of a pre-existent spiritual cosmos?"

Supporter of Rudolf Steiner's "spiritual science," Hauschka is lapidary in his approach when he states that the elements as we know them are already corpses, the residue of life forms. Though chemists can derive oxygen, hydrogen and carbon from a plant, they cannot derive a plant from any combination of these or other elements. "What lives," says Hauschka, "may die; but nothing is created dead."

Hauschka, who also duplicated many of Heerzele's experiments, found that plants could not only generate matter out of a nonmaterial sphere, but could "etherealize" it once more, noting an emergence and disappearance of matter in rhythmic sequence, often in conjunction with phases of the moon.

In Paris, Kervran, a pleasant and forthrightly cooperative man of seventy with a prodigious memory for detail, told the authors that powerful energies are at work in the germination process of seeds which synthesize enzymes, probably by transmuting matter within them. His experiments have also convinced him that lunar forces are extremely important in germination, though botanists have long asserted that only warmth and water are required.

"We cannot deny the existence of something just because we don't know about it," said Kervran. "The kind of energies to which the great Austrian natural scientist and clairvoyant Rudolf Steiner refers as cosmic etheric forces must exist if only from the fact that certain plants will only germinate in springtime no matter what amounts of heat and water are administered to them during other parts of the year. There are varieties of wheat said to germinate only as the days lengthen, but, when days are artificially lengthened, the wheat does not always germinate."

We do not know what *matter* really is, says Kervran. We do not know what a proton or an electron is *made of*, and the words serve only to cloak our ignorance. He suggests that inside atomic nuclei may lie forces and energies of a totally unexpected nature and that a physical theory to explain the low energy transmutations with which he deals must be sought, not in the hypotheses of classical nuclear physics based on powerful interactions, but in the field of hyperweak interactions in which there is no assurance of the operation of the established laws of conservation of energy or even the existence of a mass/energy equivalent.

Physicists, says Kervran, are mistaken in claiming that physical laws are the same for the living as for inanimate matter. Many physicists declare, for instance, that a negative entropy, a force which in biology would build up matter, is an impossibility, since the second principle of thermodynamics of Carnot-Clausius, regarding the breakdown of energy, states that there is only positive entropy, i.e., that the natural state of matter is chaos and that all things run down and become random, losing heat and not acquiring it.

In contradiction to the physicists, Wilhelm Reich held that the accumulators he built to collect an energy, which he named "orgone," permanently raised the temperature inside their tops, thus making nonsense of the second law of thermodynamics. Despite the fact that he demonstrated the phenomenon to Albert Einstein in his house in Princeton, and that Einstein confirmed the phenomenon, though he could not account for it, Reich was considered mad.

Reich maintained that matter is created from orgone energy, that under appropriate conditions matter arises from mass-free orgone, and that these conditions are neither rare nor unusual. All of this further suggests that in living nature there exists, below the level of Lavoisier's classical molecular chemistry, a deeper level of nuclear chemistry which associates and dissociates nucleons, the components of atomic nuclei. In molecular combinations heat energy is produced. At the nuclear level a much more powerful energy, that of fission or fusion as in A or H bombs, must be added. What remains unexplained is why these fantastic energies are not released in biological transmutations.

Science et Vie has postulated that if plasma-type nuclear reactions take place in bombs, in nuclear reactors and in stars, then there must be a wholly different type of reaction, specifically utilized by life, which brings about fusion in a strangely quiet way. The magazine suggests the analogy of a strongbox which can be opened by dynamite or by a combination lock. Like the lock, the atomic nucleus can prove stubborn when confronted with blind violence but pliable to skillful manipulation. The secret of life, so long suspected by vitalists, is as much a secret as the locksmith's combination. The cleavage between the animate and the inanimate is to be found at the level of manipulation of the nuclear lock. It appears that, whereas man has to use dynamite, plants and other living organisms know the combination.

Kervran also wonders whether microorganisms can even take sand and make it fecund. After all, he maintains, humus comes today from organic matter but at one time there was no organic matter on earth.

This raises the question of whether Dr. Wilhelm Reich was not on the track of the discovery of the century when he purported that he had observed at the microscope energetic vesicles or "bions" which are not alive but "carry biological energy." Exposed to sufficiently high temperatures and made to swell, all matter, even sand, undergoes vesicular disintegration, wrote Reich, and the resulting vesicles can later develop into bacteria.

Kervran, who has now retired from his duties as one of France's more eminent professors in order to embark on the career of a determined alchemist, asks why chemically pure reactions such as the combination of one atom of nitrogen and one atom of oxygen can be realized in a test tube only at extremely high temperatures and pressures whereas living organisms can perform the same feat at room temperature. He feels that the biological catalysts known as enzymes are in some way responsible.

In a yearbook entitled *Alchemy: Dream or Reality?* published in 1973 in Rouen by the students of the prestigious Institut Nationale Superieur de Chimie Industrielle, Kervran writes that microorganisms are a concentration of enzymes. Their ability to transmute elements is not a mere hooking of peripheral electrons to form bonds as in classical chemistry but involves a fundamental alteration of the nucleus of elements.

Most transmutations have been observed to take place within the first twenty elements of the periodic table. They further always seem to involve hydrogen or oxygen. Thus the transmutation of potassium to calcium is accomplished through the addition of a hydrogen proton.

Kervran expects the phenomena he describes, and the data he supplies, to irritate chemists because it involves, not the displacement of electrons in the peripheral atomic layers and the chemical bonding in molecules which lie at the heart of their discipline, but the alteration in structural arrangements of atoms induced by enzyme activities in living matter. Since this takes place within atomic nuclei, a new science distinct from chemistry is involved. Though strange at first sight, the new language is so simple that the average high school student can easily follow it. Thus, if one has sodium with eleven protons written $_{11}Na$ and oxygen with eight protons written $_8O$ one need only add the protons together to get nineteen, the number which exists in potassium written $_{19}K$.

Following this reasoning, calcium (Ca) can come from potassium (K) with the interaction of hydrogen (H) according to the formula $_1H$ plus $_{19}K$ equals $_{20}Ca$, or from magnesium with the interaction of oxygen in $_{12}Mg$ plus $_8O$ equals $_{20}Ca$, or from silicon with the interaction of carbon in $_{14}Si$ plus $_6C$ equals $_{20}Ca$.

Since nature's atom smashing, according to Kervran, is performed by biotic life, microorganisms are thus nature's prime mover in maintaining balance in soils.

In Kervran's view some transmutations are biologically beneficial, others dangerous. Since the harmful ones can be countered, the whole problem of deficiencies in the soil remains to be reassessed. Indiscriminate application of NPK fertilizers to the land can alter the content in plants of just those elements necessary to healthful nutrition. In this connection, Kervran cites the work of an American researcher, who, knowing nothing of Kervran's theory of biological transmutations, found that in hybrid corn too rich in potassium the content of molybdenum decreases. "What *are* the optimal quantities of these two elements in plants?" asks Kervran, then continues: "This does not appear to have been studied, and there is not only one answer, since values differ not only between species but between varieties of the same species."

Even if potassium fertilizers were no longer available to agriculturalists, Kervran says, this would represent no catastrophe since microorganisms could produce potassium from calcium. If yeasts and molds for penicillin are already being produced on an industrial scale, why not factories for growing microorganisms for the transmutation of elements? Already in the late 1960s Dr. Howard Worne started Enzymes, Inc., at

Cherry Hill, New Jersey, where microorganisms bombarded with strontium 90 were being mutated so as to produce enzymes that would transmute waste carbon into usable carbon simply by having microorganisms ingest one material and excrete a new one. Dr. Worne is now in New Mexico using microorganisms to transform solid waste from garbage and stockyards into humus for the compost-hungry Western states and methane gas for the energy-hungry Eastern states.

The understanding of the phenomena of biological transmutation, though as yet unrecognized by the majority of the world's agriculturalists, seems to have been anticipated by the advocates of biological cultivation, who, above all, realized that a price must be paid for *reliance on chemistry in a biological context.* Cultivation based on classical chemistry alone, stresses Kervran, fails wherever intensive and abusive methods are employed. The marked crop increases, such as those for the Illinois corn, can thus last only a certain time.

Though not applied as abusively as in America, where huge areas have been lost to cultivation because of a surfeit, even the more limited European use of artificial fertilizers has led, says Kervran, to a mounting lack of resistance in plants to pests. The increase of infestation is no more than a consequence of biological imbalance.

"Classical soil scientists and agronomists attached to the dogma that biology equals chemistry," writes Kervran, "cannot conceive that all that is in plants has not been put into the soil. They are not the people to advise farmers; farmers should be guided by the enlightened and intelligent agriculturalists who have long recognized the division between a purely chemical and biological agriculture. They might then achieve their own conversion, and carry out some of the experiments described in this book for themselves. If they are men of good faith, they will admit their past errors, but one doesn't ask that much—only that they act."

Pointing out that the great English astromomical physicist Fred Hoyle gave up the theory of the steady state universe which he utilized for nearly a quarter of a century and which made him famous, Kervran notes that Hoyle himself has recognized that if future observations confirm that physics has taken a wrong direction then "the properties of matter, the laws of chemistry, for example, would be completely changed."

It is in bulletins such as that of the British Soil Association that Kervran sees articles confirming his ideas of biological transmutation in the soil. In the French analog of this bulletin, *Nature et Progrès,* one researcher reports that, after analyzing month by month for one year the phosphorus content of identical soils, one benefited by fermented compost containing no phosphorus and the other by phosphorus-rich farmyard manure, the first sample had 314 milligrams of phosphorus at the year's end as against only 205 milligrams for the second. The researcher concluded: "Therefore the soil containing the greater amount of phosphorus was the one without any external supply of this mineral. A miracle of the living soil."

If Dr. Barry Commoner sees the buyers of artificial fertilizer becoming "hooked" on their product, Kervran says the same thing for plants. Offering them chemicals, he writes, is simply drugging them to achieve higher yields—for a time. He compares this process to stimulating human appetites with an *apéritif* and then not following it up with a meal.

Louis-Victor de Broglie, winner of the Nobel Prize for his prediction of the wave properties of the electron, has said: "It is premature to want to assess vital processes according to the very insufficient physio-chemical concepts of the nineteenth or even the twentieth centuries." Kervran, who puts this quotation at the start of the British edition of his book, adds: "Who is to say in which present-day branch of physics 'mental energy,' the strength of will or character, should be placed? One can associate memory with information and negative entropy with cybernetics (or should it be chemistry?) but nothing tells us if intelligence itself will not someday be expressed by a physical or chemical law."

Jean Lombard, a geologist, in a preface to Kervran's second book, *Natural Transmutations,* published in 1963, stated that Kervran had opened up a wide field, which in itself could lead to clarification of confusions in geological theory. Lombard also wrote: "The true workers of science, who are always ready to welcome new suggestions, sometimes ask themselves if the greatest obstacle to the progress of science is not bad memory on the part of scholars; they wish to remind the latter that some of their predecessors were burnt at the stake because of proposed 'interpretations' which have now become foremost truths. If pioneers of science were still being burnt, I would not give much for Louis Kervran's skin."

Reviewing Kervran's third book, *Low Energy Transmutations*, published in 1964, Professor René Furon, of the Faculty of Sciences at Paris University, wrote: "This book completes the two previous ones. It can no longer be denied that nature makes magnesium out of calcium (in some cases the reverse takes place); that potassium can come from sodium; and that carbon monoxide poisoning can occur without inhalation of CO gas."

It appears that outside France, not Western, but Japanese scientists have been the first to take Kervran's work seriously. When Hisatoki Komaki, a professor of science, read a Japanese translation of Kervran's book *Biological Transmutations*, he tied Kervran's findings into ancient Eastern cosmology and wrote to Kervran to say that the transmutation of sodium, a *yang* element, into potassium, a *yin* element, was of far-reaching interest, more especially since Japan has a paucity of potash deposits but ample supplies of sea salt.

Komaki abandoned his teaching to become head of a biological research laboratory at the Matsushita Electric Company and informed Kervran that he would try to confirm the sodium-to-potassium reaction and interest his collaborators in applying it on an industrial scale. Komaki's research proved to him that various microorganisms, including certain bacteria and two species each of molds and yeasts, were capable of transmuting sodium into potassium and that the yield of bacteria themselves was enormously raised when only a small amount of potassium was added to the cultures. Komaki has placed on the market a product made of brewer's yeast which, applied to composts, raises the potassium content in them. How this process relates to the action of Biodynamic sprays as conceived by Rudolf Steiner and developed by Ehrenfried Pfeiffer remains to be determined.

Kervran's work is also attracting important notice in the Soviet Union. Professor A. P. Dubrov of the Institute of Earth Physics of the USSR Academy of Sciences, who has been working on the links between radiosensitivity in animals and the geomagnetic field, wrote to Kervran at the end of 1971 to suggest that the magnetic field of the earth itself might well play an important role in biological transmutation, and that elements might be affected depending on whether biological forms are oriented north-south.

In 1971, a Russian book, *Problems of Transmutations in Nature*, was published in a limited edition in Yerevan, capital of the Armenian Republic. Its editor, V. B. Neiman, notes in a lead article, "Transmutations in Nature: The Present Status of the Problem and Objects for Further Study," that the fundamental problems of entropy and negentropy must be re-examined, and maintains that the diversity of elements on earth is due to a series of nuclear transmutations with analogous processes applied to biological phenomena.

Neiman dug out the most extraordinary quotation from Lenin's *Materialism and Empirocriticism*, proving that the father of the Soviet Union tried to incorporate in his materialistic philosophy a notion more palatable to vitalists and mystics than to hard-core Communist pragmatists. "However miraculous, from the viewpoint of common sense," wrote Lenin, "the conversion of imponderable ether to ponderable matter may seem, it is but a further confirmation of dialectic materialism."

In the same collection, P. A. Korol'kov contributed an essay on the "Spontaneous Metamorphism of Minerals and Rocks," in which he shows how silicon can be converted to aluminum. In his summary of a conference held in July, 1972, devoted to chrome deposition in the Urals, Siberia, Kazakhstan, and the Soviet Far East, Korol'kov comes to the conclusion that the traditional geological views on the genesis of chromite and associated ores do not accord with new data presented at the conference.

"The fact is," writes Korol'kov, "that we are witnesses and participants in a scientific-technological revolution, that is, we are living in a time in which we are being subjected to a radical revision, not of minutiae, but of the basic status of an inherited natural science. The time has come to recognize that any chemical element can turn into another, under natural conditions. And I am not alone in maintaining this. I know a dozen persons in the USSR who hold the same views."

If Soviet scientists are coming around to a whole new view of matter

—and even citing Lenin on the possibility of its manufacture by the ether itself—it would seem that the ecological revolution so necessary to safeguard the future of humanity, and pleaded for in the United States since Fairfield Osborn wrote *Our Plundered Planet* shortly after World War II, may have a chance of taking place despite the host of adversaries who see in it the demise of their personal fortunes.

In a review of the American edition of Kervran's book for the International College of Applied Nutrition, V. Michael Walczak, M.D., an internist practicing in Studio City, California, said of Kervran's work: "It offers a totally different approach to our understanding of nutritional supplementation of the elements and how it functions in the physiologic and biochemical pathways of our bodies. It attempts to prove that our concepts of simple supplementation for deficiencies is not only questionable, but in serious error."

Though many nutritionists untrained even in simple chemistry are giving people huge and unnecessary doses of calcium because it is the mineral in largest quantity in the body, Walczak, who is now limiting his practice to internal metabolism and nutrition, states that his own research shows that 80 percent of his patients—with diets supplemented or unsupplemented—have *too much* calcium and too few trace minerals with respect to calcium. The lack of trace elements in soils, and in foods, Walczak maintains, leads to an imbalance in enzyme function.

Walczak says he is preventing disease by administering the right amounts of enzymes, hormones, vitamins, and minerals, which together he calls "the key to life," and also curing a host of degenerative diseases. He concludes that the "gold" which the medieval alchemists tried for centuries to derive from lead may very well turn out to be the secret for obtaining good health and long life.

Walczak's views are supported by Richard Barmakian, a nutritionist in nearby Pasadena, who wrote to Kervran's American publishers that the U.S. version of *Biological Transmutations* should prove to be "the most significant work of this century, scientifically and possibly otherwise." It was only after he had read the book that Barmakian thought he might at last get to the core of the problem of calcium-metabolism abnormalities and deficiencies which he says are "so tragically prevalent in pseudo-civilized countries of the world today and especially in the U.S.A."

This view was echoed by *Organic Gardening and Farming*, now published by J. I. Rodale's son, Robert, which stated that Kervran had showed that current chemical treatment of the soil is totally wrong and is rapidly destroying the quality of the soil worldwide: "We're sure that as our understanding of the life processes involved in organic farming grows, the scientific community will be in for many surprises." The economist Charles Walters, Jr., publisher of *Acres USA*, also concurs: "Louis Kervran has opened a door. His works have received important recognition from Russians, Japanese, French and Chinese who don't have to ask the United States Department of Agriculture and the petrochemical firms what to think, as is the case with too many extension agents, land grant colleges and farmers under the thumb of bank examiners."

If doctors, nutritionists, editors, and economists in the United States are now beginning to see in Kervran the herald of a new age, as are professional scientists abroad, it may be that a revolution is at hand. Perhaps the time is near when the dictators of nutritional and agricultural policies, who have forced upon all natural life, from the smallest microorganisms to human beings, a drenching of chemicals to the point where the only recourse against adulterated food products is the growing of one's own private garden under natural conditions, will have to listen to the prophets who have warned against the chemification of the soil since the beginning of this century.

In an age in which science itself has become so specialized and the science of life, or biology, so molecular that our technological society seems to be producing a crowd of white-coated "idiot savants" who plead lack of competency in all but their own narrow divisions of knowledge, the broad outlooks of Goethe, Pfeiffer, Howard, Commoner and Voisin and the new discoveries by Louis Kervran may be the one antidote to catastrophe.

PART V

THE RADIANCE OF LIFE

CHAPTER 18

Dowsing Plants for Health

On the brighter side of life, a French engineer, André Simoneton, has found a straw which may keep the population of the planet from going under; his device, usable by man, woman, or child, is designed to make it possible to select healthy food from bad before ingesting it: it is a simple pendulum attached to a short piece of string used by diviners of water, lost objects, or the future.

For millennia the art or science of dowsing with forked stick or pendulum has been practiced by Chinese, Hindus, Egyptians, Persians, Medes, Etruscans, Greeks, and Romans. In the Renaissance it was revived by such notables as Goethe's predecessor as Director of Mines in Saxony, Christopher von Schenberg, who had his portrait painted holding a dowsing rod, a custom emulated in modern time by Lloyd George, who had himself photographed in the same pose.

Though dowsing has not yet been accepted as a science in America, in France it is no longer relegated to the domain of the witch and warlock—despite the fact that over the centuries many a French dowser has paid with his life for practicing "sorcery." Among the more celebrated victims were Jean du Chatelet, Baron de Beausoleil, and his dowser wife Marine de Bertereau, who, working under the protection of Maréchal d'Effiat, Louis XIV's superintendent of mines, discovered several hundred profitable mines in France only to be arrested for sorcery and succumb in prison, she in Vincennes, he in the Bastille. The persecution has continued in France mostly against doctors who find themselves dragged before tribunals for perpetrating dowsing cures on patients officially declared uncurable.

That dowsing is no longer considered anathema by the Church is thanks largely to the efforts of a long series of French abbés such as Mermet, Bouly, Vallemont, Richard, Carrie, Descosse, and Ferran, and the recent intercession in Rome of such an eminent churchman as Cardinal Tisserant.

In the scientific community the art is now on the fringe of recognition thanks to professors such as Yves Rocard of the Collège de France, head of the physics department of the prestigious Ecole Normale Supérieure, who is recognized not only as a brilliant physicist but as an admirable dowser. His book on the science of dowsing, *Le Signal du Sourcier*, as yet unpublished in English, has been translated in the Soviet Union where geologists have recently been dowsing for minerals from airplanes and helicopters, and also locating underground archeological artifacts.

The Mecca for dowsers in Europe is located in a small Parisian side street, now lost between the luxury of the Faubourg Saint Honoré and the tourist-ridden arcades of the rue de Rivoli, appropriately named for Saint Roch, canonized for protecting the populace against various pestilences. The actual Kaaba is an old curiosity shop called the Maison de Radiesthesie, *"radiesthesie"* being generic for dowsing and for the search for radiations beyond the electromagnetic spectrum, an appellative given to the art by the Abbé Bouly, who coined it from the Greek for "sensitivity" and the Latin for "radiance."

On the shelves of this now venerable institution, run for the last half century by Alfred Lambert and his wife, are scores of books on dowsing —dowsing for water, for objects, and for health. In addition to those written by Catholic clergymen, there are others by aristocrats such as Count Henry de France and Count André de Belizal and by several distinguished French physicians.

There are also brass and mahogany showcases protecting various exotic machines, some simple, some sophisticated, designed to tune in, amplify or shield radiations, healthy or toxic. The machines are used mostly by doctors from all over the world for diagnostic and curative purposes, though the fundamental instrument in each case is the simple pendulum. These lie in stacked drawers on velvet cushions designed in many shapes and sizes from various materials, including ivory, jade, and octagonal quartz or crystal, though any weight on any string or chain is said to be effective.

In the United States, Dr. Zaboj V. Harvalik, a professional physicist recently retired from his post as scientific adviser to the U.S. Army's Advanced Material Concepts Agency to devote himself to private research, has turned his attention to the dowsing phenomenon and to how physical theory might help to explain it. As chief of the research committee of the American Society of Dowsers, Harvalik is helping to break down fifty years of prejudice in official circles against dowsing as a "quack art."

At his home on the banks of the Potomac River in Lorton, Virginia, Harvalik has made meticulous tests to reveal for the first time that dowsers react with varying degrees of sensitivity to polarized electromagnetic radiation, artificial alternating magnetic fields in a frequency range from one to one million cycles per second and to DC magnetic fields. Harvalik is convinced that dowsers pick up magnetic field gradients whether they are trying to find water, underground pipes, wires, tunnels, or geological anomalies.

Dowsing, however, appears to extend far beyond the detection of flowing water or the magnetic field gradients thought to be associated with water currents. In its broadest definition it is simply *searching*—for anything. The former president of the American Society of Dowsers, John Shelley, before his premature death in 1972, amazed his fellow naval reserve officers when at the end of a training session at the Pensacola, Florida, Naval Air Station he was able, by using only a small dowsing rod, to locate his government salary check, which his colleagues had conspired with the help of the paymaster to hide somewhere in a huge two-story naval building with dozens of rooms branching out of its corridors.

Gordon MacLean, a research chemist for Pine State By-Products in Portland, Maine, who still works full time despite his eighty-odd years, will take any visitor out to the Coast Guard lighthouse at Portland Head and with his "divining" rod accurately predict when the next oil tanker on its way into Portland harbor will appear on the horizon and where.

Perhaps the most celebrated American dowser is Henry Gross, also of Maine, to whose feats Kenneth Roberts, the American historical novelist, devoted three books in the 1950s. Like the French abbots, Gross is an expert at dowsing from maps. Sitting at his kitchen table, he pinpointed on a map of the British-governed island of Bermuda, on which no source of water had been found, just those spots where he said drilling would produce it. To everyone's amazement, Gross was correct.

To physicists like Harvalik the forces at work in *map* dowsing, which do not appear to be related to the magnetic gradients operative in *field* dowsing, are totally inscrutable. Obviously a dowser is contacting some source of information which can provide accurate data on areas—or parts of space—far removed from his own physical location. Rexford Daniels, whose Interference Consultants Company of Concord, Massachusetts, has been pioneering the study for twenty-five years of how proliferating electromagnetic emissions interfere with one another and may work harmful environmental effects on man, states that he has become convinced that some overall force exists in the universe which is itself intelligent and provides answers. Daniels theorizes that this force operates through a whole spectrum of frequencies not necessarily linked to the electromagnetic spectrum and that human beings can mentally interact with it. To Daniels dowsing is simply an as yet imperfectly defined though exceedingly useful communications system. In his eyes an important task confronting man now is to check out the system in all of its aspects.

The specific technique of dowsing food for freshness and vitality was learned by engineer Simoneton, now also in his eighties—though he looks like a successful French businessman in his sixties—from another extraordinary Frenchman, André Bovis, a fragile tinker who died in his native Nice during the Second World War. Bovis is most widely known for his experiments with pyramids built to the dimensions of the Great Pyramid of Cheops, which he found would mysteriously dehydrate and mummify dead animals without decomposing them, especially if they were placed in a pyramid at the relative height of the King's Chamber, or one third of the way from the base to the summit.

Basic to Bovis' theory is that the earth has positive magnetic currents running north to south, negative magnetic currents running east to west. He says that these currents are picked up by all bodies on the surface of the earth, and that *any* body placed in a north-south position will be more or less polarized, depending on its shape and consistency. In human bodies these telluric currents, both positive and negative, enter through one leg and go out through the opposite hand. At the same time cosmic currents from beyond the earth enter through the head and go out through the other hand and foot. The currents also go out through the open eyes.

All bodies containing water, says Bovis, accumulate these currents and can radiate them slowly. As the currents go out and act and react against other magnetic forces in objects, they affect the pendulum held by the dowser. Thus the human body, as a variable condenser, acts as a detector, selector and amplifier of short and ultra-short waves; it is a go-between for the animal electricity of Galvani and the inanimate electricity of Volta.

At the same time the pendulum, says Bovis, acts as a perfect lie detector in that if a person is frankly saying what he thinks about some subject, it will not affect the radiations and thus not affect the pendulum; but anyone saying something different from what he is thinking changes the wavelengths, making them shorter and negative.

Bovis developed a pendulum from a similar device which he says was used by the ancient Egyptians, made from crystal with a fixed metal point suspended on a double strand of red and violet silk. He called it "paradiamagnétique" because it is sensitive to objects which are either attracted or repelled by a magnet. Bodies which are attracted, such as iron, cobalt, nickel, magnesium, chrome, or titanium, he called paramagnetic; those which are repelled, such as copper, zinc, tin, lead, sulfur and bismuth, he called diamagnetic. By placing a small magnetic field in the form of a solenoid between the dowser and the pendulum he claimed to be able to pick up very faint currents such as those emanating from a nonfecundated egg. He explained the use of red and violet strands as increasing the sensitivity of his pendulum on the grounds that red light vibrations are the same as the atomic vibrations of iron, which are paramagnetic, and those of violet being the same as copper, which are diamagnetic.

Bovis found that with his pendulum he could tell the intrinsic vitality and relative freshness of different foods within their protective skins because of the power of their radiations. To measure with his pendulum the varying radiant frequencies produced by foods Bovis developed a *biomètre*, or simple ruler arbitrarily graduated in centimeters to indicate microns, which are thousandths of a millimeter, and angstroms, which are a hundred times smaller, covering a band between zero and ten thousand angstroms.

By placing a piece of fruit or vegetable, or any kind of food, at one end of the ruler, Bovis could watch his swinging pendulum change directions at a certain distance along the ruler, which gave him an indication of the degree of the food's vitality. According to Bovis the limit of any object's radiance is overcome at some point by the general telluric field surrounding it, and can thus be measured. Dowsers maintain that any two objects of the same material and size placed a yard or so apart will create two fields which will repel each other at a halfway mark easily noted with a pendulum. Increasing the size of one of the objects will cause its field to move closer to the smaller object.

Simoneton found that food which radiates 8,000 to 10,000 angstroms on Bovis' biomètre would also cause a pendulum to turn at the remarkable speed of 400 to 500 revolutions per minute in a radius of 80 millimeters. Foods which radiate between 6,000 and 8,000 spun it at a rate of 300 to 400, with a radius of 60 millimeters. Meats, pasteurized milk, and overcooked vegetables, which radiate less than 2,000 angstroms, have not sufficient energy to make the pendulum spin.

For those who might complain about the arbitrary selection of angstroms for measuring the relative radiant vitality of objects, Louis Kervran, in a preface to Simoneton's book, *Radiations des Aliments,* points out that the angstrom is no more arbitrary than the calorie used in nutrition—a calorie being the quantity of heat required to raise the temperature of one gram of water one degree centigrade. All systems of measurement, says Kervran, are conventional; Bovis' angstrom merely made it easy to distinguish between the radiant value of fermented cheese, which reads at 1,500, and that of fresh olive oil, which reads at 8,500. In any case, Kervran adds, the wavelengths emitted by fruits and vegetables and other biochemical foodstuffs which are picked up with the pendulum are of totally unknown nature, apparently outside the electromagnetic spectrum. It is simply the fact that they are measurable by dowsing methods which remains of great practical value.

According to Bovis, wavelengths broadcast by an object are picked up by the nerves in a human arm and then amplified by means of a pendulum swinging at the end of a string. Impressive proof of this has been established in Montreal by Jan Merta, whose laboratory experiments clearly indicate that a minute muscular movement occurs in the area of the wrist a fraction of a second after a change in the encephalograph has been registered. Merta has also designed a dowsing device, which can be placed not only in the hands but on the arms, shoulders, head, legs, or feet, or any other part of the body where it can be balanced.

In line with Bovis and Lakhovsky, Simoneton reasoned that if human nerve cells can receive wavelengths they must also be transmitters: senders and receivers must be able to enter into resonant vibration with each other in order to pick up a transmission. Lakhovsky likened the system to two well-tuned pianos: when a note is struck on one it will cause the same note to vibrate on the other.

Some dowsers say that the prime sensor in the human body may be located in the area of the solar plexus. This appears to be borne out by Harvalik's most recent research. To shield parts of the human body from the effects of the ocean of magnetic forces surrounding it, Harvalik took an eight-foot-by-ten-inch strip of highly effective magnetic shielding (made from a Co-Netic AA Perfection Annealed sheet 0.025 inches thick, produced by the Magnetic Shield Division of the Perfection Mica Company) and rolled it into a two-layered cylinder which could be lowered around the body to shield head, shoulders, torso, or pelvic area.

With the shield covering his head, Harvalik walked blindfolded across a level area known to produce dowsing signals and obtained a strong reaction over each of three dowsing zones. The same reactions were obtained with his head exposed but his shoulders shielded. Gradually lowering the shield, Harvalik found that he could pick up dowsing signals until he reached an area between the 7th and 12th rib, that is to say from sternum to navel.

"These measurements," says Harvalik, "suggest that dowsing sensors must be located in the region of the solar plexus and that perhaps there are additional sensors in the head or brain."

Dr. J. A. Kopp of Ebikon, Switzerland, who for years has been working with dowsing techniques to locate geopathogenic zones that seem to be related to high incidences of cancer, reported in 1972 that a German engineer, in an experiment analogous to those of Harvalik, had himself carried horizontally on a stretcher over a dowsing zone. As his head passed the dowsing zone, the rod was undisturbed; when his solar plexus was above the same zone, the dowsing rod immediately reacted.

Using a pendulum to establish the relative radiance of different foods was a technique developed by Simoneton as a matter of life or death. During the First World War he underwent five operations. One dark night lying on a stretcher by a hospital train he overheard two medics whispering in the shadows cast by a kerosene lantern that he was so severely tubercular there was no chance of his recovery. A forced diet of rich food ruined his liver and gave him other unpleasant side effects. Barely surviving the ministrations of the medics, Simoneton discovered Bovis' system of selecting fresh and vital foods from poisonous fare. In a short time he rid himself not only of the TB but of its side effects and became so healthy that years later, at sixty-six and sixty-eight he still fathered children, and at seventy was still playing tennis.

As a young engineer Simoneton had been drafted into the French army to work on the new science of radio, which, says Simoneton, was in those days at about the level that dowsing is today. During World War I Simoneton worked alongside such electrical luminaries as physicist Louis de Broglie, who was to establish that every particle, down to a photon of light, is associated with a specific wavelength.

With this background Simoneton had enough electrical engineering and radio knowledge not to dismiss Bovis as a quack, and was able to establish empirically that with Bovis' system he could measure specific wavelengths from foods that indicated both vitality and freshness. Milk, which he measured at 6.5 thousand angstroms when fresh, lost 40 percent of its radiation by the end of twelve hours and 90 percent by the end of twenty-four. As for pasteurization, Simoneton found that it killed the wavelengths dead. The same he found true of pasteurized fruit and vegetable juices. Garlic juice, when pasteurized, coagulated like dead human blood and its vibrations dropped from around eight thousand angstroms to zero.

On the other hand freezing fresh fruit and vegetables has the effect of prolonging their life; on defrosting they resume their radiance at almost the same level as when they were iced. Food placed in a refrigerator will deteriorate, but at a much slower pace. Unripe fruits and vegetables in a refrigerator may actually increase in radiance as they slowly mature.

Dehydrated fruit was found by experiment to retain its vitality; if soaked in "vitalized" water for twenty-four hours, even several months after drying, it would reradiate almost as strongly as when freshly picked. Canned fruits remained perfectly dead. Water turned out to be a very strange medium: normally unradiant, it was capable of being "vitalized" by association with minerals, human beings, or plants. Some waters, such as those at Lourdes, Bovis found, in 1926, to radiate as high as 156,000 angstroms. Eight years later some of the same water still registered 78,000 angstroms. The Czech-born psychic Jan Merta holds that the rind from apples, pears, and other fruits and vegetables, when left to soak in a glass of water overnight, releases healthful vibrations into the water which can then be drunk to provide better nourishment than the rind itself, which has little or no effect on Simoneton's pendulum.

To simplify life for readers of his book, Simoneton divided foods into four general classes. In the first he placed those foods whose radiant wavelength he found higher than the basic human wavelength of 6,500 angstroms, going up to 10,000 or higher. These include most fruits, which run between 8,000 and 10,000 at the peak of their maturity, and vegetables if eaten fresh from the garden. Simoneton noted that by the time most vegetables get to the market in town they have lost one-third of their potency; by the time they have been subjected to cooking, they have lost another third.

Simoneton says fruits are filled with solar radiation in the healthful light spectrum between the bands of infrared and ultraviolet, and that their radiance rises slowly to a peak while ripening, then gradually decreases to zero at putrefaction. The banana, which is healthily edible for about eight days out of a span of twenty-four between the time it is picked and when it starts to rot, gives off optimum vibrations when it is yellow, not so good when green, and very low when black.

Anyone who has lived in pineapple-growing areas of the world such as the Hawaiian islands knows that a pineapple picked and eaten at the precise time of its ripening—a period lasting no longer than a few hours —has a delicious taste which amazes people who have only eaten store-bought fruit picked long before they come to maturity.

Vegetables are most radiant if eaten raw, two raw carrots being better than a plateful of cooked ones. The potato, which has a radiance of only 2,000 angstroms when raw (perhaps because it grows underground hidden from the sun), mysteriously rises to 7,000 angstroms when boiled and all the way to a very healthy 9,000 when baked. The same applies to other tubers.

Legumes, such as peas, beans, lentils, or chickpeas, rate 7,000 to 8,000 when fresh. Dried they lose most of their radiance. They become heavy, indigestible, and hard on the liver, says Simoneton. To benefit from legumes they too should be eaten raw and freshly picked. Optimum results, says Simoneton, come from their juices, especially if drunk at 10 A.M. and 5 P.M. when they are easily digested and do not tire the system but nourish it.

On Simoneton's scale wheat has a radiance of 8,500 angstroms; when cooked this rises to 9,000. He says wheat can and should be eaten in a variety of ways rather than simply in bread. Whole-wheat flour should be mixed into pies, tarts, and other pastries with butter, eggs, milk, fruits, and vegetables. Baked in a wood-burning oven, bread gives off even better radiations than if cooked with coal or gas.

Olive oil was found by Simoneton to have a high radiance of 8,500, and to be extremely long-lasting. Six years after pressing it still gives off around 7,500. Butter, which radiates about 8,000, is good for about ten days before it starts to fall off, reaching bottom in about twenty days.

Ocean fish and shellfish are good foods with a bright radiance from 8,500 to 9,000 especially if caught fresh and eaten raw. This includes crabs, oysters, clams, and other shellfish. Lobsters, says Simoneton, are best cut in half while live and broiled on a wood fire. Fresh water fish is much less radiant.

In Simoneton's second category he places foods radiating from 6,500 down to 3,000 angstroms. These include eggs, peanut oil, wine, boiled vegetables, cane sugar, and cooked fish. He rates a good red wine between 4,000 and 5,000, and says it is a better drink than devitalized city water, and certainly better than coffee, chocolate, liquor, or pasteurized fruit juices, which have virtually no radiance.

Echoing Nichols, Simoneton says that, whereas the juice of a fresh sugar beet gives 8,500 angstroms, refined beet sugar can fall as low as 1,000, and the white lumps that get wrapped in papers are down to zero.

Of meats, the only one that makes Simoneton's list of edible foods is freshly smoked ham. Freshly killed pork radiates at 6,500, as does all animal meat; but once it has been soaked in salt and hung over a wood fire its radiance rises to 9,500 or 10,000 angstroms. Other meats are almost pointless to eat; they are an exercise in tough digestion, which wears out rather than vitalizes the eater, requiring him to drink coffee to keep from falling asleep.

Cooked meats, sausages, and other innards are all in Simoneton's third category along with coffee, tea, chocolate, jams, fermented cheeses, and white bread. Because of their low radiation they do one little or no good, says Simoneton.

In his fourth category are margarines, preserves, alcohols, liquors, refined white sugar, and bleached white flour: all dead as far as radiations are concerned.

Applying his technique for measuring wavelengths directly to human beings, Simoneton found that the normal healthy person gives off a radiance of about 6,500 or a little higher, whereas the radiations given off by tobacco smokers, alcohol imbibers, and carrion eaters are uniformly lower. Bovis claimed that cancer patients give off a wavelength of 4,875, which, he noted, was the same wavelength as that of over-refined white French bread before the Second World War.

However, because a cancer victim will radiate this low level long before any overt symptom of his disease is in evidence, Bovis pointed out that it is possible to take remedial steps well before the ailment has made serious inroads into the body's cellular tissue.

It is Bovis and Simoneton's thesis that human beings should eat fruit, vegetables, nuts, and fresh fish that give off radiations higher than their own normal 6,500, if they wish to energize themselves and feel healthy. They believe that low-radiance foods, such as meats and bad bread, instead of bringing vitality to the body, sap the body of its existing vitality and that that is why one can feel heavy and devitalized from a meal one expected to replenish one's energy.

From the fact that most microbes read well below 6.5 thousand angstroms, Simoneton, like Lakhovsky, deduces that they can only affect a human being whose vitality has been lowered to a point where cells resonate at their wavelength, whereas a body with a healthy vitality remains immune to attack by microbes. This gives a *raison d'être* for deadly microbes in an ordered universe. The same principle, no doubt, explains why plants whose radiance has been reduced by chemical fertilizers are subject to attack by pests.

It struck Simoneton that the therapeutic marvels attributed since the dawn of history to herbs, flowers, roots, and barks might not be due simply to their chemical content, but the healthy wavelengths they radiate. Though the apothecary's shelves are still stocked with chemical derivatives from plants and herbs, their curative powers no longer appear so miraculous. The secret of their potency seems to have been lost.

Old wives and hermits are still reputed to know and understand the mysterious healing powers of plants, but they must have acquired their knowledge by some extra sense, or the woods would be strewn with the corpses of accidented sages, poisoned by belladonna, deadly nightshade and a host of other noxious weeds.

Simoneton believes the day will soon come when vaccines are made not from the bodies or carcasses of animals but from the radiant juice of plants. To set the world right Simoneton envisages doctors with headphones like radio operators, able to diagnose by the frequencies they receive from patients just what ails them, able to broadcast to them just the frequencies required to set things right.

Perhaps the most informed doctor in the healing power of plants was Paracelsus, who acquired his lore from old European herbalists, from wise men of the East, but primarily from the direct study of nature. According to his "doctrine of sympathetic resemblances" all growing things reveal through their structure, form, color, and aroma, their peculiar usefulness to man. Paracelsus recommended that a physician sit quietly in a meadow, relax and soon notice "how the blossoms follow the motion of the planets, opening their petals according to the phases of the moon, by the cycle of the sun, or in response to distant stars."

A modern follower of Paracelsus who turned out to be an extraordinary wizard with herbs and plants was a young London doctor, Edward Bach, who gave up a handsome practice as a physician on Harley Street in the 1930s to take to the woods and fields in search of a better cure for his fellow human beings. Like Paracelsus who sought to restore health by natural means so that it would not be necessary for the sick first to recover from their ailment and then have to recover from the cure, Bach rebelled against the idea that medicine should be painful and unpleasant. Noting that in most hospitals in England the so-called remedies gave the patient great pain and often did him more harm than good, he was determined to find remedies in nature that would neither be harmful nor unpleasant. He sought a remedy that would be gentle, sure, and would result in healing of both mind and body.

Like Paracelsus and Goethe, Bach was convinced that true knowledge was to be gained not through man's intellect, but through his ability to see and accept the natural, simple truths of life. Paracelsus had asserted that the further you search the greater you will realize the simplicity of all creation, and advised physicians to search within themselves for the spiritual insight that would lead them to sense and recognize the energies of plants.

In the summer of 1930 Bach turned the key on his lucrative practice and took to the highway, wandering through the English countryside and into the wild mountains of Wales in search of the wildflowers he was convinced contained the secret to healing both the spiritual and physical ailments of aberrant mankind. Like Paracelsus he was convinced that disease of the body is due not primarily to physical causes, but to disturbing moods or states of mind which interfere with the normal happiness of the individual, moods which if allowed to continue lead to a disturbance of the functions of the bodily organs and tissues with resulting ill health.

With Paracelsus, Bach believed that everything that lives radiates, and with Simoneton, he realized that plants with high vibrations were able to raise the lowered vibrations of human beings. As he put it, "herbal remedies have the power to elevate our vibrations, and thus draw down spiritual power, which cleanses mind and body, and heals." Bach compared his remedies to that of beautiful music or arrangements of color, or any gloriously uplifting medium that gives inspiration; his cure was not to attack the disease, but to flood the body with beautiful vibrations from wild herbs and flowers, in the presence of which "disease would melt away as snow in the sunshine."

Myrna I. Lewis, coauthor with Robert N. Butler, M.D., of a new book, *Aging and Mental Health,* was amazed when recently taken by the Soviets on a visit to several sanitariums in the Black Sea city of Sochi to find aging Soviet citizens, afflicted with a variety of ills, both physical and mental, being treated not with drugs but with vibrations from flowers in greenhouses where they were led to smell specific blooms so many minutes a day. They were also being treated with music played in their rooms and the sound of the sea recorded on tapes.

Fundamentally, Bach maintains that it is up to the sick person to change his mind about his own illness, but that healthy aesthetic vibrations help him recover his desire to be well. Bach felt that a long bout of fear or worry could deplete an individual's vitality to the point where his body lost its natural resistance to disease, and was thus in a state to become the prey of any infection and any form of illness. "It is not the disease which needs the treatment," said Bach. "There are no diseases; only sick people."

Although he was convinced that plants with the right medical properties were to be found among the simple wildflowers of the countryside, Bach was out to find those with the greatest power, capable of being more than palliatives, actually able to restore health to mind and body.

The first flower he tested for its medicinal properties was the yellow-spired agrimony *(Agrimonia eupatoria)*, a common wildflower which grows in abundance on the grassy verges of country roads and fields throughout England. Its small blooms are golden with many stamens of the same hue. Bach found an infusion of it to be a great remedy for worry, for the restless tormented state of mind so often hidden behind outward cheerfulness. Next he experimented with the striking blue flower of chicory, which he found a remedy for overconcern, especially for others, and discovered that it brought calmness and serenity. Bach's remedy for extreme fear was the administration of a dose of the elixir of rockrose. As his discoveries and ministrations progressed, Bach felt he was on the verge of discovering an entirely new system of medicine. On impulse or instinct he went to the Welsh wilderness, where he found two beautiful plants: the pale mauve impatiens, and the golden-flowered mimulus, growing in profusion near a mountain stream. Both turned out to be powerful medicines.

During his months in Wales, Bach felt his senses quickening, becoming more developed. Through a finely developed sense of touch he was able to feel the vibrations and power emitted by any plant he wished to test. Like Paracelsus, if he held a petal or bloom in the palm of his hand or placed it on his tongue he could feel in his body the effects of the properties within that plant. Some had a strengthening, vitalizing effect on his mind and body; others would give him pain, vomiting, fevers, rashes, and the like. His instinct told him that the best plants would be found blooming in the middle of the year, when the days are longest and the sun at the height of its power and strength. The plants he chose were the most perfect of their kind, their bloom beautiful in shape and hue, growing in profusion.

Perhaps Bach had read that Paracelsus on his estate at Hohenheim had captured dew on plates of glass, gathering the dew under various configurations of the heavenly bodies, believing the water to carry within it the energy of these planetary combinations, or perhaps he had a flash of intuition. At any rate, early one morning as he walked through a field upon which the dew still lay heavy, it struck Bach that each dewdrop must contain some of the properties of the plant upon which it rested; the heat of the sun, acting through the fluid, would serve to draw out these properties until each drop was magnetized with power. He realized that if he could obtain the medicinal properties of the plants he was seeking in this way, the resulting remedies would contain the full, perfect, and uncontaminated power of the plants, and they might heal as no medical preparations had been known to heal before. Collecting the dew from certain flowers before the sun had caused evaporation, he tried it on himself, shaking the drops from various flowering plants into small bottles, filling some with the dew from flowers which had been in full sunlight, some from those still in shade, although the latter never seemed as potent as the ones in the sun.

Though many of the flowers did not contain the healing properties he sought, Bach found the dew from each plant held a definite power of some kind, and deduced that the sun's radiation was essential to the process of extraction. As collecting sufficient dew from individual flowers could be laborious he decided to pick a few blooms from a chosen plant and place them in a glass bowl filled with water from a clear stream, leaving them standing in the field in the sunlight for several hours. To his delight he found that the water became impregnated with the vibrations and power of the plant and was very potent. To potentize his water Bach would choose a summer day with no clouds to obscure the sun's light and heat. Taking three small plain glass bowls filled with fresh water, he set them in a field where the flowering plants were growing, then selected the most perfect blossoms and placed them on the surface of the water. To lift the blooms from the water without touching the fluid with his fingers he used two blades of grass. The water was then transferred by means of a small lipped phial to bottles. When half-full the rest of the bottle was filled with brandy designed to preserve the mixture. Before the next experiment Bach would destroy both bowls and phials.

Altogether Bach produced thirty-eight remedies and wrote a philosophic booklet to go with them. Thousands of patients throughout England and the world were to vouch for their efficacy, and many thousands still depend on this elixir of flowers to cure them of innumerable ailments.

The work of Maurice Mességué, a sophisticated Frenchman born of peasant stock in a remote section of Gascony known as the Gers, parallels that of Bach. Taught by his father, who took him as a child on herb-collecting trips all over the countryside, Mességué went on to become a famous herbal healer successfully treating hundreds of patients including such notables as the president of the French Republic, Edouard Herriot, and artist Jean Cocteau. Among the afflictions he cured were such baffling ones as a withered arm on a beautiful young girl and the apparent inability to talk in a child of twelve. Most of Mességué's cures were effected by having his patients soak their extremities in infusions of wild plants. Hounded into court on many occasions for practicing medicine without a medical degree, Mességué fought back because he felt he could not abandon the thousands of sufferers who pleaded for his assistance. An account of his life with many anecdotes about his encounters with world figures appears in three best-selling books he has written on the subject of plants.

Another sensitive who can feel the radiations from flowers has gone Bach and Mességué one better, saying he can transfer radiations direct from a blooming flower into a bowl of water without in any way harming the plant on which it grows.

A ruddy-cheeked Scotsman, very independent, Alick McInnes was born and lives on a sheep farm in the shadow of the castle of the Thane of Cawdor, surrounded by gently rolling hills and a fortune in peat bog —which he cannot dig or burn because by Scottish tradition it all belongs to the Thane. Blindfolded, McInnes can put his hand over a ripe bloom and tell from the wavelength of its radiation just what plant it is and what its medical properties may be. In India, where he spent thirty years working for the British Raj, McInnes got his first introduction to the fact that plants not only give off radiations which are sensible to humans, but are themselves sensitive to the radiations given off by humans; this he discovered when he visited the Bose Institute near Calcutta.

By the entrance to the Institute stands a luxuriant *Mimosa pudica*. Visitors are requested to pick a small frond from this compliant horticultural guinea pig and place it in one of Bose's complicated machines, which provides a schematic pattern of the vibrations of the plant on a sheet of paper. A visitor is then asked to place his wrist inside the machine and watch as a duplicate of the pattern is produced, demonstrating that mimosa is so sensitive it can pick up and faultlessly reflect individual human radiations.

As McInnes interprets the phenomenon of human and plant radiations, each individual member of either kingdom modifies or qualifies with his own wavelength the fundamental energy radiating through him. The same applies, says McInnes, down to the finest particle of matter: "Everything radiates wavelengths which can be identified as sound, color, form, movement, perfume, temperature and intelligence."

McInnes says the radiations from some flowers are circular, others go from left to right, others from right to left. Some go up and down; others down and up; some go diagonally from left to right; others in the opposite direction. Some feel cold; others warm. But the same flower species always gives off the same radiation. McInnes says he has found it possible to transfer flower radiations to water, where the radiations will stay more or less indefinitely. He has some bottles with radiations still effective after twenty years. Each flower species has a time when its radiations can best be transferred to water, usually, though not always, when the flowers are at the peak of their maturity, which is also usually near a full moon.

Potencies, as McInnes calls the radiations which are transferred to water, can be taken from the rose around midsummer, or June 21, and from the dandelion around the Easter full moon. When conditions are right, transfer of the radiations is instantaneous, and McInnes, wrinkling his weatherbeaten lips into a wise smile, says the water can actually be seen to change, "an awe-inspiring experience never to be forgotten." Far from damaging the plant, McInnes says that just at that moment when its potency is transferred to water, other members of the same species for miles around brighten up and appear to grow more vigorously than before. The resulting potentized water McInnes calls an Exultation of Flowers, which he says is not a specific for the treatment of any diagnosable disease, but operates in a subtle way on the radiations coming through the human body, on animal or the soil, and in so doing raises the vitality of the person, animal, or soil concerned. When vitality is raised to the necessary level, says McInnes, illness disappears.

McInnes prescribes his Exultation to be taken by mouth, so many drops at a time for varying conditions, as a salve for cuts and burns and other problems of the skin, and as a tonic diluted in one's bath. He says that although he has been asked to do so he has never attempted to find individual flowers, or groups, that would be helpful in the treatment of a particular disease. He figures it more worthwhile to work on the concept that all illness has a common cause, and strives for a preparation that will, ultimately, bring results to every illness, no matter what the diagnosis. The decision as to whether potencies from any particular flower should be included in the forty-odd varieties in his Exultation has been made by McInnes by feeling the radiations emanating from the particular potency concerned. He finds that not all can be mixed successfully. Some seem to cancel each other out; others disturb the mixture; others upset the temper of the radiations already in the preparation. McInnes is amazed at how many differing radiations he has managed to combine in a harmonious whole.

As the radiations in Exultation of Flowers are not identifiable by ordinary methods of analysis based on the identification of chemical ingredients, and as so far the impulses cannot be identified by any measuring instrument available in Britain, McInnes has been obliged by a court action instituted by the Scottish health authorities to label his bottles "Guaranteed Chemical Composition—100% water, without herbal or chemical ingredients." Pointing out that magnetized steel and ordinary steel show the same chemical ingredients but are obviously quite different from each other, McInnes still hopes some new method will be devised to identify the radiations.

McInnes says his Exultation is just as good for a cow with milk fever in Scotland as it is for a man with asthma in California or a woman stung by a wasp in New Zealand. It can be used on a baby with a stomach ache, on a hive of bees with "foul brood," on strawberry plants with "June yellows" or on hens which have eaten poisoned grain. Sprayed onto the soil McInnes says it increases the activity and quality of soil bacteria. But he warns that gardens which have been treated with chemical fertilizers will take longer to respond "because the whole polarity of the soil has been geared to decay." He says the vibrations of his Exultation channel fresh energy into the soil which counteracts disease, blight, and pests.

In the more than sixteen years since Exultation of Flowers was first offered to the public, many thousands of letters have been received reporting success in the treatment of pretty well every diagnosable disease. Philosophically McInnes believes that all forms of life are created to live in harmony, but mankind has so misused this dominion over created things that there is now disharmony everywhere, which is expressed in physical disease in human, animal, and plant life, the life forces coming from the Source of Creation becoming more and more distorted. Believing that in the Golden Age the lion would lie down with the lamb, he describes how, when he lived in Uganda, he would watch hundreds of animals making tracks through the elephant grass toward the salt licks, with carnivores such as leopards and panthers trotting alongside tiny timorous deer that in other circumstances would tremble and run away.

In South India, where McInnes spent a couple of weeks as the guest of Ramana Mohan Maharshi at his ashram at the foot of the holy hill Arunachalam, famed in Hindu mythology for many centuries, every evening when the Maharshi would go out for a walk, within seconds of his crossing the threshold of his residence, cattle tied up in stalls in the nearby village, about half a mile away, would struggle to get out of their bonds. Released by the villagers they careered along the road to accompany the old man on his walk, followed by all the dogs and children of the village.

Before the procession had gone very far wild animals, says McInnes, joined it from the jungle, including several varieties of snakes. Thousands of birds appeared, almost blotting out the sky, including tiny tits, huge kites and other birds of prey, heavy-winged vultures, all flying in harmony around the Maharshi on his walk. When he returned to his room, said McInnes, all the birds, animals, and children would quietly disappear. To achieve such an atmosphere worldwide, McInnes realizes, would be quite a feat. His Exultation would have to help produce vegetation of such an improved nutritive quality that the lion could feed on it before he would happily lie down with the lamb. McInnes sees no reason such a food plant could not be encouraged by some new Burbank to grow in abundance.

There will also have to be an increase in the sensitivity of humanity, says McInnes, to the point where the sacrifice of animals to sport becomes wholly intolerable, as well as the mass slaughter of animals in total terror in abattoirs. Better food must be more easily obtainable in such abundance that half-starved and semi-brutalized men no longer need to eat meat or demand work of half-dead, diseased, and suffering animals; in other words, we must cease to be a planet of jailors and chain-gang drivers.

As everything created is interdependent, says McInnes, it follows that what affects one form of life must affect all other forms as well. "If we deliberately cause suffering and disease in other lives, we increase our own suffering and disease." All creation, says McInnes, is affected by the disease inflicted on laboratory animals in what he believes to be a futile and foredoomed attempt to combat illness. All creation is tormented through the ghastly agonies which the vivisectionist inflicts on helpless creatures. Any relief of illness supposed to be removed by knowledge gained at the expense of such agonies will, says McInnes, be paid for many times over in increased suffering in some other part of the Whole. All creation suffers when plants in their millions are burnt by chemical weed killers.

Just as every created thing takes a knock for every victim of war or every inmate tortured in a concentration camp, so every created thing takes a knock when a rabbit dies of human-induced myxomatosis, or a plant dies in agony, deliberately diseased with toxic chemicals. "All of life," says McInnes, "is one. There is no exception."

CHAPTER 19

Radionic Pesticides

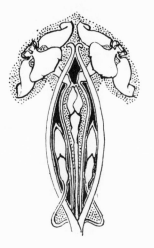

Simoneton's dream that doctors with earphones would one day diagnose patients simply by tuning in to the frequencies given off by their ailing organs and then be able to cure them by broadcasting to the organs more healthful vibrations has turned out to be closer to fact than fiction. However, because the mechanism appears to be as explosive as TNT and as amenable to the spread of death and disease as it is to the spread of life, the findings have been discreetly scotched by both the political and scientific establishments.

At the end of the nineteenth century Dr. Albert Abrams, the son of a successful San Francisco merchant from whom he had inherited a vast fortune, traveled to Heidelberg to study advanced medicine. In Naples young Abrams watched the famous Italian tenor Enrico Caruso flick a wine glass with his finger to produce a pure tone, then step back and by singing the same note shatter the glass. This impressive feat awoke in Abrams the idea that he might have stumbled on a fundamental principle which could be tied into medical diagnosis and healing.

At the University of Heidelberg's medical school, from which he was to receive top honors and the gold medal, Abrams met a Professor de Sauer, who was engaged—many years before Gurwitsch had happened on "mitogenetic radiation"—in a bizarre series of experiments with plants. De Sauer told Abrams that, while transplanting onion seedlings, he had inadvertently left some of the uprooted onions next to those still growing in one of several flats. Two days later he noticed that the seedlings growing on the side of the flat next to the dying plants were different in appearance from those on the opposite side. De Sauer could not explain the reason for the difference but Abrams was convinced that the onion roots were emitting some strange form of radiation and linked this in his mind with the resonance phenomenon behind Caruso's voice-shattered glass.

Abrams returned to the United States to teach pathology at Stanford University's medical school, of which he was later to become director of medical studies. A superb diagnostician and master of the art of percussion, he would tap the body of a patient to produce resonating sounds, which became clues to whatever ills might be afflicting the patient. One day Abrams noticed that when a nearby X-ray apparatus was switched on without warning it dulled the resonant note he was getting from his tapping. Perplexed, Abrams rotated his patient and discovered that the strange dulling occurred only while the man faced east and west, but that when he was aligned north and south the percussion note was continuously resonant. There seemed to be a relationship between the geomagnetic field and—as with the grains researched by Pittman in Alberta—the electromagnetic fields of individuals. Abrams later discovered a similar effect was produced by a man with a cancerous ulcer of the lip, even when the X-ray machine was not operating.

After several months of experimentation with persons afflicted with various maladies, Abrams concluded that nerve fibers in the epigastric region not only react by contracting to the stimulus of X-rays generated from a machine several yards distant, but appear to be in a state of permanent contraction in the case of a patient suffering from cancer, except when the patient is oriented in a north-south direction. Because of this similarity, Abrams concluded that the contractions, due in the first case to radiant energy rippling from an X-ray instrument, were in the second case taking place in response to vibrating molecules which were collectively forming the cancerous growth.

Abrams asked his houseboy, Ivor, who had accompanied him to class, to step onto the lecture platform, strip to the waist, and face west. As he tapped the boy just above the navel, Abrams told his students to listen carefully to the hollow, resonant quality of the note he was obtaining. He then asked one young doctor to hold a specimen of cancerous tissue in light contact with Ivor's forehead, applying it for a few seconds, removing it, and applying it again. As Abrams continuously percussed the abdomen, the class was amazed to hear the note change from resonance to dullness each time the specimen was placed on Ivor's forehead, apparently because of a contraction of muscle fibers. When Abrams substituted a tuberculous specimen for the cancerous one, the resonance of the note did not change. But when he began tapping an area just below the navel, the same effect was produced. Abrams was forced to the conclusion that unknown waves from diseased specimens could be received and recorded by a healthy human body and that they somehow altered the character of its tissues.

After months of work, Abrams was able to show that a series of what he called "electronic reactions," varying from cancerous and tuberculer to malarial and streptococcal, could be pinpointed on different areas of the trunk of a healthy person like Ivor. This led him to proclaim that the time-honored idea that disease was of cellular origin was out of date and must be discarded. Instead, he maintained it was because the molecular constituents of cells undergo a structural alteration, specifically a change in the number and arrangement of their electrons, that they develop characteristics which only later become visible at the microscope. Exactly what caused the alteration Abrams did not know, nor does anyone today. He nevertheless suspected that forces could be discovered for correcting what he considered to be intramolecular aberrations, and even for preventing their occurrence.

Abrams next found that the radiation from a pathological specimen could be transmitted, like electricity, over a six-foot wire. When a skeptical doctor challenged Abrams to find the exact location of a tuberculosis infection in his lung for which he had been receiving treatment in a sanitarium, Abrams immediately had the man hold one disc against his forehead and got another student to pass the second disc over the subject's chest until the percussing note changed in tone. The baffled man admitted Abrams had located the infection within centimeters.

Since one spot on the trunk of a healthy subject reacted to not just one but several pathological specimens, Abrams next began to conceive of an instrument which might differentiate between the wavelengths of all specifically diseased tissues. After months of research, he worked out what he called a "reflexophone," an instrument very much like the rheostat—a continuously variable electrical resistor used to regulate current—that could emit sounds varying in pitch and thus obviate the necessity of having to tap a specific point on a body.

Different diseases could now be read from the dial: 55 for a syphilitic specimen, 58 for sarcomatous tissue, and so on. Abrams asked his assistant to mix up the specimens and found he could infallibly select or "diagnose," by checking the readings on his indicator.

Abrams' developments to this point ran not only decades ahead of, but directly counter to, the prevailing medical philosophy of his day. His statement that "as physicians we dare not stand aloof from the progress made in physical science and segregate the human entity from other entities of the physical universe" was as incomprehensible to most of his medical colleagues as were the later pronouncements of Lakhovsky and Crile.

An even more fantastic revelation came when Abrams found he could diagnose the ills of the human body with his instrument from a single drop of the body's blood. Furthermore, by apparently inducting the effect from one reflexophone to another which contained three rheostats calibrated in units of 10, 1 and 1/25, he was able to determine not only from what disease a person was suffering but *to what stage it had advanced.*

Even more fantastic, Abrams found that if a woman was afflicted with a breast cancer, he could determine from her blood spot alone in which breast the cancer was located, merely by having a healthy percussed subject point with his fingertips to his own breasts. In exactly the same way, Abrams could reveal the exact site of tubercular or any other diseased condition whether focused in the lungs, bowel, bladder, one of the vertebrae; in fact, wherever in the body.

One day while Abrams was demonstrating to a class the reaction induced by the blood of a malarial patient, he suddenly turned and said, "Well, there are upwards of forty of you physicians present, and probably all of you would prescribe quinine to a patient suffering from this disease, but can any one of you offer any scientific reason for so doing?" There being no reply, Abrams took out a few grains of sulfate of quinine and put them where the blood drop had been in the device. It produced exactly the same percussion note as malaria. He then placed the malarial material in the container *together* with a grain or so of quinine wrapped in tissue paper. Now the percussion which had produced a dull sound indicating malaria gave a resonant sound. To his amazed class Abrams put forward the suggestion that radiations emitted by quinine molecules *exactly canceled* those from malarial molecules, that the effect on malaria of quinine was due to an unsuspected electrical law which should become the subject of intensive research. Various other known antidotes behaved similarly—mercury against syphilis, to cite but one example.

Abrams knew that if he could devise a wave-emitting instrument, similar to a wireless broadcasting station, which could alter the character of the waves transmitted by malarial or syphilitic tissue, he might cancel them out as effectively as did quinine or mercury.

Though at first he believed "this was beyond the wit of man," he eventually built an "oscilloclast" with the help of a friend, Samuel O. Hoffman, a distinguished radio research engineer who had achieved fame in World War I by devising a unique method for detecting German zeppelins approaching the U.S. coast even at a great distance. This oscilloclast or "wave breaker" could emit specific waves capable of curing human afflictions by apparently altering or canceling out radiations emitted by various diseases. By 1919 Abrams began teaching its use to physicians, who, because neither they nor Abrams could exactly explain how it effected cures, regarded it as nothing short of miraculous.

In 1922, Abrams reported in the *Physico-Clinical Journal* that for the first time he had effected over telephone wires the diagnosis of a patient miles away from his office, using nothing more than a drop of blood from the patient and analysis of its vibratory rates by his instruments. This somewhat eerie claim finally aroused the ire of the AMA, which published a defamatory article impugning Abrams in its journal as a quack, an article which was parroted in England in the *British Medical Journal*. This caused Sir James Barr, past president of the British Medical Association, who had been successfully using Abrams' methods in his own practice, to write in reply: "You very seldom quote from the *Journal of the American Medical Association* and one might have expected that when you did you would have chosen a more serious subject than an ignorant tirade against an eminent medical man, against, in my opinion, the greatest genius in the medical profession." Barr concluded that one day "medical editors and medical men will begin to perceive that there was more to Abrams' vibrations than was dreamt of in their philosophy."

Abrams' greatest discoveries were that all matter is radioactive and that the generated waves can be picked up across space by using human reflexes as detectors; also, that in many conditions of disease dull patches are consistently found at specific spots on afflicted patients' bodies.

When Abrams died in 1924, the vilification against him continued in the United States in eighteen separate and consecutive issues of *Scientific American*. One of the worst insinuations was that the "Abrams box" had been devised for no other purpose than to make a financial killing by selling it to naïve physicians and an unsuspecting public. No one noted that Abrams, a millionaire in his own right, had written to Upton Sinclair, one of his American defenders, that he would donate his devices to, and work unremunerated for, any institute which would develop the "Abrams box" in the interests of humanity.

The sanctions against Abrams and his work scared off all but a small minority of American doctors, most of whom were independent-minded chiropractors or, as they like to be called, "drugless physicians."

But a generation after Abrams' death one of these, living in the San Francisco Bay area, was visited by Curtis P. Upton, a Princeton-trained civil engineer whose father was a partner of Thomas Alva Edison. Upton's engineering mind led him to wonder whether the strange device used to cure human affliction might not be applied to pest control for agriculture. In the summer of 1951 he and his Princeton classmate William J. Knuth, an electronics expert from Corpus Christi, Texas, drove into the cotton fields of the thirty-thousand-acre Cortaro-Marana tract near Tucson, Arizona. Together they unloaded from the back of their truck a mysterious boxlike instrument about the size of a portable radio, complete with dials and a stick antenna. Only this time they went one better than Simoneton and McInnes. They would attempt to affect the field not directly but through the medium of photographs.

An aerial photograph of the field was placed on a "collector plate" attached to the base of the instrument, together with a reagent known to be poisonous to cotton pests. The dials were set in a specific manner. The object of the exercise was to clear the field of pests without recourse to chemical insecticides. The theory behind the system—as "way out" as anything so far reported on the nature of plants—held that the molecular and atomic makeup of the emulsion on the photograph would be resonating at the identical frequencies of the objects they represented pictorially. Though the American engineers did not know it, the same discovery had been made by Bovis in the 1930s. By affecting the photograph with a reagent known to be poisonous to cotton pests the Americans believed the cotton plants in the field could be immunized against the pests. Because the amount of poisonous reagent used was infinitesimal compared to the number of acres photographed, the reagent was thought to act in the same way that trace dosages of dilution function in Homeopathic Medicine.

Homeopathy is a method of treatment founded by Christian Samuel Hahnemann, a physician of note born in Meissen in Saxony in 1755. Hahnemann, who was also a chemist, a linguist, a translator of medical works, and the author of a comprehensive apothecaries' lexicon, got himself into serious trouble with the then equivalent of the FDA by his discovery that small doses of what can cause the symptoms of a disease in human beings can also cure them. The original discovery was made by chance when the Countess of Cinchon, wife of the Spanish Viceroy to Peru, was relieved of malaria with an infusion of bark from a local tree which produced symptoms in her identical with those of malaria. Thereafter known as "cinchon bark," the remedy was sold by monks in Spain to the rich for its weight in gold and given to the poor for nothing.

Spurred by this novel approach to medicine, Hahnemann made a methodical search for plants, herbs, barks, or any substance, including snake venom, which could produce symptoms similar to those of a known disease, and by administering them in small doses produced some near miracle cures. He found belladonna to be a remedy against scarlet fever, pulsatilla against measles, and gelsemium against influenza. Quite as extraordinary as Hahnemann's cures was his next discovery, that the more he diluted a remedy the more potent and effective it became, even if diluted to an infinitesimal one million to one. Rudolf Hauschka explains the phenomenon by suggesting that if matter is a condensation or a crystallization of cosmic forces, these forces would naturally revert to being more powerful as they were liberated from their material casing like jinns from a bottle.

A careful chemist, Hahnemann would start by diluting the tincture of some bark, root, resin, seed, or gum with ninety-nine parts of pure alcohol. This would give him what he called a one-centesimal potency. He would then dilute one part of this liquid into ninety-nine parts of a diluent. The third time round he would have a tincture that was only one millionth part of the diluent. The result, for some even to him mysterious reason, was far more potent. Hauschka explains part of Hahnemann's secret as being in the rhythmic, mathematical fashion in which he shook his dilutions, rhythm having the same effect it has on humans of freeing the spirit from the clutches of the body.

But the authorities made short shrift of Hahnemann. Already in bad odor with his fellow physicians because he considered bleeding and cupping his patients to be a crime, Hahnemann next incurred the wrath of his fellow apothecaries when they saw the threat to their profits from the sale of drugs in such minute quantities. The moment Hahnemann's discovery was given to the public in the journal of Goethe's personal physician, Dr. Hufeland, the Guild of Apothecaries (forerunners of today's pharmacists and the "detail men" who each year press hundreds of new pills on doctors) saw to it that Hahnemann was brought before a court, found guilty, forbidden to dispense medicine, and compelled to leave town.

In Tucson in 1951, it would have been hard to find a scientist who would bet the small change in his pocket that Upton and Knuth's protective process could offer them any safeguards against marauding pests. Yet the two engineers pursued their course, repeating the process with aerial photographs covering the entire four thousand acres owned by the Cortaro Management Company, one of Arizona's biggest cotton growers. The company executives were gambling that, if the twelve varieties of pests that normally attacked their million-dollar crop could be kept at bay with so simple a device, they could save up to $30,000 a year in operating costs by eliminating the use of insecticide sprays.

In the fall, the Tucson *Weekend-Reporter* ran an illustrated two-page spread headlined: "Million Dollar Gamble Pays Off for Cotton Man." The article stated that a "Buck Rogers type of electronic pest control" had allowed Cortaro to achieve an almost 25 percent increase in per-acre yield of cotton over the state average. W. S. Nichols, president of the Cortaro Management Company, stated in an affidavit that the treated cotton also seemed to have approximately 20 percent more seed: "This may possibly be the result of not destroying the bees, upon which the radionic process seems to have no effect." Nichols further remarked that his hoe hands had noted an almost complete absence of snakes in the areas subjected to the strange treatment.

On the East Coast of the United States, one of Upton's Princeton classmates, Howard Armstrong, who had become an industrial chemist with many inventions to his credit, decided to try his friend's method in Pennsylvania. After taking an aerial photograph of a cornfield under attack by Japanese beetles, he cut one corner off the photo with a pair of scissors and laid the remainder together with a small amount of rotenone, a beetle poison, extracted from the roots of a woody Asian vine which the Japanese call "roten," on the collector plate of one of Upton's radionic devices.

After several five- to ten-minute treatments with the machine's dials set to specific readings, a meticulous count of beetles revealed that 80–90 percent of them had died or disappeared from the corn plants treated through the photo. The untreated plants in the corner cut away from the photo remained 100 percent infested.

After witnessing this experiment, B. A. Rockwell, director of research for the Pennsylvania Farm Bureau Cooperative Association in Harrisburg, wrote: "To control insect pests at a distance of thirty miles with no danger to man, plants or animals would perhaps be an accomplishment heretofore unrivaled in the scientific control of insects injurious to vegetation. To an individual with 19 years experience in the research field this feat appeared unreal, impossible, fantastic, and crazy. Yet careful counts by the writer of the treated corn plants and untreated corn plants indicated definitely that the kill ratio was 10 to 1 in favor of the treated plants."

Upton, Knuth, and Armstrong combined their talents and the first letters of their names to form UKACO, Inc. The new company's goal was to relieve farmers of unwanted pests by the new method, as scientifically inexplicable as it was simple and inexpensive. The company received the backing of General Henry M. Gross, one of Harrisburg's most distinguished citizens, head of the Selective Service Board for the State of Pennsylvania.

In the West, Upton and Knuth contracted with forty-four artichoke growers to treat their crop against plume moths. The contracts were written on the basis of "no control—no pay." All the growers paid the service charge of one dollar an acre, a tiny fraction of the costs of conventional spraying. In Pennsylvania Rockwell stated: "Since farmers usually do not pay for a service unless there is value received, this is the best testimonial for the UKACO process which has come to my attention."

Convinced that a radical new development for controlling pests was in the offing, Rockwell arranged contracts with his fellow farmers to run a long series of experiments under his supervision. In 1949 at the cooperative's "Camp Potato" in Potter County, and at the Fairview farmstead in Easton, potato crops treated by the UKACO process yielded 30 percent more than those fields sprayed seven times with conventional insecticides, the saving in chemicals also greatly adding to the value of the crop.

The following year the Farm Bureau's research division operatives, having learned to operate the UKACO equipment themselves, got yields 22 percent greater than in the insecticide-treated fields. In tests at Hershey Estates Farm No. 40, and the bureau's own poultry farm, a pair of cornfields showed, by actual count of cornstalks, 65 percent control of second-brood European corn borer, an efficiency never approached with any other treatment.

In Eatonville, Florida, the director of agriculture for the Hungerford School for Boys, a graduate in agriculture from Tallahassee University, also successfully used the UKACO method to eliminate pestilent worms from the school's cabbage patch and flea beetles from its turnip plants.

At this point, the new insecticideless method of treating crops piqued the curiosity of the United States Department of Agriculture's research station at Beltsville, Maryland, one of whose officials, Dr. Truman Hienton, called General Gross to say that he would like to find out exactly how UKACO was achieving its results. When Hienton and two of his Ph.D. colleagues arrived in Harrisburg, they were informed that the principle behind the machine seemed somehow to be related to that of radio broadcasting. But when UKACO's Howard Armstrong was asked at what wavelength he was broadcasting his treatments, he could only say he did not know. The mystified scientists shook their heads dubiously and returned to Beltsville.

In the summer of 1951 Armstrong traveled through the Cumberland Valley treating corn and anything else the farmers wanted him to treat. He was so successful that when insecticide salesmen visited the farms under treatment they were informed their products were no longer needed. The farmers themselves operated many of the treating devices which were left by Armstrong on their farms. This evidently raised the hackles of the American insecticide industry, which responded that winter to UKACO's new technology in the same way that the British fertilizer industry had to Sir Albert Howard's recommendations. *Agricultural Chemicals,* the industry's mouthpiece, printed an article in its January, 1952, issue, panning the UKACO process as fraudulent. When asked about the article's claim that his test results could not be duplicated by "disinterested agencies," the Pennsylvania farm bureau's Rockwell replied: "I've studied enough science to know a dead Japanese beetle when I see one."

In March of 1952, fifty York County agricultural leaders assembled, with a skeptical glint in their eyes, to hear R. M. Benjamin, executive secretary of the Pennsylvania Farm Bureau, tell them during a two-hour meeting how they could kill or chase away various insect pests by what seemed to be remote electronic control. Benjamin supplied testimonials to back up his story, one of them signed by the Secretary of Agriculture for Pennsylvania, Miles Horst, who reported highly effective results on a rose-of-Sharon bush in his garden which had been infested by Japanese beetles. Though many in the audience at first heckled Benjamin, and one jeeringly remarked that perhaps the cornfields should be injected with "a dose of faith," before the end of the meeting all present became convinced that the new methods should be given a trial the following summer.

When the York *Dispatch,* which had printed an account of the meeting, requested an opinion on the UKACO process from the U.S. Department of Agriculture in Washington, it was surprised to learn that the department put no faith in the process. F. C. Bishopp, assistant chief of the Agricultural Research Administration's Bureau of Entomology and Plant Quarantine, claimed in a letter that one of the bureau's field men had observed the experiments run by Knuth and Upton in the Southwest and found that the insects were *not controlled.* Bishopp added that "though we have not had an opportunity to carefully examine the device, or conduct any properly designed tests of it . . . a number of adverse reports on tests set up by the company have also reached us." He cited an article in the *Arizona Farmer* headlined "Electronic De-Bugger Flops—Promoter of Magic Black Box Leaves Texas Panhandle When Cotton Farmers Find It Didn't Work."

A week later, Bishopp, realizing that tests planned for the summer of 1952 were to proceed as scheduled and, evidently feeling that he had not made his point convincingly, wrote a second letter to the York *Dispatch*, in which he stated in part: "From our limited knowledge of the use of radiation in control of insects we frankly feel that the claims of this company are exaggerated. The question naturally arises as to why the company should proceed with large-scale tests without having competent authorities evaluate the method. We are anxious that unsound methods not be permitted to divert the farmer's attention, at this critical time, from recognized sound insect control practices." Bishopp's aim was evidently to use his authoritative position to prejudge and condemn a process of which he admitted he had no firsthand knowledge.

Rockwell never denied that the radionic process was *not always* successful. He himself stated plainly to the newspaper that certain tests could fail because of interference from standing irrigation pipes, high-tension wires, leaky transformers, wire fences, radar, plant pots, and various soil conditions, and added that, because the patents for UKACO devices had not yet been granted, he was not at liberty to turn one over to the Beltsville research center.

The same spring, the three UKACO partners and General Gross organized a nonprofit foundation to carry on their pest-control work. Because of the homeopathic quality of the reagents used, the nonprofit entity was called the Homeotronic Foundation, at the suggestion of Dr. William J. Hale, former chief of research in organic chemistry for the Dow Chemical Corporation.

In the meantime, despite Bishopp's statements, the USDA's Dr. Hienton again called General Gross to say that he had heard extremely favorable reports on Armstrong's work in the Cumberland Valley the previous year and wondered what his Beltsville agricultural research station could do to assist UKACO's further efforts. Gross suggested that the government research body send five representatives to work all summer with five UKACO operatives, each one of whom was to treat fields in a separate Pennsylvania county. By constant observation of the method of treatment and results obtained, they should be able to determine firsthand whether the UKACO work was all that it claimed to be.

Instead of accepting Gross's offer, Hienton decided to commission a USDA field worker in New Jersey, Dr. E. W. Seigler, and an assistant to oversee the UKACO operations on a sporadic basis.

During the 1952 growing season field corn was treated on 1,420 acres belonging to 61 farmers on 81 separate holdings in five counties; 78,360 individual corn stalks were examined. Officers of the new Homeotronic Foundation worked with several Pennsylvania Farm Bureau officials and one from the Farm Bureau Association of the State of Ohio.

The USDA officials finally put in an appearance on August 7. Dr. Seigler randomly selected one cornfield in York County owned by the Bittinger Cannery and checked the treated corn against the untreated. In four rows totaling 400 plants he found 346 silks damaged by beetles in the untreated section but only 65 silks damaged in the treated section. In another field, owned by the Pennsylvania Farm Bureau poultry farm cooperative, results were 339 and 64. Checks in other areas also testified to the success of the new methods, with the exception of one field where the process inexplicably did not seem to work. Overall results indicated that 92 percent success in the control of Japanese beetles, and 58 percent for corn borers was achieved.

The UKACO team was happy that the results had now been checked by the United States agricultural authorities. But the USDA's Dr. Seigler asked UKACO to refrain from publishing any results in the *Pennsylvania Farm Bureau Journal* until Beltsville had had time to issue their own report. When, after a number of weeks, no report was forthcoming from the USDA research station, General Gross called Beltsville to ask for thirty copies. Instead of mailing them, Bishopp sent a curt letter to Rockwell stating that, since no count had been made *before* the treatment had begun, the reports sent back from Pennsylvania by his own research men were valueless.

As the Pennsylvanians knew that Beltsville was well aware that the pictures had been taken and treatment started long before there was any appearance of either corn ears or Japanese beetles, they found the attitude of the USDA surprising. It seemed that the USDA was intent on killing the UKACO process in the bud. When several very large prospective customers called Beltsville for an opinion about it, they were informed that the whole thing was a fake that had produced no results whatsoever.

Armstrong next learned from the West Coast that representatives of insecticide companies in concert with USDA employees had been visiting farmers who used the UKACO process and telling them it was an outright fraud. The UKACO team came to the conclusion that Beltsville was directly and intentionally preventing them from proceeding with their work and that lobbyists of the insecticide industry in Washington were putting extreme pressure on the government to stamp out the new pest-control methods which were so dangerously threatening to put them out of business. So effective was the campaign that UKACO had difficulty soliciting new clients among farmers, who were becoming convinced by an army of USDA agents that there was nothing to the Upton-Knuth-Armstrong treatments.

Meanwhile Upton, whose patent application had been rejected for "lack of convincing evidence in the record from qualified experts with scientific backgrounds," submitted a twenty-two-page addendum to support his claim. The addendum pleaded that "it is difficult to precisely define the nature and mechanism of the novel methods" and postulated that the process "comprehends the study and use of certain fundamental energy sources capable of affecting molecules, atoms and electrons through their characteristic harmonic potency resonance frequencies in which every particle of matter exhibits its own characteristic frequency under a controlled polarity in a magnetic field of motion."

In support of their allegations, the inventors cited the work of Dr. Edward Purcell, co-winner with Dr. Felix Bloch of a 1952 Nobel Prize in physics, who published an article in the November 15 issue of *Science News Letter* on the characteristic resonant frequency of elements when resonated in selected magnetic fields, and a report on the work of Dr. Bloch, wherein he succeeded, by a process he designated "nuclear induction," in turning atomic particles into what, in effect, were infinitesimal radio transmitters, whose broadcasts, if highly amplified, could be detected in loudspeakers. There was little doubt in Upton's mind that his "radiotonic treatment," as he called it, made use of the type of energy involved in the Bloch study, which, as Upton wrote, had "not heretofore been recognized by science—particularly in its applications to molecular structures of the complex nature of plant and animal life."

Holding that the work of electronic experts and the detection of potentials by means of delicate apparatus had long since proven the existence and the measurability of various amplitudes of electrical potentials in living creatures, Upton referred to the writings of Drs. George Washington Crile and Harold Saxton Burr.

When all this failed to get the patent accepted, General Gross brought into play his contacts on the boards of some of the nation's largest industrial companies and was able to introduce the process to the consideration of important scientists in the U.S. Government, including Vannevar Bush, science adviser to President Eisenhower. When Gross explained to them UKACO's accomplishments and said they were based on the idea that every particle has its own generic frequency, as Dr. Crile had so stoutly maintained, the scientists responded heatedly that the UKACO-obtained results were impossible.

Though Gross politely suggested that the scientists come to Harrisburg and talk with Rockwell and the farmers whose crops had been "radiotonically" protected and see the results for themselves, they declined his invitation. Gross had no more success with the director of the Carnegie Institution in Washington, who flatly told him that there was nothing in the science of electronics to suggest that the UKACO process could work.

Dr. Willard F. Libby, who devised the carbon-14 dating technique, and who was soon to win the Nobel Prize in chemistry, after hearing Gross out, discouragingly yet perhaps accurately told him that it would take more than a million dollars to research the "box."

What also may have alarmed the government was the idea that if a host of insects could be affected, even killed, simply by radiating a poison at them via a picture of the plants which they were attacking, then the same technique could be militarily applied to concentrations of troops or even the populations of whole cities in wartime. All this discouragement, added to the studied and seemingly successful efforts of governmental and industrial moguls to wean farmers away from the new approach to insect control, finally forced UKACO to close its doors. But the story of what came to be called "radionics" was only beginning.

Thirty years before the demise of the UKACO enterprise, a young engineer for the Kansas City Power and Light Company, T. Galen Hieronymus, who was one of the first to be granted an amateur radio operator's license before World War I, was asked by one of his neighbors, a Dr. Planck, to machine various parts for some instrumentation which required precise components, such as strips of silver plate, cut to exact proportions down to the millimeter, and carefully wound coils. Beyond referring to a mysterious medical genius in San Francisco with whom he had studied fantastic new techniques to treat disease, Planck did not enlighten his young machinist as to the purpose of the new instruments he was helping to build. It was only after Planck died and his wife asked Hieronymus to come to the house to look over a workroom full of strange equipment and, because she had no use for it, select whatever he wanted, that Hieronymus learned the real purpose of the equipment he had been machining, and that the name of the unknown surgeon was Albert Abrams.

Meanwhile a vivacious young Los Angeles chiropractor, Dr. Ruth Drown, was also making refinements on Abrams' devices. Drown's most startling accomplishment was her development of a camera which could be used to take pictures of organs and tissues of patients using nothing but a drop of their blood, even when the patients were hundreds or thousands of miles from her office. Even more startling, she could take pictures in "cross-section," which cannot be done with X-rays. Though she received a British patent for this twenty-first-century apparatus, Dr. Drown's claim was relegated by FDA authorities to the realm of science fiction and her equipment was confiscated in the early 1940s. To make sure that her plight was suitably publicized, the same authorities saw to it that reporters from *Life* magazine were on the scene. After the *Life* story presented her as a charlatan, Dr. Ruth Drown died of grief—an unrecognized genius.

While Drown was working in California, still another of Abrams' followers, a Chicago doctor, G. W. Wiggelsworth, with the help of his brother, an electronics engineer who at first looked upon the oscilloclast as an outright fraud but finally became convinced of its efficacy, went on to improve the "Abrams box" by substituting for resistance coils variable condensers, a change which he found vastly improved the tuning. Wiggelsworth christened his new device a "pathoclast" or disease breaker, the users of which banded together into a Pathometric Association.

In the 1930s Glen Wills, an Arkansas chiropractor, successful businessman, and promoter, who pioneered the method of raising broiling chickens in cages or "batteries," heard Hieronymus lecture on electronic theory before the Pathometric Association. Wills bought out Wiggelsworth's Pathometric Association and asked Hieronymus if he could build a modified and more complex version of the pathoclast.

Hieronymus had earlier made a detailed study of his own of strange energies emitted, not from healthy or diseased tissues, but from metals. Working on his theory, he took sterling-silver objects, such as broken spoons, pepper-and-salt shakers, and anything else he could steal from his wife, and buried them in the Kansas prairie.

Knowing the location of the hidden silver, Hieronymus then "worked backward," as he says, trying to find the emanations from it. To his surprise, he discovered that every so often he could find *no energy* emanating from the silver, and wondered if someone might have dug up his hoard. A few hours later the energy would be radiating as strongly as ever.

Hieronymus' eclectic mind next wondered whether the energy was undetectable at given times because it was radiating not upward out of the earth but downward toward the earth's center. To find out, he took an eight-foot copper-clad steel ground rod and sledge-hammered it at an angle into the ground so that it would extend below the silver hoard. When the rod was at the level of the silver or below it, his device, to which the rod was attached, indicated a surge of energy; when he pulled the rod some distance above the silver, no energy was registered.

By repeatedly taking measurements over weeks, Hieronymus found that the energy from the silver seemed to be diverted downward for a few hours every two and a half days. Checking in an almanac he discovered that the cycle of diversions in some ways correlated with phases of the moon. What Pfeiffer had discovered about lunar influence with respect to plants seemed also to be applicable to metals.

Further work with buried metal also convinced Hieronymus that these energies were, like those in Abrams' experiments, strongly influenced by magnetic attraction. Thus, at least two twentieth-century researchers, one a medical man, like Mesmer, the other a laboratory researcher, like Reichenbach, appeared to have rediscovered the link between mineral magnetism on the one hand and "animal magnetism" on the other.

Hieronymus suspected that the unknown energy emitted from metals might be somehow linked to sunlight; since it could be transmitted over wires, it might have an effect on the growth of plants.

To find out, Hieronymus placed some aluminum-lined boxes in the pitch-dark cellar of his Kansas City house. Some boxes he grounded to a water pipe and connected by separate copper wires to metal plates on the outside of the house exposed to full sunlight. Other boxes were left unconnected. In all of them Hieronymus planted seed grain. In the connected boxes the seeds grew into sturdy green plants. The seeds in the unconnected boxes had no trace of green and were anemic and drooping.

This brought Hieronymus to the revolutionary conclusion that whatever caused the development of chlorophyll in plants could not be sunlight itself but something associated with it, which, unlike light, was transmittable over wires. He had no idea at what frequency this energy might be located on the electromagnetic spectrum, or even if it was related to it.

As Hieronymus continued to build instruments for the doctors, and to experiment with them, he grew more and more convinced that the energy being modulated by the devices had little to do with electromagnetism. This notion became a certainty when he found the device itself was short-circuited if bathed in light rays from the sun just as electrical circuits in a radio are shorted by being plunged into a bath of water.

Hieronymus next designed a special analyzer, first with lenses, finally with a prism, by means of which he could identify, from the radiations they emitted, many of the elements on Mendeleyev's periodic chart. He found that the energy, when refracted through a prism, behaved in the same manner as light, except that the angles of refraction were much more acute, and that the energy from various elements came through at angles of refraction in the same order as the contents of their nuclei. His ability to detect a substance from its radiation alone convinced Hieronymus that disease was destroyed by the Abrams device and its descendants "through a radiative attack on the binding energy which holds molecular structures together."

The frequency of emanation, or angle of refraction, is in exact proportion to the number of particles in the nucleus of an element, says Hieronymus. The range of frequencies or angles of refraction from complex substances can thus be used to disclose what they contain. The energy emitted does not, like electromagnetic energy, attenuate inversely as the square of the distance from its source. It radiates out only a certain distance depending on the object from which it is emitted, on the direction it takes, and even on the time of day of its measurement. Something varies the amount of radiation emitted in the same way that fog, smoke or other materials altering the density of the air in our atmosphere vary the intensity of light from whatever source.

Trying to describe this radiation Hieronymus first came up with the cumbersome explanation: "Energy obeying some of the laws of *electricity* but not all of them, and some of the laws of *optics*, but not all of them." To obviate the repetition he finally coined the term *"eloptic energy."*

This energy, he concluded, though independent of, was somehow affiliated with, electromagnetic energy. Because of the difference, Hieronymus inferred that their spectra of frequencies were necessarily related. He decided to refer to eloptic energy in all its wavelengths as a *fine medium* which, as he wrote, "might be the same as that which used to be described by electronic engineers and physicists as 'the ether' put in action at higher harmonics than so far experienced."

In the early 1940s Hieronymus applied for a patent. The invention to which he put claim was basically a method and an apparatus "relating to the art of detecting the presence of, and measuring the intensity or quantity of, any known element of material matter, singly or in combination, whether in solid, fluid or gaseous form." For those who might rush to duplicate his idea, there was an important qualification in the application which stated that the *"apparatus preferably relies upon the element of touch and, therefore, the skill of the operator."*

This was because the operator had to stroke a detector which, substituting for the abdomen of Abrams' subject, was, in the abstruse language required by the patent office: "preferably an electrical conductor coated with a material having such characteristics that under influence of energy flowing through the conducting portion, the coating will change its surface tension or viscosity, or in some manner give evidence of the presence of the energy flowing through the conducting portion by producing a greater drag or resistance to the movement of any part of the body of the operators thereover, such as the hand or fingers."

What actually happened at the detector, to increase and decrease its drag at the touch of the operator, was not understood, but, as the text lamely explained, "the apparatus functions . . . and, therefore, a positively acting analyzer for atomic radiations is produced even though the principle upon which it is based is not fully known."

When he was invited in 1946, less than a year after Hiroshima and Nagasaki had been blasted, to describe his new process over Kansas City's radio station WHAM, Hieronymus paid full tribute to Abrams. "About twenty years ago a discovery was made by a California man," he said, "that was so hard to believe and more especially by those who did not wish to believe it, that the world was set back by their disbelief for many years. There were a few of those following along who took the original idea to the point where today it is as important, in fact, more important to mankind than the atomic bomb because the latter means destruction of humanity and the other idea means the lengthening of life and the alleviation of disease."

The bacteriologist Otto Rahn, whose book on radiation from living things had so puzzled his colleagues ten years before, after examining Hieronymus' process and experiments, wrote to the inventor: "Since those radiations hold the secret of life, they also hold the secret of death. At present, very few people know about the possibilities, and very few know *all* the facts. It seems imperative that those few keep their knowledge to themselves, and divulge only as much as is necessary to perform the immediate applications to cure disease. Your discoveries open up great possibilities, as tremendous as those of the atom bomb, and just like atomic energy, these radiations may be used for the bad as well as for the good of humanity." In the meantime, the *Saturday Evening Post* published a rehash of the more than twenty-year-old *Scientific American* series in a snide article "The Wondrous Box of Dr. Abrams," authored by a Robert M. Yoder, who falsely claimed that Abrams had risen to "fame and fortune selling a sealed box."

Part of the motive for this hatchet job was revealed by Hieronymus in his answering letter to the *Post's* editor, Ben Hibbs. "This is a controversial subject," wrote Hieronymus, "only because it involves the pocketbook of a large group of people who might be harmed financially should the truth of the present day status of the little black box be made generally known to the public. The unfortunate part of the situation at the moment is that a large pressure group is still fighting tooth and nail to keep the known facts from being presented and I just wonder if the article in the *Saturday Evening Post* wasn't instigated by that group."

The letter appeared in a booklet, *The Truth about Radionics and Some of the Criticism made about it by its Enemies,* published by a group which, because it applied the new term "Radionics" to the therapies being practiced on the basis of Abrams' finding, called itself the International Radionics Association.

In 1949 Hieronymus was awarded United States patent number 2,482,773 for the "Detection of Emanations from Materials and Measurement of the Volumes Thereof." Other patents were later issued in the United Kingdom and Canada.

The story of UKACO and the Homeotronic Foundation is further complicated by the fact that, at one point during the work, Hieronymus went to Harrisburg to consult with and assist Armstrong and his collaborators. Hieronymus told the authors that the device incorporating the amplifier which he had built for Wills was used in Pennsylvania with almost 100 percent success. However, according to Hieronymus, the UKACO group could not understand his notion that a new "eloptic energy" might be involved and preferred to proceed on the theory that the device worked solely on electromagnetic or electronic principles.

When they made further adaptations on his device, says Hieronymus, they began to get less than perfect results. The lack of a perfect record, however, was more than overshadowed in Hieronymus' eyes by observations which shook him profoundly. At the Hershey farms, together with a UKACO representative he selected three ears of corn on each of which a corn worm was munching.

Isolating the ears so that the worms could not escape, Hieronymus began to treat them with his radionic broadcaster. He states that, after three days of treatment for ten minutes per hour round the clock, two of the corn worms were reduced to mush but the third was still wobblily intact. Another twenty-four hours of the same treatment and the stubborn worm was also mush. All that remained of the others was just "wet places" on the corn ears.

Hieronymus was so stunned by the lethal potential of the tuned radiation that he resolved never to reveal everything about the makeup of his devices or their operation until he could one day find serious researchers of impeccable character to help him elucidate the exact potentials of his discoveries.

Having for years measured the states of the human body and its organs radionically, Hieronymus and his wife, Louise, operator of the device, decided in 1968 to check the ongoing conditions of the first men ever to go on a trip to the moon.

They ordered photographs of the three astronauts from Washington and, after inserting them one at a time in their instrument, claimed they were not only able to track and monitor all physiological functions of the astronauts from the earth to the moon and back, but to determine that the transmitting energy could neither be shielded by the metal shell of the capsule nor affected by the great distance from Mother Earth or her satellite. They said they were also able to measure the effects of high "G" stress on the astronauts during take-off and re-entry as well as the effects of living in a weightless—zero "G"—environment for an extended period.

The Hieronymuses' most startling claim was the discovery of what they term a *lethal radiation belt round the moon,* which during the landing of Apollo 11 apparently extended from an altitude of roughly sixty-five miles down to approximately fifteen feet above the moon's surface. While the astronauts were traveling through or within this belt, Hieronymus noted a drop in the vitality as measured by his wife on the "box." But when two of the astronauts got out of the capsule and climbed down the ladder onto *luna firma*, he says the trends showed a spectacular turnaround.

In following later flights of the Apollo series, Hieronymus found that the lower level of the mysterious lethal atmosphere was as high as two miles above the moon's surface. Hieronymus believes further that its altitude may alter depending on a given time period or on its exact position above various spots on the moon's surface, or both, but states that extensive observations will be required to confirm this.

No less interesting was Hieronymus' confirmation that the energy he was picking up from the spacemen appeared not to be related to any of those on the electromagnetic spectrum. When the capsule was on the far side of the moon relative to the earth, no radio or other telemetered signals could be transmitted back to the Houston base. The astronauts were thus out of contact with their earthbound guides. Not so with Hieronymus, who says he was able to monitor them during this period on his analyzer. On the other hand, when the capsule was on the far side of the moon relative to the sun, i.e., in the moon's shadow, radio signals were easily sent to and received from earth, whereas Hieronymus' analyzer went "dead" and could pick up nothing. This seemed to confirm the idea, hit upon by Hieronymus when he was growing plants in his cellar, that the energy received by his analyzer was in close association, if not carried on, sunlight rays.

A German-born engineer, Rolf Schaffranke, working as a propulsion expert for American corporations contracting with NASA in Huntsville, Alabama, who as a young student watched the launching of the first man-made rocket, the V-2, from the secret German base at Peenemünde, wrote of Hieronymus' experiment: "Sounds absolutely crazy. Yet it really happened. Numerous observers are firmly convinced that the experiment is repeatable. Repeatable anywhere, any time, with as many witnesses present as desired."

Wondering whether eloptic energy could be carried not only on light rays from our sun but on those from all cosmic bodies including planets, Hieronymus took a ten-power telescope from an ordinary navigational sextant onto the roof of his house in Lakemont, Georgia, and fixed it so that it could be constantly directed at any spot in the heavens.

After focusing on Venus, he replaced the telescope's eyepiece with a metal disc penetrated by a hole, and soldered a wire to the edge of the disc to conduct what he believed was eloptic energy down into the house to the radionic device operated by his wife. Mrs. Hieronymus began to run tests similar to those which had measured the vitality rates of the astronauts' bodily parts and systems so as to see if there was anything that gave a similar response on the Venusian surface. Of the thirty-five wavelengths received from astronauts' organs and systems, half seemed to be tunable from Venus, the others not at all.

Perplexed by these findings, the Hieronymuses were suddenly struck that they might be receiving energies from parts, not of animals, but of plants. So they began running analyses on the organs of earthly plants *as if they were human beings.*

Checking three trees, a mango, a willow, and a pine, Hieronymus found that while they all had what appeared to be the equivalent of lungs, pineal, thymus, and pituitary glands, adrenals, thyroids, stomachs, a colon wall, a prostate, ovaries, and a nervous system, there were strange differences among them. The mango alone, for instance, seemed to have something akin to a lymphatic system, but, unlike both the willow and the pine, no duodenum or spleen.

Hieronymus next checked Bermuda grass, which he knew does not propagate by seeding itself but extends endlessly underground. Sure enough, no sex organs could be detected for the grass according to his readings, though a weed registered ovaries even when he had removed its seeds. Strangely, the Bermuda grass seemed to have the analog of an appendix.

The readings from Venus set on the tunings for each organ or system, or analog thereof, clearly indicated some structure on Venus similar to that of earthly plants. Hieronymus concludes that there may well be a form of Venusian plant life, though he has no idea what kind, or why the vitality of its organs seems to be more than twice that of the earth plants he has tested; nor has he any idea whether such "plants" may have no more than what occultists call etheric or astral bodies.

By the summer of 1973, as a result of the publication of a series of articles about him and his work in U.S. magazines devoted to the unexplained, Hieronymus began to attract wider interest; his correspondence mushroomed with letters and calls asking for further information.

Still keenly aware of Rahn's post-Hiroshima warning, and remembering with awe the corn borers reduced to no more than "wet spots," Hieronymus is still leery of revealing all he knows. As he stated to the authors: "While we are not intending to hold back scientific investigation, we are not going to broadcast complete information on our technology to the general public so that people can play around with it irresponsibly any more than we would advocate giving dynamite and matches to small children. If a group of responsible people will help us to run a proper and broad investigation of eloptic energy for the good of mankind, I will be glad to cooperate and tell them all I know."

CHAPTER 20

Mind Over Matter

About two decades before UKACO's efforts to help the farmers of Pennsylvania were put to rout by the chemical manufacturers and the USDA, a book appeared in the United Kingdom called *The Chain of Life* by the British surgeon Guyon Richards, who had built up wide experience in medical problems as physician in charge of an entire district for the Indian medical service.

He was stimulated by the theories of a colleague, Captain Sandes, who introduced him to the little-known benefits of ionization and its remarkable effects on the treatment of disease, a branch of science later developed in Germany and more particularly in the USSR, but almost wholly neglected in other countries. Richards became, as he put it, "electrically-minded," and proceeded to make detailed galvanometric studies of plants and people in health and disease. Of Abrams, Richards said it was a pity that the very invention of the oscilloclast had, because its curative properties could not be exactly explained, obscured from the medical profession the important issues which Abrams had raised.

Richards' book restimulated interest in radionics among a small coterie of imaginative British doctors who wanted to experiment with the new healing process. Looking for an engineer who could help them build the strange new equipment, they sought out an "English Hieronymus" and found him in the person of an Oxonian, George De La Warr, a psychically-gifted civil engineer.

Having built a series of instruments covered in black leather, which came to be known as "black boxes," about a year following the demise of UKACO, the work of which they had no inkling, De La Warr and his osteopath wife, Marjorie, found that they could affect the growth of diseased or undernourished plants by focusing "radionic" energy straight at them through a lens system, thus substantiating the claim of Hieronymus, of whom they were also unaware, that it was optically refractable. Like the UKACO partners, the De La Warrs found that they could obtain equally successful results either by directly radiating a plant or by beaming energy to it through one of its leaves or even its photograph. Why this should be so remained a mystery to the De La Warrs, who could only state: "It is still problematical whether it is the apparatus, the photographic emulsion or the presence of a specific operator that produces the effects—or a combination of all these factors."

De La Warr further theorized that in addition to radiations of light the emulsion on the negative receives from the subject other radiations, the precise nature of which was unknown. There was also evidence that a relationship perdured between a plant and a leaf detached from it, or the expressed juice of that plant, just as it existed between one of Abrams' patients and his blood spot.

"It would appear," wrote De La Warr, "that each molecule of matter is capable of producing a tiny electrical voltage that is specific to itself, and which 'transmits' rather like a tiny radio transmitter-receiver. A collection of molecules, therefore, is capable of transmitting a generic pattern. This means that the signal from a plant or human is quite individual, and that each plant or person will receive a transmission on their own generic pattern. It is here that the photograph plays its part, as it is thought that the emulsion on the negative retains the generic pattern of the object photographed and can be induced to re-radiate as a carrier. Thus, with a photograph of a plant in circuit it is possible to affect that plant at a distance."

The theory was in no way airtight, but the results obtained by radionics were fantastic. Realizing that the presence of living organisms in the soil is a prerequisite to good husbandry, the De La Warrs wondered if they could treat the soil itself through the cells living within it by radiating energy patterns effectively equivalent to plant nutrients. To attempt this they determined to photograph the soil of garden plots, treat the photos radionically, then plant vegetables in the treated soil to see how they would fare.

They began with cabbages. Selecting two sites eighty feet apart, in the curtilage of their laboratory, they removed all the topsoil. This they thoroughly sieved and mixed to eliminate any possibility of soil variation, then spread it back on the sites, allowing it to settle for a week.

On the 27th of March, 1954, they began a month-long treatment of one site by radiating its photograph daily in their darkroom, leaving the other site untreated. This treatment accomplished, they planted four young cabbages, selected for their similarity, into the soil of each site. For two weeks no difference in the rate of growth was observable, causing them to have doubts about the procedure. Thenceforth to the end of June, the cabbages in the treated soil continued to grow larger than those left to grow normally. Photographs taken some four weeks before maturity revealed that the plants in the treated site were *three times larger* than those left to grow normally.

Encouraged by this success, the De La Warrs decided to repeat the experiment on a larger scale. They noticed that in one strip of garden three rows of peas thirty-seven feet long were growing so uniformly as to leave little doubt that the soil was of equal consistency throughout.

The peas were uprooted and the site prepared for fresh planting. The strip was divided into fifteen plots, six of which were photographed from a bird's eye view and treated radionically every day for one month. Two plots were left untreated; seven others were used as buffers.

At the beginning of August, ninety-six Early English winter-resisting broccoli plants, all seven inches high, were set out, six to a plot. The radionically treated plots were rephotographed with the plants in them and irradiated daily until the experiment was concluded in mid-January, 1955, after snow and ice had apparently stopped all growth. Accurate weighing of the plants under the scrutiny of an expert from Oxford University's Department of Agriculture, Dr. E. W. Russell, who observed the experiment from beginning to end, revealed that an average 81 percent increase in total crop yield had been obtained for the treated plants compared to the nontreated controls.

After successfully experimenting with lettuces, suggested by Russell because they were fast-growing, the De La Warrs next decided to broadcast treatment from their laboratories to a garden at Old Boars Hill, two miles from Oxford. They laid out an equilateral plot, divided it into four squares, and planted broad-leaf beans in each square. A single square was photographed and irradiated from the beginning of May to the beginning of August, 1955. At the end of the test, the height of the bean plants grown in the treated square was 9½ inches greater than in any of the other squares, and the number of pods greater than for all the other plants combined.

Further to extend the distance between the soil treated and the laboratory, the De La Warrs cooperated with a carrot grower in Scotland. Soil samples taken from seventeen acres of a twenty-two-acre field were irradiated at Oxford each day throughout the growing season. When the carrots were pulled from the earth, those treated weighed out 20 percent heavier than the ones which were left alone. Pleased as they were with the astonishing results they were obtaining, the De La Warrs still had no idea why the radiation from their equipment affected the growth of various vegetables so favorably.

During the next growing season in 1956, they decided to ascertain whether an inert substance, if irradiated and mixed with soil, could reradiate the nutritive energy patterns to the seeds during germination and growth. The substance they selected was "vermiculite," a micaceous silica sold by the building industry as an insulator, which was both chemically inert and insoluble in water. To treat it they blew it into the air for seven hours in front of a radionic apparatus normally used for therapeutic purposes on humans.

They then mixed the treated vermiculite with a grass-seed mixture containing rye, cocksfoot, and other varieties. The proportions were two parts vermiculite to one part grass seed by weight. The mix was sown in two boxes; an identical mixture, containing untreated vermiculite, was sown in two similar boxes. The soil was the same throughout. The results, as confirmed by a leading agricultural firm, showed that the treated vermiculite produced a crop 186 percent heavier in moist weight, with a protein content 270 percent higher, an extraordinary gain for any farmer.

Milford oats, seeded with treated vermiculite in a yard-square plot at a rate equivalent to 252 pounds to the acre, when harvested five months later produced at an estimated rate of *two tons to the acre* or a crop *270 percent larger* than that obtained from an untreated square. More uncannily, oat seeds grown in a beaker of nothing but distilled water containing not a single nutrient nevertheless grew luxuriously if treated vermiculite was added to the water.

At this point a nationally known plant-breeding establishment requested to perform tests with the treated vermiculite on various types of seed. Under the firm's rigid test conditions, the phenomenal increases in growth obtained by the De La Warrs were no longer apparent.

Instead of dejection, this news brought the De La Warrs to a stunning realization: perhaps the plants had been responding all along *not* to the radiations from their machines but indirectly to the human beings involved in the experiments!

To test this idea they called up the plant-breeding firm and obtained permission to run the very same tests the firm had performed on exactly the same plots. To the amazement of the establishment's horticultural staff, the De La Warrs were successful in increasing growth with treated vermiculite to a significant degree but, try as they would, the professional plant growers could not repeat the De La Warrs' success.

After three years of intense labor with plants, and out-of-pocket costs of some $20,000, the De La Warrs had at last stumbled onto the crux of the problem. A human factor of immense importance was confusing the issue. To determine the extent of this factor they again mixed vermiculite into the soil of potted oats. Their assistants, who daily poured measured quantities of water onto the seeds, were told which pots contained the treated substance, which the untreated. What they were *not* told was that none of the vermiculite used had in any way been irradiated and was as inert as when brought from the supplier.

Though every one of the oat seeds had received no nutrient energy other than that provided by the soil itself, the De La Warrs were excited to note that the seedlings in those pots which the assistants *believed* to contain treated vermiculite were coming up faster than the others. Human belief that a plant might grow faster was apparently acting as a nutrient to actually produce faster growth. Thought was a food!

De La Warr, who considered this experiment the most important he had ever run, found himself face to face with a shattering new reality with the most far-reaching implications: *the mind of a human being could affect cell formation!*

When De La Warr described this experiment to one of Great Britain's leading physicists and suggested that a universal energy could be evoked by the proper attunement of one's thoughts, he was told curtly: "I do not believe you, Mr. De La Warr. If you can affect the number of atoms in a growing plant by your thought process, we must revise our concept of what constitutes matter."

"Indeed we must," said De La Warr, "even if such revision poses a whole overhaul of existing knowledge. How, for instance, could this energy be incorporated into mathematical equations? What would happen to the law of the conservation of energy?"

When De La Warr realized that the real key to getting plants to flourish was simply asking them to do so, he published an article in his journal, *Mind and Matter,* entitled "Blessing Plants to Increase their Growth," asking readers to produce evidence to support his own experimental results, which were so at variance with accepted and current materialistic atomic theory.

One of the most crucial steps in a fifteen-step procedure outlined in the article was that in which the experimenter was to hold bean seeds in his hands and invoke a blessing, varying according to his faith or denomination, in a reverent and purposeful manner. Though warmly received by readers, the article evoked a harsh reply from officials of the Roman Catholic Church, who took umbrage because, as they pointed out, it was inadmissible for anyone below the rank of deacon to perform any act of blessing. Laymen were supposed only to ask the Creator to perform a blessing. To still the waters of protest, the De La Warrs renamed their experiment "Increasing the Rate of Plant Growth by the Mental Projection of an Undefined Energy."

Many of their readers reported success similar to that attained in America by the Reverend Franklin Loehr, whose 700 experiments on the effect of prayer on plants, conducted by 150 persons, using 27,000 seeds, under the auspices of Loehr's Religious Research Foundation in Los Angeles, are reported in his book *The Power of Prayer on Plants.* Loehr showed that the growth rate of plants could be accelerated as much as 20 percent when individuals singly or in concert visualized the plants as thriving under ideal conditions. Though their experiments seemed to be acceptable from the evidence and pictures presented, the results were ignored by scientists on the basis that Loehr and his assistants had no scientific training and used relatively crude methods to measure growth.

However, Dr. Robert N. Miller, an industrial research scientist and former professor of chemical engineering at Georgia Tech, began a series of experiments in 1967 with Ambrose and Olga Worrall, whose feats of healing have become celebrated in the United States. Using an extremely accurate method of measuring plant growth rates developed by Dr. H. H. Kleuter of the United States Department of Agriculture, with accuracies up to one thousandth of an inch per hour, Miller, working in Atlanta, Georgia, asked the Worralls to direct their thoughts at rye seedlings from Baltimore, some 600 miles away.

Whereas the growth rate of a new blade of rye grass had been observed by Miller to stabilize at 0.00625 inch per hour, after he asked the Worralls to think of the seedling at exactly 9 P.M., the trace on a graph indicating growth rate began immediately to deviate upward and by 8 A.M. the following morning the grass was growing at a rate 84 percent faster. Instead of growing the expected ¹⁄₁₆ inch in the interval, the seedling had sprouted more than ½ inch. Miller reported that the dramatic results of his experiment suggest that the sensitive experimental technique could be used to measure accurately the effect of mind over matter.

The mysteries of how the human mind may act through radionic devices such as those of UKACO, Hieronymus, or De La Warr are yet to be explained. In an amazing development, the late John Campbell, editor of *Astounding Science Fiction*—since become *Analog Science Fiction/Science Fact*—determined in the 1950s that a circuit diagram of Hieronymus' machine drawn in India ink worked as well as the machine itself. "Your electronic circuit," he wrote to Hieronymus, "represents a *pattern of relationships.* The electrical characteristics are unimportant and can be dropped out completely."

Voysey, an English dowser, corroborated the evidence by pointing out that if he traces a line with pencil on paper, thinking strongly that this mark will represent a certain metal, his pendulum will react to the drawn line exactly as if it were the metal.

After a prolonged study of radionic devices sponsored by the Foundation for the Study of Consciousness set up by Arthur M. Young, inventor of the Bell helicopter, Frances Farrelly, who ran her own college for medical laboratory technicians, also came to the conclusion that the devices were not necessary to achieve effects. While working in England with a Harley Street physician, she found she could walk toward a patient with her hands outstretched and feel within her own body where the patient had trouble. As she says: "I was beginning to run the instrument in my head, or mentally only." Since then, Farrelly has been able to make diagnoses of ills of individuals not only without a radionics device but without a blood spot or a photograph or anything at all. The mental image of a patient held in her mind is sufficient. She calls this a "resonating reflex phenomenon."

In the summer of 1973 Farrelly's talents were put to test in Prague when one of the participants in the First International Conference on

Psychotronics—a Czech logism for the effects of mental energy on matter—lost a wallet in the cavernous four-story Railway Workers' Building, site of the conference. Within minutes, Farrelly tracked it down, pinpointing its exact location inside a box at the back of a dark closet where a cleaning woman had placed it for safekeeping.

The following day she was confronted by a professor from the Czechoslovak Academy of Sciences who gave her a chip of mineralized rock and asked her before a large audience if she could state its origin and age. Rubbing the table before her to get a radionic type "stick," Farrelly, after putting a dozen questions to herself, stated that the mineral in question came from a meteor and was about 3,200,000 years old, answers which exactly matched the most considered conclusions of expert Czech minerologists.

During her stay in England, Farrelly was intrigued that the De La Warrs seemed to have radionically detected that every living plant has a critical rotational position (CRP), which is apparently established by the earth's magnetic field as the seed sprouts out of the ground. If the seedling is transplanted in such a way that it continues to grow in its CRP, it will thrive better than plants which have been transplanted out of that orientation. This phenomenon was also independently discovered by Hieronymus, who found that a reading on the dials of his radionic device was maximum when the plant was rotated in a given position with respect to a compass rose.

The De La Warrs had also found that, because of this apparent relationship with the geomagnetic field, a plant has a pattern of radiation around it. Nodal points within this pattern or web which seem to concentrate the field of radiation can be located by a portable detector with a probe and a rubbing plate similar to that on their radionics device.

In England Frances Farrelly found that with a simple dowsing pendulum she could locate on a tree and in the domelike geometric pattern around it nodal points of energy which could expose X-ray film.

This field of energy may be related in some way to a magnetic field, since both can be detected with dowsing methods. In Lorton, Virginia, the authors witnessed the incredible sensitivity to a magnetic field as displayed by Wilhelm de Boer, a *Rutenmeister*, or master dowser, who lives in the Hanseatic city of Bremen, West Germany. When Dr. Zaboj Harvalik asked de Boer to walk through a magnetic field which could be switched on or off, each time the field was on de Boer's tiny dowsing rod delicately held in his fingertips would revolve. When the field was off, the rod would not move.

With the same rod de Boer measures the auras of trees and people. First backing off from a large oak, he then advanced toward it until he was about twenty feet away, at which point the rod flipped downward. On a smaller tree de Boer had to approach more closely before there was any reaction from the rod.

"This energy coming out of a large oak can temporarily increase the strength of a human aura, or a person's vitality," said de Boer, demonstrating that it extended some nine to ten feet outward from Harvalik's chest but was double that length after Harvalik hugged a big oak for two minutes. De Boer related how the "Iron Chancellor" of Germany, Bismarck, at the advice of his personal physician, would put his arms around a tree for up to half an hour to recover from the fatigue of pressing duties.

Harvalik stated that the aura de Boer was measuring might not be the same as that seen around human beings by sensitives, to which the Britishers, Dr. Walter Kilner and Oscar Bagnall, devoted much attention, since it seemed to extend further from the body. As Harvalik put it: "We don't really know exactly what this extended aura is and we certainly have no way to analyze it in a physics laboratory, at least not yet."

Whether the auric field as measured by de Boer is the same as the one which contains the "nodal points" as revealed on film by Frances Farrelly is also as yet unanswerable. It appears that when the material substance with which the field is associated is broken up, the field goes with the individual parts which remain in contact even at a distance. This led the De La Warrs to wonder if a slip cut from a plant and rooted would benefit from the radiations emitted by its "mother" or pine away in the absence of such radiation. Incinerating a mother plant, roots and all, they found that its motherless children did not thrive as well as similar shoots taken from a mother which was permitted to continue growing.

Most incredible to J. I. Rodale, who successfully repeated the De La Warrs' experiment, was the allegation that the mother plant did not necessarily have to be growing near her children for them to benefit from her "protection." The mother could apparently be in the next city, the next country, across the ocean, or anywhere on earth. If so, suggested Rodale, it would tend to indicate that all living things, including human babies, get protective radiations from their mothers, that radiations might underlie "love at first sight" and that people with "green thumbs" are emitting radiations beneficial to their plants.

That an energy comes from the hands of a healer—as was claimed of Jesus Christ—and that this energy can increase the growth of plants seems to have been proved in a scientific experiment on sprouting seeds by Dr. Bernard Grad, a research biochemist at Allan Memorial Institute of Psychiatry of McGill University in Montreal. Taking the "healing controversy" into his laboratory, he performed some careful experiments with the cooperation of a retired Hungarian Army colonel, Oskar Estebany, who became aware of his own extraordinary healing powers during the Hungarian revolt against the Soviet occupation of his country in 1956.

Grad's meticulous experiments, written up in the *Journal of the Society for Psychical Research* and the *International Journal of Parapsychology*, indicated that the sprouting of grains and the total amount of green plant issuing therefrom could be significantly increased when compared to controls, by watering them with a solution sealed in bottles and exposed only to the healing energy of Estebany's hands.

In his first rigidly controlled experiments Grad convinced himself that by holding the cages of wounded mice, but not actually touching the animals themselves, Estebany could heal their wounds faster than if the mice were exposed to heat or left untreated. Estebany also could retard the growth of goiters produced in the mice by iodine-deficient diets and goitrogens and hasten their disappearance when the mice were returned to a normal diet.

Grad wondered what results might be obtained from subjects other than Estebany. From the many patients available at the institute he chose a twenty-six-year-old woman with a depressive neurotic reaction and a thirty-seven-year-old man with a psychotic depression. He also selected a psychiatrically normal man of fifty-two. What Grad sought to ascertain was whether a solution held for thirty minutes in the hands of a normal individual would cause plants to grow at a faster rate than a solution held for the same amount of time by neurotics and psychotics.

After the threesome had held sealed bottles of saline solution, their contents were poured on barley seeds embedded in soil. Grad found that the little plants watered by the saline solution held by the normal human being grew significantly faster than those held by the psychiatric patients, or by a control group left untreated. The plants treated by the psychotic grew the slowest. Contrary to Grad's expectations, the plants treated by the neurotic grew at a slightly higher rate than the controls.

Grad noticed that when the psychotic was given the sealed bottle to hold he expressed not the slightest reaction or emotion, whereas the neurotic immediately inquired about the reason for the procedure and, when told, responded with an expression of interest and what Grad termed a "brightening of mood." Grad also observed that she lovingly cradled the bottle in her lap as a mother would a child. Grad reached the conclusion that "the important fact for the purpose of the experiment was not the state of her general diagnosis but of her mood *at the time* she was holding the bottle." In his detailed account of the experiment Grad reported to the American Society for Psychical Research that it would seem that a negative mood, such as depression, anxiety, or hostility while treating the solutions would result in an inhibition of cell growth when plants were watered with that solution.

Grad saw the implications of his experiment to be far-reaching. If a person's mood could influence a saline solution held in the hands, it seemed natural to assume that a cook's or housewife's mood could influence the quality of food prepared for a meal. He recalled that in various countries menstruating milkmaids were not permitted in that part of the dairy where cheese was being prepared because of a presumed unfavorable effect on the bacterial cultures, and that during their menstrual periods women have been held to influence negatively the canning of perishables, the stiffening of egg white, and the survival of cut flowers. If Grad's experiments were correct, it was not the menstruation but the depression created by it in certain women that had the effect, a discovery which removes from the realm of prejudice to the realm of science the biblical injunction against "unclean" women.

The whole subject of radionics and the part played by the action of the human mind—and whether it interacts with various radionics devices designed by De La Warr, Hieronymus, Drown, Abrams and others —stands on the very frontier of physics and metaphysics and the no-man's land which lies between them.

As Galen Hieronymus said to the authors: "Is the force and its manipulation basically in the realm of the psychic? We know that powerful psychics such as Frances Farrelly can produce results with no help whatsoever from a device. But others seem to be helped by a radionics instrument even when, like the De La Warrs, they have well-developed psychic powers."

Hieronymus has tried his best to separate the action of the human mind from whatever the various "boxes" do to interact with it. "I can take an ordinary empty cigar box and mount a tuning dial on top of it," he says. "By properly setting the dial at a given tuning, some psychics have been able to cure a given disease. I think they do this because they *believe* that they are *using* the box when, in reality, they are using only psychic ability.

"On the other hand, we are able without question to run analyses of ill persons and, having made our diagnoses, give information to third parties on how to set dials on healing instruments when those persons know nothing about radionics and are merely following instructions. The proper setting of the dials seems to have important effects. So there are two sides to the question which await resolution." Hieronymus says that a good friend, an Episcopal minister in Florida, received a hand-carved ebony cross from the family of an old Scottish vicar who had died in Great Britain. Touched, he replaced the metal cross which he normally wore around his neck with the ebony cross each time he offered holy services. A short time later he told Hieronymus that he felt exhaustingly depleted after each church service.

As a long-time "radionic detective," Hieronymus questioned his friend whether he had not done something different during the services which seemed so to fatigue him. When the clergyman remembered the substitution of crosses, Hieronymus tested his friend's vitality with and without the ebony rood around his neck. Whenever the black cross was worn, the minister's vitality dropped almost to the zero point on the device's dials.

Hieronymus suggested to his friend that he exorcise the gift cross. This accomplished, the minister no longer felt any debilitating effects. The two friends concluded that negative thoughts from the old vicar had lodged in the ebony cross and the energy therefrom was affecting its new owner.

The experiments run on certain strange figurines made of baked clay, stone, and bone discovered at Acámbaro in the Mexican state of Guanajuato by Waldemar Julsrud offer impressive evidence that matter can receive malevolent energy and store it for long periods of time, perhaps thousands of years.

Professor Charles H. Hapgood in his manuscript, *Reports from Acámbaro*, says of the huge Julsrud collection, numbering over 33,000 artifacts, that it cannot be identified with any of the known cultures of Mexico but suggests relationships not only with specific Indian tribes of the Western Hemisphere but also with peoples of the south Pacific and Africa. Researchers sponsored by Arthur M. Young's foundation selected a few examples which appeared to the eye as most evilly weird. After putting them individually in cages together with mice, they found that the tails of some of the mice turned black and fell off and that other animals died after only a night's exposure to the objects. There was evidently a malevolent energy—of a kind usually associated with voodoo—present in the evil-looking artifacts which was capable of destroying a mouse.

If mental intercession can act malevolently to destroy life, it is also clear, as the radionic process proves, that it can act benevolently to enhance life. In his unique paper, "Radionics, Radiesthesia and Physics," published by the Academy of Parapsychology and Medicine, Professor William A. Tiller, chairman of the Department of Material Science at Stanford University, who devoted part of a year-long stay in England to the study of radionics at the De La Warr laboratories, presents a model to explain how the process works.

The basic idea in radionics [writes Tiller] is that each individual, organism, or material radiates and absorbs energy via a unique wave field which exhibits certain geometrical, frequency and radiation-type characteristics. This is an extended force field that exists around all forms of matter whether animate or inanimate. A useful analogy here is the physical atom that is continually radiating electromagnetic energy in the form of waves because of its oscillating electrical dipole movement and its thermal vibrations. The more complex the material, the more complex the wave form. Living things, like humans, emit a very complex wave spectrum of which parts are associated with the various organs and systems of the body.

Tiller holds that if the millions of new cells born in our bodies each day come into being in the presence of fields polarized by the radionic process, they tend to grow in a healthier configuration, which weakens the original field of an abnormal or diseased structure. Continued treatment eventually molds the healthy organ structure and the condition is healed.

Following Hindu Yoga philosophy, Tiller postulates further that there are seven principles operating in man, each of which constitutes a different type of substance that obeys a unique set of natural laws. These he lists as the *physical*, which most of us simply call the "body"; the *etheric*, or what the Russians have termed the "bioplasmic"; the *astral*, or emotional body, followed by three separate intuitive, intellectual, and spiritual *minds;* and finally *pure spirit* or divine mind.

"These substances are presumed to exist everywhere in nature and to interpenetrate with the human body, i.e., they all exist within the physical atom and organize themselves within the body," writes Tiller, who adds that if one thinks of seven transparent sheets containing seven different circuit patterns, each of a different color, and then overlays them, one can thus visualize the complete organization of the different levels of substance in the body. Although the different energy fields perturb each other only in a small way, they can be influenced to do so in a strong way, says Tiller, *by the agency of mind.*

Tiller points out that the seven endocrine centers of the physical body —the gonads, cells of Lydig, adrenals, thymus, thyroid, pineal, and pituitary—are paralleled in Hindu philosophy by seven energy vortices, or *chakras*, which are linked in the etheric body by a current of vitality. This current, says Tiller, is associated with the meridians of acupuncture and the points on them which, though known to the Chinese millennia ago, have only recently been detected with an instrument that measures electrical resistance.

> One of our goals [continues Tiller] is to arrange our etheric/physical system so as to deliver maximum power to the physical body from the environmental energy stream. One reason for wanting to tune the chakra/endocrine system relates to the transmitting of spiritual and healing qualities into the earth environment. These seven endocrine centers have been called our sacred centers and through them we radiate transmitting information of a quality (frequency) associated with that center.

Tiller offers the example of the thymus gland, the center supposed to control the quality of love in all its spectral range. He postulates that an entity radiates from this gland a field that is broadcast through space and is absorbed in the corresponding gland by another entity. This stimulates the gland and generates some biological activity within the organism. If the second entity radiates an in-phase vibration back to the first, then the love consciousness can form a bond between them. Most of us, in Tiller's view, are confined to expressing love in so limited a way that it is radiated at small power and has a restricted range of expression such that only a few individuals will receive the radiation and be aware of it. But, as Tiller puts it, "if the entity has built himself to radiate at large power and over a very broad band of the spectral distribution, then many, many entities will receive this radiation, be aware of this love and be nourished by it." Tiller's statement fits well with Rexford Daniels' idea that altruism has a higher, and perhaps more powerful, set of frequencies than egotism.

It also echoes the latest conclusions of Marcel Vogel:

> A thought is an act of creation. It is what we are here for, to create, to bring into being ourself by means of thinking. The way a thought can be observed and measured by a simple life form, a plant, shows a wonderful relationship between man and plant. When we love, we release our thought energy and transpose it to the recipient of our love. Our primary responsibility is to love.

Another researcher to accept the power of the mind is a neurologist and medical electronics expert, Dr. Andrija Puharich, who has recently reported some of the most awe-inspiring feats of psychic, or mental, power yet to confront physicists, psychologists, and other academicians. Author of *The Sacred Mushroom* (Doubleday, New York, 1959), which dealt with the effects of hallucinogenic plants, such as peyote, a decade before the world's younger generation became absorbed with mind-bending drugs, from marijuana to LSD, and of *Beyond Telepathy* (Darton, Longman and Todd, London, 1962) a decade before studies of direct idea transference from one human mind to another were considered anything but crazy by the "responsible" scientific community, Puharich has now discovered a truly remarkable psychic in the body of a young Israeli, Uri Geller, whose abilities have startled hundreds of audiences and left most open-minded scientists aghast at their implications.

Under rigorous test conditions, Geller has been able to unfailingly locate an iron ball or water hidden in one of ten identical sealed metal cans without touching the cans, to move solid objects at a distance without the use of any energy known to physics, to bend at a distance dense metal objects, such as a solid silver Mexican coin, as if they were plastic in his hands, to repair broken watches and get them running without having ever opened their cases, to shatter a set of watchmaker's screwdrivers made of a special alloyed steel, and even to cause objects to vanish from their locations and reappear somewhere else. Geller can also affect at will the material recorded on a magnetic tape, such as that used in television.

Puharich has now organized a multi-disciplinary international group of scientists to assess the abilities of Geller and of perhaps thousands of other people who would reveal similar gifts if they were taken seriously rather than considered freaks. A theoretical group which will take the results of the experiments and seek to mathematically provide physical constructs for them is being led by physicist Dr. Edward Bastin, member of the "Epiphany Philosophers" at Cambridge University in England and originator of the most advanced quantum theory.

The group will be asking such fundamental questions as: How can a coin disappear? What kind of space, or lack of it, is involved? What are the energetics which operate during Geller's transformations and vanishings?

As Puharich told Connie Best, author of an article on Geller, "The Man Who Bends Science":

> We're trying to develop a model to explain how all these atoms can be taken apart. There are theories of annihilation and so on in microphysics, but there is no theory in the world that can explain this on a macroscopic scale. How can you take all these atoms apart or infinitely compress them to the point where they are so tiny they are invisible, have the thing parked in some unknown space, and then get the atoms back reassembled?

Geller not only can miraculously affect the so-called inanimate world but the world of living things as well. Before reliable witnesses he has placed his hands over a rosebud for slightly longer than a quarter of a minute, then opened them to reveal the rose in full and radiant bloom. As Connie Best comments:

> Physics is precise, unbending. Yet Uri Geller is finding loopholes in science wide enough to pluck a rose out of. Uri Geller is bending physics, forcing it to take account of the so-called 'paranormal' powers of the mind. How much will physics have to change? If the readings of meters reflect the wishes of lab assistants, if the presence of an experimenter is enough to embarrass sub-atomic particles, how are we to know where we stand?

As the Serbian-born American inventor and genius, Nikola Tesla, stated before his death: "The day science begins to study nonphysical phenomena, it will make more progress in one decade than in all the previous centuries of its existence."

Perhaps that decade is upon us.

CHAPTER 21

Findhorn and the Garden of Eden

The most advanced experiment involving communication with plants has now developed in a remote corner of northern Scotland, with results more radiant than have been achieved by any other means. On a barren, wind-blown patch of gorse and sand overlooking the Firth of Moray, a seedling community has taken root which may flourish into a marvel of the Aquarian Age.

Three miles as the raven croaks from the battlements of Duncan's castle at Forres, and just south of the heath where the three witches prophesied to Macbeth that he would be Thane of Glamis and Cawdor, an ex-RAF squadron leader turned hotelkeeper decided to take up residence with his wife and three young sons in the derelict corner of a caravan park on Findhorn Bay—a rubbish heap of old tin cans, broken bottles, brambles, and gorse bushes.

Tall, ruddy, with the gentle manner of an English headmaster and the dress of a country squire, Peter Caddy, who once walked two thousand miles through the Himalayas, crossing Kashmir deep into Tibet, has been a follower since young manhood of a school of adepts whose object is to bring back beauty and wonder to this planet. Illumined by the dictates of his conscience, or as he chose to call it, the will of an all-powerful creative force revealed to him by his clairvoyant wife, Eileen, Caddy pulled up roots and moved to Findhorn one snowy November day in 1962. Accompanying the Caddys was another sensitive, Dorothy Maclean, who had left the Canadian Foreign Office to study Sufism.

For some time the Caddys had been intent upon radically changing their lives by turning away from mundane occupations and materialist pursuits in order to enter upon what Caddy calls a long period of training and preparation. During this period they planned to surrender everything, including all personal volition, to a being they term "Unlimited Power and Love," whose will is manifest to them through the guidance of a deceased Rosicrucian master whom they recognized in the flesh as Dr. G. A. Sullivan, and in the spirit as Aureolus, or St. Germain, or the Master of the Seventh Ray.

To be fair, the place in which the Caddys least expected to settle was the unsightly, overcrowded encampment of mobile houses known as Findhorn Caravan Park. For years they had hurried past it on their way to and from Forres. Now some mysterious force was overriding their aversion. Following what appeared to be crystal guidance, they wheeled an old caravan onto the site of their new home—less than half an acre in a hollow not far from the main cluster of trailers, a patch of land composed mainly of sand and gravel, constantly swept by gale-force winds, protected only partially by tufts of broom and quitch grass which kept the sand from blowing away, and shaded by a belt of spiny fir trees.

With winter coming it was a dismal prospect. Following the concept of the monks who used to build their monasteries by hand, putting love and light into the fabric of the building with every stone they laid, the Caddys cleaned their rickety trailer from top to bottom and polished all the furniture, pouring in vibrations of love to cancel out the negative vibrations they considered to be inevitable in structures built by people interested only in money. Cleansing and hand painting the caravan was a first step toward the creation of their own center of light.

As none of the Findhorn pioneers was employed, and their meager resources would carry them through only one dark and clammy Scottish winter, they dreamed of springtime and establishing a garden, partly to increase the protective shield of light round them and partly as a source of healthy nourishment.

Short days and long nights Caddy pored over gardening books, which he found contradictory in their recommendations. Written for horticultural enthusiasts living mostly on the mild southern coast of England, they were irritatingly irrelevant. When Easter rolled around to herald a renaissance of the land, the arid, all but lifeless soil surrounding their caravan seemed hopeless for growing anything comestible. Caddy, who had never sown a vegetable seed in his life, felt like Noah when guided to build an ark where there was no water; but he dutifully persisted. Either guidance was to be followed to the letter or they might as well return to the world of business. His Rosicrucian masters had taught him one prime rule of life: "To love where I was, love whom I was with, and love what I was doing."

To receive the arcane guidance on which the infant community planned its every move, Eileen would rise regularly at midnight and meditate for several hours, bundling herself in an overcoat against the chill of the Scottish nights, taking refuge in the only place that could afford her absolute tranquillity, the trailer park's frigid toilet. Eileen had read in a book that everyone receives his spiritual name at some point in life and that only then can he begin his spiritual work in earnest. In 1953 she had felt the word Elixir branded on her forehead; so she adopted the name, and from then on her guidance was constant.

In her clairvoyant vision Elixir saw seven cedarwood bungalows clustered together, in the midst of a splendid garden, all trim and neat. How this vision was to materialize in the constricted squalor of the caravan site remained a mystery. Yet all were prepared to put their faith in her clairvoyance.

The prospect of creating a garden seemed a superhuman task. The ground was made of fine, dusty sand and gravel in which nothing grew but tough pointed grass. Elixir received guidance that each time you put a spade into the ground you put in your own vibrations, that the right vibrations acted as a magnet to draw in like vibrations. Peter Caddy cheerfully dug a strip of quitch turf three feet wide by nine feet long and laid it to one side. He then dug down eighteen inches, accumulating a pile of sand and gravel. In the clean trench he placed the strip of quitch turf upside down and broke it up with his spade. This was to insure that the turf would not sprout its way back up to the surface, but provide nourishment as it disintegrated.

Repeating the operation with two more trenches, Caddy had a garden nine feet by nine. His problem was to get water into the soil, a far more difficult job than he imagined. The sand was so fine the water poured onto it simply went into globules like quicksilver. Only by dint of the most assiduous patience, by spraying the surface over long periods with a very fine spray, was it possible to impregnate the soil sufficiently for it to hold the moisture. More stones and gravel had to be raked out; finally the plot was ready for seeding. According to the local agricultural experts and the available textbooks on gardening, nothing could be grown in the Findhorn soil except perhaps a few lettuces and radishes. Scanty fare for a family which had become accustomed at their hotel to daily steak or duck washed down with good red wine.

Fortunately Elixir had been warned by her guidance that man is eating the wrong food, drinking the wrong drink, thinking the wrong thoughts, and making his body gross instead of a body of light. They were to eat less dense food and begin to concentrate on making a real garden, the fruit and vegetables of which, combined with honey and wheat germ, would constitute the fare in the new age of refined bodies.

Conscientiously Caddy planted his lettuce seeds in an inch-deep furrow made with the handle of his spade, placing the seeds a foot apart, then raked them over. To sit in the sun and watch their garden grow the Findhorners needed a fence, to fend off the ever-present winds blowing across the Moray Firth, and a level concrete patio. Sand they had in abundance, but no cement, nor any money for its purchase.

Lumber for a slatted fence appeared as if by miracle from a man who was dismantling his garage. As soon as the fence was up a neighbor ran over to say that some barely damaged bags of cement had fallen from a truck across the road. In a short while they had a fenced patio from which to admire—not thriving young lettuce, but stunted apparitions, attacked by wireworms.

What to do? Caddy had been warned by Elixir's guidance not to use chemical insecticides. A neighbor chanced to pass and informed him of a pile of seasoned soot just outside the entrance to the caravan park, an admirable antidote to wireworms.

Caddy spread it carefully, without taking into account the wind which that night blew it through the caravan, into hair, books, and clothing. Luckily it rained and the soot was washed into the soil. By the end of May they were eating luscious lettuces and radishes.

As Elixir's guidance informed them that chemical fertilizers were toxic to the human body, a compost heap was essential if they were to grow a greater variety of vegetables. Only, where to obtain the ingredients? A pile of rotting grass was donated by a neighbor. A nearby farmer, grateful for a rescued sheep, gave Caddy a large load of cow manure. A friend who owned a riding stable allowed them to follow his horses with bucket and shovel. A nearby distillery supplied them with free peat dross and cummings, a natural barley-germ fertilizer. Seaweed they gathered free from the beach. A bale of hay, dropped from a passing truck almost at the gate of the park as if from heaven, served to cover the piles of compost.

Relying on such "supermundane assistance," the Findhorners acted as if they were endowed. As one of them wrote: "We could have been negative and said the soil was useless—as it was. Instead we put hard work and positive thought into everything we did." Caddy began working from morning till night, putting sweat and radiations into the soil, his object to grow sufficient vegetables and salads to provide a large part of their diet in the months to come. Along with pure air, sunlight, sea bathing, and plenty of cold, pure water, they hoped gradually to purify their bodies and endow them with energy, on the theory that the more refined their bodies became the more they would be able to absorb cosmic energies and the less solid food they would need.

The Findhorners planted watercress, tomatoes, cucumbers, spinach, parsley, squash, and asparagus. As a living wall against an unruly Dalmatian they planted hedges of blackberries and raspberries round their garden, which began to spread beyond the caravan till it covered two acres of ground, every bit of soil of which had to be manufactured from old turf and new compost, every square inch manhandled several times in the process.

Within two months the results were stunning the neighbors, who, not knowing of the spirit in which the Caddys were going about their gardening, could not understand what was happening, especially when the Caddys' cabbages and Brussels sprouts were the only ones in the area to survive a plague of cabbage-root grubs which eat away at the roots of the plants, and their harvest of black currants grew healthily by the bushel, whereas the crop largely failed in the rest of the county.

Findhorn lunches began to consist of salads with over twenty ingredients; surplus quantities of lettuce, radishes, spinach, and parsley were disposed of round the county, which was suffering a shortage. Their evening meals included two or three vegetables from the garden, grown without fertilizer or insecticides, freshly picked and freshly cooked. Stews from garden vegetables consisted of onions, leeks, garlic, carrots, parsnips, rutabagas, turnips, artichokes, kohlrabi, celery, squash, potatoes, flavored with all kinds of herbs.

Elixir was told to let her mind dwell on each ingredient when making a salad, or a ratatouille, that her thoughts and feelings were important in the continuing cycle of life. She was to appreciate whatever she was doing, whether peeling a carrot or podding a pea, and to consider each pea or bean a living thing in her hands. Of the peelings and garbage nothing was to be wasted. All was to go back into the compost and the soil, constantly increasing the live vibrations. The only drawback to this life was that when they were obliged to go into town, or on a short holiday, they found it very difficult to support normal food. Elixir became so sensitive it was painful for her to go near the noxious vibrations of so-called civilization.

When midsummer came they were ready to preserve quantities of raspberries, blackberries, and strawberries, putting up altogether a hundred pounds of jam. They pickled fifteen pounds of red cabbage, and large quantities of cucumbers. In a newly built garage they stored potatoes, carrots, beets, and shelves full of shallots, garlic, and onions. During the winter they prepared the earth for the following season and planted more fruits, altogether some twenty species, including apples, pears, plums, greengages, cherries, apricots, loganberries, and boysenberries. By May of 1964 the fruit trees and bushes were bursting into bud.

When estimating the number of red cabbages the Findhorners would need for the following season Caddy calculated that with an average weight of three or four pounds they would require no more than eight. To the Findhorners' amazement, when the cabbages matured one of them weighed thirty-eight pounds and another forty-two. A sprouting broccoli, mistakenly planted as a cauliflower, grew to such enormous proportions that it provided vegetables for weeks; when eventually pulled out of the ground it was nearly too heavy to be lifted.

It began to dawn on Caddy that there might be some greater underlying purpose behind what was happening at Findhorn, that they must be involved in some mysterious pioneering venture, some larger experiment in group living, that the garden might be the nucleus of some larger experiment in New Age living, a sort of training course in the realization that Life is a Whole.

In June of 1964 when the county horticultural adviser came to take a sample of the soil for analysis, his first comment on arrival was that the soil would require a dressing of at least two ounces of sulfate of potash per square yard. Caddy replied that he did not believe in artificial fertilizers, that he was happy using compost and wood ash. The adviser said that would be totally inadequate.

Six weeks later, when the adviser returned bringing the results of the analysis which had been carried out in Aberdeen, he acknowledged with some bewilderment that the analysis had found no deficiencies in the soil sample. All necessary elements, including rare trace elements, were present. The adviser was so astonished by the results that he asked Caddy to take part in a broadcast about the garden in which the adviser would take the chair and an experienced gardener using conventional methods with chemical fertilizers would debate with Caddy. Caddy says that at the time he still did not feel it appropriate to expound to the public on the subject of the spiritual side of their endeavor and again he attributed the success solely to organic manure and compost.

By now they were growing sixty-five different kinds of vegetables, twenty-one fruits, and over forty herbs, both culinary and medicinal. For some time Dorothy Maclean had also been receiving extraordinary spiritual guidance of her own and had adopted the spiritual name of Divina. She learned from the aromatic plants in the garden that their unique wavelengths could serve special functions for humans, affecting different parts of human anatomy as well as the human psyche, some plants being good for wounds, others for eyesight, others for human emotions. She realized that by raising the quality of her own vibrations she might eventually open the doors to a whole new spiritual realm of plant life. It became clear to her that human thinking, human passion, human anger, human kindliness and affection, all have far-reaching effects on the world of plants, that they are most susceptible to human thoughts and emotions, which affect their energy. Poisonous and bad-tempered moods have as depressing an effect on plants as happy, uplifting frequencies have a beneficial effect. It occurred to her also that bad effects could come back to humans as they ate the produce they had infected with bad vibrations. Thus the whole cycle could become viciously descending, leading to more and more misery, pain, and disease, or hopefully ascending, leading to greater joy and greater light.

Divina says she realized that the most important contribution that man can make to a garden—even more important than water or compost—is the radiation he puts into the soil while cultivating it, such as love, and that every member of a group has something to contribute in the way of radiations—strength, happiness, and so on. Everything that comes into a human being through inspiration of one sort or another goes out again modified in wavelength, tone, and timber by the will of the person involved; he or she can improve the quality of what is sent out and increase the brilliance of its wavelength.

At the same time Divina realized that the soil and plants are constantly being affected by radiations from the earth itself and from the cosmos, each of which contributes to its fertility, without which both soil and plants would be sterile; these radiations, she realized, were more fundamental than chemical elements or microbiotic organisms, radiations that are subject fundamentally to the mind of man. Man appeared to have the role of a demi-god; by cooperating with nature he might find no limit to what could be achieved on this planet.

In the spring of 1967 Elixir—who still received the overall policy guidance for the venture—was told that the garden was to be extended even further and made into a place of beauty with the planting of many kinds of flowers. The center was to be expanded and new bungalows built. The vision she had first received on arriving at Findhorn was now beginning to materialize. Money for neat cedarstrip bungalows turned up as if by miracle, and the bungalows were soon surrounded by impeccable flower gardens.

In 1968, when Findhorn was visited by a number of accomplished gardeners and agricultural experts, they were amazed at what they found, remarking they had never seen such a uniformly high standard in all sections of a garden. The growth and color of the flowers in the new herbaceous borders were so remarkable that the visitors were at a loss to explain the phenomena, considering the poverty of the soil and the rigorous northern climate. When Sir George Trevelyan, who for twenty-four years had run the famed Adult Education Foundation at Attingham, dropped in at Easter he was amazed by the quality of the daffodils and narcissi growing in beds crowded with shorter flowers, all as beautiful and large as he had ever seen, their brilliant colors of a scintillating quality. He found the root vegetables the best he had ever tasted, and was surprised to find fruit trees of all sorts in blossom, as well as a vigorous young chestnut standing eight feet high among broad-leaved trees and shrubs thriving on the landward slope of windswept dunes.

As a member of the Soil Association, with an interest in the organic method, Sir George said he had seen enough to know that compost and straw mulch alone mixed with poor and sandy soil were not enough to account for such a garden. There must, said he, be some Factor X to be taken into consideration, adding that if so much could be accomplished at Findhorn in such a short time the Sahara could be made to blossom.

In June of 1968, Miss Armine Wodehouse, of the Radionic Association, who ran a commercial truck garden in Wales for twenty years, visited Findhorn and was amazed at the lush crops she found, especially when she noted the pure sand thinly spread with compost and the powerful winds that swept uninterruptedly across the garden. She felt the strawberry plants would arouse the admiration of any gardener, and was surprised to find moisture-loving asters and primulas, which are notoriously thirsty, thriving in such soil.

Mrs. Elizabeth Murray, an independent organic gardener and member of the Soil Association, who visited Findhorn in July of 1968, felt that the radiant health of the trees, flowers, fruit, and vegetables was far beyond the ordinary. She felt the compost was of such poor quality when mixed with sand that it could not explain the superb produce, which for size, quality, and flavor was superior to anything she had ever seen anywhere. She too was sure that such results could not have been attained on such barren soil simply by good husbandry and compost.

Lady Mary Balfour, sister of Lady Eve, who describes herself as an "ordinary gardener of the organic school," spent twenty-four hours at Findhorn in September of 1968 and wrote: "The weather throughout was grey and at times wet. Yet in retrospect I can see that garden in brilliant sunshine without a cloud in the sky, which must be due to the extraordinary brilliance of the blooming flowers I saw there. The flower beds were all a compact mass of color."

Lady Cynthia Chance, a follower of Rudolf Steiner's Biodynamic farming methods, was astounded when Peter Caddy told her he did not need to apply Steiner's methods, that he had a more direct spiritual way of obtaining the same results. A United Nations agricultural expert and professor of agriculture at various universities, Professor R. Lindsay Robb, when he visited Findhorn just before Christmas went on record to say that "the vigor, health and bloom of the plants in the garden at midwinter on land which is almost a barren powdery sand cannot be explained by the moderate dressings of compost, nor indeed by the application of any known cultural methods of organic husbandry. There are other factors and they are vital ones."

At which point Peter Caddy broke down and let out to Sir George Trevelyan the secret of their success at Findhorn. He said that Dorothy Maclean, or Divina, had managed to get into direct contact with the devas or angelic creatures who control the nature spirits that are said by clairvoyants to be everywhere at work nurturing plant life. Sir George, an advanced student of the arcane, of astrology and the hermetic sciences, admitted he was aware that a number of sensitives claimed to be in touch with the devic world and to be working with it, that Rudolf Steiner had founded his Biodynamic methods on such knowledge. Far from scoffing at Caddy's explanation, he was prepared to give it credence and to validate it by suggesting that conscious investigation of such worlds is of the utmost importance to our understanding of life, and especially our understanding of the life of plants.

In short order Peter Caddy put out a series of pamphlets describing the true nature of the experiments at Findhorn. Divina contributed detailed descriptions of the messages she said she received directly from the devas, of which she described whole hierarchies responsible for every fruit and vegetable, for every flower and weed. Here was a Pandora's box more phenomenal than the one opened in New York by Backster.

Findhorn quickly developed into a community of over a hundred disciples. Young spiritual leaders turned up to preach the gospel of a New Age, and a college was founded in the community to teach the tenets of this New Age. What had started as a miraculous little garden appeared to be turning into a true center of light for the Aquarian Age, visited annually from every continent of the globe.

Parting the veil into other worlds and other vibrations beyond the limits of the electromagnetic spectrum may well go a long way to explain the mysteries which are incomprehensible to physicists who limit their looking to what they can see with their physical eyes and their instruments. In the more ethereal world of the clairvoyant, who claims to have mastered the art of etheric and astral vision, a whole new series of vistas opens up around plants and their relation to man, to the earth, and to the cosmos. The growth of seeds and plants, as Paracelsus intimated, may indeed be affected very strongly by the position of the moon, the positions of the planets, their relation to the sun and to the other stars of the firmament.

Fechner's animistic vision of plants being ensouled becomes less of a wild conceit, as does Goethe's concept of a prototype plant. Burbank's knowledge that whatever man wishes he can produce with the aid of nature or Carver's insistence that nature spirits abound in the woods and take part in the growth of plants may have to be reviewed in the light of the discoveries of the Theosophists and especially of such extraordinary seers of nature spirits as Geoffrey Hodson. The ancient wisdom, as detailed by seers like Mesdames Helena P. Blavatsky and Alice A. Bailey, throws quite another light on the energy of bodies, both of humans and of plants, as well as the relation of individual cells to the entire cosmos.

The secret behind Pfeiffer's Biodynamic compost, which has been proved so highly effective scientifically, turns out to be a homeopathic wonder based on a fairyland creation of Rudolf Steiner's organic brews made by burying cow horns filled with cow dung and deer bladders filled with nettles and camomile leaves. Steiner's anthroposophy, or Spiritual Science, throws such a light on plant life and agriculture as to make scientists root in their tracks.

Aesthetically, the world of the devas and the nature spirits turns out to be even more full of color and sound and perfume than the creations of Scriabin and Wagner, their gnomes, nymphs, and undines, their fire, water, earth, and air spirits closer to reality than the Holy Grail and the eternal quest it engendered. As Dr. Aubrey Westlake, author of *Pattern of Health*, describes our imprisoned state, we are locked in a "valley of materialistic concepts, refusing to believe there is anything other than the physical-material world of our five senses. For we, like the inhabitants of the country of the blind, reject those who claim to have 'seen' with their spiritual vision the greater supersensible world in which we are immersed, dismissing such claims as 'idle fancies' and advancing far 'saner' scientific explanations."

The attraction of the seer's supersensible world, or worlds within worlds, is too great to forgo, and the stakes too high, for they may include survival for the planet. Where the modern scientist is baffled by the secrets of the life of plants, the seer offers solutions which, however incredible, make more sense than the dusty mouthings of academicians; what is more, they give philosophic meaning to the totality of life. This supersensible world of plants and man, only touched on in this volume, will be explored in another, *The Cosmic Life of Plants.*

Bibliography

Abrams, Albert. *New Concepts in Diagnosis and Treatment.* San Francisco: Philopolis Press, 1916.

―――. *Iconography: Electronic Reactions of Abrams.* San Francisco, 1923.

Acharya Jagadis Chandra Bose. (Transactions of the Bose Research Institute, Calcutta, volume 22.) Calcutta: Bose Institute, 1958.

Acres USA, a Voice for Eco-Agriculture. (Monthly newspaper.) Raytown, Mo.

Adam, Michel. *La Vie et les Ondes; l'oeuvre de Georges Lakhovsky.* Paris: E. Chiron, 1936.

Adamenko, Viktor. "Living Detectors (on the Experiments of K. Bakster)," *Tekhnika Molodezhi,* no. 8, 1970, pp. 60–62 (in Russian).

Adams, George, and Olive Whicher. *The Living Plant and the Science of Physical and Ethereal Spaces.* Clent, Worcestershire, England: Goethean Science Foundation, 1949.

Albus, Harry. *The Peanut Man.* Grand Rapids, Michigan: Wm B. Eerdman Pub. Co., 1948.

Albrecht, William A. *Soil Fertility and Animal Health.* Webster City, Iowa, 1958.

———. *Soil Reaction (pH) and Balanced Plant Nutrition.* Columbia, Missouri, 1967.

Alder, Vera Stanley. *The Secret of the Atomic Age.* London: Rider, 1958–1972.

Aldini, Giovanni. *Orazione di Luigi Galvani.* Bologna: Monti, 1888.

Allen, Charles L. *The Sexual Relations of Plants.* New York, 1886.

Andrews, Donald Hatch. *The Symphony of Life.* Lee's Summit, Missouri: Unity Books, 1967.

Applewhite, P. B. "Behavioral Plasticity in the Sensitive Plant, Mimosa," *Behavioral Biology,* vol. 7, Feb. 1972, pp. 47–53.

Arditti, Joseph, and Dunn, Arnold. *Experimental Plant Physiology: Experiments in Cellular and Plant Physiology.* New York: Holt, Rinehart and Winston, 1969.

Audus, L. J. "Magnetotropism: A New Plant Growth Response," *Nature,* Jan. 16, 1960.

Bach, Edward. *Heal Thyself.* Ashingdon, Rochford, Essex, England: C. W. Daniel Co. Ltd.

———. *The Twelve Healers and Other Remedies.* Ashingdon, Rochford, Essex, England: C. W. Daniel Co. Ltd., 1933.

Backster, Cleve. "Evidence of a Primary Perception in Plant Life," *International Journal of Parapsychology,* vol. 10, no. 4, Winter 1968, pp. 329–348.

———. "Evidence of a Primary Perception at Cellular Level in Plant and Animal Life," unpublished. Backster Research Foundation, Inc., 1973, 3 pp.

Bacon, Thorn. "The Man who Reads Nature's Secret Signals," *National Wildlife,* vol. 7, no. 2, Feb.-Mar. 1969, pp. 4–8.

Bagnall, Oscar. *The Origin and Properties of the Human Aura.* New York: University Books, 1970.

Baitulin, I. O., Inyushin, V. M., and Scheglov, U. V. "On the Question of Electrobioluminescence in Embryo Roots," *Bioenergetic Questions—and Some Answers,* Alma Ata, 1968 (in Russian).

Balfour, Lady Eve B. *The Living Soil.* London: Faber & Faber, 1943.

Balzer, Georg. *Goethe als Gartenfreund.* Munich: Bruckmann, 1966.

Barnothy, Madeleine F. (ed.). *Biological Effects of Magnetic Fields.* New York: Plenum Press, 1964.

Barr, Sir James (ed.). *Abram's Methods of Diagnosis and Treatment.* London: W. Heinemann, 1925.

Basu, S. N. *Jagadis Chandra Bose.* New Delhi: National Book Trust, 1970.

Beaty, John Yocum. *Luther Burbank, Plant Magician.* New York: J. Messner, Inc., 1943.

Bentley, Linna. *Plants That Eat Animals.* London: Bodley Head, 1967.

Bertholon, M. L'Abbé. *De l'Electricité des Végétaux.* Alyon, 1783.

Bertrand, Didier. *Recherches sur le Vanadium dans les Sols et dans les Plantes.* Paris: Jouve et Cie, 1941.

Best, Connie. "The Man Who Bends Science." . . . *And It Is Divine.* Denver, Colorado: Shri Hans Productions, May 1973.

Bhattacharya, Benoytash. *Magnet Dowsing or The Magnet Study of Life.* Calcutta, India: K. L. Mukhopadhyay, 1967.

"Billions of Transmitters Inside Us? An Unknown Bio-information Channel has Been Discovered: Using this 'Wireless Telegraph,' the Cells of the Organism Transmit Danger Signals." *Sputnik,* May 1973, pp. 126–130.

Bio-Dynamics (periodical). Stroudsburg, Pa.: Bio-Dynamic Farming and Gardening Association.

Bird, Christopher. "Dowsing in the USSR." *The American Dowser,* Aug. 1972.

――――. "Dowsing in the USA: History, Achievement, and Current Research." *The American Dowser,* Aug. 1973.

Boadella, David. *Wilhelm Reich: The Evolution of His Work.* London: Vision Press, 1972.

Bock, Hieronymus. *Teütsche Speiszkammer.* Strassburg: W. Rihel, 1550.

Bontemps, Arna. *The Story of George Washington Carver.* New York: Grosset & Dunlap, 1954.

Bose, D. M. "J. C. Bose's Plant Physiological Investigation Relating to Modern Biological Knowledge," *Transactions of the Bose Research Institute,* vol. 37. Calcutta: Bose Research Institute, 1947–48.

Bose, Jagadis Chandra. *Izbrannye Proizvedeniya po Razdrazhimosti Rastenii.* I. I. Gunar (ed.), 2 vols. Moscow: Izdatel'stvo Nauka, 1964.

――――. "Live Movements in Plants." *Transactions of the Bose Research Institute,* vols. 1–6. New York: Longmans, Green & Co., 1918–1931.

――――. *Response in the Living and Non-Living.* New York: Longmans, Green & Co., 1902.

――――. *Plant Response as a Means of Physiological Investigation.* New York: Longmans, Green & Co., 1906.

――――. *Researches in Irritability of Plants.* New York: Longmans, Green & Co., 1913.

――――. *The Physiology of the Ascent of Sap.* New York: Longmans, Green & Co., 1923.

――――. *The Physiology of Photosynthesis.* New York: Longmans, Green & Co., 1924.

――――. *The Nervous Mechanism of Plants.* New York: Longmans, Green & Co., 1926.

――――. *Plant Autographs and Their Revelations.* New York: Longmans, Green & Co., 1927.

――――. *Motor Mechanisms of Plants.* New York: Longmans, Green & Co., 1928.

――――. *Growth and Tropic Movements of Plants.* New York: Longmans, Green & Co., 1929.

――――. "Awareness in Plants." *Consciousness and Reality: The Human Pivot.*

Charles Musès and Arthur M. Young (eds.). New York: Outerbridge and Lazard, Inc., 1972, pp. 142–150.

Boulton, Brett. "Do Plants Think?" *The Ladies' Home Journal*, May, 1971.

Bovis, André. Pamphlets on dowsing privately printed in Nice, 1930–1945.

Bragdon, Lillian J. *Luther Burbank, Nature's Helper.* New York: Abingdon Press, 1959.

Brier, Robert M. "PK on a Bio-electrical System," *Journal of Parapsychology*, vol. 33, no. 3, Sept. 1969, pp. 187–205.

Brown, Beth. *ESP with Plants and Animals: A Collection of True Stories that Glow with the Power of Extrasensory Perception.* New York: Essandess Special Edition, 1971.

Brown, Jr., Frank A. "The Rhythmic Nature of Animals and Plants." *American Scientist*, vol. 47, June 1959, p. 147.

Brunor, Nicola. *La medicina e la teoria elettronica della materia.* Milan: Instituto editoriale scientifico, 1927.

Budlong, Ware T. *Performing Plants.* New York: Simon & Schuster, 1969.

Burbank, Luther. *The Training of the Human Plant.* New York: The Century Co., 1907.

———. *My Beliefs.* New York: The Avondale Press, 1927.

———. *How Plants Are Trained to Work for Man.* New York: P. F. Collier & Son, 1921.

Burbank, Luther, with Hall, Wilbur. *The Harvest of the Years.* Boston and New York: Houghton Mifflin, 1927.

Burr, Harold Saxton. *Blueprint for Immortality: The Electric Patterns of Life.* London: Neville Spearman Ltd., 1972.

Camerarius, Rudolf Jakob. *Über das Geschlecht der Pflanzen (De sexu plantorum epistula).* Leipzig: W. Engelmann, 1899.

Carson, Rachel. *Silent Spring.* Boston: Houghton Mifflin, 1962.

Chase, Thomas T. "The Development and Use of Electronic Systems for Monitoring Living Trees," M.S. Thesis, Department of Electrical Engineering, University of New Hampshire, November 1972, 48 pp.

Clark, Laurence. *Coming to Terms with Rudolf Steiner.* Rickmansworth, Herts., England: Veracity Ventures Ltd., 1971.

Cocannouer, Joseph A. *Weeds: Guardians of the Soil.* New York: Devin-Adair Co., 1964.

Commoner, Barry. *The Closing Circle.* New York: Bantam Books, 1971.

Conrad-Martius, Hedwig. *Die "Seele" Der Pflanze.* Breslau: Frankes Verlag, 1934.

Cremore, John Davenport. *Mental Telepathy.* New York: Fieldcrest Pub. Co., 1956.

Crile, George Washington. *The Bipolar Theory of Living Processes.* New York: Macmillan, 1926.

———. *The Phenomena of Life: A Radio-Electrical Interpretation.* New York: W. W. Norton, 1936.

Crow, W. B. *The Occult Properties of Herbs.* London: The Aquarian Press, 1969.

Culpeper, Nicholas. *Culpeper's English Physician & Complete Herbal Remedies.* North Hollywood, Calif.: Wilshire Book Co., 1972.

Darwin, Charles R. *The Power of Movement in Plants.* New York: Da Capo Press, 1966.

———. *Insectivorous Plants.* London: J. Murray, 1875.

———. *The Movements and Habits of Climbing Plants.* New York: D. Appleton and Co., 1876.

———. *The Variation of Animals and Plants Under Domestication.* New York: D. Appleton and Co., 1896.

Davis, Albert Roy, and Bhattacharya, A. K. *Magnet and Magnetic Fields.* Calcutta: K. L. Mukhopadhyay, 1970.

Day, G. W. Langston, and De La Warr, George. *Matter in the Making.* London: Stuart, 1966.

———. *New Worlds Beyond the Atom.* London: Stuart, 1956.

De Beer, Sir Gavin. *Charles Darwin: Evolution by Natural Selection.* Garden City, N.Y.: Doubleday, 1967.

De La Warr, George. "Do Plants Feel Emotion?" *Electrotechnology,* April, 1969.

———. "Seeds Respond to Sound of Music," *News Letter,* Radionic Centre Organization, Spring 1969, pp. 6–7.

De La Warr, George, and Baker, Douglas *Biomagnetism.* Oxford: De La Warr Laboratories, 1967.

De La Warr, Marjorie. "Thought Transference to Plants." *News Letter,* Radionic Centre Organization, Autumn 1969, pp. 3–11.

———. Plant Experiments—Series 2." *News Letter,* Radionic Centre Organization, Summer 1970, pp. 1–72.

Dibner, Bern. *Alessandro Volta and the Electric Battery.* New York: F. Watts, 1964.

———. *Galvani-Volta; A Controversy That Led to the Discovery of Useful Electricity.* Norwalk, Conn.: Burndy Library, 1952.

———. *Dr. William Gilbert.* New York: Burndy Library, 1947.

Dixon, Royal. *The Human Side of Plants.* New York: Frederick A. Stokes Co., 1914.

Dixon, Royal, and Brayton, Eddy. *Personality of Insects.* New York: Charles W. Clark Co., 1924.

Dixon, Royal, and Fitch, Franklyn E. *Personality of Plants.* New York: Bouillon-Biggs, 1923.

Dodge, Bertha Sanford. *Plants That Changed the World.* Boston: Little, Brown, 1959.

Dombrovskii, B., and Inyushin, V. M. "This Experiment Calls for Thought" (on the Experiments of C. Backster). *Tekhnika Molodezhi,* no. 8, 1970, p. 62 (in Russian).

"Do Plants Feel Emotion?" in *Ahead of Time*, Harry Harrison and Theodore J. Gordon (eds.). Garden City, N.Y.: Doubleday, 1972, pp. 106–116.

"Do Plants Have Feelings? Researcher Is Communicating." Bardwell, Kentucky, *Carlisle County News*, March 8, 1973.

Dowden, Anne Ophelia. *The Secret Life of the Flowers*. New York: Odyssey Press, 1964.

Drown, Ruth Beymer. *The Theory and Technique of the Drown H.V.R. and Radiovision Instruments*. (Private Printing.) Los Angeles: Artists' Press, 1939.

———. *The Science and Philosophy of the Drown Radio Therapy*. Los Angeles, 1938.

Du Hamel du Monceau, Henri Louis. *La Physique des Arbres*. 1758.

Du Plessis, Jean. *The Electronic Reactions of Abrams*. Chicago: Blanche and Jeanne R. Abrams Memorial Foundation, 1922.

Du Puy, William A. *Wonders of the Plant World*. Boston: D. C. Heath & Co., 1931.

Ellicott, John. *Several Essays Towards Discovering the Laws of Electricity*. London, 1748.

Elliott, Lawrence. *George Washington Carver: The Man Who Overcame*. Englewood Cliffs, N.J.: Prentice-Hall, 1966.

Electroculture in Plant Growth. Compiled by the staff of *Organic Gardening and Farming*. Emmaus, Pa.: Rodale Press, 1968.

Emrich, Hella. *Strahlende Gesundheit Durch Bio-electrizität*. Munich: Drei-Eicken Verlag, 1968.

"ERA: Electronic Reactions of Abrams," *Pearson's Magazine*, 1922.

Esall, Katterine. *Plants, Viruses and Insects*. Cambridge: Harvard University Press, 1961.

"ESP: More Science, Less Mysticism," *Medical World News*, vol. 10, no. 12, Mar. 21, 1969, pp. 20–21.

Fairchild, David. *The World Was My Garden*. New York and London: Charles Scribner's Sons, 1938.

Faivre, Ernest. *Oeuvres Scientifiques de Goethe*. Paris: L. Hachette, 1862.

Farb, Peter. *Living Earth*. New York: Harper Colophon Books, 1959.

Farrington, Benjamin. *What Darwin Really Said*. New York: Schocken Books, 1966.

Faulkner, Edward H. *Plowman's Folly*. Norman, Oklahoma: University of Oklahoma Press, 1943–63.

Fechner, Gustav Theodor. *Nanna Oder über das Seelenleben der Pflanzen*. Leipzig: Verlag von Leopold Voss, 1921. (1st edition, 1848.)

———. *Zend-Avesta, Pensieri Sulle Cose Del Cielo e Dell'Al Di La*. Milan: Fratelli Bocca, 1944.

———. *Life After Death*. New York: Pantheon Books, 1943.

———. *Elements of Psychophysics*. New York: Holt, Rinehart and Winston, 1966.

Fenson, D. S. "The Bio-electric Potentials of Plants and Their Functional

Significance, I: An Electrokinetic Theory of Transport." *Canadian Journal of Botany*, vol. 35, 1957, pp. 573–582.

————. "The Bio-electric Potentials of Plants and Their Functional Significance, II: The Patterns of Bio-electric Potential and Exudation Rate in Excised Sunflower Roots and Stems." *Canadian Journal of Botany*, vol. 36, 1958, pp. 367–383.

————. "The Bio-electric Potentials of Plants and Their Functional Significance, III: The Production of Continuous Potentials Across Membranes in Plant Tissue by the Circulation of the Hydrogen Ion." *Canadian Journal of Botany*, vol. 37, 1959, pp. 1003–1026.

————. "The Bio-electric Potentials of Plants and Their Functional Significance, IV: Some Daily and Seasonal Changes in the Electric Potential and Resistance of Living Trees." *Canadian Journal of Botany*, vol. 41, 1963, pp. 831–851.

Findhorn News (periodical). Findhorn Bay, Forres, Mordy, Scotland: Findhorn Foundation.

Foster, Catherine Osgood. *The Organic Gardener*. New York: Vintage Books, 1972.

Francé, Raoul Heinrich. *Pflanzenpsychologie als Arbeitshypothese der Pflanzenphysiologie*. Stuttgart: Frankh, 1909.

————. *Das Sinnesleben der Pflanzen*. Stuttgart: Kosmos Geselschaft der Naturfreunde, 1905.

————. *La Vita Prodigosa delle Piante*. Milan: Genio, 1943.

————. *Plants as Inventors*. New York: A. and C. Boni, 1923.

————. *The Love Life of Plants*. New York: A. and C. Boni, 1923.

————. *Germs of Mind in Plants*. Chicago: Charles H. Kerr & Co., 1905.

Freedland, Nat. *The Occult Explosion*. New York: Berkley Pub. Corp., 1972.

Friend, Rev. H. Ideric. *Flowers and Flower Lore* (Vol. II). London: George Allen and Co. Ltd.

Fryer, Lee, and Simmons, Dick. *Earth Foods*. Chicago: Follett, 1972.

Galaxies of Life: The Human Aura in Acupuncture and Kirlian Photography. Krippner Stanley and Daniel Rubin (eds.). New York: Interface, 1973.

Gallert, Mark L. *New Light on Therapeutic Energies*. London: James Clarke & Co. Ltd., 1966.

Galvani, Luigi. *Commentary on the Effect of Electricity on Muscular Motion— A Translation of Luigi Galvani's De Viribus Electricitatis in Motu Musculari Commentarius*. Cambridge, Mass.: E. Licht, 1953.

————. *Opere Scelte*. Torino: Unione Tipografico Editrice Torinese, 1967.

Geddes, Patrick. *The Life and Work of Sir Jagadis C. Bose*. London: Longmans, Green & Co., 1920.

Gilbert, William. *De Magnete*. New York: Dover Pubs., 1958.

Goodavage, Joseph F. *Astrology, The Space-Age Science*. West Nyack, N.Y.: Parker Pub. Co., 1966.

Grad, Bernard. "A Telekinetic Effect on Plant Growth." *International Journal of Parapsychology*, vol. 5, no. 2, 1963, pp. 117–133.

————. "A Telekinetic Effect on Plant Growth, II: Experiments Involving Treatment of Saline in Stoppered Bottles." *International Journal of Parapsychology,* vol. 6, no. 4, 1964, pp. 473–98.

————. "Some Biological Effects of the 'Laying on of Hands': A Review of Experiments with Animals and Plants." *Journal of the American Society for Psychical Research,* vol. 59, no. 2, 1965, pp. 95–127.

Graham, Shirley, and Lipscomb, George. *Dr. George Washington Carver, Scientist.* New York: Julian Messner, Inc., 1944.

Grayson, Stuart H., and Swift, Sara. "Do Plants Have Feelings? Cleve Backster's Remarkable Experiments Suggest Heretofore Unknown Levels of Consciousness in Living Things." *Dynamis,* vol. 1, nos. 6–7, Nov.-Dec., 1971, pp. 1–8.

Grohmann, Gerbert. *Die Pflanze als Lichtsinnesorgan der Erde und Andere Aufsätze.* Stuttgart: Verlag Fries Geistesleben, 1962.

Guilcher, Jean Mickel. *La vie Cachée des Fleurs.* Paris: Flammarion, 1951.

Gumpert, Martin. *Hahnemann: The Adventurous Career of a Medical Rebel.* New York: L. B. Fischer, 1945.

Gunar, Ivan I., et al. "On the Transmission of Electrical Stimulation in Plants." *Izvestiya* (News) of the Timiryazev Academy of Agricultural Sciences, USSR, no. 5, 1970, pp. 3–9 (in Russian with summary in English).

————. "The Evaluation of Frost and Heat Resistance of Plants Through Their Bioelectric Reactions." *Izvestiya* (News) of the Timiryazev Academy of Agricultural Sciences, USSR, No. 5, 1971, pp. 3–7 (in Russian with summary in English).

————. "Bioelectric Potentials of Potato Tubers in Varying Phytopathological States." *Izvestiya* (News) of the Timiryazev Academy of Agricultural Sciences, in Russian with summary in English, USSR, no. 6, 1971, pp. 212–213.

————. "Electro-Physiological Characteristics of Reproduction and the Combined Values for Hybrids of Winter Wheat in Connection with Frost Resistance," *Doklady* (Reports) of the Lenin Academy of Agricultural Sciences, in Russian, USSR, No. 9, Sept. 1971.

————. "The Influence of Thermic Factors on the Dormancy Potentials of the Root Epidermal Cells of Winter Wheat." *Izvestiya* (News) of the Timiryazev Academy of Agricultural Sciences, in Russian with summary in English, USSR, no. 2, 1972, pp. 12–19.

Gupta, Monoranjon. *Jagadis Chandra Bose, A Biography.* Chaupatty, Bombay; Bharatiya Vidya Bhavan, 1964.

Gurvich, Aleksandr G. *Mitogenetic Radiation; Physico-chemical Bases and Applications in Biology and Medicine.* In Russian. Moscow: Medgiz, 1945.

————. *The Theory of the Biological Field.* In Russian. Moscow: Sovyetskaya Nauka, 1944.

————. *Mitogenetic Analysis of the Biology of the Cancer Cell.* In Russian. Moscow: All-Union Institute for Experimental Medicine, 1937.

Gurwitsch, A. and L. *L'Analyse Mitogénétique Spectrale*. Paris: Hermann, 1934.

Gurwitsch, A. G. *Mitogenetic Analysis of the Excitation of the Nervous System*. Amsterdam: N.V. Noord-Hollandsche Uitgeversmaatschappij, 1937.

Haase, Rudolf. *Hans Kayser. Ein Leben für die Harmonik der Welt*. Basel, Stuttgart: Schwabe, 1968.

Hahn, Fritz. *Luftelektrizität Gegen Bakterien für Gesundes Raumklima und Wohlbefinden*. Minden: Albrecht Philler Verlag, 1964.

Hahnemann, Samuel. *The Chronic Diseases, Their Specific Nature and Homoeopathic Treatment*. New York: W. Radde, 1845.

Halacy, Jr., Daniel S. *Radiation, Magnetism and Living Things*. New York: Holiday House, 1966.

Hall, Manly Palmer. *The Mystical and Medical Philosophy of Paracelsus*. Los Angeles: Philosophical Research Society, 1969.

Hapgood, Charles H. *Reports from Acámbaro*. (Unpublished manuscript.)

Harvalik, Z. V. "A Biophysical Magnetometer-Gradiometer." *The Virginia Journal of Science*, vol. 21, no. 2, 1970, pp. 59–60.

Hashimoto, Ken. *Chobutsurigaku Nyumon*. (Work in Japanese on fourth dimension.) Tokyo, 1971.

――――. *Choshinrigaku Nyumon*. (Work in Japanese on psychical research.) Tokyo, 1964.

Hauschka, Rudolf. *The Nature of Substance*. London: Vincent Stuart Ltd., 1966.

Henslow, George. *The Origin of Floral Structure Through Insects and Other Agencies*. New York: D. Appleton & Co., 1888.

Hieronymus, Louise and Galen. *Tracking the Astronauts in Apollo "11" with Data from Apollo "8" Included. A Quantitative Evaluation of the Well-being of the Three Men Through the Period from Two Days Before Liftoff Until the Quarantine Ended—A Consolidated Report*. Self-published, Sept. 4, 1969.

Hieronymus, T. Galen. *Tracking the Astronauts in Apollo "8." A Quantitative Evaluation of the Well-being of the Three Men Through the Period from Two Days Before Liftoff Until Two Days After Splashdown—A Preliminary Report*. Self-published, Dec. 30, 1968.

――――. *The Truth about Radionics and Some of the Criticism Made about It by Its Enemies*. Springfield, Mo.: International Radionic Association, May 1947.

Hill, Harvey Jay. *He Heard God's Whisper*. Minneapolis: Jorgenson Press, 1943.

Howard, Sir Albert. *The Soil and Health*. New York: Schocken Books, 1972.

――――. *The War in the Soil*. Emmaus, Pa.: Organic Gardening, 1946.

Howard, Sir Albert, and Yeshwant, D. Wad. *The Waste Products of Agriculture: Their Utilization as Humus*. London and New York: Oxford University Press, 1931.

Howard, Walter L. *Luther Burbank: A Victim of Hero Worship*. Waltham, Mass.: Chronica Botanica Co., 1945.

———. *Luther Burbank's Plant Contributions.* Berkeley, Calif.: University of California, 1945.

Hudgings, William F. *Dr. Abrams and the Electron Theory.* New York: Century Co., 1923.

Human Dimensions (periodical). Buffalo, N.Y.: The Human Dimensions Institute, Rosary Hill College.

Hunt, Inez, and Draper, Wanetta W. *Lightning in His Hand—The Life Story of Nikola Tesla.* Denver: Sage Books, 1964.

Hutchins, Ross E. *Strange Plants and Their Ways.* New York: Rand McNally & Co., 1958.

Hyde, Margaret O. *Plants Today and Tomorrow.* New York: Whittlesey House, 1960.

Inglis, Brian. *The Case for Unorthodox Medicine.* New York: Berkley Medallion Books, 1969.

Innes, G. Lake. *I Knew Carver.* Self-published, 1943.

Inyushin, Vladimir M., and Fedorova, N. N. "On the Question of the Biological Plasma of Green Plants." Thesis, in Russian. USSR: Alma Ata, 1969.

Jenness, Mary. *The Man Who Asked God Questions.* New York: Friendship Press, 1946.

Jimarajadasa, Curuppmullagé. *Flowers and Gardens (A Dream Structure).* Adyar, Madras, India: Theosophical Publishing House, 1913.

Joachim, Leland. "Plants—The Key to Mental Telepathy." *Probe, the Unknown,* no. 47329, Dec. 1972, pp. 48–52.

Journal for the Study of Consciousness. Santa Barbara, Calif.

Journal of Paraphysics. Downton, Wiltshire, England: Paraphysical Laboratory.

Journal of the Drown Radio Therapy. Hollywood, Calif.

Karlsson, L. "Instrumentation for Measuring Bioelectrical Signals in Plants," *The Review of Scientific Instruments,* vol. 43, no. 3, Mar. 1972, pp. 458–464.

Kayser, Hans. *Die Harmonie der Welt.* Vienna: Akademie für Musik und Darstellende Kunst, 1968.

———. *Akroasis: The Theory of World Harmonics.* Boston: Plowshare Press, 1970.

———. *Harmonia Plantarum.* Basel: B. Schwabe & Co., 1943.

———. *Vom Klang der Welt.* Zurich-Leipzig: M. Niehans, 1937.

Kervran, C. Louis. *Biological Transmutations.* London: Crosby Lockwood, 1972.

———. *A la Découverte des Transmutations Biologiques, une Explication des Phénomènes Biologiques Aberrants.* Paris: Le Courrier du Livre, 1966.

———. *Preuves Relatives à L'existence de Transmutations Biologiques, Échecs en Biologie à la loi de Lavoisier d'invariance de la Matiere.* Paris: Maloine, 1968.

———. *Transmutations Biologiques; Metabolismes Aberrants de l'azote, le Potassium et le Magnésium.* Paris: Librairie Maloine, 1962.

———. *Les Transmutations Biologiques en Agronomie.* Paris: Maloine, 1970.

_____. *Biological Transmutations.* Binghamton, N.Y.: Swan House Publishing Co., 1972.

_____. "Alchimie d'hier et D'aujourd'hui," *L'Alchimie, Rêve ou Réalité,* Revue des Ingénieurs de L'Institut National Supérieur de Rouen, 1972–73.

Kilner, Walter J. *The Human Atmosphere; or the Aura made Visible by the Aid of Chemical Screens.* New York: Rebman Co., 1911.

King, Francis. *The Rites of Modern Occult Magic.* New York: Macmillan, 1970.

Kirlian, Semyon D. and Valentina H. "Investigation of Biological Objects in High-Frequency Electrical Fields." *Bioenergetic Questions—and Some Answers.* Alma Ata, USSR, 1968.

_____. "The Significance of Electricity in the Gaseous Nourishment Mechanism of Plants," in *Bioenergetic Questions—and Some Answers.* Alma Ata, USSR, 1968.

Kraft, Ken and Pat. *Luther Burbank: The Wizard and the Man.* New York: Meredith Press, 1967.

Kreitler, Hans and Shulamith. "Does Extrasensory Perception Affect Psychological Experiments?" *Journal of Parapsychology,* vol. 36, no. 1, Mar. 1972, pp. 1–45.

Kunz, F. L. "Feeling in Plants." *Main Currents of Modern Thought.* May-June 1969.

Lakhovsky, Georges. *La Cabale; Histoire d'une Découverte (L'oscillation Cellulaire.)* Paris: G. Doin, 1934.

_____. *La Formation Néoplasique et le Déséquilibre Oscillatoire Cellulaire.* Paris: G. Doin, 1932.

_____. *La Matière.* Paris: G. Doin, 1934.

_____. *La Nature et ses Merveilles.* Paris: Hachette, 1936.

_____. *L'Origine de la Vie.* Paris: Editions Nilsson, 1925.

_____. *L'oscillateur à Longeurs D'onde Multiples.* Paris: G. Doin, 1934.

_____. *L'oscillation Cellulaire; Ensemble des Recherches Experimentales.* Paris: G. Doin, 1931.

_____. *La Science et le Bonheur.* Paris: Gautier-Villars, 1930.

_____. *La Terre et Nous.* Paris: Fasquelle, 1933.

L'Alchimie, Rêve ou Réalité. Revue des Ingénieurs de L'Institut National Supérieur de Rouen, 1972–73.

Lawrence, L. George. "Biophysical AV Data Transfer." *AV Communication Review,* vol. 15, no. 2, Summer 1967, pp. 143–152.

_____. "Interstellar Communications Signals." *Information Bulletin* No. 72/6. San Bernardino, Calif. Ecola Institute.

_____. "Interstellar Communications: What are the Prospects?" *Electronics World,* Oct. 1971, pp. 34 ff.

_____. "Electronics and the Living Plant." *Electronics World,* Oct. 1969, pp. 25–28.

_____. "Electronics and Parapsychology." *Electronics World,* April, 1970, pp. 27–29.

_____. "More Experiments in Electroculture." *Popular Electronics*, June, 1971, pp. 63–68, 93.

_____. "Experimental Electro-Culture." *Popular Electronics*, Feb. 1971.

Leadbeater, C. W. *The Monad.* Adyar, Madras, India: Theosophical Pub. House, 1947.

Lehrs, Ernst. *Man or Matter.* New York: Harper, 1958.

Lemström, Selim. *Electricity in Agriculture and Horticulture.* London: The Electrician Pub. Co., 1904.

Lepinte, Christian. *Goethe et l'Occultisme.* (Publications de la Faculté des Lettres de l'Université de Strasbourg.) Paris: Societe d'Edition les Belles Lettres, 1957.

Lewis, Joseph. *Burbank the Infidel.* New York: Freethought Press Assn., 1930.

Linné, Carl von. *Flower Calendar.* Stockholm: Fabel, 1963.

_____. *Reflections on the Study of Nature.* Dublin: L. White, 1784.

Loehr, Rev. Franklin. *The Power of Prayer on Plants.* New York: Signet Books, 1969.

Luce, G. G. *Biological Rhythms in Psychiatry and Medicine.* U.S. Public Health Service Pub. No. 2088, 1970.

Lund, E. J. *Bioelectric Fields and Growth.* Austin: University of Texas Press, 1947.

Lyalin, O., and Pasiehngi, A. P. "Comparative Study of Bioelectric Response of a Plant Leaf to Action of CO and Light." Agrophysics Research Institute, V.I. Lenin All-Union Academy of Agricultural Sciences, Leningrad. Bulletin issued by the Institute of Plant Physiology, Academy of Sciences of the Ukrainian SSR, Kiev, Mar. 6, 1969.

Mackay, R. S. *Bio-Medical Telemetry.* New York: John Wiley, 1970.

Magnus, Rudolf. *Goethe as a Scientist.* New York: H. Schuman, 1949.

Manber, David. *Wizard of Tuskegee.* New York: Crowell-Collier, 1967.

Mann, W. Edward. *Orgone, Reich and Eros.* New York: Simon & Schuster, 1973.

Marha, Karel; Musil, Jan; and Tuhà, Hana. *Electromagnetic Fields and the Life Environment.* San Francisco: San Francisco Press, 1971.

Marine, Gene, and Van Allen, Judith. *Food Pollution: The Violation of our Inner Ecology.* New York: Holt, Rinehart & Winston, 1972.

Markson, Ralph. "Tree Potentials and External Factors," in Burr, H. S., *Blueprint for Immortality: The Electric Patterns of Life.* London: Neville Spearman, 1972, pp. 166–184.

Martin, Richard. "Be Kind to Plants—Or You Could Cause a Violet to Shrink." *The Wall Street Journal*, Jan. 28, 1972, pp. 1, 10.

Matveyev, M. "Conversation with Plants." *Nedelya.* Weekend supplement of *Izvestia*, no. 17, April 17, 1972 (in Russian).

McCarrison, Sir Robert. *Nutrition and National Health.* London: Faber & Faber Ltd., 1944.

McGraw, Walter. "Plants Are Only Human." *Argosy*, June 1969, pp. 24–27.

Merkulov, A. "Sensory Organs in the Plant Kingdom." *Nauka i Religiya (Science and Religion)*, no. 7, 1972, pp. 36–37, in Russian.

Mermet, Abbé. *Principles and Practice of Radiesthesia*. New York: Thomas Nelson, 1935–59.

Mesmer, Franz Anton. *Le Magnétisme Animal*. Paris: Payot, 1971.

———. *Memoir of F. A. Mesmer, Doctor of Medicine, on His Discoveries*. Mt. Vernon, N.Y.: Eden Press, 1957.

Mességué, Maurice. *C'est la Nature qui a Raison*. Paris: R. Laffont, 1972.

———. *Cherches et tu Trouveras*. Paris: La Passerelle, 1953.

———. *Des Hommes et des Plantes*. Paris: R. Laffont, 1970.

Meyer, Warren. "Man-and-Plant Communication: Interview with Marcel Vogel." *Unity*, vol. 153, no. 1, Jan. 1973, pp. 9–12.

Miller, Robert N. "The Positive Effect of Prayer on Plants." *Psychic*, vol. 3, no. 5, Mar.-Apr. 1972, pp. 24–25.

Milne, Lorus and Margery. *The Nature of Plants*. Philadelphia: J. B. Lippincott, 1971.

Mind and Matter. (Quarterly periodical.) Oxford, England: The De La Warr Laboratories.

Mitchell, Henry. "Spread a Little Sunshine and Love and Reap Sanity from Plants That Really Care," *The Washington Post*, July 1, 1973, pp. G1, G4.

Morgan, Alfred P. *The Pageant of Electricity*. New York: D. Appleton Century Co., 1939.

Mother Earth. Journal of the Soil Association, London.

Murr, L. E. "Physiological Stimulation of Plants Using Delayed and Regulated Electric Field Environments." *International Journal of Biometeorology*, vol. 10, no. 2, pp. 147–53.

———. "Mechanism of Plant-Cell Damage in an Electrostatic Field." *Nature*, vol. 201, no. 4926, March 28, 1964.

Naumov, E. K., and Vilenskaya, L. V. *Soviet Bibliography on Parapsychology (Psychoenergetics) and Related Subjects*, Moscow, 1971. Translated from Russian by the Joint Publications Research Service, JPRS No. 55557, Washington, D.C., May 28, 1972, 101 pp.

Natural Food and Farming. (Monthly journal.) Atlanta, Texas: Natural Food Associates.

Neiman, V. B. (ed.) *Problems of Transmutations in Nature: Concentration and Dissipation*. (Collection of papers.) In Russian. Erevan, Armenia, USSR: Aiastan Pub. House, 1971.

Nicholson, Shirley J. "ESP in Plants," *American Theosophist*, pp. 155–158.

Nichols, J. D. *Please Doctor, Do Something!* Atlanta, Texas: Natural Food Associates, 1972.

Nollet, M. L'Abbé. *Recherches sur les Causes Particulieres des Phénomènes Electriques*. Paris, 1754.

———. *Lettres sur L'Electricité*. 1753.

Norman, A. G. "The Uniqueness of Plants." *American Scientist*, vol. 50, no. 3, Autumn 1962, p. 436.

Northern, Henry and Rebecca. *Ingenious Kingdom.* Englewood Cliffs, N.J.: Prentice-Hall, 1970.

Obolensky, George. "Stimulation of Plant Growth by Ultrasonic Waves." *Radio-Electronics,* July 1953.

O'Donnell, John P. "Thought as Energy." *Science of Mind,* July 1973, pp. 18–24.

Old and New Plant Lore. Smithsonian Scientific Series. New York: Smithsonian Institution Series, Inc., 1931.

Organic Gardening and Farming. (Monthly journal.) Emmaus, Pa.: Rodale Press.

Osborn, Fairfield. *Our Plundered Planet.* Boston: Little, Brown, 1948.

The Osteopathic Physician, Oct. 1972 (special issue devoted to Kirlian photography and bioenergetics).

Ostrander, Sheila, and Schroeder, Lynn. *Psychic Discoveries Behind the Iron Curtain.* New York: Bantam Books, 1970.

Ott, John N. *My Ivory Cellar—The Story of Time-Lapse Photography.* Self-published, 1958.

———. *Health and Light—The Effects of Natural and Artificial Light on Man and Other Living Things.* Old Greenwich, Conn.: Devin-Adair, 1973.

Paracelsus. *Sämtliche Werke von Theophrast von Hohenheim gen. Paracelsus.* 20 vols. Munich: R. Oldenbourg, 1922–65.

Parasnis, D. S. *Magnetism.* London: Hutchison, 1961.

Parker, Dana C., and Wolff, Michael F. "Remote Sensing." *International Science and Technology,* July 1965.

Payne, Alan. " 'Secret Life of Plants' Revealed by Biologist." *Performance,* vol. 1, no. 41, Mar. 29, 1973.

Pekin, L. B. *Darwin.* New York: Stackpole Sons, 1938.

Pelt, Jean-Marie. *Evolution et Sexualité des Plantes.* Paris: Horizons de France, 1970.

Perkins, Eric. *The Original Concepts of the Late Dr. Albert Abrams.* A lecture delivered to the Radionic Association, March 17, 1956. Burford, Oxon, England: Radionic Association.

Pfeffer, Wilhelm. *Pflanzenphysiologie.* Leipzig: W. Engelmann, 1881.

Pfeiffer, Ehrenfried. *The Compost Manufacturer's Manual.* Philadelphia: Pfeiffer Foundation, 1956.

———. *Sensitive Crystalization Processes: A Demonstration of Formative Forces in the Blood.* Dresden: E. Weisesbuchhandlung, 1936.

———. *The Earth's Face and Human Destiny.* Emmaus, Pa.: Rodale Press, 1947.

———. *Formative Forces in Crystalization.* New York: Anthroposophic Press, 1936.

———. *Practical Guide to the Use of the Bio-Dynamic Preparations.* London: R. Steiner Pub. Co., 1945.

———. *Weeds and What They Tell.* Bio-Dynamic Farming and Gardening Association, Inc.

Philbrick, Helen, and Gregg, Richard. *Companion Plants and How to Use Them.* Old Greenwich, Conn.: Devin-Adair Co., 1966.

Philbrick, John and Helen. *The Bug Book: Harmless Insect Controls.* Self-published, 1963.

Picton, Lionel James. *Nutrition and the Soil: Thoughts on Feeding.* New York: Devin-Adair, 1949.

Pierrakos, John C. *The Energy Field in Man and Nature.* New York: Institute of Bioenergetic Analysis, 1971.

Pressman, A. S. *Electromagnetic Fields and Life.* New York and London: Plenum Press, 1970.

Priestley, Joseph. *The History and Present State of Electricity with Original Experiments.* London, 1767.

Pringsheim, Peter, and Vogel, Marcel. *Luminescence of Liquids and Solids and Its Practical Application.* New York: Interscience Pubs., 1943.

Preuss, Wilhelm H. "Aus 'Geist und Stoff,' die Arbeiten von Herzeles ," in Hauschka, Rudolf, *Substanzlehre,* V. Klosterman, Frankfurt am Main, 1942.

Prevention: The Magazine for Better Health. (Monthly journal.) Emmaus, Pa.: The Rodale Press.

Puharich, Andrija. *The Sacred Mushroom: Key to the Door of Eternity.* Garden City, N.Y.: Doubleday, 1959.

————. *Beyond Telepathy.* London: Darton, Longman and Todd, 1962.

Pullen, Alice Muriel. *Despite the Colour Bar.* London: S.C.M. Press Ltd., 1946.

Pushkin, V. N. "Flower Recall," *Znaniya Sila,* Nov. 1972, in Russian.

Rahn, Otto. *Invisible Radiations of Organisms.* Berlin: Gebrüder Borntraeger, 1936.

Ravitz, L. J. "Periodic Changes in Electromagnetic Fields," *Annals, New York Academy of Sciences,* vol. 46, 1972, pp. 22–30.

Regnault, Jules Emile J. *Les Methodes d'Abrams.* Paris: N. Maloine, 1927.

Reich, Wilhelm. *The Discovery of the Orgone: Volume I, The Function of the Orgasm, Sex-Economic Problems of Biological Energy.* New York: Orgone Inst. Press, 1942.

————. *The Discovery of the Orgone: Volume II, The Cancer Biopathy.* New York: Orgone Inst. Press, 1948.

Reichenbach, Karl L. F., Freiherr von. *The Odic Force; Letters on Od and Magnetism.* New Hyde Park, N.Y.: University Books, 1968.

————. *Physico-Physiological Researches on the Dynamics of Magnetism, Heat, Light, Electricity and Chemism, in Their Relations to Vital Force.* New York: J. S. Redfield, 1851.

Retallack, Dorothy. *The Sound of Music and Plants.* Santa Monica, Calif.: De Vorss and Co., 1973.

Richards, Guyon. *The Chain of Life.* London: John Bale Sons and Danielsson Ltd., 1934.

Robbins, Janice and Charles. "Startling New Research from the Man Who

'Talks' to Plants." *National Wildlife*, vol. 9, no. 6, Oct.-Nov. 1971, pp. 21–24.

Rocard, Y. *Le Signal du Sourcier*. Paris: Dunod, 1963.

Rodale, J. I. *The Healthy Hunzas*. Emmaus, Pa.: Rodale Press, 1949.

Russell, Sir Edward John. "The Soil as a Habitat for Life." In Smithsonian Institution Annual Report 1962.

Russell, Walter B. *The Russell Genero-Radiative Concept*. New York: L. Middleditch, 1930.

──────. *The Universal One*. New York: Briefer Press, 1926.

──────. *The Secret of Light*. New York: Self-published, 1947.

Sanderson, Ivan T. "The Backster Effect: Commentary." *Argosy*, June 1969, p. 26.

Scott, Bruce I. H. "Electricity in Plants." *Scientific American*, Oct. 1962, pp. 107–115.

Scott, Cyril Meir. *Music, Its Secret Influence Throughout the Ages*. New York: S. Weiser, 1969.

Scott, G. Laughton. "The Abrams Treatment," in *Practice; an Investigation*. London: G. Bles, 1925.

Selsam, Millicent. *Plants That Move*. New York: Morrow, 1962.

──────. *Plants That Heal*. New York: Morrow, 1959.

Semenenko, A. D. "Short Term Memory of Plants," in Russian. Institute of Photosynthesis, Academy of Sciences of USSR and Timiryazev Academy, Inst. of Plant Physiology, Academy of Science of USSR, Nov. 1968.

Sergeyev, G. A. "Principles of Mathematical Modulation of Bioplasmic Radiations of a Living Organism," in Russian; in the anthology *Voprosy Bioenergetiki*, Kazakh State University, Alma Ata, USSR, 1969.

Shaffer, Ron. "Your Plants May Be Perceptive," *The Washington Post*, April 18, 1972.

Sherrington, Sir Charles Scott. *Goethe on Nature and Science*. Cambridge, England: Cambridge Univ. Press, 1942.

Simonéton, André. *Radiations des Aliments, Ondes Humaines, et Santé*. Paris: Le Courrier du Livre, 1971.

Singh, T. C. N. "On the Effect of Music and Dance on Plants." *Bihar Agricultural College Magazine*, vol. 13, no. 1, 1962–63, Sabour, Bhagalpur, India.

Sinyukhin, A. M., and Gorchakov, V. V. "Role of the Vascular Bundles of the Stem in Long-Distance Transmission of Stimulation by Means of Bioelectric Impulses." *Soviet Plant Physiology*, vol. 15, no. 3, May-June 1968, pp. 477–487. In Russian.

Skutt, H. R.; Shigo, A. L.; and Lessard, R. A. "Detection of Discolored and Decayed Wood in Living Trees Using a Pulsed Electric Current." *Canadian Journal of Forest Research*, vol. 2, 1972.

Soloukhin, Vladimir. *Trava. (Grass.)* In Russian, serialized in *Nauka i Zhizn*, nos. 9–12, 1972.

"Some Plants are 'Wired' for Growth: Electricity in the Garden." *The Washington Post*, Feb. 13, 1968, p. 34.

Spangler, David. *Revelation, The Birth of a New Age.* Findhorn, Scotland: Findhorn Pubs., 1971.

Spraggett, Allen. *Probing the Unexplained.* New York: World Pub. Co., 1971.

Steiner, Rudolf. *Agriculture.* London: Biodynamic Agricultural Assn., 1924–1972.

Stephenson, W. A. *Seaweed in Agriculture and Horticulture.* London: Faber and Faber, 1968.

Sutherland, Halliday. *Control of Life.* London: Burns Oates, 1951.

Swanholm, A. L. *The Brunler-Bovis Biometer and Its Uses.* Los Angeles: De Vorss, 1963.

Sykes, Friend. *Food, Farming and the Future.* Emmaus, Pa.: Rodale Press, 1951.

————. *Humus and the Farmer.* London: Faber and Faber, 1946.

Synge, Patrick. *Plants with Personality.* London: Lindsay Drummond Ltd., 1939.

Taylor, J. E. *The Sagacity and Morality of Plants.* London: Chatto & Windus, 1884.

Thomas, Henry. *George Washington Carver.* New York: Putnam, 1958.

Thompson, Sylvanus. *Magnetism in Growth.* (8th Robert Boyle Lecture) London: Henry Frowde, 1902.

Tiller, William A. "On Devices for Monitoring Non-Physical Energies." (Unpublished article, 41 pp.)

————. "Radionics, Radiesthesia and Physics." *Proceedings of the Academy of Parapsychology and Medicine, Symposium on the Varieties of Healing Experience,* 1971.

Tompkins, Peter, and Bird, Christopher. "Love Among the Cabbages: Sense and Sensibility in the Realm of Plants." *Harper's Magazine,* Nov. 1972, pp. 90–96.

Turner, Gordon. "I Treated Plants not Patients." *Two Worlds,* vol. 92, no. 3907, Aug. 1969, pp. 232–234.

Voisin, André. *Soil, Grass and Cancer.* New York: Philosophical Library, Inc., 1959.

Volta, Alessandro. *Opere Scelta di Alessandro Volta.* Torino: Unione Tipograficoeditrice Torinese, 1967.

Voprosy Bioenergetiki. (Problems of Bioenergetics.) In Russian. Kazakh State University, Alma Ata, USSR, 1969.

Watson, Lyall. *Supernature.* Garden City, N.Y.: Anchor Press, 1973.

Weeks, Nora. *The Medical Discoveries of Edward Bach, Physician.* Ashingdon, Rochford, Essex, England: C. W. Daniel Co. Ltd.

Weinberger, Pearl, and Measures, Mary. "The Effect of Two Sound Frequencies on the Germination and Growth of a Spring and Winter Wheat," *Canadian Journal of Botany.*

Westlake, Aubrey T. *The Pattern of Health; A Search for A Greater Understanding of the Life Force in Health and Disease.* London: V. Stuart, 1961.

"What Noise Does to Plants." *Science Digest,* Dec. 1970, p. 61.

Wheaton, Frederick Warner. "Effects of Various Electrical Fields on Seed

Germination," Ph.D. dissertation, Iowa State University, Ames, Iowa, 1968.

Wheeler, F. J. *The Bach Remedies Repertory.* Ashingdon, Rochford, Essex, England: C. W. Daniel Co. Ltd.

Whicher, Olive, and Adams, George. *Plant, Sun and Earth.* Stuttgart: Verlag Freies Geistesleben.

White, John W. "Plants, Polygraphs and Paraphysics." *Psychic,* vol. IV, no. 2, Nov.-Dec., pp. 12–17, 24.

Wickson, Edward J. *Luther Burbank, Man, Methods and Achievements.* San Francisco: Southern Pacific Co.

"The Wonderful World of Plants." *Za Rubezhom,* no. 15, April 7–13, 1972, pp. 28–29. In Russian.

Wrench, G. T. *The Wheel of Health.* New York: Schocken Books, 1972.

Yogananda, Paramahansa. *Autobiography of a Yogi.* New York: Rider, 1950.

Index

fertilizers *(cont'd)*
Organic agriculture), 137–8, 219, 227ff., 243, 251, 256–7, 261ff.
Fetisov, V. M., 70–1
Findhorn (Scotland), 361–71
Finland, 175–6
Fliess, Wilhelm, 197
Fontes, Randall, 32
Food and Drug Administration, 250, 254–6, 267, 333
Food, Farming and the Future (Sykes), 232
food, human, viii–ix, 68, 126ff., 138–9, 364ff.; health and, 139, 224ff., 231, 234, 238–9, 241ff., 253ff., 268, 272–3, 285, 290–1; meats, chemicals and, 250–1; meats, dowsing, 305–6; dowsing, 300ff.; minerals and trace elements, 238, 243, 246ff., 251, 256, 290–1; organic, 139, 224ff., 231, 234, 238ff., 253ff., 261, 266–7, 270–1, 354ff.; pesticides and, 249, 253, 255; processed, 245–50, 255–6; production, *see* Productivity; proteins, 250–2; vitamins, 225, 243ff., 256
force fields, 172, 200–13, 357; *see also* Auras; Radionics; *subjects*
Ford, Frank, 261
Ford, Henry, 141
Formation of Vegetable Mould through the Action of Worms (Darwin), 234–5
formative forces, 243–4
forms, metamorphosis of, 111ff., 161–2
Foster, Sir Michael, 87
Foundation for Study of Consciousness, 350, 356
Fourth State of Matter (Grishchenko), 204
France, 55, 86, 101–2, 107, 116, 166–71, 184–6, 189–90, 196, 221–2, 236, 275–88, 291, 295–307, 311
France, Raoul, ix–xi, xiii–xiv, 108
Franklin, Benjamin, 167, 171, 175
Freud, Sigmund, 124, 197
Fryer, Lee, 268
Funk, Casimir, 225
Furon, René, 288

Galvani, Luigi, 4, 169–70, 195–6, 209, 299
galvanometry: eggs, 15–16, 29–30; plants, 3ff., 21ff., 32, 40ff., 65; polarity changes, 41
Gardeners' Chronicle, 174
Gardini, Professor, 167–8
Garner, John, 140
Gassner, J. J., 170

Gauss, Karl Friedrich, 51
Geddes, Patrick, 99–100
Geitel, Hans, 174
Geller, Uri, 359–60
genetics, 127
geomagnetism, *see* Gravity; Polarity and orientation
Germany, 55, 97, 105–25, 161–2, 166, 172–4, 196, 223, 277–8, 323–5, 343
germination, 282; lunar cycle and, 197, 282; orientation and, 182, 351; psychic energy and, 351–2; radiation and, 59–60, 173–4; radionics and, 346–7, 351–2
giantism, 189–90
Gilbert, William, 165, 166, 170, 172, 184, 277
Gilgit Agency (Afghanistan), 224–6
Goethe, Johann Wolfgang von, x, 109–19, 120, 162, 174, 245, 291, 372
Goldstein, Norman, 32
Goodavage, Joseph F., 53
Graber, Glenn, 268–72
Grad, Bernard, 353–5
Grass (Soloukhin), 72–5, 236
gravity, 166, 182; levity, 117–18; radiation of metals and, 334; *see also* Polarity and orientation
Great Britain, *see* United Kingdom
Greece, Ancient, 105, 161, 164, 172–3, 295
Greenwell, Sir Bernard, 230
Gregory, William, 172
Grishchenko, V. S., 204
Gros, Charles, 51
Gross, Henry, 298
Gross, Henry M., 326–32
growth, 97–9, 101; direction tendencies, 116–18; fertilizers, *see* Fertilizers; light spectrum and, 189ff.; metamorphosis, 111ff., 161–2; parapsychology and, 59–60; photography, time-lapse, 188ff.; radiation and, 59–60, 167ff., 178ff., 187ff.; radionics and, 344ff.; sound waves and, 59–60, 145ff.; thought and/or prayer and, 19–20, 348ff.; *see also* Productivity
Gunar, Ivan Isidorovich, 64–5, 72, 76–7
Gurwitsch, Alexander, 54–5, 187, 188, 195, 197–9, 204, 318

Haeckel, Ernst, 109
Hagaseth, Gaylord T., 152
Hahnemann, Christian Samuel, 323–5
Halacy, D. S., 173
Halbleib, Ernest, 267–8
Hale, William J., 329

Lakhovsky, Georges, 184–8, 301, 306, 320
Lamarck, Jean, 109
Lambert, Albert and Mrs., 297
Langman, Louis, 196
Latscha Filialbetriebe, 270
Lavoisier, A. L., 275–6, 281, 283
Lawrence, L. George, 35, 46–51, 53–62, 151, 187
League of Nations Committee on Intercultural Cooperation, 102
Lebedinskii, A. V., 77
Lehrs, Ernst, 111–13, 117–18
Lemonnier, Pierre Charles, 167, 174
Lemström, Selim, 175–7, 183
Lenin, 289–90
Lepinte, Christian, 110
Lewis, Myrna I., 308
Libby, Willard F., 332
Liebeg, Baron Justus von, 223–4
Life, 333
life-fields, 196–7
Life Force, 24
light, 118–19, 189; flashes, plant, 174; frequencies and effects of, 189ff.; response to, 57, 64, 92; sun, biorhythm and, 163–4
Linnaeus (von Linne), Carl, ix, 108, 162
Linnean Society, 90–1
Lipsett, Mortimer, 250
Literaturnaya Gazetta, 75
Little Book of Life After Death (Fechner), 121–2
Lloyd George, David, 296
Locker, Arthur, 148
Lodge, Sir Oliver, 102, 186, 183
Loehr, Franklin, 349
Lombard, Jean, 287–8
Low Energy Transmutations (Kervan), 288
Lund, E. J., 187
Lundberg brothers, 266–7

Maclean, Dorothy (Divina), 362, 368–71
MacLean, Gordon, 298
magnetism, 164–7, 209–10; dowsing, 296ff., 351–2; radiation of metals and, 334–5; *see also* Animal (s); magnetism; Polarity and orientation
Mairan, Jean-Jacques D. de, 163–5
malevolence, 355–6
Man or Matter (Lehrs), 111–13
Mangeldorf and Bros., Inc., 149
Marconi, Guglielmo, 48, 84, 98
Marine, Gene, 248
Mary Reynold Babcock Foundation, 15
Matin, Le, 101–2
matter: forms, Yogic, 357–8; nature and creation of, 275ff.

Matveyev, M., 66–8
Maxwell, James Clerk, 83–4
Mayer, Jean, 255
Mayron, Lewis W., 195
McCarrison, Sir Robert, 224–6, 230–1, 238–9, 242
McGarey, William, 65
McInnes, Alick, 311–16
McKibben, E. G., 181
Measures, Mary, 151–2, 157
Medical World News, 14–15
medicine and medical professions, 139; acupuncture, 205; diagnostic techniques, 196, 199, 204, 210ff., 297, 317ff., 333; dowsing, 296–7, 302, 306ff.; faith healers, 208–9; herbal healing, 306–14, 324–5; homeopathy, 323–5; ionization, 343–4; mesmerism, 170–1; nutrition and disease, 224ff., 239, 241ff., 353–6, 290–1; pathoclast, 334; pesticides, 253; radiation, pathology and, 318–23; radiobiology, 186–8; sound therapy, 308; *see also* Health, human
memory, 9, 68–9, 72
Mendel, Johann, 127
Mendeleyev, Dmitri, 275
mental energy, *see* Thought, human
Merkulov, A., 68–9
Merta, Jan, 59, 209–10, 301, 303–4
Mesmer, Franz Anton, 19, 170–1, 188, 195–6, 209
Mességué, Maurice, 311
metals: electricity and, 169–71; molecular reaction, 85ff.; radiation, eloptic, 334–7
metamorphosis of plants, 111ff., 161–2
Mexico, 356
microorganisms, 235, 251–2, 284–6, 288
microscopy, 20
Midwest, 218–21, 267–8
Miller, Howard, 11
Miller, Robert N., 349–50
Milstein, George, 158–9
Mind and Matter, 348
minerals and trace elements: dowsing, 295ff.; nutrition, 238, 243, 246ff., 251, 256, 290–1; transmutation, 275ff.
mitogenetic radiation, 54–5, 318
Molisch, Hans, 102
Molitorisz, Joseph, 178–9
Monteith, Henry C., 207
Montelbono, Tom, 26
moon: cycle, effects of, 197, 282; radiation belt, 339–40
morphology, 111ff., 161–2
Moss, Thelma, 203–8, 213

74 75 10 9 8 7 6 5 4